SECOND EDITION

GIRLS, WOMEN, AND CRIME

To the many women who work passionately and relentlessly to improve the lives of female offenders. This book is dedicated to you and to one such "warrior" in general: Kimberly Bolding.

SECOND EDITION

GIRLS, WOMEN, AND CRIME

SELECTED READINGS

EDITORS

MEDA CHESNEY-LIND • LISA PASKO

University of Hawaii at Manoa *University of Denver*

Los Angeles | London | New Delhi
Singapore | Washington DC

Los Angeles | London | New Delhi
Singapore | Washington DC

FOR INFORMATION:

SAGE Publications, Inc.
2455 Teller Road
Thousand Oaks, California 91320
E-mail: order@sagepub.com

SAGE Publications Ltd.
1 Oliver's Yard
55 City Road
London EC1Y 1SP
United Kingdom

SAGE Publications India Pvt. Ltd.
B 1/I 1 Mohan Cooperative Industrial Area
Mathura Road, New Delhi 110 044
India

SAGE Publications Asia-Pacific Pte. Ltd.
33 Pekin Street #02-01
Far East Square
Singapore 048763

Acquisitions Editor: Jerry Westby
Editorial Assistants: Erim Sarbuland and Laura Cheung
Production Editor: Melanie Birdsall
Typesetter: C&M Digitals (P) Ltd.
Proofreader: Christine Dahlin
Indexer: Gloria Tierney
Cover Designer: Gail Buschman
Marketing Manager: Katie Winter
Permissions Editor: Karen Ehrmann

Printed in the United States of America

Library of Congress Cataloging-in-Publication Data

Girls, women, and crime : selected readings / [edited by] Meda Chesney-Lind, Lisa Pasko. — 2nd ed.

p. cm.
Includes bibliographical references and index.

ISBN 978-1-4129-9670-9 (pbk. : acid-free paper)

1. Female offenders. 2. Women prisoners. 3. Female juvenile delinquents. 4. Criminology. 5. Feminism. I. Chesney-Lind, Meda. II. Pasko, Lisa.

HV6046.G57 2013
364.3′74—dc23   2011042893

This book is printed on acid-free paper.

12 13 14 15 16 10 9 8 7 6 5 4 3 2

BRIEF CONTENTS

DETAILED CONTENTS

INTRODUCTION

This collection of readings makes several assumptions about gender and crime, and it aims to collect research that reflects these orientations. First, the collection assumes that gender matters in crime and crime policy, and, more specifically, that gender must be theorized in order to do good criminological research. For most of the last century, gender, if considered at all, was one variable among the many studied. Never was the social context of patriarchy considered when exploring the causes of crime, and rarely was the growing literature on gender consulted. As chapters in this collection attest, there is burgeoning research that does not reflect these shortcomings.

Second, as the title shows, *Girls, Women, and Crime* assumes that the problems of girlhood are salient in the lives of adult women, and therefore it is vital that good research on "offending" women must include perspectives on both juvenile delinquency and crime. Usually, these issues are addressed in separate books, thus missing critical developmental links. Using a variety of academic and professional perspectives, the authors of these readings investigate the myriad problems and decisions girls and women face when they commit delinquent and criminal offenses and enter the justice system. Two central questions in these readings are (1) How does gender matter in crime and the justice system? and (2) What characterizes women's and girls' pathways to crime? In answering these key queries, the authors reveal the complex worlds female offenders must often negotiate—worlds frequently riddled with violence, victimization, discrimination, and economic marginalization.

Girls, Women, and Crime addresses four critical areas of work in the field of gender and crime. Part I, Gender and Criminological Theorizing: Gender at the Forefront, provides examples of research that examines the gender and crime interface in feminist criminological theory. The first two readings in this section look at different ways of conceptualizing gender and patriarchy in furthering the understanding of victimization and criminal behavior, and the last two readings explore aspects of contemporary feminist thought and activism that have the potential for profound implications in mainstream criminology and for significant impact on the field.

Part II, Female Juvenile Delinquents: Victimization, Delinquency, and the Juvenile Justice System, presents current research on girls, delinquency, and the justice system. No discussion of female delinquency would be complete without a discussion of girls' family dynamics, peer relationships, and experiences with physical, sexual, and emotional abuse. Accordingly, the first three chapters in this section examine how instability, disrupted families, school problems, and encounters with violence place girls on a trajectory toward offending, court involvement, and correctional placement. While girls' needs have been largely ignored throughout the history of juvenile justice, a focus on gender-specific programming has emerged in recent years, due to the strength and persistence of advocates and scholars in the area. The final installment in this section explores gender-specific programming for girl offenders, focusing on the aspects that must be included and the challenges that should be addressed.

Part III, The Woman Offender: Women's Experiences With Drugs, Crime, and Violence, considers the lives and situations of adult women and the criminal justice system. As with work on girls, no discussion of this topic can neglect the critical role of victimization and survival strategies in the lives of these women. The first reading—a discussion of female homicidal behavior—analyzes why some women resort to lethal violence to end abusive relationships and why others—who are the majority of abused women—do not. The second chapter is a qualitative study of female sex workers and illuminates the various techniques the women use to avoid sexual, health, and physical safety risks. The last two readings look at the impact of the illicit drug economy and drug policy on the lives and choices of women drug users or traffickers. The last reading documents, among other things, how the war on drugs has evolved into an indirect and undeclared war on women, particularly African American women.

Part IV, The Female Offender and Incarceration: Before, During, and After Incarceration, explores critical aspects of another unacknowledged national crisis: soaring increases in girls' and women's imprisonment in the United States. Prisons and youth correctional facilities were built to house dangerous men and law-violating boys, but they also increasingly house large numbers of girls and women. In a system that has long ignored the female offender, gender differences often cause serious difficulties. The readings in this section cover a variety of issues facing girls and women behind bars, from the Prison Rape Elimination Act and the culture of doing time to the struggles of negotiating re-entry into former communities. The section includes readings that underscore the challenges facing girls and women before, during, and after incarceration.

The readings in *Girls, Women, and Crime* provide a sampling of what the last three decades of feminist criminology have produced in the area of theory, girls' violence and delinquency, women's crime, and justice responses to female offending. We hope it will be clear from a reading of these assembled chapters that criminological theory, as well as research into crime more generally, will benefit from a more sophisticated approach to the study of gender and crime. In short, in crime and crime policy—as in life in general—gender matters.

PART I

GENDER AND CRIMINOLOGICAL THEORIZING

Gender at the Forefront

Traditionally, criminology has largely been a study of male crime and male victimization. Intellectual theorizing about crime and crime policy has actually been a type of theorizing about male deviance and criminality, with little to no attention paid to the role of gender. Women's and girls' experiences with crime, deviance, and victimization were at the periphery of scholarly inquiry, female crime was overlooked almost completely, and female victimization was ignored, trivialized, and minimized. Feminist criminology challenged the overall androcentric nature of traditional criminology by pointing to the repeated exclusion and misrepresentation of women and girls in criminological theory.

Feminist criminology places gender at the center of criminological theorizing. It recognizes how patriarchal power relations and inequality differentially affect men and women both in their criminal activities and in their experiences with victimization. It demonstrates how gender matters, not only in terms of one's pathways into and out of crime, but also in how the criminal justice system responds to the offenders under its authority. Gender is no longer a mere demographic variable or a brief footnote. Suddenly, men have gender, too, and male behavior is no longer considered the "normal" response to life.

The readings in this section represent criminological theorizing that keeps gender in the forefront. The first two readings underscore the merger of gender studies and gender theory with criminology. Summarizing the major models of feminist inquiry during the 1980s, Kathleen Daly presents an evaluation of the benefits and limitations of such theorizing for criminology. Through these modes of thought, she demonstrates how gender can be conceptualized as more than an attribute, how it is produced by social practices and situations, and how it is entwined with other social relations (namely, race and class). In the second reading, Lyn Mikel Brown, Meda Chesney-Lind, and Nan Stein apply feminist critical thought to understanding female violence, relational aggression, and bullying. The authors examine the consequences of the degendering and decontextualizing female violence and victimization and show the various ways anti-bullying programs in schools reinforce sex role stereotypes and structural inequities.

The last two readings showcase directions for feminism and activism in the field of criminological research and policy. Dana M. Britton discusses feminism's initial and ongoing impact on criminology and its emerging contributions both inside and outside the field and trends in emerging research. Hillary Potter's chapter examines one such emerging trend—Black feminist criminology. Using an integrated approach to understanding African American women's experiences with intimate partner abuse, Potter shows how Black feminist criminology offers a fresh and more comprehensive consideration of African American women's experiences with and responses to domestic violence.

Chapter 1

Different Ways of Conceptualizing Sex/Gender in Feminist Theory and Their Implications for Criminology

Kathleen Daly

At a recent feminist conference held at the Australian National University, I was struck by the varied vocabularies and assumptions used to discuss sex and gender. There is nothing unusual about seeing differences among women and feminists when we speak and write, but the categories of difference I saw took a new form. They were not marked by the familiar distinctions of liberal, radical and socialist-feminist; nor by identity politics in terms of a speaker's self-declared race-ethnicity, sexuality, nationality, physical ability, and the like. Nor were they ordered—at least not explicitly—by method and epistemology, including feminist arguments 'for' or 'against' postmodern ways of theorizing. What I observed set in motion a rethinking of the ways that sex and gender are conceptualized in feminist theory and in criminology. They can be termed 'class-race-gender,' 'doing gender' (and subsequently, 'doing difference'), and 'sexed bodies.' In describing and presenting these modes of feminist enquiry, I do not want to suggest that they cover the field.[1] Rather, I wish to clarify the contributions and limits of each to criminological knowledge.

My essay has two parts. In the first, I sketch major challenges to feminist theory that emerged in the 1980s concerning the production of knowledge and truth claims. This can be termed the 'knowledge problem' for feminism. The second describes three modes of feminist enquiry that responded, in part, to the challenges of the 1980s.

Source: Daly, K. (1997). Different ways of conceptualizing sex/gender in feminist theory and their implications for criminology. *Theoretical Criminology, 1*(1), 25–51.

Author's Note: For their careful reading and comments on an earlier draft, I thank Piers Beirne, Moira Gatens, Stuart Henry, Lisa Maher, Heather Strang and Rebecca Stringer. Portions of this paper were presented at the British Criminology Conference (July, 1995) and the Australian National University, Law Faculty Seminar (October, 1995) (Daly, 1995a), where comments by Angela McRobbie, Rebecca Dobash, Kathy Laster and Barbara Sullivan were especially helpful.

CHALLENGES TO FEMINIST THEORY

Engaging academic feminism in the 1960s and 1970s was how and whether sex, gender and 'women' could be linked or 'added on' to liberal and Marxist theories. A burgeoning literature developed that compared liberal, radical, Marxist and socialist feminist perspectives (see, for example, Jaggar, 1983; Sargeant, 1981). In 'Feminism and Criminology,' Meda Chesney-Lind and I appended an overview of these perspectives on the 'causes' of inequality and strategies for social change (Daly and Chesney-Lind, 1988: 536–8). We did so reluctantly: while we wished to show that a range of feminist positions was possible, we worried the typology would become fixed precisely when it was unravelling.[2] It became apparent by the mid-1980s that the task for feminist theory was no longer how 'to remove "biases" [from Marxism and liberalism] but to see this "bias" as intrinsic to the structure of the theories in question' (Gatens, 1996: 60).

Shifting Ground in the 1980s

In the 1980s, feminist theory was especially influenced by scholars in philosophy and literature. This signalled a shift from the socio-cultural and historical emphases of the 1970s, when scholars began to 'uncover' women's histories and to reveal ethnographic diversity and commonality in women's lives. Michele Barrett (1992) characterizes this shift as moving from 'things' to 'words.' In the 1970s, feminist scholars had referred to *women* or *women's experiences* unproblematically, and they had stressed the importance of distinguishing biological sex from socio-cultural gender, and of developing a comprehensive feminist theory that might replace liberal, Marxist or psychoanalytical theories. But those efforts became untenable in the 1980s. A related critical challenge came from women marginalized by feminist theory and from a variety of postmodern/poststructuralist texts and theorists.[3] These developments set in motion questions about how feminist knowledge is and should be produced and evaluated.

Early critiques of racism (hooks, 1981) and heterosexism suggested a failure of previous feminist scholarship to reflect on its own 'white solipsism' (Rich, 1979: 299) and 'compulsory heterosexuality' (Rich, 1980). Just when some feminist scholars sought to develop a women's standpoint on knowledge, drawing either from Marxist terminology of proletarian consciousness (Hartsock, 1983) or women's bifurcated consciousness (Smith, 1979, 1987), the grounds for claiming a singular women's standpoint began to dissolve. Increasing attention was given to differences among women, which spawned what was termed *identity politics*: naming who one 'was' in terms of social location or 'identity,' with a particular set of experiences and viewpoints, and hence, different knowledges 'about women.' Voices that had been excluded from or ignored within feminist thought—e.g. self-identified radical women of color (Moraga and Anzaldua, 1983) and black feminists (Collins, 1986), among others (Cole, 1986)—gained presence in the 1980s, giving notice to the dominant white, middle-class voices of feminist thought that theirs was not the only feminist analysis in town.[4]

Feminists who drew from postmodern thought also challenged the term *woman*, though for the reason that it lacked a stable and unified referent.[5] But, like the early critiques from women marginalized by feminist thought, which raised questions about whose knowledge or 'experience' was legitimate, feminists working with postmodern texts raised questions about power in the production of knowledge.

Several major feminist literary theorists—Jane Gallop, Marianne Hirsch and Nancy Miller—discussed the role of feminist critique and their fears of being criticized by other scholars. As Gallop admitted,

> I realize that the set of feelings that I used to have about French men I now have about African-American women. Those are the people I feel inadequate in relation to and try to please in my writing. (Gallop et al., 1990: 363–4)

Gallop's comment suggests that her feminist literary analysis was *first* affected by French men and *then* by black women.[6] I suspect this chronology was common for US feminist literary scholars. Certainly, it was more so for this group than for US feminists in sociology, who responded first to the charge of racism in feminist thought and who were relatively more resistant to postmodern influences. These different histories of coming to terms with 'French men and black women' have important consequences for how we think through the problem of 'difference' (both among and between men and women) and the degree to which postmodern/poststructuralist theoretical terms are embraced.[7]

For feminists in sociology, the problem of difference is commonly understood to mean mapping variation in women's (and men's) lives, of documenting power and resistance in interaction, and of assuming that one's engagement in social structures (and especially, class, race-ethnicity, gender, sexuality and age) matter in shaping one's consciousness, patterns of speech, behavior and capacity to affect social structures. In sociological empirical terms, difference is hardly novel; it is another way to theorize variability and power in social life. For literary scholars, the problem of difference is more often understood primarily as a discursive construction, its elements being binary oppositions in language, the construction of the 'masculine' and 'feminine' as constitutive of hierarchical sexual difference, and for some, an interest in the unconscious psyche. This contrast renders these approaches more oppositional than I would like, but two observations can be made.

First, humanities scholars set the feminist theoretical agenda in the 1980s; they were quicker than social science scholars to work with postmodern texts and theorists and, as such, they were more interested in the ways in which language and discourse set limits on what could be known. One result of the dominance of the humanities in the production of feminist knowledge is that scholars may not appreciate—indeed they may misunderstand—the practices of empirical social research. Another is that the work exhibits a form of theoretical imperialism or theoreticism, where the primary activity is discussion of concepts in the abstract.

Second, and more speculatively, I suspect that many humanities scholars read the race critique through postmodern terms, whereas the order may have been reversed for those in sociology (and kindred social sciences), who read the race critique through modern terms and who took on postmodern texts later. There have, of course, been different directions taken by feminist scholars in response to critique from within and from without. My point here is to note a confluence between the 'problem of difference' in feminist theory and a problem of power in the production of feminist knowledge. It is illustrated by Maria Lugones (a philosopher and Latina), who describes how 'white women' addressed the problem of difference:

> White women conceived [not] noticing us as a theoretical problem, which they label the problem of difference. . . . But white women theorists seem to have worried more passionately about the harm the claim does to theorizing than about the harm the theorizing did to women of color. The 'problem of difference' refers to feminist theories—these theories are the center of concern. The attempted solutions to the 'problem of difference' try to rescue feminist theorizing from several . . . pitfalls that would render it false, trivial, weak, and so on. (Lugones, 1991: 41)

As Lugones suggests, the problem of difference was framed by many feminist theorists solely as a problem for theory. Whereas she locates this tendency as stemming from 'white women's theorizing,' I see it stemming from a disciplinary-based theoreticism, especially evident in philosophy, but which may also have a class and racial nexus.[8] In comparison to philosophy, there was a larger group of feminists in sociology who called for 'incorporating' class-race-gender into the curriculum and research (see Andersen and Collins, 1992).[9] That incorporation is not without problems (see Piatt, 1993), but it remains a major theoretical point of entry, especially for feminists of color, and a strategy for coalitional knowledge-building across groups.

Contrary to the claims of radical feminism of the early 1970s, Moira Gatens (1996: 62) suggests that it would be naive to think that feminists can produce 'pure or non-patriarchal theory.' This issue is central to the knowledge problem for feminism: it invites a rethinking of how we adjudicate among competing claims about 'women' or 'women's experiences.' Are some better than others, and how do we decide?

Empiricist-Standpoint-Postmodern Feminisms

In the mid-1980s, Sandra Harding made an important contribution when she compared different epistemologies in producing feminist knowledge: empiricist, standpoint and postmodern (Harding, 1986, 1987). She noted the paradox (Harding, 1986: 24) that feminism was a political movement for social change and yet feminist researchers were producing knowledge in the natural and social sciences that was more 'likely to be confirmed by evidence' than previous scientific claims. Harding wondered, 'How can such politicized research be increasing the objectivity of inquiry? On what grounds should these feminist claims be justified?' She suggested that there were two 'solutions' (empiricism and standpointism) and one 'agenda for a solution' (postmodernism).

By *feminism empiricism,* Harding referred to improvements in knowledge by removing sexist and androcentric biases. This meant to 'correct' but not to transform the methodological norms of science. Such a stance was dominant in 1970s feminist social science work, including criminology; and it remains strong in the 1990s. An unfortunate legacy in Harding's analysis is the choice of the term *empiricism* in light of its connotations in social research.[10] In the social sciences, *empiricist* or *empiricism* are distinguished from *empirical.* The former terms refer to non-theorized empirical enquiry: that which exhibits the 'imperialism of the technique' or that which assumes a firm foundation of knowledge through observation (Wagner, 1992). However, one can do empirical work without being empiricist or without assuming an epistemology of empiricism. It seems crucial, then, that the term empirical not be tied to a particular epistemology. It is as large as 'text,' and both can stand in a constructive tension in the practice of social research.

By *feminist standpoint,* Harding (1986: 26) referred to how 'women's subjugated position provides the possibility of more complete and less perverse understandings' than the dominant position of men. This 'standpoint' is informed by women's experiences as understood from the perspective of feminism; thus, it can be taken by both men and women. Several problems are immediately evident. Can there be just one feminist standpoint if subjugated experiences vary by class or race, etc.? And, 'Is it too firmly rooted in a problematic politics of essentialized identities?' (Harding, 1986: 27).

The possibility of a feminist standpoint in law was most explicitly theorized by Catharine MacKinnon (1982, 1983), who contrasted a Marxist ontology of exploited and alienated labor (that of a nongendered proletariat) with a radical feminist ontology of exploited and alienated sexuality (that of women). Her arguments have been discussed and criticized at length by others (see, for example, Smart, 1989) so I will not repeat them here. Despite its problems, the idea of a feminist or women's standpoint remains popular. It has evolved, shifting from an initial justificatory claim of superior feminist knowledge to anti-elitist claims of 'women's gendered experiences' (Fineman, 1994). It continues to resonate with the variety of 'hyphenated' feminisms—black (or African-American) feminism, Native American feminism, and the like—as scholars identify and validate a set of subjugated experiences and knowledges (see, e.g. Collins, 1990); and it is relevant for those examining the consequences of 'lived sexed bodies' for the 'sexualization of all knowledges' (Grosz, 1995: 36, 43). This larger set of positions congenial with standpointism reflects postmodern strains that soon become evident in standpoint thinking (Harding, 1986: 27).

By *feminist postmodernism,* Harding referred to a heterogeneous set of critiques of Enlightenment thought with its associated hierarchical dualisms (mind over body and reason over emotion, among others), disembodied claims of truth 'innocent of power,' and assumptions of a stable, coherent self (see Flax, 1990: 41–2). During the 1980s, US feminist engagement with postmodern texts and theorists was emergent; more developed analyses and debates soon followed (e.g. Butler and Scott, 1992; Nicholson, 1990).

One cannot make sense of feminist knowledge debates today without reference to postmodern ways of thinking about multiple and partial knowledges. For example, Harding (1990: 93) suggests that 'the knowing subject of feminist empiricism inadvertently but inevitably is in tension with Enlightenment assumptions,' and she views the modernist assumptions embedded in standpoint epistemologies and the postmodern skepticism of science, as reflecting 'converging approaches to a postmodernist world' (Harding, 1987: 295). Like other commentators, she notes that many modernist assumptions are embedded in postmodern texts and that feminist thinkers had already been challenging the assumptions of Enlightenment knowledge without benefit of postmodern thought (see Bordo, 1993; Carrington, 1994; de Lauretis, 1990; Henry and Milovanovic, 1996: Ch. 2; Seidman, 1994).

Discourse and 'A Real World Out There'

Modern/postmodern boundaries are more often blurred than sharp in feminist knowledge debates. However, for those engaged in social research, important tensions remain concerning the status of 'the real' or the 'extra-discursive' in connection (or disconnection) to 'discourse.' Cain (1995: 70) puts the matter this way:

> Do we emphasize the privilege or necessity of a downsider perspective, or do we buy in to the full postmodern package as a way of dealing with the differences within the downsider group?

By the 'full postmodern package,' Cain refers to a tendency to accord 'primal ontological status ... to texts (or discourses) ... ' (p. 70). She suggests that the fallacies of epistemological primacy ('human knowledge calls the world') and epistemological privilege ('the social world has no potency outside of discourse'), which are present in many postmodern texts, 'arrogant[ly] place human knowledge at the centre of the universe.' Cain argues for

> an autonomous existence for the material world, ... which ... include[s] not only untouched stars and virgin forest, artefacts with a knowledge component such as houses, fields, cakes, gardens, radios, bicycles, and income tax forms, but also social relations. (p. 74)

She envisions an 'empirical argument about the unthought and unspeakable relationships which yet have (so much) power' and thus, she wants to claim an ontology for social relations which 'like discourse ... exist powerfully in a state of radical and uncaused autonomy' (p. 75). She suggests a methodological strategy of 'mapping ... the articulations between relationships and knowledge/discourse.' She sees this strategy as implicit in Foucault's earlier work on discourse and the extra-discursive (see also Cain, 1993) and proposes that 'genealogy needs a sociology, as sociology has needed to understand the autonomy and power of the text' (p. 75).

Cain's arguments assist me in several ways. First, she recreates a space within postmodern thought for 'a real world out there,' although not a world that is transparent or knowable to an observer in empiricist terms. She terms her approach 'realist feminist,' which she links to a relational standpointism that is not given by biology but by social relations and an act of political will (Cain, 1993: 88–94; see also Cain, 1986, 1990). Second, she offers a way to see the limits of discourse analysis and, as such, challenges current hierarchies in feminist

knowledge: of words 'over' things and of philosophy and literature 'over' the social sciences.[11] I do not think it is coincidental that Cain's (1995) interest in reconciling 'apparently incompatible ontologies' (p. 73) has been forged from reflecting on the subjugated knowledges both of First World women in the metropole and of Third World men and women in the postcolonial Caribbean.

How has research in criminology been affected by these shifts in feminist thought? In the 1970s and 1980s feminist research on Real Women challenged the androcentrism of the field, as scholars filled knowledge gaps about women law-breakers, victims and criminal justice workers. By the 1990s, several scholars signalled a shift in interest from Real Women to The Woman of criminological or legal discourse (see Smart, 1990a, 1992). This reflected a move toward postmodern thinking on crime, courts and prisons, which is evident in the works of Bertrand (1994), Howe (1990, 1994), Smart (1995), Worrall (1990), and A. Young (1990, 1996). While sympathetic to postmodern texts, others have not wanted to abandon Real Women; they include Cain (1989), Carlen (1985, 1988), Carrington (1990), Daly (1992), Joe and Chesney-Lind (1995), and Maher and Daly (1996). Those studying violence against women may be especially resistant to letting go of Real Women because their voices and experiences have only recently been 'named' (compare Marcus, 1992 and Hawkesworth, 1989; see Radford et al., 1996). I am, of course, simplifying here, but I do so to highlight where feminist debate remains keen, both within and outside criminology, on the politics of knowledge. By retaining Real Women, feminists may take 'the ground of specifically *moral* claims against domination—the avenging of strength through moral critique' (Brown, 1991: 75). Real Women can be mobilized as 'our subject that harbors truth, and our truth that opposes power' (p. 77).[12] But for others, Real Women, their moral grounds and 'truths,' must be set aside (Smart, 1990b, as discussed below). Concurring with Smart, Brown asks

> What is it about feminism that fears the replacement of truth with politics ... privileged knowledge with a cacophony of unequal voices clamoring for position? (Brown, 1991: 73)

A good deal, many reply (e.g. di Leonardo, 1991; di Stefano, 1990; Harding, 1987). And that is why the knowledge problem continues to be contentious for feminist theory and politics. One response has been sketched by Smart (1995: 230–2), who now admits that while we 'need to address this Woman of legal [or criminological] discourse, . . . this kind of analysis alone gives me cause for concern.' She suggests that discourse analysis of, for example, 'the raped woman is of little value unless we are also talking to women who have been raped' (p. 231). To Smart, this is not the same as asserting some truth about Real Women, but rather to be cognizant that 'women discursively construct themselves' (p. 231).[13]

Let me summarize and reflect on my argument in this first section. I identified problems resulting from a dominance of the humanities in feminist work: theoretical imperialism, insufficient attention to and a misreading of social science enquiry, and analyzing women's 'differences' solely in linguistic or discursive terms. I would not wish to claim superiority of 'the empirical' or of social science enquiry. Such a position does not reflect what I have learned from feminist work in philosophy, literature and media studies. Nor does it reflect my interests to develop interdisciplinary 'hybrid knowledges' that break down disciplinary boundaries (Seidman, 1994: 2). It is to say that social science research has a key role to play in feminist knowledge and that empirical enquiry can be as radical and subversive as deconstruction.

THREE MODES OF FEMINIST ENQUIRY

The challenges to feminist theory in the 1980s, both by women marginalized by its terms and by postmodern texts, were not isolated. They were part of a general mood to unsettle social theory and to re-engage a critique of positivist social science (Seidman, 1994). Thus, we would expect to see reworkings of old concepts and the emergence of new ones. Two ways of reconceptualizing sex/gender in feminist enquiry—'class-race-gender' and 'doing gender'—have been developed by feminists in the social sciences, especially those in sociology. 'Sexed bodies' has been developed by feminists in philosophy, and more generally, by re-readings of Foucault.

Class-Race-Gender

My work has been most influenced by class-race-gender or what I have come to term *multiple*

inequalities (Daly, 1993; 1995a). In the 1980s, it was not French men but black women whose critique of feminist thought had the greater influence on my thinking. Class-race-gender need not be interpreted literally to mean a sole focus on these three relations; its meaning can be stretched to include others, e.g. age, sexuality and physical ability. For many scholars, the term retains an allegiance, though not complete fealty, to notions of determining structures of inequality. For example, Pat Carlen (1994: 139–40) suggests the need to theorize inequalities that 'both recognizes and denies structuralism.' The term varies in application across and within the disciplines: from statistical analyses of wages and law-breaking for particular sub-groups (e.g. King, 1988; Simpson, 1991) to biographical and autobiographical storytelling forms (e.g. Abrams, 1991; Lorde, 1984; Pratt, 1984; Williams, 1991). In the US, class-race-gender is used to denote a more inclusive college-level curricula (see, for example, Belkhir et al., 1994 and the new journal *Race, Sex & Class)*, and it has become a popular title in marketing readers in women's studies (e.g. Andersen and Collins, 1992; Jaggar and Rothenberg, 1993; Ruiz and DuBois, 1994). While, on balance, curricula change and new readers are a good thing,[14] they are but a small slice of a wider class-race-gender project.

Class-race-gender conceptualizes inequalities, not as additive and discrete, but as intersecting, interlocking and contingent. In the US, class-race-gender emerged from the struggles of black women in the Civil Rights Movement; it came into academic institutions (and especially sociology) in the late 1970s through articles and books by women of color. This early body of work not only critiqued ethnocentrism in feminist theory, but also established a rhetorical ground for women of color (see, e.g. Baca Zinn et al., 1986; Combahee River Collective, 1979; Dill, 1983).

Conceptualizing multiple relations of inequality has only just begun (for a recent effort in criminology, see Schwartz and Milovanovic, 1995). It will not take the same form as previous efforts to theorize 'systems of inequality' (as in relationships of capitalism and patriarchy). And while its proponents often claim its 'greater inclusiveness,' we should expect that like other ideas, it is 'condemned to be haunted by a voice from the margins . . . awakening us to what has been excluded, effaced, damaged' (Bordo, 1990: 138). Like others (e.g. Anthias and Yuval-Davis, 1992; Collins, 1993) I see the project as mapping the salience and contingency of gender, class, race-ethnicity, and the like, both separately and together. For Floya Anthias and Nira Yuval-Davis (1992: 99), this means 'specifying] the mechanisms by which different forms of exclusion and subordination operate.' For Patricia Hill Collins (1990: 226–7), it means showing how social relations operate in a matrix of domination at three levels: personal, group and systemic. Authors' uses of terms such as *power* and *social structure* may vary: they range from earlier, more deterministic understandings of power as something individuals 'possess' in varying degrees, depending on their location in social structures external to them (e.g. Davis, 1981) to recent understandings, which are more context-dependent. These recent ways of conceptualizing social structure as fluid pose major challenges to previous understandings of power, subordination and human emancipation (see Collins, 1990; Henry and Milovanovic, 1996: Chs. 2–3; Yeatman, 1995).

Bordo (1990: 145) observes that the 'analytics of class and race . . . do not seem to be undergoing the same deconstruction' as gender and women. I would agree: relatively less intellectual discussion has been devoted to showing the lack of a unified referent for racial and class categories compared to those for gender. One reason is an under-theorization of race-ethnicity and its links to other social relations, e.g. the 'gendering' of race or the 'racializing' of gender. This is one of several building blocks in developing a class-race-gender analysis in criminology, but as yet, movement has been slow. Discomfort levels are high, not coincidentally because criminologists are so 'white' and advantaged, while the subjects of their crime theories more often are not (despite some attention to organizational crime). Moreover, scholars of color in criminology have only recently been in a position to challenge the white-centered assumptions of the field and to develop anti-racist theoretical and research agendas (see Russell, 1992; Walker and Brown, 1995; Young and Greene, 1995).

There are many ways to work with the idea of multiple inequalities. One is to use it to transform research and writing practices in the social sciences (see Daly, 1993, 1994). For example, to show how racial discrimination 'works,' one could use Richard Delgado's (1989) method of presenting multiple accounts of the 'same event.' In this case, Delgado describes what happened when a black man was interviewed for a job at a law school. The multiple perspectives of the participants, as orchestrated by Delgado, bring the white reader into the story in such a way that racial discrimination toward the black man becomes visible to the white reader as part of his/her routine interpretations and practices. Delgado offers a nuanced picture of how race relations routinely work to disadvantage black job applicants through the organizational frame of 'neutral' job criteria. This kind of multi-perspectival approach could also be used by authors in communicating research findings and, as such, class-race-gender can be a vehicle by which to develop collaborations across academic-community locations and identities (see Austin, 1992; Daly and Stephens, 1995).

To date, class-race-gender has been most vividly revealed through literary and story-telling forms (see, for example, Bell, 1987; Delgado, 1989; Jordan, 1985; Lubiano, 1992; Pratt, 1984; Williams, 1991).[15] Unlike a good deal of traditional social science, these works reveal (1) the shifting salience of race, class, gender, nation and sexuality, and the like as one moves through space and time, and (2) the different world-views or lenses that participants bring to social encounters. A major question is whether one can bring these literary or storytelling forms into research practices in sociology and criminology. It may be possible, if researchers use narrative modes of reasoning (see Richardson, 1990; Stivers, 1993; Ewick and Silbey, 1995).

The contribution of class-race-gender to criminology is an insistence that everyone is located in a matrix of multiple social relations, i.e. that race and gender are just as relevant to an analysis of white men as they are to black women. With an emphasis on contingency, one can explore the varied positions of 'black women'—as offenders, victims, and mothers and wives of offenders and victims—to 'white justice' (Daly, 1995b). And as Lisa Maher (1995: Ch. 9) demonstrates in her ethnographic research on women drug-users in New York City, one can reveal varied angles of vision for African- and European-American women and Latinas in neighborhood drug markets. Class-race-gender can also be used to politicize and problematize knowledge in collaboration with others. In this regard, Collins (1993) is right to emphasize the piecing together of work by different scholars as bits in a wider mosaic; the quest to theorize the 'totality' of multiple inequalities is ill-founded. One set of theoretical problems, discussed by

Anthias and Yuval-Davis (1992: 17), is how to relate the 'different oncological spheres' of class, race and gender divisions, while simultaneously showing the ways they intermesh in concrete situations. Another challenge is to identify new vocabularies to discuss multiple, intersecting or interlocking inequalities. Otherwise, we may easily slip into additive, mechanical analyses of power, oppression and the heaping of disadvantage and advantage.

Doing Gender

Candace West and Donald Zimmerman (1987) coined the construct 'doing gender' to describe gender as a 'situated accomplishment':

> [Gender is not the] property of individuals . . . [but rather] an emergent feature of social situations: . . . an outcome of and a rationale for . . . social arrangements . . . a means of legitimating [a] fundamental division . . . of society. [Gender is] a routine, methodical, and recurring accomplishment (p. 126) . . . not a set of traits, nor a variable, nor a role [but] itself constituted through interaction, (p. 129)

R. W. Connell (1987, 1995) and James Messerschmidt (1993) have developed linkages between 'doing gender' (more precisely, 'doing masculinity') and gender relations of power. Susan Martin and Nancy Jurik (1996) have also utilized 'doing gender' in their analysis of women and gender in justice system occupations. All four authors have elements of 'class-race-gender' in their work. They view structure as ordering interaction, and interaction as producing structure, drawing on Anthony Giddens' (1984) efforts to transcend the sociological dualism of interaction and social structure.[16]

In 1995, West and Fenstermaker published 'Doing Difference,' in which they attempt to incorporate 'doing gender' with 'class-race-gender.' Rather than viewing each relation of class or race or gender as a 'structure of oppression,' they propose that the whole be viewed as 'experience.' Thus, every social encounter, no matter who the participants are, can be conceptualized as being classed, raced and gendered. The terms used in 'doing gender' are extended without modification to 'doing race' or class. For example, the authors say that

the accomplishment of race (like gender) does not necessarily mean 'living up' to normative conceptions of attitudes and activities appropriate to a particular race category; rather, it means engaging in action at the risk of race assessment. (West and Fenstermaker, 1995: 23–4)

Later that year, several scholars replied to West and Fenstermaker's article (Collins et al., 1995). Critics objected that it ignored power and oppression, as it did resistance and conflict (Collins et al., 1995: 491–4, 497–502).

What vexed the critics, in part, was that the 'isms' of inequality—racism, classism, etc.—were not sufficiently addressed with West and Fenstermaker's version of social constructionism. Also vexing was that gender or race, etc. could be viewed merely as an accomplishment or performance. In this regard, Barrie Thorne (1995: 498–9) noted similarities between 'doing gender' and Judith Butler's (1990) discussion of gender as the performance of sex; both, in her view, neglected the importance of seeing gender (and other social relations) as extending 'deep into the unconscious . . . and outward into social structure and material interests.'[17]

Some feminist skepticism toward 'doing gender' lies in a desire to retain 'structures of power' that both precede and are produced by gender or race, etc. as 'accomplishments.' Whether sex and gender are understood to be produced in interaction or in discourse, feminist critiques (specifically, by sociologists) are based on retaining some semblance of social structure or materialism. As we shall see, some feminists using 'sexed bodies' also wish to include a form of materialism ('materiality'), but its constituents are the body and sexual difference.

Messerschmidt (1993) applied 'doing gender' in his analysis of crime as 'a resource for doing masculinity in specific social settings . . . ':

> Crime . . may be invoked as a practice through which masculinities (and men and women) are differentiated from one another. . . . [It] is a resource that may be summoned when men lack other resources to accomplish gender. (p. 85)

Whereas West and Zimmerman (1987: 137) had focused on how the doing of gender 'creat[es] differences between . . . women and men' that materialize as 'essential sexual natures' (p. 138),

Messerschmidt suggested that the doing of gender also produces multiple forms of masculinity and crime.

One problem Messerschmidt encounters is how to conceptualize crime as a gendered line of social action without once again establishing boys and men as the norm, differentiating themselves from all that is 'feminine.' Although masculine subjectivity and lines of action may be described with these terms (see Jefferson, 1994), it is disputable that feminine subjectivity and lines of action could be. Specifically, would the claim that crime is a 'resource for doing femininity'—for women and girls 'to create differences from men and boys or to separate from all that is masculine'—have any cultural resonance? Probably not. But nor should theories necessarily have to employ symmetrical sex/gender terms. That is to say, arguments that crime is a resource or situation where masculinities are produced may be useful: they normalize crime but problematize men and masculinity.

In applying 'doing gender' to criminological research, scholars will have to let go of thinking about gender or race, etc. as attributes of persons and examine how situations and social practices produce qualities and identities associated with membership in particular social categories. Despite the creative efforts of some to employ doing gender in quantitative analyses of self-reported delinquency (e.g. Simpson and Elis, 1995), it is better suited to analyses of social interaction. Researchers will need to be mindful that categories taken from theorizing masculinity may be inappropriately applied to femininity. Gender categories are not neutral, and the terms used to describe men and women 'doing gender' are not likely to be interchangeable. These are major points for those using the 'sexed bodies' construct.

Sexed Bodies

Gatens (1996: 67) observes that 'there is probably no simple explanation for the recent proliferation of writings concerning the body.' She credits Foucault's work on the (male) body as a site of disciplinary practices, coupled with that of feminist social scientists, who showed that even the most privileged women have not attained equality with men in the 'public sphere.'[18] Perhaps feminists would need to face, yet again but in different ways, 'questions of corporeal specificity' (p. 68). The trick, Gatens suggests, is

to acknowledge 'historical realities ... without resorting to biological essentialism' (p. 69):

> The present capacities of female bodies are, by and large, very different from the present capacities of male bodies. It is important to create the means of articulating the historical realities of sexual difference without thereby reifying these differences. (p. 69)

Feminists have been analyzing a large philosophical literature on 'the body' and its connection with 'the mind' (see, for example, Butler, 1993; Gatens, 1996; Grosz, 1994, 1995). Sexed bodies are theorized in several ways: some emphasize the discursive construction of 'sex,' including cultural inscription on bodies, whereas others work at the edges of the 'materiality of sex' and 'culture.' For the moment, I will focus on the latter in reviewing three interrelated themes: the sex/gender distinction, power as productive of gender and sexual difference, and dualisms in western philosophy.

Sex/Gender. In 1983 Gatens challenged the familiar distinction between sex (the biological categories of 'male' and 'female') and gender (the social categories of 'masculinity' and 'femininity' that are linked to sex) (reprinted in Gatens, 1996: Ch. 1). She was critical of the assumption that 'the mind of either sex is initially a neutral, passive entity, a blank slate on which are inscribed various social "lessons."' The 'alleged neutrality of the body, the postulated arbitrary connection between femininity and the female body, masculinity and the male body' troubled Gatens because it 'encourage[s] ... a neutralization of sexual difference and sexual politics ... and the naive solution of resocialization' (p. 4, Gatens's emphasis). Moreover, by denying sex-specific corporeality, key differences are overlooked 'between feminine behavior or experience that is lived out by a female subject and feminine behavior or experience that is lived out by a male subject (and vice versa with masculine behavior)' (p. 9).

Power. Drawing on but moving beyond Foucault's account of 'the manner in which the micropolitical operations of power produce socially appropriate bodies,' Gatens (1996: 70) proposes that we view gender as

> not the effect of ideology or cultural values but as the way in which power takes hold of and

constructs bodies in particular ways. . . . The sexed body can no longer be conceived as the unproblematic biological and factual base upon which gender is inscribed, but must itself be recognized as constructed by discourses and practices that take the body both as their target and as their vehicle of expression.

Gatens's conceptualization of gender as 'the way in which power takes hold of bodies and constructs them in particular ways' raises questions for the relationship between social construction and materiality, which Butler (1993) takes up:

> To claim that sex is already gendered, already constructed, is not yet to explain in which way the 'materiality' of sex is forcibly produced. What are the constraints by which bodies are materialized as 'sexed,' and how are we to understand the 'matter' of sex? . . . (p. xi)

Butler proposes a 'return to the notion of matter, not as site or surface, but as a process of materialization' (p. 9) and suggests we should ask, 'Through what regulatory norms is sex itself materialized?' (p. 10).

Dualisms. Elizabeth Grosz (1994) argues that current understandings of 'the body' reflect dualisms in western thinking, and by rethinking 'the body,' subjectivity can be reconceptualized. She rejects the view of the body as 'natural' or having a 'presocial' existence and, simultaneously, she rejects the view of the body as '*purely* a social, cultural, and signifying effect lacking its own weighty materiality' (p. 21, Grosz's emphasis). (As such, she takes issue with feminist approaches she terms egalitarian and social constructionist.) She wants to

> . . . deny that there is the 'real' material body on the one hand and its various cultural and historical representations on the other. . . . These representations and cultural inscriptions quite literally constitute bodies and help to produce them as such. (p. x)

Grosz uses the metaphor of a mobius strip to suggest the 'inflection of mind into body and body into mind . . . the torsion of the one into the other . . . [the] uncontrollable drift of the inside into the outside and outside into the

inside' (p. xii). Terms such as 'embodied subjectivity' and 'psychical corporeality' (p. 22) might be used to characterize this inflection.

Why are sexed bodies and corporeality important? When viewing the mind as 'linked to, perhaps even part of, the body' and 'bodies themselves as always sexually (and racially) distinct, . . . then [we can see that] the very forms that subjectivity takes are not generalizable.' We therefore cannot assume 'universalist ideals of humanism' nor can we produce and evaluate knowledges that are not 'sexually determinate, limited, finite' (Grosz, 1994: 20).

'Sexed bodies' is excellent for revealing the 'neutralization and neutering of . . . [sex] specificity' and with it the 'cultural and intellectual effacement of women' (Grosz, 1994: ix). Its practitioners are on weaker ground, however, when they attempt to connect, in a theoretical sense, sexual difference and racial, cultural and class divisions. Grosz suggests that interconnections be viewed as 'interlocking'—using similar terms as Collins (1990) and West and Fenstermaker (1995)—and like these theorists, she is concerned that class, race, etc. should not be conceived as 'autonomous structures which then require external connections' (p. 20). A major difference is what is being explained. For Collins, it is inequality and oppression; for Grosz, it is sexual difference and multiple subjectivities.

Grosz argues (1994: 18) that scholars working with a sexed bodies construct share 'a commitment to a notion of the fundamental, irreducible differences between the sexes' and while they acknowledge that 'class and race differences may divide women, sexual differences demand social recognition and representation.' Arguing against those who say that theirs is an essentialist analysis, Grosz suggests that the task is to undermine the dichotomy between 'sex as an essentialist and gender as a constructionist category' (p. 18).

Grosz and colleagues' work on sexed bodies is one way the construct can be used. Another emphasizes cultural inscription *on* the body (see review in Howe, 1994: 194–205). The work I shall consider is Carol Smart's (1990b) on the production of sexed bodies in legal discourse.

Smart is interested in how 'law constructs and reconstructs masculinity and femininity, and maleness and femaleness' that produce a 'common-sense perception of difference' (p. 201). One sees affinity between Smart's claim that legal discourse produces gender and that of West and Zimmerman for whom situations produce gender; but there are key differences. Smart wants to consider how 'law constructs sexed (and not simply gendered) subjectivities' (p. 202), that is, 'the sexed body' (p. 203).[19] She does so by examining rape and rape trials. Smart's (1990b) article was published at around the same time that analyses of the 'matter' or 'materiality of sex' were emerging; this may explain why she does not engage with authors like Grosz who viewed 'sexed bodies' neither as natural nor as signifying effects of culture. Instead, Smart analyzes the sexed body as produced both by legal and feminist discourse: the 'natural' sexed woman, who during a rape trial becomes a victimized sexed body. In feminist discourse this is the body of the eternal victim, whereas in legal discourse, it is the deserving victim (pp. 207–8). Smart cautions that it will be difficult for feminists to 'construct rape differently' because the effort to 'deconstruct the biological/sexed woman is silenced by the apparition of law's sexed woman to whose survival it is unwillingly tied' (p. 208). In other words, feminist efforts to challenge rape law will be thwarted by law's discursive power.

'Sexed bodies' can contribute to criminology in several ways. We can see that gender categories 'neuter' sexual difference, both in research and in policy. For research, we might explore how the 'sensual attractions' of crime (Katz, 1988) are differently available to and 'experienced' by male/female bodies and masculine/feminine subjectivities. We could analyze the variable production of sexed (and racialized, etc.) bodies across many types of harms (not just rape) or for other sites of legal regulation such as family law. We could take Howe's (1994) theoretical lead by investigating women's bodies as the object of penality. For policy, 'sexed bodies' is useful for showing that reputedly gender-neutral policies are tied to specific male bodies. Sexed bodies may worry some feminists because the construct seems to revisit the spectre of biologism and body types that has long haunted criminology. This need not be the case. Sexed bodies calls attention to how we 'experience' sexual difference and its relationship to gender. It also calls attention to dualisms in western philosophy and how dualisms such as reason/emotion, mind/body and male/female are constituted in and through law, science and criminology.

A problem with sexed bodies is the strong temptation to see social life primarily through a lens of sexual difference. It is not just that feminist analyses may unwittingly collude with say, legal discourse in 'reifying these differences' (Gatens, 1996: 69), as Smart's (1990b) analysis reveals so well. Nor that for those who take 'phallocentric culture' as the start point, the recommended strategy of 'thinking outside the confining concept of the natural/sexed woman' (Smart, 1990b: 208) may be foreclosed by its own terms. From an empirical point of view, the problem is that claims such as 'the utterances of judges constantly reaffirm [the natural/sexed woman]' and 'almost every rape trial tells the same story' (Smart, 1990b: 205–6) are theoretical claims. While they may help us see a pattern of discursive power, they should be seen as open to empirical enquiry not asserted as ahistorical discursive 'fact' (see Carrington, 1994 on this point). A second problem is that variation and particularity in sexed bodies (by race or age, etc.) is posited by theorists but not explored with care. As a consequence, sex and gender are foregrounded whereas other socially relevant divisions are accorded secondary status.

CONCLUSION

I have highlighted the different contributions and trajectories that class-race-gender, doing gender and sexed bodies take, but I have also endeavored to identify points of convergence. 'Class-race-gender' and 'doing gender' share a common sociological heritage, the former emphasizing social relations of inequality and the latter, the production of social categories in interaction. Thus, scholars have drawn from each to get around the sociological 'macro-micro level' problem and the structure-agency dualism. Most feminist scholars today are concerned with linking sex/gender to other social relations and with making particular (not generic) claims about women or men. Those working with 'class-race-gender' have begun to articulate what the linkages might look like and to conduct empirical research along these lines. Those working with 'sexed bodies' continue to challenge the thinking of 'class-race-gender' and 'doing gender' analysts by emphasizing that sexual difference is qualitatively different from other social categories and divisions. The 'sexed bodies' construct takes several forms: one relies on discursive power inscribing 'sex' on bodies (e.g. Butler, 1990), and another aims to bring a 'materiality' to the cultural construction of 'the body' (e.g. Bordo, 1993; Butler, 1993; Grosz, 1994).

Recent interest by feminist philosophers in 'materiality' reflects, I would argue, a recognition of the failure of discourse theory or deconstruction alone to adequately represent social relations and human existence. It also signals a need to rethink the relationship between 'the discursive' and 'the real' in feminist and allied social theories, a development I welcome. Therefore, I would disagree with Charles Lemert (1994: 274), who proposes that sociologists (and criminologists) ignore our 'thirst for reality, and consider it . . as though it were . . . a huge, ugly but plausibly discursive text.' We may do better by working the boundary between 'the discursive' and 'the real world out there,' not seeing either as prior or foundational. This would permit greater openness to theoretical and methodological innovation. It may also require reconciling 'apparently incompatible ontologies,' as Cain (1995: 73) suggests, and challenging the dominance of the humanities in contemporary feminist and allied social theories. Theoretical space must surely be large enough to include 'French men' and 'black women' and many, many others.

Notes

1. Any such typology is likely to reflect one's disciplinary background with its 'core' set of texts and theories; these are modified further by national and academic milieux. Many other typologies are possible, e.g. those arraying psychoanalytical and literary theories, or highlighting disciplinary debates. My typology draws largely from sociology. Readers will appreciate that my sketch of shifts and disciplinary differences in feminist thought that is done with broad brush strokes.

2. Even in the better discussions in US undergraduate textbooks and readers (Beirne and Messerschmidt, 1995: 550–61; Price and Sokoloff, 1995: 1–3), this typology remains in place.

3. Following Seidman (1994: 2) I use the terms modern and postmodern 'to refer to broad social and cultural patterns and sensibilities that can be analytically distinguished for the purpose of highlighting social trends.' Elements of each may be embedded in the other, but among those associated with modern are 'the claim of the exclusive truth-producing capacity of science,' centered and transcendental subjects

and causal relations; for postmodern, a rejection of Enlightenment theories of knowledge, decentered subjects or multiple subject positions, and non-causal relations. Most scholars working with a postmodern sensibility term their analyses 'poststructuralist,' which signals an interest to deconstruct hierarchical binary oppositions in language and to analyze the role of discourse in 'shaping subjectivity, social institutions, and politics' (Seidman, 1994: 18). I shall use postmodern and poststructuralist loosely and interchangeably, although others have suggested ways of distinguishing them (see Smart, 1995: 1–15; see also Henry and Milovanovic, 1996: 1–15; Schwartz and Friedrichs, 1994).

4. As Lise Vogel (1991) suggests, some members of the second generation of feminist scholars, who came into the academy in the mid-1980s, can also be criticized for their poor revisionist history of 1960s and 1970s feminist thought, one major strand of which did address class and racial-ethnic divisions.

5. Also raised was the problem of essentialism in feminist thought (see de Lauretis, 1990; Grosz, 1990; Martin, 1994). I see this problem as far more relevant for feminist philosophers than for social researchers. Whereas the former reflect on 'woman' or 'women' as analytical categories, the latter assume and describe variability in particular women studied (see Roseneil, 1995, on this point).

6. Her particular reference is to Jacques Lacan and Deborah McDowell (Gallop et al., 1990: 364). There are, of course, several 'French women' who have been highly influential in feminist thought (see Spivak, 1992).

7. This claim is impressionistic and is based on reading the major US feminist journals (*Signs* and *Feminist Studies*) in the past two decades; it could be explored empirically. Many feminist scholars might also say that 'French men and black women' had a simultaneous impact on their thinking.

8. Major feminist philosophers themselves have made the same point (Bordo, 1993: 285–300; I. Young, 1994: 717).

9. Evidence for this claim comes from several sources. First, sociology has been the disciplinary home for more feminists of color than has philosophy; and it was feminists of color who put race (and class-race-gender) on the agenda. Second, institutional support, including materials for curriculum integration, was developed by sociologists at a key US center in Memphis State University. In general, 'incorporation' of race-ethnicity did not require a fundamental rethinking of the canon in sociology (or in history or anthropology) to the same degree as it did in philosophy and literature.

10. Naffine (1994: xi–xxx) has developed a modified version of this knowledge typology; she uses the terms empiricism and empirical interchangeably.

11. This hierarchy is also in place when one says that words 'contain' things. See Norris (1992: 28–31)

for other critical realist arguments and Bordo's (1993: 291) critique of discursive foundationalism in which 'language swallows everything up, voraciously, a theoretical pasta machine through which the categories of competing frameworks are pressed and reprocessed as "tropes."'

12. Brown (1991) gives a good characterization of how Real Women is mobilized by feminists, but she argues that it should be set aside.

13. One problem with positing The Woman of legal or criminological discourse is the assumption of a single or overarching discourse. I prefer the notion of discordant discourses; but in any event, this should be open to empirical enquiry, not presupposed.

14. In the readers just cited, articles describe a particular group at a particular time, but the editors identify no historical or relational linkages between them. These readers tend to reinforce notions of 'experience' and 'identity politics,' which have been ably challenged by postmodern feminist scholars (e.g. Scott, 1992).

15. To me these are excellent examples of class-race-gender in action, but the authors may not claim them as such.

16. As such, I see more discussion of 'structure' in Connell, Messerschmidt, and Martin and Jurik than in the original West and Zimmerman (1987) article.

17. Thorne (1995: 498) said that 'Butler [who] writes within the tradition of poststructuralism seems to be unaware of sociological analyses of . . . gender, which predated her work by more than a decade' (see also Epstein, 1994). Young's (1994) philosophical argument of gender as 'seriality' has affinities with 'doing gender.'

18. By contrast, Bordo (1993: 17) suggests that 'the body' was a preoccupation of feminist scholars prior to the influence of Foucault.

19. In a more recent essay, Smart (1995: 228–30) discusses law as a 'gendering practice' and a 'sexing practice,' which 'work alongside' each other. The former 'render[s] women as perpetually feminine, [and the latter makes] women perpetual "biological" women' (p. 229). Smart uses 'sexed bodies' to refer to the ways that women (more often than men) are constructed as 'sex' or simply as 'mere bodies' by legal discourse. Grosz (1994) discusses the women/body equivalence as one of several elements of 'sexed bodies.'

References

Abrams, Kathryn (1991) 'Hearing the Call of Stories,' *California Law Review* 79(4): 971–1052.

Andersen, Margaret L. and Patricia Hill Collins (eds.) (1992) *Race, Class, and Gender: An Anthology*. Belmont, CA: Wadsworth.

Anthias, Floya and Nira Yuval-Davis (1992) *Racialized Boundaries: Race, Nation, Gender, Colour and Class and the Anti-Racist Struggle*. New York: Routledge.

Austin, Regina (1992) '"The Black Community," Its Lawbreakers, and A Politics of Identification,' *Southern California Law Review* 65: 1769–1817.

Baca Zinn, Maxine, Lynn Weber Cannon, Elizabeth Higginbotham, and Bonnie Thornton Dill (1986) 'The Costs of Exclusionary Practices in Women's Studies,' *Signs: Journal of Women in Culture and Society* 11(2): 290–303.

Barrett, Michele (1992) 'Words and Things: Materialism and Method in Contemporary Feminist Analysis,' in Michele Barrett and Anne Phillips (eds.) *Destabilizing Theory*, pp. 201–19. Stanford: Stanford University Press.

Beirne, Piers and James W. Messerschmidt (1995, 2nd edn) *Criminology*. San Diego: Harcourt Brace Jovanovich.

Belkhir, Jean, Suzanne Griffith, Christine Sleeter and Carl Allsup (1994) '*Race, Sex, Class* & Multicultural Education: Women's Angle of Vision,' *Race, Sex & Class* 1(2): 7–22.

Bell, Derrick (1987) *And We Are Not Saved*. New York: Basic Books.

Bertrand, Marie-Andree (1994) '1893–1993: From La Donna Delinquente to a Postmodern Deconstruction of the "Woman Question" in Social Control Theory,' *The Journal of Human Justice* 5(2): 43–57.

Bordo, Susan (1990) 'Feminism, Postmodernism, and Gender-Scepticism,' in Linda J. Nicholson (ed.) *Feminism/Postmodernism*, pp. 133–56. New York: Routledge.

Bordo, Susan (1993) *Unbearable Weight: Feminism, Western Culture, and the Body*. Berkeley: University of California Press.

Brown, Wendy (1991) 'Feminist Hesitations, Postmodern Exposures,' *differences: A Journal of Feminist Cultural Studies* 3(1): 63–84.

Butler, Judith (1990) *Gender Trouble: Feminism and the Subversion of Identity*. New York: Routledge.

Butler, Judith (1993) *Bodies That Matter: On the Discursive Limits of 'Sex.'* New York: Routledge.

Butler, Judith and Joan W. Scott (eds.) (1992) *Feminists Theorize the Political*. New York: Routledge.

Cain, Maureen (1986) 'Realism, Feminism, Methodology, and Law,' *International Journal of the Sociology of Law* 14: 255–67.

Cain, Maureen (ed.) (1989) *Growing Up Good*. Newbury Park: Sage.

Cain, Maureen (1990) 'Realist Philosophy and Standpoint Epistemologies or Feminist Criminology as a Successor Science,' in Loraine Gelsthorpe and Allison Morris (eds.) *Feminist Perspectives in Criminology*, pp. 124–40. Philadelphia: Open University Press.

Cain, Maureen (1993) 'Foucault, Feminism and Feeling: What Foucault Can and Cannot Contribute to Feminist Epistemology,' in Caroline Ramazanoglu (ed.) *Up Against Foucault*, pp. 73–96. New York: Routledge.

Cain, Maureen (1995) 'Horatio's Mistake: Notes on Some Spaces in an Old Text,' *Journal of Law and Society* 22(1): 68–77.

Carlen, Pat (ed.) (1985) *Criminal Women: Autobiographical Accounts*. Cambridge: Polity Press.

Carlen, Pat (1988) *Women, Crime and Poverty*. Philadelphia: Open University Press.

Carlen, Pat (1994) 'Gender, Class, Racism, and Criminal Justice: Against Global and Gender-Centric Theories, For Poststructuralist Perspectives,' in George S. Bridges and Martha A. Myers (eds.) *Inequality and Social Control*, pp. 134–44. Boulder: Westview Press.

Carrington, Kerry (1990) 'Aboriginal Girls and Juvenile Justice: What Justice? What Justice,' *Journal for Social Justice Studies* 3: 1–18.

Carrington, Kerry (1994) 'Postmodern and Feminist Criminologies: Disconnecting Discourses?' *International Journal of the Sociology of Law* 22: 261–77.

Cole, Johnetta B. (ed.) (1986) *All American Women: Lines That Divide, Ties That Bind*. New York: Free Press.

Collins, Patricia Hill (1986) 'Learning From the Outsider Within: The Sociological Significance of Black Feminist Thought,' *Social Problems* 33(6): 14–32.

Collins, Patricia Hill (1990) *Black Feminist Thought: Knowledge, Consciousness, and The Politics of Empowerment*. London: Unwin Hyman.

Collins, Patricia Hill (1993) 'Toward a New Vision: Race, Class, and Gender as Categories of Analysis and Connection,' *Race, Sex, and Class* 1(1): 25–45.

Collins, Patricia Hill, Lionel A. Maldonado, Dana Y. Takagi, Barrie Thorne, Lynn Weber and Howard Winant (1995) 'Symposium: On West and Fenstermaker's "Doing Difference,"' *Gender & Society* 9(4): 491–506.

Combahee River Collective (1979) 'The Combahee River Collective Statement,' in Zillah Eisenstein (ed.) *Capitalist Patriarchy and the Case for Socialist Feminism*, pp. 362–72. New York: Monthly Review Press.

Connell, R. W. (1987) *Gender and Power*. Stanford: Stanford University Press.

Connell, R. W. (1995) *Masculinities*. St Leonards, NSW: Allen & Unwin.

Daly, Kathleen (1992) 'Women's Pathways to Felony Court: Feminist Theories of Lawbreaking and Problems of Representation,' *Southern California Review of Law and Women's Studies* 2(1): 11–52.

Daly, Kathleen (1993) 'Class-Race-Gender: Sloganeering in Search of Meaning,' *Social Justice* 20(1–2): 56–71.

Daly, Kathleen (1994) 'Criminal Law and Justice System Practices as Racist, White, and Racialized,' *Washington & Lee Law Review* 51(2): 431–64.

Daly, Kathleen (1995a) 'Where Feminists Fear to Tread? Working in the Research Trenches of Class-Race-Gender,' paper presented at the annual meeting of the British Criminology Conference, Loughborough, July.

Daly, Kathleen (1995b) 'Black Women, White Justice,' paper presented to the Law and Society Summer Institute, Niagara-on-the-Lake, Ontario, June.

Daly, Kathleen and Meda Chesney-Lind (1988) 'Feminism and Criminology,' *Justice Quarterly* 5(4): 497–538.

Daly, Kathleen and Deborah Stephens (1995) 'The "Dark Figure" of Criminology: Toward a Black and Multi-Ethnic Feminist Agenda for Theory and Research,' in Nicole Hahn Rafter and Frances Heidensohn (eds.) *International Feminist Perspectives in Criminology*, pp. 189–215. Philadelphia: Open University Press.

Davis, Angela (1981) *Women, Race, and Class*. New York: Vintage.

de Lauretis, Teresa (1990) 'Upping the Anti [*sic*] in Feminist Theory,' in Marianne Hirsch and Evelyn Fox Keller (eds.) *Conflicts in Feminism*, pp. 255–70. New York: Routledge.

Delgado, Richard (1989) 'Storytelling for Oppositionists and Others: A Plea for Narrative,' *Michigan Law Review* 87: 2411–41.

di Leonardo, Micaela (1991) 'Introduction,' in Micaela di Leonardo (ed.) *Gender at the Crossroads of Knowledge: Feminist Anthropology in the Postmodern Era*, pp. 1–48. Berkeley: University of California Press.

Dill, Bonnie Thornton (1983) 'Race, Class, and Gender: Prospects for an All-inclusive Sisterhood,' *Feminist Studies* 9: 131–50.

di Stefano, Christine (1990) 'Dilemmas of Difference: Feminism, Modernity, and Postmodernism,' in Linda J. Nicholson (ed.) *Feminism/Postmodernism*, pp. 63–82. New York: Routledge.

Epstein, Steven (1994) 'A Queer Encounter: Sociology and the Study of Sexuality,' *Sociological Theory* 12: 188–202.

Ewick, Patricia and Susan S. Silbey (1995) 'Subversive Stones and Hegemonic Tales: Toward a Sociology of Narrative,' *Law & Society Review* 29(2): 197–226.

Fineman, Martha (1994) 'Feminist Legal Scholarship and Women's Gendered Lives,' in Maureen Cain and Christine B. Harrington (eds.) *Lawyers in a Postmodern World*, pp. 229–46. Buckingham: Open University Press.

Flax, Jane (1990) 'Postmodernism and Gender Relations in Feminist Theory,' in Linda Nicholson (ed.) *Feminism/Postmodernism*, pp. 39–62. New York: Routledge.

Gallop, Jane, Marianne Hirsch and Nancy K. Miller (1990) 'Criticizing Feminist Criticism,' in Marianne Hirsch and Evelyn Fox Keller (eds.) *Conflicts in Feminism*, pp. 349–69. New York: Routledge.

Gatens, Moira (1996) *Imaginary Bodies: Ethics, Power, and Corporeality*. New York: Routledge.

Giddens, Anthony (1984) *The Constitution of Society: Outline of the Theory of Structuration*. Oxford: Polity Press.

Grosz, Elizabeth (1990) 'A Note on Essentialism and Difference,' in Sneja Gunew (ed.) *Feminist Knowledge: Critique and Construct*, pp. 332–44. London: Routledge.

Grosz, Elizabeth (1994) *Volatile Bodies: Toward a Corporeal Feminism*. St Leonards, NSW: Allen & Unwin.

Grosz, Elizabeth (1995) *Space, Time and Perversion: The Politics of Bodies*. St Leonards, NSW: Allen & Unwin.

Harding, Sandra (1986) *The Science Question in Feminism*. Ithaca: Cornell University Press.

Harding, Sandra (1987) 'The Instability of the Analytical Categories of Feminist Theory,' in Sandra Harding and Jean F. O'Barr (eds.) *Sex and Scientific Inquiry*, pp. 283–302. Chicago: University of Chicago Press.

Harding, Sandra (1990) 'Feminism, Science, and the Anti-Enlightenment Critiques,' in Linda J. Nicholson (ed.) *Feminism/Postmodernism*, pp. 83–106. New York: Routledge.

Hartsock, Nancy (1983) 'The Feminist Standpoint: Developing the Ground for a Specifically Feminist Historical Materialism,' in Sandra Harding and Merrill Hintikka (eds.) *Discovering Reality*, pp. 283–310. Dordrecht: Reidel.

Hawkesworth, Mary E. (1989) 'Knowers, Knowing, Known: Feminist Theory and Claims of Truth,' *Signs: Journal of Women in Culture and Society* 14(3): 533–57.

Henry, Stuart and Dragan Milovanovic (1996) *Constitutive Criminology: Beyond Postmodernism*. London: Sage.

hooks, bell (1981) *Ain't I a Woman? Black Women and Feminism*. Boston: South End Press.

Howe, Adrian (1990) 'Prologue to a History of Women's Imprisonment: In Search of a Feminist Perspective,' *Social Justice* 17(2): 5–22.

Howe, Adrian (1994) *Discipline and Critique: Towards a Feminist Analysis of Penality*. New York: Routledge.

Jaggar, Alison (1983) *Feminist Politics and Human Nature*. Totowa, NJ: Rowman & Littlefield.

Jaggar, Alison and Paula Rothenberg (eds.) (1993, 3rd edn) *Feminist Frameworks*. New York: McGraw-Hill.

Jefferson, Tony (1994) 'Theorizing Masculine Subjectivity,' in Tim Newburn and Elizabeth A. Stanko (eds.) *Just Boys Doing Business? Men, Masculinities and Crime*, pp. 10–31. New York: Routledge.

Joe, Karen A. and Meda Chesney-Lind (1995) '"Just Every Mother's Angel": An Analysis of Gender and Ethnic Variations in Youth Gang Membership,' *Gender & Society* 9(4): 408–30.

Jordan, June (1985) 'Report from the Bahamas,' in June Jordan (ed.) *On Call: Political Essays*, pp. 39–49. Boston: South End Press.

Katz, Jonathan (1988) *Seductions of Crime: Moral and Sensual Attractions of Doing Evil*. New York: Basic Books.

King, Deborah K. (1988) 'Multiple Jeopardy, Multiple Consciousness: The Context of a Black Feminist Ideology,' *Signs: Journal of Women in Culture and Society* 14(1): 42–72.

Lemert, Charles C. (1994) 'Post-Structuralism and Sociology,' in Steven Seidman (ed.) *The Postmodern Turn: New Perspectives on Social Theory*, pp. 265–81. New York: Cambridge University Press.

Lorde, Audre (1984) *Sister Outsider*. Trumansburg, NY: The Crossing Press.

Lubiano, Wahneema (1992) 'Black Ladies, Welfare Queens, and State Minstrels: Ideological War by Narrative Means,' in Toni Morrison (ed.) *Raceing Justice, Engendering Power*, pp. 323–63. New York: Pantheon.

Lugones, Maria C. (1991) 'On the Logic of Pluralist Feminism,' in Claudia Card (ed.) *Feminist Ethics*, pp. 35–44. Lawrence: University Press of Kansas.

MacKinnon, Catharine (1982) 'Feminism, Marxism, Method, and the State: An Agenda for Theory,' *Signs: Journal of Women in Culture and Society* 7(3): 515–44.

MacKinnon, Catharine (1983) 'Feminist, Marxism, Method, and the State: Toward Feminist Jurisprudence,' *Signs: Journal of Women in Culture and Society* 8(4): 635–58.

Maher, Lisa (1995) 'Dope Girls: Gender, Race and Class in the Drug Economy,' PhD Thesis, Rutgers University, New Jersey.

Maher, Lisa and Kathleen Daly (1996) 'Women in the Street-Level Drug Economy: Continuity or Change?' *Criminology* 34(4): in press.

Marcus, Sharon (1992) 'Fighting Bodies, Fighting Words: A Theory and Politics of Rape Prevention,' in Judith Butler and Joan W. Scott (eds.) *Feminists Theorize the Political*, pp. 385–403. New York: Routledge.

Martin, Jane Roland (1994) 'Methodological Essentialism, False Difference, and Other

Dangerous Traps,' *Signs: Journal of Women in Culture and Society* 19(3): 630–57.

Martin, Susan E. and Nancy C. Jurik (1996) *Doing Justice, Doing Gender.* Newbury Park: Sage.

Messerschmidt, James W. (1993) *Masculinities and Crime: Critique and Reconceptualization of Theory.* Lanham, MD: Rowman & Littlefield Publishers.

Moraga, Cherrie and Gloria Anzaldua (eds.) (1983, 2nd edn) *This Bridge Called My Back: Writings by Radical Women of Color.* New York: Kitchen Table Press.

Naffine, Ngaire (1994) 'Introduction,' in Ngaire Naffine (ed.) *Gender, Crime and Feminism,* pp. xi–xxx. Brookfield, VT: Dartmouth Publishing Company.

Nicholson, Linda (ed.) (1990) *Feminism/ Postmodernism.* New York: Routledge.

Norris, Christopher (1992) *Uncritical Theory: Postmodernism, Intellectuals and the Gulf War.* London: Lawrence & Wishart.

Piatt, Anthony M. (1993) 'Beyond the Canon, with Great Difficulty,' *Social Justice* 20(1–2): 72–81.

Pratt, Minnie Bruce (1984) 'Identity: Skin Blood Heart,' in Elly Bulkin, Minnie Bruce Pratt and Barbara Smith (eds.) *Yours in Struggle,* pp. 11–63. Ithaca, NY: Firebrand Books.

Price, Barbara Raffel and Natalie J. Sokoloff (eds.) (1995, 2nd edn) *The Criminal Justice System and Women.* New York: McGraw-Hill.

Radford, Jill, Liz Kelly and Marianne Hester (1996) 'Introduction,' in Marianne Hester, Liz Kelly and Jill Radford (eds.) *Women, Violence and Male Power,* pp. 1–16. Philadelphia: Open University Press.

Rich, Adrienne (1979) 'Disloyal to Civilization: Feminism, Racism, Gynophobia,' in Adrienne Rich (ed.) *On Lies, Secrets, and Silence,* pp. 275–310. New York: Norton.

Rich, Adrienne (1980) 'Compulsory Heterosexuality and Lesbian Existence,' *Signs: Journal of Women in Culture and Society* 5(4): 631–60.

Richardson, Laurel (1990) 'Narrative and Sociology,' *Journal of Contemporary Ethnography* 19(1): 116–35.

Roseneil, Sasha (1995) 'The Coming of Age of Feminist Sociology: Some Issues of Practice and Theory for the Next Twenty Years,' *British Journal of Sociology* 46(2): 191–205.

Ruiz, Vicki L. and Ellen Carol DuBois (eds.) (1994, 2nd edn) *Unequal Sisters.* New York: Routledge.

Russell, Katheryn K. (1992) 'Development of a Black Criminology and Role of the Black Criminologist,' *Justice Quarterly* 9: 667–83.

Sargeant, Lydia (ed.) (1981) *Women and Revolution: A Discussion of the Unhappy Marriage of Marxism and Feminism.* Boston: South End Press.

Schwartz, Martin D. and David O. Friedrichs (1994) 'Postmodern Thought and Criminological Discontent: New Metaphors for Understanding Violence,' *Criminology* 32(2): 221–46.

Schwartz, Martin D. and Dragan Milovanovic (eds.) (1995) *Race, Gender, and Class in Criminology: The Intersections.* New York: Garland.

Scott, Joan W. (1992) ' "Experience," ' in Judith Butler and Joan W. Scott (eds.) *Feminists Theorize the Political,* pp. 22–40. New York: Routledge.

Seidman, Steven (1994) 'Introduction,' in Steven Seidman (ed.) *The Postmodern Turn: New Perspectives on Social Theory,* pp. 1–23. New York: Cambridge University Press.

Simpson, Sally S. (1991) 'Caste, Class, and Violent Crime: Explaining Differences in Female Offending,' *Criminology* 29(1): 115–35.

Simpson, Sally S. and Lori Elis (1995) 'Doing Gender: Sorting Out the Caste and Crime Conundrum,' *Criminology* 33(1): 47–81.

Smart, Carol (1989) *Feminism and the Power of Law.* New York: Routledge.

Smart, Carol (1990a) 'Feminist Approaches to Criminology, or Postmodern Woman Meets Atavistic Man,' in Loraine Gelsthorpe and Allison Morris (eds.) *Feminist Perspectives in Criminology,* pp. 70–84. Philadelphia: Open University Press.

Smart, Carol (1990b) 'Law's Power, the Sexed Body, and Feminist Discourse,' *Journal of Law and Society* 17: 194–210.

Smart, Carol (1992) 'The Woman of Legal Discourse,' *Social and Legal Studies* 1(1): 29–44.

Smart, Carol (1995) *Law, Crime and Sexuality: Essays in Feminism.* London: Sage.

Smith, Dorothy E. (1979) 'A Sociology for Women,' in Julia A. Sherman and Evelyn Torton Beck (eds.) *The Prism of Sex: Essays in the Sociology of Knowledge,* pp. 135–87. Madison: University of Wisconsin Press.

Smith, Dorothy (1987) *The Everyday World as Problematic: A Feminist Sociology.* Toronto: University of Toronto Press.

Spivak, Gayatri Chakravorty (1992) 'French Feminism Revisited: Ethics and Polities,' in Judith Butler and Joan W. Scott (eds.) *Feminists Theorize the Political,* pp. 54–85. New York: Routledge.

Stivers, Camilla (1993) 'Reflections on the Role of Personal Narrative in Social Science,' *Signs: Journal of Women in Culture and Society* 18 (2): 408–25.

Thorne, Barrie (1995) Symposium participant, *Gender & Society* 9(4): 497–9.

Vogel, Lise (1991) 'Telling Tales: Historians of Our Own Lives,' *Journal of Women's History* 2(winter): 89–101.

Wagner, David G. (1992) 'Daring Modesty: On Metatheory, Observation, and Theory Growth,' in Steven Seidman and David G. Wagner (eds.) *Postmodernism and Social Theory*, pp. 199–220. Cambridge, MA: Blackwell.

Walker, Samuel and Molly Brown (1995) 'A Pale Reflection of Reality: The Neglect of Racial and Ethnic Minorities in Introductory Criminal Justice Textbooks,' *Journal of Criminal Justice Education* 6(1): 61–83.

West, Candace and Sarah Fenstermaker (1995) 'Doing Difference,' *Gender & Society* 9(1): 8–37.

West, Candace and Don H. Zimmerman (1987) 'Doing Gender,' *Gender & Society* 1(2): 125–51.

Williams, Patricia J. (1991) *The Alchemy of Race and Rights: Diary of a Law Professor*. Cambridge: Harvard University Press.

Worrall, Anne (1990) *Offending Women*. New York: Routledge.

Yeatman, Anna (1995) 'Interlocking Oppressions,' in Barbara Caine and Rosemary Pringle (eds.) *Transitions: New Australian Feminisms*, pp. 42–56. Sydney: Allen & Unwin.

Young, Alison (1990) *Femininity in Dissent*. London: Routledge.

Young, Alison (1996) *Imagining Crime*. London: Sage.

Young, Iris Marion (1994) 'Gender as Seriality: Thinking About Women as a Social Collective,' *Signs: Journal of Women in Culture and Society* 19(3): 713–38.

Young, Vernetta D. and Helen Taylor Greene (1995) 'Pedagogical Reconstruction: Incorporating African-American Perspectives into the Curriculum,' *Journal of Criminal Justice Education* 6(1): 85–104.

Chapter 2

PATRIARCHY MATTERS

Toward a Gendered Theory of Teen Violence and Victimization

Lyn Mikel Brown, Meda Chesney-Lind, and Nan Stein

Concern about girls' aggression and violence has rarely been higher, largely because the general public feels that girls' violence is increasing at a remarkable rate. The media have played a central role in this perception, not only in showcasing girls' violence, but also by providing the public with the explanation for this perplexing "new" phenomenon. Take the extensive media coverage of the hazing incident at suburban Chicago's Glenbrook High School in spring of 2003, or a more recent example from San Francisco. In this latter instance, the *San Francisco Chronicle* ran a front-page story warning residents about the "Hill Girls," a "violent clique of about 20 young women" who "prey on women" (Hendrix, 2003). Police there said they were "surprised by the savagery of the attacks," noting that although gang members sometimes selectively singled out their victims because of personal vendettas, "other victims appear to be randomly selected such as one woman who brushed up against one of the gang members on a bus. She was attacked after leaving the bus."

According to the article, the officers linked the girls to "15 incidents" and wanted the group, "whose members are African American" labeled a "criminal street gang." One gang officer continued, "these women are extremely violent, and they are not locking themselves into distinct boundaries" (Hendrix, 2003, p. A2). The officers also claimed that this was a new challenge for the city: "We know there are all-girl gangs in other cities, but this is the first we have seen in San Francisco" (Hendrix, 2003, p. A1). Later reporting would reveal that the most serious injury caused by this girl gang was a "broken elbow" and that actually the gang wasn't new. In fact, the "Potrero Hill Posse," a group of African American girls from a public housing project in the area, was first documented over a decade earlier in an ethnographic study of gangs in San Francisco (Lauderback, Hansen, & Waldorf, 1992; Ryan, 2003).

Most media treatments link the increase in girls' violence to girls becoming more like boys (the "dark" side, if you will, of girls' and women's quest for equality). As an example, the *Boston*

Source: Mikel Brown, L., Chesney-Lind, M., & Stein, N. (2007). Patriarchy matters: Toward a gendered theory of teen violence and victimization. *Violence Against Women, 13*(12), 328–345. Copyright © SAGE, Inc.

Authors' Note: The authors are listed in alphabetical order.

Globe Magazine ran an article that proclaimed on its cover, over huge red letters that said BAD GIRLS, "girls are moving into the world of violence that once belonged to boys" (Ford, 1998), and from the *San Jose Mercury* comes a story entitled "In a new twist on equality, girls' crimes resemble boys'" and features an opening paragraph that argues,

> Juvenile crime experts have spotted a disturbing nationwide pattern of teenage girls becoming more sophisticated and independent criminals. In the past, girls would almost always commit crimes with boys or men. But now, more than ever, they're calling the shots. (Guido, 1998, p. 1B)

The media are often eager to showcase "bad girls," and not infrequently their violence is linked to women seeking equality with men, with the assumption that as an exorable part of that process they will become more like men in areas like crime and violence. This position is actually decades old. In fact, since early in the past century, criminologists have been issuing dire warnings that women's demand for equality would result in a dramatic change in the character and frequency of women's crime (Pollak, 1961; Smart, 1976). Implicit in this "masculinization" theory of women's violence (Pollock, 1999) is the companion notion that contemporary theories of violence (and crime more broadly) need not really attend to gender, but can simply "add women and stir." That is, it assumes that the same forces that propel men into violence will also increasingly produce violence in girls and women. Moreover, the masculinization framework lays the foundation for responding to girls' and boys' violence "equally" or in gender-neutral ways.

In this chapter, we interrogate the role that the sex-gender system plays in shaping both the violence and victimization of girls and as key policies related to these issues. We argue that steep increases in girls' arrests are not the product of girls becoming more like boys. Instead, it is the case that forms of girls' minor violence that were once ignored are now being criminalized with serious consequences, particularly for girls of color. Shifting gears from the criminal to the civil side of the legal system, we then explore how "gender neutral" relabeling of girls' victimization in schools, a site of much violence against girls, is extremely problematic. Renaming

"sexual harassment" as "bullying" tends to psycho-pathologize gender violence while simultaneously stripping girl victims of powerful legal rights and remedies under civil law, particularly federal law Title IX. To illustrate, we critically review an Office of Juvenile Justice and Delinquency Prevention (OJJDP) "model" anti-bullying program used in communities across the U.S., the Bullying Prevention Program developed by Dan Olweus.

THINKING CRITICALLY ABOUT GIRLS' ARREST TRENDS

To understand the renewed focus on girls' violence, it is important to review the crime trends that drew media attention to youth violence over the past decade. After a period of some stability in the 1980s, the violent crime rate for juveniles soared in the early 1990s, with a nearly 300% growth in the youth homicide rate between 1983 and 1994 (Synder & Sickmund, 1999). The vast majority of violent perpetrators and victims during the youth violence epidemic were boys and young men of color, so the media coverage of the "epidemic" was initially focused on boys. By the mid-1990s, though, boys' arrests began to decline, whereas girls' arrests did not—a fact that was also not lost on the media. They discovered, as did the rest of the country, that what came to be known as the "crime drop" (Blumstein & Wallman, 2000) was, in reality, a male crime drop, at least among youth.

Between 1992 and 2003, girls' arrests increased 6.4%, whereas arrests of boys actually decreased by 16.4%. Although decreases were seen across many crimes of violence for both boys and girls, the period saw a 7% increase in girls' arrests for aggravated assault, but a 29.1% decrease in boys' arrests for this offense. Likewise, arrests of girls for assault climbed an astonishing 40.9% when boys' arrests climbed by only 4.3% (Federal Bureau of Investigation, 2003).

Concomitant with these arrest increases were increases in girls' referrals to juvenile courts from police and other sources (e.g., school officials and parents). Between 1990 and 1999, the number of delinquency cases involving girls increased by 59% (from 250,000 to 398,600) compared to a 19% increase for males; from 1,066,900 to 1,274,500 (Stahl, 2003). Looking at specific offense types, the report observed: "The growth in cases involving females outpaced the growth in cases involving males in all offense categories. For both males and females, simple assault cases increased more than any other person offense (136% for females and 80% for males)" (Stahl, 2003, p. 1).

Finally, and most significantly, the detention of girls (a focus of three decades of "deinstitutionalization" efforts) has suddenly increased. Between 1989 and 1998, girls' detentions increased by 56% compared to a 20% increase seen in boys' detentions, and the "large increase was tied to the growth in the number of delinquency cases involving females charged with person offenses (157%)" (Harms, 2002, p. 1).

Clearly, more girls were arrested in the last decade, and they were being arrested for "non-traditional" offenses such as assault and aggravated assault. At first glance, it seemed that the media hype about bad girls was not an exaggeration after all; girls were closing the gender gap in violence, just like they were closing the gap in sports participation. Are girls becoming more like boys when it comes to violence? If so, what should our response be? To many policy makers and practitioners, it seems only fair to treat girls the same way they would treat boys. After all, they're acting like boys.

ARE GIRLS REALLY GETTING MORE VIOLENT?

Actually, there are several reasons to be highly skeptical about the notion that the recent increases in girls' arrests mean that girls are getting more violent. As an example, several self-report data sources reveal that boys' and girls' violence decreased dramatically in the late 1990s, thus indicating that the youth violence epidemic had significantly waned for both boys and girls. Most interesting, these self-reports indicate that girls' rates of violence decreased more dramatically than boys' rates, a direct contradiction to the trends seen in female juvenile arrests.[1]

The Centers for Disease Control and Prevention (CDC) has been monitoring youthful behavior in a national sample of school-aged youth in a number of domains (including violence) at regular intervals since 1991 in a biennial survey, the Youth Risk Behavior Survey. A quick look at data collected over the last decade reveals that although 34.4% of girls surveyed in 1991 said that they had been in a physical fight in the last year, by 2001 that figure had dropped to 23.9% or a 30.5% decrease in girls' fighting. Boys' violence also decreased during the same period, but less dramatically, from 50.2% to 43.1%, a 14.1% drop (CDC, 1992–2002).

There are other reasons to be skeptical of the arrest data; notably, studies of other systems that also monitor injury and mortality apparently do not show dramatic increases in violent victimization. Males and Shorter (2001) have reviewed hospital admission data and vital statistics maintained by the health department over the past decades in San Francisco and they note decreases, not increases, in girls' injuries and mortality rates. More broadly, victimization data collected by the National Crime Victimization Survey (NCVS) show decreases in violent victimization among females (15.7% decrease) from 1999 to 2000 and 2001 to 2002, and also decreases in the violent victimization of youths. In fact, the second greatest *decrease* in violent victimization was reported by youth aged 12 to 15 (Rennison & Rand, 2003), a rate that approached the decrease noted in the violent victimization of individuals aged 50 to 64 (27.8%).

Finally, there are the arrest data on forms of violence, other than assault and aggravated assault. Surely if girls were getting more violent generally, one would expect that trend to manifest itself in other crimes of violence, such as robbery and murder (particularly because aggravated assault is supposed to involve "severe" or aggravated bodily injury" including either a weapon or "means likely to produce death or great bodily harm") (Federal Bureau of Investigation, 2003, p. 454). Yet, consistently, arrests of girls for other serious crimes of violence, including the most lethal, have shown decreases, not increases. As an example, arrests of girls for the offense of murder actually decreased by 42.8% in the period between 1993 and 2002, and female robbery arrests were down by 36.2% (FBI, 2003). If girls were simply getting more violent overall, wouldn't this eventually show up in other forms of the same behavior? These data, too, suggest that something else, something specific to the arrest process in the area of assaults, is changing. And here we approach the equity question again, but arguably from a different angle: What little we know about actual trends in girls' violence suggests that someone's behavior *has* been changing, but it is likely not girls, but rather those who police and monitor girls' behavior (e.g., police, teachers, and parents) who are acting differently. Moreover, it may well be the desire to punish girls' violence as if it is the same as boys' violence that has, in fact, produced much of the run up in girls' arrests.

SHIFTING ENFORCEMENT PRACTICES

If girls' behavior is not becoming more violent, then what explains the huge increases in female arrests for violence? Elsewhere, it has been noted that there are three forces likely at work: "relabeling" (sometimes called "bootstrapping") of girls' status offense behavior from noncriminal charges such as "incorrigibility" to assaultive charges, "rediscovery of girls' violence," and "upcriming" of minor forms of youth violence, including girls' physical aggression. (For a full discussion of these issues, see Chesney-Lind & Belknap, 2004.) Let's take each in turn.

Girls have traditionally been arrested for status offenses (noncriminal offenses such as "runaway," being "incorrigible," and "person in need of supervision"), but many of us suspect that girls engaged in these behaviors are now being relabeled as violent offenders, partially as a consequence of parents being advised to do so should they wish their defiant daughters arrested and detained, and partially as a result of changing police practices.

Some researchers now blame much of the increase in the arrests of both girls and women for assault to arrests of girls and women for domestic violence (Greenfeld & Snell, 1999). In California, for example, arrests of girls and women for domestic violence increased from 6% of the total in 1988 to 16.5% in 1998 (Bureau of Criminal Information and Analysis, 1999). Significantly, race also plays a role, here; African American girls and women had arrest rates for domestic violence roughly three times that of White girls and women in 1998 (Bureau of Criminal Information and Analysis, 1999).

Reviews of girls' case files clearly indicate the role family violence plays in girls' arrests for assault. Acoca's (1999) assessment of 1,000 girls' files from different points in the juvenile justice system in four California counties found that although roughly one third of these girls were charged with "person offenses," the majority of these involved assault rather than robbery or more serious crimes of violence. Furthermore, "a close reading of the case files of girls charged with assault revealed that most of these charges were the result of nonserious, mutual combat, situations with parents." In many cases, she contends, "the aggression was initiated by the adults." Acoca noted that in one case, "father lunged at her while she was calling the police about a domestic dispute. She [girl] hit him." In another case, "She [girl] was trying to sneak out of the house at night, but mom caught her and pushed her against the wall." Finally, she reports that some cases were quite trivial in nature, including a girl arrested "for throwing cookies at her mother" (Acoca, 1999, pp. 7–8).

In a number of these instances, the possibility that the child, not the parent, is actually a victim cannot be completely ignored, particularly when girls and defense attorneys continue to report such a pattern. Marlee Ford, an attorney working with the Bronx Defenders Office, commented, "Some girls have been abused all their lives. . . . Finally, they get to an age where they can hit back. And they get locked up" (quoted in Russ, 2004, p. 20).

Less direct, but still confirmatory evidence of the same pattern can be found in Canada, where a recent national review of youth charged with "violent crimes" found that "two-thirds of female youths were charged with common assault compared to just under half (46%) of male youths" (Savoie, 1999, p. 1).

Then there is the fact that girls have always been more violent than their stereotype as weak and passive "good girls" would suggest, so that the periodic "discoveries" of their violence are pretty much part of a media staple (some call this "man-bites-dog" journalism). Self-report data, as noted earlier, have always shown clearly that girls do get into fights, and they even occasionally carry weapons. As an example, in 2001, about a quarter of girls reported that they were in a physical fight, and about 1 in 20 carried a weapon. Until recently, girls' aggression, even their physical aggression, was trivialized rather than criminalized. Law enforcement, parents, social workers, and teachers were once more concerned with controlling girls' sexuality than they were with their violence, but recent research suggests that may be changing.

The notable increase in youthful violence seen in the early 1990s was waning by the end of that decade, but recall that the 1990s ended with dramatic and, many would say, atypical school shootings such as the events at Columbine High School in Littleton, Colorado, in April of 1999. The combined effect of these events was to produce legions of school policies to formally contain and officially respond to youth violence, particularly around and in schools (for a full discussion of these issues, see Chesney-Lind & Irwin, 2004). Upcriming refers to policies (e.g., "zero-tolerance policies") that have the effect of increasing the severity of criminal penalties associated with particular offenses, like minor forms of school bullying and fighting.

Criminologists have long known that arrests of youth for minor or "other" assaults can range from schoolyard tussles to relatively serious, but not life-threatening assaults (Steffensmeier & Steffensmeier, 1980). Currie (1998) adds to this the fact that these "simple assaults without injury" are often "attempted" or "threatened" or "not completed." A few decades ago, schoolyard fights and other instances of bullying were largely ignored or handled internally by schools and parents.

But at a time when official concern about youth violence is almost unparalleled and "zero tolerance" policies proliferate, school principals are increasingly likely to call police onto their campuses. As an example, in Pennsylvania, school districts refer any child who threatened violence or was violent to juvenile court (Schwartz & Rieser, 2001). It should come as no surprise that youthful arrests in this area are up as a consequence, with both race and gender implications. Specifically, although African American children represent only 42% of public school enrollment, they constitute 61% of the children charged with a disciplinary code violation. And these violations have serious consequences; according to a U.S. Department of Education report, 25% of all African American students nationally were suspended at least once over a 4-year period (Harvard Civil Rights Project, 2000, p. vi).

Simpkins, Hirsch, Horvat, and Moss (2004) focus their attention on what they describe as the "obvious but unexplored connection between abuse and school failure for girls" (p. 19). Interviews with 44 girls in detention in Philadelphia, 63% of whom were African American, found that "truancy, suspension, poor grades or expulsion is almost universal"

(p. 19). Girls who were suffering abuse were not able to get help at school, according to their interviews; instead, they were either ignored or yelled at or bullied by other youth. Finally, some began acting out, because "girls often respond to interpersonal problems with aggressive behavior" (Beyer, cited in Simpkins et al., 2004, p. 28). This aggression, which is "a common defense against helplessness among traumatized delinquent girls," then becomes a reason for their expulsion and detention.

Focus groups with delinquent girls in Ohio training schools found that girls' attempts to protect themselves from sexual harassment have also resulted in girls being expelled from school (Belknap, Dunn, & Holsinger, 1997). In one instance, a girl told school authorities that an older boy in the school was following her as she walked to and from school and that she was afraid of him. The school refused to look into it, but when the girl put a knife in her sock to protect herself getting to and from school, the school's "no tolerance" code for weapons resulted in her incarceration, despite the fact that it was her first offense.

Upcriming, like zero tolerance policies, can have very troubling implications for economically marginalized communities, because youth in these communities have always been heavily monitored and policed. The relabeling and upcriming of girls' minor offenses (including status offenses such as "incorrigibility") to assault and other criminal offenses have been particularly pronounced in the official delinquency of African American girls (Bartollas, 1993; Robinson, 1990). This practice also facilitates the incarceration of girls in detention facilities and training schools, something that would not be possible if the girl were arrested for noncriminal status offenses.

Returning to San Francisco, where the media panic about the "Hill Girls" flourished, Males (2003) found that African American girls' arrest rates there for felonies are three times higher, for robbery seven times higher, and for felony drugs 10 times higher, than for girls in Los Angeles. In fact, according to Males, African American girls in San Francisco make up just 2% of California's black girls, but they comprise fully 12% of the state's female arrests for robbery. Commenting on the pattern, Males noted, "Forget the evil streets of South Central and East Oakland—the Mission and Hunter's Point are where the new

Criminal Girl rides. In fact, *robbery rates among San Francisco girls are almost as high as for Los Angeles boys!*" (Males, 2003, p. 1).

Not surprisingly, these same patterns showed up in San Francisco detention statistics, where the city saw a 64% increase in girls' detentions coupled with a 12.5% decrease in boys' detentions between 1992 and 2000. Again, this pattern dramatically varied by ethnic group: Detention of White girls was actually down slightly in San Francisco, but there was a 90% increase in the number of African American girls detained and a 209% increase in the detentions of Hispanic girls. Other girls of color were also at higher risk of detention as we entered the new millennium (Males, 2003).

Perhaps the pattern found in San Francisco and hinted at in other research explains why, nationally, amidst rising detentions of girls, it is girls of color who are increasingly likely to be detained. According to the American Bar Association and National Bar Association (2001), African American girls make up nearly half of those in secure detention, and they are also far less likely than their White counterparts to have their cases dismissed; 7 out of 10 cases involving White girls were dismissed compared to 3 out of 10 of African American girls. Although not as specific in terms of gender, the same pattern appears to be found in the detention of Latino youth; according to a Michigan State University study, between 1983 and 1991, the age of Latino and Latina youth in public detention centers increased by 84%, compared to an 8% increase for White youth and a 46% increase for youth overall (Villarruel et al., 2002). One researcher, examining these racialized patterns, noted, "Not since slavery have we witnessed a system so effective at arresting Black womanhood as today's juvenile justice system" (Morris, 2002, p. 1).

In short, criminalizing girls' violence, such as the justice system's earlier efforts to criminalize their sexuality, has had an enormous impact on girls and juvenile justice. But although the earlier policing of girls was justified by gender *difference*, today's pattern is masked as gender *equity*. The results of what might be called "vengeful equity," though, are clearly as disadvantageous to girls as the earlier pattern of inequality. In both systems, girls are the clear losers, and neither affords them the justice promised by a system that purports to seek the "best interest of the child."

FROM THE CRIMINAL JUSTICE SYSTEM TO THE PUBLIC SCHOOL SYSTEM

In the same ways that girls are disadvantaged in the criminal justice system, their rights have been eroded in the civil arena of law. Our schools, 30 years after the passage of federal law Title IX, are still filled with abundant examples of student-to-student gender-based harassment and violence. Despite continuing guidance on federal law Title IX (sex discrimination in education) from federal agencies and the federal courts, including the U.S. Supreme Court (*Davis v. Monroe*), results from surveys attesting to the ugly entrenchment of sexual and gender harassment in our schools (American Association of University Women Foundation and Harris Interactive, 2001; GLSEN, 2004; Human Rights Watch, 2001), and laws at both the federal and state levels that require attention and compliance from school officials, our nation's schools are riddled with examples of conduct that qualifies as gender-based harassment or violence. Yet sexual or gender-based harassment rarely shows up in any of the standard analyses of school violence; gender is the missing discourse of rights.

As noted earlier, the nation was mesmerized by the shootings at Columbine High School, and in an effort to make sense of this horrific, but very rare event, the public became convinced that it was, somehow a harbinger of things to come. Overnight, reports appeared on the topic of "school violence," with many urging that schools take measures that allegedly make a school safer by passing state laws on bullying and/or suspending and expelling more students under the "one strike, you are out" mentality of zero tolerance. This approach has taken over the good senses of the educational and legislative establishments. What has gotten lost in this surge of reports and frenzy to reduce a rather expansive notion of bullying in schools are the rights of students to go to school in an environment that is gender-safe, and free from gender-based harassment and violence.

Our disagreement with the extremely popular framework of bullying is that it both degenders harassment and removes it from the discourse of rights by placing it into a more psychological, pathologizing realm. Our objections to these anti-bullying efforts embodied both in the new laws and the training efforts that have accompanied them are multiple: (a) they largely do not hold school administrators liable in the same ways to resolve the problems that federal law Title IX requires, but instead put the onus of solving the problem on the victim; (b) most of these anti-bullying laws are overly broad and arbitrary, with the result that students are suspended or expelled from schools for a variety of minor infractions; and yet (c) sometimes egregious behaviors are framed as bullying when, in fact, they may constitute illegal sexual or gender harassment or even criminal hazing or assault.

There are two broad consequences of these antibullying laws. The first is to further degender school safety by the use of the gender-neutral term "bullying." Although sometimes employing psychotherapeutic language (as bullying is a term that has been transplanted from 30 years in the psychological literature), antibullying legislation may serve to undermine the legal rights and protections offered by antiharassment laws. A second consequence is to shift the discussion of school safety away from a larger civil rights framework that encompassed both racial and sex discrimination and harassment to one that focuses on, pathologizes, and in some cases, demonizes individual behavior: the bully (Stein, 2001b, 2003).

In the United States, the discourse around bullying is a relatively new phenomenon, in large part imported from the Europeans and the research conducted there since the 1970s (e.g., Ahmad & Smith, 1994; Olweus, 1993). Prior to the emphasis on bullying as a new trend for U.S. educators and researchers, redress of injustices and wrongs were addressed through civil and constitutional rights (Whalen & Whalen, 1985). Sexual harassment and sex discrimination laws grew out of the larger civil rights movement of the 1960s, and the equal employment rights movement of the 1960s and 1970s (Baker, 2004; Farley, 1978; Hoff, 1991; MacKinnon, 1979, 2001; O'Connor, 1980). However, those linkages and legacies are now in jeopardy: The discourse of bullying may eclipse the rights discourse (Stein, 2003).

Consider the case that was heard in the U.S. Supreme Court in 1999, the details of which demonstrate the implications of the bully versus harassment distinction. LaShonda Davis was repeatedly touched, grabbed, and verbally harassed by a male classmate in her fifth-grade class. The boy, who is only known by his initials, G. F., repeatedly attempted to touch LaShonda's breasts and genital area, rubbed against her in a sexual manner, constantly asked her for sex and, in one instance, put a doorstop in his pants to simulate an erection and then came at her in a sexually suggestive manner (Brake, 1999). By no stretch of the imagination was this boy subtle or was his behavior ambiguous; rather, it was persistent and unrelenting. Should these behaviors have been called bullying or sexual harassment? The answer to this question has vitally important consequences for LaShonda, for her assailant, and for the teachers and school administrators.

LaShonda did not respond passively to the boy's behavior. Besides telling G.F. to stop, she also told her teachers. Her parents also complained to her teachers and asked to have LaShonda's seat moved. But her teachers and school officials did nothing, not even separate the two students who sat next to each other. G. F.'s behavior was clearly affecting LaShonda, both psychologically and academically. After several months of this harassment, LaShonda's grades fell and she wrote a suicide note. Her parents filed a criminal complaint against the boy and also a federal civil rights lawsuit against the school district for permitting a sexually hostile environment to exist. In the criminal action, the boy pled guilty to sexual battery. And after 5 years of legal battles and appeals, the U.S. Supreme Court, in a 5–4 decision, ruled that schools are liable for student-to-student sexual harassment if the school officials knew about the sexual harassment and failed to take action (*Davis v. Monroe County Board of Education*, 1999).

It is highly unlikely that if these behaviors had been framed as bullying, LaShonda's case would have ever been heard in a federal court, let alone in the U.S. Supreme Court. As it was, the conduct that was inflicted on her, by both the male classmate and the treatment that she received from school personnel, was framed as civil rights violations. To have viewed this conduct as bullying would have relegated her case to the principal's office, a place where she had not received justice or redress prior to filing a federal lawsuit or a criminal complaint. Moreover, the context and timing of the *Davis* decision proved to be crucial. It came one month after the shootings at Columbine High School (April 1999), putting the subject of sexual harassment in schools into the midst of the national conversation about school safety.

THE RESEARCH ARENA: HARASSMENT OR BULLYING?

A typical example of the problems associated with the conflation of bullying and harassment can be found in the April 24, 2001, issue of the Journal of the American Medical Association (JAMA; Nansel et al., 2001). This study of nearly 16,000 6th through 10th graders from public and private schools came from a larger sample of those who had filled out a World Health Organization instrument administered in 1998 in 30 countries. To be applicable, the original instrument had to use questions and definitions that would make sense in all of the 30 participating countries. Thus, behaviors that legally could be sexual harassment or assault in the United States were framed as bullying for purposes of this survey; for example: being hit, slapped or pushed, spreading rumors, or making sexual comments. Again, terms used in the survey had to conform to definitions in 30 countries, from France to Indonesia (Best, 2002).

In the United States, the results showed that nearly 30% of the sample reported moderate or frequent involvement in bullying, either as the bully (13%), one who was bullied (10.6%), or both (6.3%). Males were more likely than females to be both perpetrators and targets of bullying.

But the term "sexual harassment" was never raised, not by the researchers nor in the accompanying article in JAMA written by public health researchers (Spivak and Prothrow Smith, 2001). To engage 6th through 10th graders in this discourse of bullying without acknowledging the realities of sexual or racial harassment is to infantilize and mislead them because some of the behaviors described as bullying are, in fact, criminal conduct, or could be covered by sexual harassment or other civil rights in education laws.

Compare this JAMA article with the findings of two other studies released 2 months later, both of which received scant publicity. First, Human Rights Watch considered the harassment of gay and lesbian students in U.S. schools (*Hatred in the hallways: Violence and discrimination against lesbian, gay, bisexual, and transgender students in U.S. schools*). The second study, by the American Association of University Women Foundation and Harris Interactive (2001; *Hostile hallways II: Bullying, teasing and sexual harassment in school*), involved students the same ages as those studied in the JAMA article, who were surveyed about their experiences with sexual and gender harassment.

In both studies, the euphemism "bullying" was not used as it was in the two JAMA articles when describing behaviors that constitute sexual and gender-based harassment. In the AAUW study, sexual harassment was found to be widespread in schools, with 83% of the girls and 79% of the boys indicating that they had ever been sexually harassed. In all, 30% of the girls and 24% of the boys reported that they were sexually harassed often. Nearly half of all students who experienced sexual harassment felt very or somewhat upset afterwards, pointing to the negative impact that sexual harassment has on the emotional and educational lives of students.

In the Human Rights Watch study, 140 gay, lesbian, and bisexual students, along with 130 school and youth service personnel, in seven states were interviewed. The results showed an alarming portrait of daily human rights abuses of the students by their peers and, in some cases, by some of their teachers and administrators.

We are not proposing that the word "bullying" be purged from the language, but rather that the word be utilized in an age-appropriate way with young children. Young children, unlike teenagers, might be hard pressed to understand the concepts of sexual harassment or sexual violence. But, even if the term "bullying" is used instead of "harassment" with young children, school officials cannot dismiss their legal liability to abide by sexual harassment laws and to ensure that schools do not discriminate on the basis of sex. Moreover, to use the word "bullying" to cover some behaviors that may constitute criminal or civil violations is to perform a great disservice to young people; the word "bullying" may infantilize them, but the law will not.

On one hand, it is as if "bullying" has become the stand-in for other behaviors that school and public health officials, scholars, legislators, and researchers do not want to name, such as racism, homophobia, sexism, or hate crimes. On the other hand, this loose and liberal use of the term "bullying" may be part of a general trend to label children, particularly in a culture that tends to psycho-pathologize behaviors.

Psychologists seem to dominate the field of bullying research and largely seem unfamiliar with nearly 30 years of research from the fields of education, sociology, anthropology, and feminist legal scholarship; fields that might instead frame the bullying behaviors as gendered violence or sexual harassment. Although the bullying researchers may acknowledge the existence of sexual harassment in schools, they generally only cite surveys or court decisions from the U.S. Supreme Court and largely have ignored a wealth of studies and articles from researchers who have employed widely different methodologies and have long argued for a gendered critique of children's behaviors. Included among the scholars who have conducted relevant research on gender are Lever (1976); Stein (1981, 1992, 1993a, 1993b, 1995, 1999, 2001a); Bogart & Stein (1987); Kimmel (1987, 1996, 2000); Thorne (1989, 1993); Eder (1985, 1997); Fineran and Bennett (1995, 1998, 1999; Fineran, 1996); Shakeshaft (Shakeshaft et al., 1995, 1997; Shakeshaft & Mandel, 2000); Lee, Croninger, Linn, and Chen (1996); Lesko (2000); and Tolman, Spencer, Rosen-Reynoso, and Porche (2003).

In addition, the omission or denial of gender from the dominant construction of school safety and violence contributes to the disproportionate focus on the most extreme, rare forms of violence, whereas the more insidious threats to safety are largely ignored (Lesko, 2000; Stein, 1995, 1999; Stein, Tolman, Porche, & Spencer, 2002). An example of this failure to factor in the saliency of gender in school violence is reflected in the many reports and analyses of the spate of school shootings, the form of school violence that has attracted the most national attention and incited the most panic (Kimmel, 2001). In general, the school shootings were widely reported in a gender-neutral way, when in fact the majority of these tragedies were perpetrated by White middle-class boys who were upset either about a break-up or rejection by a girl (e.g., Jonesboro, Arkansas; Pearl, Mississippi), or who did not meet traditional expectations and norms of masculinity (e.g., Columbine, Colorado) and were thus persecuted by their peers (Kimmel, 2001; National Research Council and Institute of Medicine, 2003; Perlstein, 1998; Vossekuil, Fein, Reddy, Borum, & Modzeleski, 2002).

This failure to consider the role of gender is also endemic to much of the bullying research. Researchers of bullying, for the most part, have unfortunately failed to consider the ways in which adolescent boys (and adult men) unmercifully police each other with rigid and conventional notions of masculinity and the imposition of compulsive heterosexuality. Not to factor in or even recognize these potent elements is to deny a central and operating feature in boy culture, namely the maniacally driven, tireless efforts to define oneself as "not gay." Researchers such as Pleck (1981), Connell (1987, 1995), Kimmel (1987, 1996, 2000, 2001), and Messner (1990) have written about this phenomenon and its consequences for several decades, yet most bullying researchers have failed to draw on their findings.

VIOLENCE IN TEENAGE RELATIONSHIPS

There are two questions on the Youth Risk Behavior Survey (YRBS), a comprehensive survey about general behavior of teens from the U.S. Department of Health and Human Services and the CDC, which asks about violence in teen dating relationships. One of those questions inquires about physical violence in a dating relationship, and the second question asks about sexual violence in a dating relationship (http://www.cdc.gov/HealthyYouth/yrbs).

Data from both versions of the YRBS (the state-by-state version and the national version, with its sample of 13,000 or so students aged 14 to 18 years old) show that in some states, up to 20% of girls experience violence from a dating partner, some physical violence and some sexual violence. For example, in Massachusetts, 20% of the girls experienced one form of the violence (Silverman, Raj, Mucci, & Hathaway, 2001). A more socially and religiously conservative state, Idaho (Idaho Department of Education, 2003), shows a safer picture; nevertheless, 10% of students report physical violence from a dating partner (7.6% females, 11.8% boys). The responses to the question about being forced to have sexual intercourse in Idaho showed 7.8% (10.5% females, and 5.2% males). Moreover, a recent analysis of the national 2001 data from 6,864 female students in grades 9 through 12 found that 17.7% of the girls reported being intentionally physically hurt by a date in the previous year (Silverman, Raj, & Clements, 2004).

Prevalence data on sexual violence in elementary and middle schools have not been consistently collected, disaggregated, or reported. Researchers lack a complete picture about the violence that children younger than 12 experience, whether that violence happens at home, in the streets, in public spaces, or at school. This lack of information may lie largely with the resistance of the parents who will not permit researchers to ask these sorts of questions to children younger than 12 years old.

Only recently have self-report data from children younger than 12 been collected. Since its origin in 1929, the FBI's Uniform Crime Reporting (UCR) system and the Bureau of Justice Statistics' NCVS did not collect information about crimes committed against persons under 12 years of age and, thus, could not provide a comprehensive picture of juvenile crime victimization (Finkelhor & Ormrod, 2000, p. 1). The new National Incident-Based Reporting System (NIBRS) is designed to replace the UCR as the national database for crimes reported to law enforcement and it now includes data about juvenile victims (Finkelhor & Ormrod, 2000). However, participation by the states and local jurisdictions is incremental and voluntary. The crime experiences of large urban areas are particularly underrepresented, and the system does not yet have a nationally representative sample (Finkelhor & Ormrod, 2000).

Nonetheless, the 1997 NIBRS data from 12 states revealed some key findings about juvenile crime and preteen victims, data that were previously uncollected. Although children younger than age 12 represent only a small percentage of all reported victims (3% of all crimes and 6% of crimes against persons), their crime profile is unusual. Sexual assault accounts for almost one third of this preteen victimization, more than twice the proportion for older juveniles, and family offenders make up one third of the offenders against this group, twice the proportion for older juveniles (Finkelhor & Ormrod, 2000).

The NIBRS study finds that although family members comprise 35% of the offenders, acquaintances comprise 56% of the offenders, and strangers 9%. Such a large percentage of crimes committed by acquaintances may indicate that, in fact, some or even a majority of these incidents may be occurring at school. Unfortunately, information about the location of the crimes is not available from this report. Once again, yet another survey provides only partial, albeit new, information in the quest to know the prevalence of sexual assaults that occur at school, during the school day, by one's peers. The quest to compose a full and accurate picture continues.

VIOLENCE, NOT BULLYING

Bullying is sometimes used as a euphemism for what we used to call sexism, racism, and homophobia. It is a term that makes adults feel more comfortable, but it doesn't do anything to stop gender harassment and sexual violence. Unfortunately, the new antibullying laws may serve to dilute the discourse of rights by minimizing or obscuring harassment and violence. When schools put the new antibullying laws and policies into practice, the policies are often overly broad and arbitrary, resulting in students being suspended or expelled from schools for a variety of minor infractions (Stein, 2001a).

On the other hand, sometimes egregious behaviors are framed by school personnel as bullying, when in fact they may constitute illegal sexual or gender harassment or even criminal hazing or assault (Stein, 2001b). In an era when school administrators are afraid of being sued for civil rights or harassment violations, as a consequence of the May 1999 decision of the Supreme Court in the *Davis* case, naming the illegal behaviors as "bullying" serves to deflect the school's legal responsibility for the creation of a safe and equitable learning environment onto an individual or group of individuals as the culprit or culprits liable for the illegal conduct (Stein, 2001b). Under the prevailing definition of bullying, almost anything has the potential to be called bullying, from raising one's eyebrow, giving "the evil eye," making faces—all culturally constructed activities—to verbal expressions of preference toward particular classmates over others. We fear that there may be a tyranny of sameness that is implicitly being proposed in this pursuit to eradicate bullying behaviors.

A TYRANNY OF SAMENESS: THE OLWEUS BULLYING PREVENTION PROGRAM

A great many schools across the country have adopted the Bullying Prevention Program developed by Norwegian psychologist Dan Olweus, chiefly because of its status as a "blueprint" or model program by the OJJDP. Such status gives the Olweus approach a legitimacy or unique standing among school-based bullying prevention approaches and thus invites careful scrutiny.

Described as a "universal intervention for the reduction and prevention of bully/victim problems" (Olweus, Limber, & Mihalic, 1999), the focus of the Olweus Bullying Prevention Program is to make a school safe by increasing staff awareness of bullying, developing school rules, stopping bullies, and protecting victims. Evaluations in Norway and in South Carolina have shown a reduced frequency in reports of bullying, improvements in school climate, and a drop in antisocial behavior such as theft, vandalism, and truancy (Olweus, 1993; Olweus et al., 1999).

But the Olweus program harbors serious weaknesses of the kind we mention above. Specifically, it offers a one-size-fits-all view of bullying, not only with respect to the motivation for bullying and the characteristics of bullies, but also the form bullying behavior is likely to take. This tyranny of sameness erodes differences that make a difference in children's lives, not only with respect to gender, but also with respect to social class, race, ethnicity, sexual identity, and ability. By assuming all bullying can be approached and dealt with psychologically or relationally, the Olweus program ignores or plays down the structural or institutional underpinnings of much bullying behavior in schools (for example, the impact of capitalism on the poor or the realities of racism in the United States on students of color). Such homogenization means that those in subordinate groups are further marginalized, because justified anger that comes from experiences of oppression or subordination carries the same valence and response in the Olweus model as anger that comes from a position of privilege and dominance over someone. Bullying that arises from such different sources can look and sound the same, but the differences matter a great deal not only to the individual, but to the kinds of relationships and institutional practices good and fair schools must foster.

How does the Olweus method enact this sameness? It does so in a number of complicated ways, not apparent at first glance amidst the trainings that focus on class meetings, discussions with bullies and victims, role-playing, and meetings with parents. First and foremost, it does so by degendering bullying behavior and, in its training materials, ignoring the important distinction between criminal harassment and bullying. Consider the case study of 14-year-old Maria, "A Victim of Bullying," excerpted from *Olweus' core program against bullying and antisocial behavior: A teachers' handbook* (Olweus, 2001, ch. 9, pp. 10–13). Teachers are told that the story of Maria, who attempted to hang herself after a "long series of physical and verbal harassment" by two boys, is based on a detailed 1993 report from a Swedish newspaper. For 2 years

> Maria had been pinched, pushed, and threatened. During woodworking class, the bullies had stabbed her with a file, tried to hit her hands with a hammer, and burned her on the neck. A common situation prior to class was that a group of students gathered around her, pushing her amongst them until she started to cry. During recess or breaks, she was chased around the schoolyard, her hair was pulled, she was called whore, witch, idiot, etc. . . . Sometimes she managed to flee to the toilet and lock the door. On several occasions she sought refuge with various teachers. Maria was completely alone at school; there was "open season" on her.

We learn that Maria's mother and other parents made attempts to contact the school, to no avail. The school denied that problems with "bullying" existed and Maria was sent to the school psychologist, who was "nice" but ineffective.

In all references to the Maria incident—the journalists' accounting, the summary of the school's reaction, and subsequent attempts to encourage the teachers and administrators reading this case to reflect on the incident as part of their training in the Olweus method (following the case are several "Items for Discussion," such as "What concrete measures should the school implement in the situation at hand?")—this case is fully accepted as a general problem of school-based "bullying." There is no serious consideration of gender-based power differences—no attempt to appreciate or unpack the differential effects of gendered insults such as "whore" and "witch;" no mention of how woodworking class typically operates as a male space; no discussion of the ways the perpetrators' aggression connects to male privilege or masculine hegemony or how Maria's responses might point to gender subordination. Most startling, there is no mention of the differences between Swedish and U.S. laws covering such gender-based harassment—indeed, no distinction made between bullying and harassment at all—and no discussion questions that draw attention to Maria's right to a school environment (in the United States) that is gender safe or the school's legal responsibility to protect Maria.

This is but one example of the way the Olweus approach feeds an ever-increasing demand for effective solutions to school-based bullying with psychologically based methods that efface social and structural forms of discrimination. Despite very general passing references to gender and social class (there are no references to race or ethnicity) in his 1993 book, *Bullying at school*, nowhere does Olweus discuss in any detail the impact of gender, race, class, or sexual identity on bullying behavior or the ways schools can unintentionally reproduce such behavior. In fact, in an attempt to assure readers that anyone can bully, social class is dismissed as a variable. And in one of the two references to gender in his book, we receive a vague and simple reference to reported gender differences in relational aggression.

When Olweus does provide examples of girls' relational aggression, he does not address female socialization or explain how gender-based power relations impact this behavior (Brown, 2003). Consider the case of Linda, a "hidden bullying situation." Again Linda's story is extracted from a press clipping, presumably from Europe (Olweus, 1993, p. 19; Olweus, 2001, chap. 3, p. 5):

> Linda, age 12, was allegedly bullied by her classmates because she was "too snobbish." Linda had made friends with another girl in the class and they were always together. The leader of the little bully gang tried to destroy this friendship and finally succeeded, with the result that Linda became quite isolated. Later another girl in the bully gang talked Linda into having a party at her home, and then made sure that no one came.

We know little to nothing about Linda with respect to social location. Given years of research on the influence of culture and social context on the socialization of girls' behavior, this would seem important information (Adams, 1999, 2001; Bordo, 1993; Brown, 1998, 2003; Debold, Brown, Wessen, & Brookings, 1999; Eder, 1985; Fine & Macpherson, 1992; Gilligan, 1991: Hey,

1997; Leadbeater & Way, 1996; Merten, 1997; Orenstein, 1994; Phillips, 2000; Thorne, 1993; Tolman, 2002; Ward, 2000; Way, 1995). Is Linda White or of color? How about the girls bullying her? Attending a school that is predominantly White, of color? Is she poor, working class, middle class? (That is, could the motivation for exclusion be connected to race or social class; in which case, how might school practices unwittingly either reinforce or effectively interrupt such behavior?) How is the "little bully gang" socially positioned in the school? (For U.S. girls, the term used to refer to the kinds of behaviors indicated in this example is usually "clique"; the difference between a gang and a clique is, itself, significant and should be interrogated.) How do ideals of feminine behavior or media images of beauty play into this case? Is there a boy involved as there is so often in incidents of girlfighting? The answers to these and other questions would address the impact of social capital and power relations that deeply impact the psychological and relational experiences of children in schools. Asking teachers to answer the more general: "Could the students have reacted in other ways?" (a follow-up question in the workbook) without first addressing the kinds of social realities impacting the perpetrators and victim is like asking them to save a child in a river without knowledge of the current, the water temperature, or the distance from shore. They can jump in, but they might not make it back safely.

The Olweus approach to bullying doesn't erase gender—after all, we know that Maria and Linda are female and we've been given a vague sense that boys are more likely to bully directly and girls more likely to bully indirectly—so much as it ignores the complexities, power differentials, and lasting impact of the current sex-gender system. But this is as bad as or worse than erasure. Olweus gives the appearance of taking gender seriously but never gets around to any substantive examination of how gendered behavior varies with social context or how intersections of race, class, or sexual identity impact gendered experiences. His few references to gender differences cite studies conducted 30 years ago by Maccoby and Jacklin and ignore a wealth of more current research. Moreover, in spite of lip service to gender, substantive descriptions of bullies, victims, and bullying behavior focus on boys and boys' behavior. Bullies are "physically stronger" and have parents that tend to use "power-assertive" techniques of childrearing. Victims have "anxious reaction patterns," are perceived as "physically weaker," and tend to be boys with close relationships with their mothers (Olweus, 1993). In this way, the Olweus Bullying Prevention Program participates in a form of symbolic annihilation (Dines & Humez, 1995; Ohye & Henderson Daniel, 1999), "the tendency to ignore certain groups in cultural representations and discourse or *only to represent them when they fit with our socially rooted conceptions of them* [italics added]" (Ohye & Henderson Daniel, 1999, p. 116). Their behavior left unexplained, girls remain firmly entrenched in sex role stereotypes, "naturally" associated with indirect forms of aggression, such as "catty" or manipulative behaviors or destroying friendships with gossip, exclusion, and other relational forms of cruelty. And because the Olweus approach does not address the impact of societal power differences, White girls, the poor, gays and lesbians, or boys and girls of color emerge primarily to mark their difference from the conventional norm. This, of course, unwittingly reproduces a social hierarchy that places White middle-class heterosexual males at the top or at the center.

Olweus (1993) declares that eradicating bullying "boils down to a matter of will and involvement on the part of adults in deciding how much bullying should take place in our schools" (p. 128). His approach depends on adults actually seeing, interpreting, and then consistently responding to what is going on among kids. But such an approach, without adequate training in the impact of the structural or systemic underpinnings of bullying, or the distinction between bullying and various forms of harassment, means that adults are likely to interpret children's behavior in ways that unwittingly perpetuate unfair school practices and contribute to the erosion of their civil rights.

Olweus is clear that bullying is about the imbalance and abuse of power. We agree. But bullying is about much more than a relational imbalance (between two children or between a child and a group of his or her peers) and the psychological consequences of such relational power inequities. The Olweus method does not account for the convoluted ways power is experienced, desired, expressed, and channeled in a sexist, racist, homophobic society, and thus his approach does not address the subterfuge of

girl-to-girl or other forms of horizontal violence perpetrated by those in historically subordinated positions in U.S. culture (Brown, 2003). Effective bully-prevention programs in the United States must start with research on diverse groups of children and take into account social location (such as gender, race, class, and sexual identity), and they must distinguish peer-to-peer bullying from more egregious forms of sexual and racial harassment.

Recent studies of this kind reveal the limits of the Olweus model. For example, Brown's (2003) study of 421 girls and young women, diverse with respect to race, class, and geographic location paints a very different portrait of what motivates and characterizes girls who fight with or bully other girls. For example, the Olweus model established the following motivations for bullying behavior: a strong need for dominance and power; hostile fundamental attitude to one's surroundings (typically the result of conflict-filled family relationships); and material and psychological rewards from their behavior, forcing victims to give them money or valuables, prestige (Olweus, 2001). Brown (2003) finds other culturally mediated motivations for girl-to-girl aggression and bullying, such as competition over media ideals of beauty and female perfection; justified (although misplaced) anger and aggression about mistreatment in school, sexual harassment, and sexual objectification; jealousies over boys; a desire for respect, for visibility and power through public performance that is either sexualized or designed to garner respect and popularity; and care taking or ensuring their own and others' protection and survival.

Similarly, Olweus (2001) characterizes bullies as children who have a strong drive to dominate and oppress other students or to get their own way; who have a more positive attitude toward violence than most; if boys, they're often physically stronger than friends and victims; have a temper or are impulsive and have a hard time conforming to rules; they appear tough and impudent and show little compassion for students they bully; they are often aggressive to adults, teachers, and parents; and they are good at talking themselves out of difficult situations. Brown (1998, 2003), finds important variations in her studies of girls, who often talk about their victims in relationally complicated ways, even feeling sorry for them and sad about the outcomes; whose fight for visibility is connected to the cultural denigration of femininity and a desire for power that adults (and the media) have told them they have a right to demand; who are less likely to be impulsive, to talk more, and to give their aggression more forethought. Girls who bully are not necessarily aggressive to adults and can appear quite civilized and "nice."

It is important to consider these differences and the culturally mediated experiences that give rise to them if a bully prevention approach is to have long-lasting effects on children's behavior. Right now girls are put in the untenable situation of receiving social power for acting in ways that objectify them, render them less significant, less visible, and less in control. Given the current sex-gender system, the answer lies less in the will of adults or their control over children than in appreciating girls' need to have more control in their lives, to feel important, to be visible, to be taken seriously, to have an effect. The best bully-prevention approaches, for girls and also perhaps for boys, would move beyond the psychological or relational and tackle social and institutional oppression by providing ways of understanding the limiting and damaging constructions of gender, race, class, and sexual identity, and working to replace them with alternative realities, critical tools, words, and ideals.

Conclusion

This chapter has reviewed the consequences of degendering violence and victimization for girls. It is widely acknowledged that the arena of violence against women has been haunted by the problems associated with constructions of "domestic violence" that ignore the context of violence against women and women's intent if they do act out violently (for a review of this literature, see Miller, 2004). Less well understood is the fact that the same problems are also appearing in treatments of girls' violence and their victimization in schools and communities.

With reference to girls' violence, there is a widespread notion that girls are becoming more violent, an impression fueled by steep increases in arrests of girls for assault. The public and, more to the point, policy makers have been repeatedly told that this phenomenon is a product of girls becoming more like boys and acting out violently. As a consequence, although girls' violence has actually been decreasing, girls' arrests for this behavior have been increasing, fueled by a series of policy changes that are criminalizing girls, particularly girls of color. Closer analysis of the impact of these practices show that contrary to the notion that these arrest trends reflect girls' "masculinization," they instead reflect emerging practices focused on control of girls in family and school settings.

Similarly, this chapter has shown that girls are disadvantaged not only in the criminal justice system, but also in school systems. The construction of bullying prevention as a solution, just as the claim that girls have become as "masculinized" as boys, effaces persistent inequities that are both structural and psychological and that find their home in our educational and legal systems. Denying that there are differences that make a difference allows the bullying ideology to have an ascendancy that defies common sense and denies the reality that living in a patriarchy matters.

Note

1. Self-report data are one of "three major ways of measuring involvement in delinquent and criminal behavior," and most scholars agree that "self-report data appear acceptably valid and reliable for most research purposes" (Thornberry & Krohn, 2000, p. 1). Focusing specifically on criterion validity, one survey of the literature found a correlation of .60 between self-reports of arrests and actual arrests; other studies have found even higher correlations (Thornberry & Krohn, 2000).

References

Acoca, L. (1999). Investing in girls: A 21st century challenge. *Juvenile Justice, 6*(1), 3–13.

Adams, N. (1999). Fighting to be somebody: Resisting erasure and the discursive practices of female adolescent fighting. *Educational Studies, 30*, 115–139.

Adams, N. (2001, April). *Girl power: The discursive practices of female fighters and female cheerleaders.* Paper presented at the annual meeting of the American Educational Research Association, Seattle, WA.

Ahmad, Y., & Smith, P. K. (1994). Bullying in schools and the issue of sex differences. In J. Archer (Ed.), *Male violence* (pp. 70–83). New York: Routledge.

American Association of University Women Foundation and Harris Interactive. (2001). *Hostile hallways II: Bullying, teasing and sexual harassment in school.* Washington, DC: Author.

American Bar Association and the National Bar Association. (2001). *Justice by gender: The lack of appropriate prevention, diversion and treatment alternatives for girls in the justice system.* Chicago: Author.

Baker, C. (2004). Race, class and sexual harassment in the 1970s. *Feminist Studies, 30*(1), 7–27.

Bartollas, C. (1993). Little girls grown up: The perils of institutionalization. In C. Culliver (Ed.), *Female criminality: The state of the art* (pp. 469–482). New York: Garland.

Belknap, J., Dunn, M., & Holsinger, K. (1997). *Moving toward juvenile justice and youth-serving systems that address the distinct experience of the adolescent female. Gender Specific Work Group report to the governor.* Columbus, OH: Office of Criminal Justice Services.

Best, J. (2002, Summer). Monster hype. *Education Next*, pp. 51–55.

Blumstein, A., & Wallman, J. (2000). *The crime drop in America.* Cambridge, UK: Cambridge University Press.

Bogart, K, & Stein, N. (1987). Breaking the silence: Sexual harassment in education. *Peabody Journal of Education*, 64(4), 146–163.

Bordo, S. (1993). *Unbearable weight: Feminism, western culture and the body.* Berkeley: University of California Press.

Brake, D. (1999). The cruelest of the gender police: Student-to-student sexual harassment and antigay peer harassment under Title IX. *Georgetown Journal of Gender and the Law, 1*(37), 37–108.

Brown, L. M. (1998). *Raising their voices: The politics of girls' anger.* Cambridge, MA: Harvard University Press.

Brown, L. M. (2003). *Girlfighting: Betrayal and rejection among girls.* New York: New York University Press.

Bureau of Criminal Information and Analysis. (1999). *Report on arrests for domestic violence in California, 1998.* Sacramento: State of California, Criminal Justice Statistics Center.

Centers for Disease Control and Prevention. (1992–2002). *Youth risk behavior surveillance—United States, 1991–2001.* Atlanta, GA: Author.

Chesney-Lind, M., & Belknap, J. (2004). Trends in delinquent girls' aggression and violent behavior: A review of the evidence. In M. Putalaz & P. Bierman (Eds.), *Aggression, antisocial behavior and violence among girls: A development perspective* (pp. 203–222). New York: Guilford.

Chesney-Lind, M., & Irwin, K. (2004). From badness to meanness: Popular constructions of contemporary girlhood. In A. Harris (Ed.), *All about the girl: Culture, power, and identity* (pp. 45–58). New York: Routledge.

Connell, R. W. (1987). *Gender and power: Society, the person and sexual politics.* Cambridge, UK: Polity Press.

Connell, R. W. (1995). *Masculinities.* Berkeley: University of California Press.

Currie, E. (1998). *Crime and punishment.* New York: Metropolitan.

Davis v. Monroe County Board of Education, 526 U.S. 629 (1999).

Debold, E., Brown, L., Weseen, S., & Brookings, G. K. (1999). Cultivating hardiness zones for adolescent girls: A reconceptualization of resilience in relationships with caring adults. In N. Johnson, M. Roberts, & J. Worell (Eds.), *Beyond appearance: A new look at adolescent girls* (pp. 181–204). Washington, DC: American Psychological Association.

Dines, G., & Humez, J. M. (Eds.). (1995). *Gender, race, and class in media: A text-reader.* Thousand Oaks, CA: Sage.

Eder, D. (1985). The cycle of popularity: Interpersonal relations among female adolescents. *Sociology of Education, 58*, 154–165.

Eder, D. (1997). Sexual aggression within the school culture. In J. Bank & P. Hall (Ed.), *Gender, equity, and schooling: Policy and practice* (pp. 93–112). New York: Garland.

Farley, L. (1978). *Sexual shakedown: The sexual harassment of women on the job.* New York: McGraw-Hill.

Federal Bureau of Investigation. (2003). *Crime in the United States, 2002.* Washington, DC: Government Printing Office.

Fine, M., & Macpherson, P. (1992). Over dinner: Feminism and adolescent female bodies. In M. Fine (Ed.), *Disruptive voices* (pp. 175–203). Albany: State University of New York Press.

Fineran, S. (1996). *Gender issues of peer sexual harassment among teenagers.* Unpublished doctoral dissertation, University of Illinois at Chicago.

Fineran, S., & Bennett, L. (1995, July). *Gender and power issues of peer sexual harassment among teenagers.* Paper presented at Fourth International Family Violence Research Conference, Durham, NH.

Fineran, S., & Bennett, L. (1998). Teenage peer sexual harassment: Implications for social work practice in education. *Social Work, 43*, 55–64.

Fineran, S., & Bennett, L. (1999). Gender issues of peer sexual harassment among teenagers. *Journal of Interpersonal Violence, 14*, 626–641.

Finkelhor, D., & Ormrod, R. (2000). *Characteristics of crimes against juveniles.* Washington, DC: U.S. Department of Justice, Office of Justice Programs.

Ford, R. (1998, May 24). The razor's edge. *Boston Globe Magazine*, pp. 13, 22–28.

Gilligan, C. (1991). Joining the resistance: Psychology, politics, girls and women. *Michigan Quarterly Review, 29*, 501–536.

GLSEN. (2004). *State of the states, 2004. A policy analysis of lesbian, gay, bisexual and transgender (LGBT) safer schools issues.* New York: Author.

Greenfeld, L. A., & Snell, T. L. (1999). *Women offenders.* Washington DC: Government Printing Office.

Guido, M. (1998, June 4). In a new twist on equality, girls' crimes resemble boys'. *San Jose Mercury*, pp. 1B–4B.

Harms, P. (2002). *Detention in delinquency cases, 1989–1998.* Washington, DC: U.S. Department of Justice.

Harvard Civil Rights Project. (2000, June). *Opportunities suspended: The devastating consequences of zero tolerance and school discipline.* Report from A National Summit on Zero Tolerance, Washington, DC.

Hendrix, A. (2003, September 3). "Hill girls" gang preys on women. Police in S.F. surprised by savagery of attacks. *San Francisco Chronicle*, pp. A1–A3.

Hey, V. (1997). *The company she keeps: An ethnography of girls' friendship.* Philadelphia: Open University Press.

Hoff, J. (1991). *Law, gender and injustice: A legal history of U.S. women.* New York: New York University Press.

Human Rights Watch. (2001). *Hatred in the hallways: Violence and discrimination against lesbian, gay, bisexual, and transgender students in U.S. schools.* New York: Author.

Idaho Department of Education. (2003). *Idaho Youth Risk Behavior Survey.* Retrieved October 24, 2004, from http://www.sde.state.id.us/yrbs

Kimmel, M. (1987). *Changing men: New directions in research on men and masculinity.* Newbury Park, CA: Sage.

Kimmel, M. (1996). *Manhood in America: A cultural history.* New York: Free Press.

Kimmel, M. (with Aronson, A.). (2000). *The gendered society reader.* New York: Oxford University Press.

Kimmel, M. (2001, March 8). Snips and snails . . . and violent urges. *Newsday*, pp. A41, A44.

Lauderback, D., Hansen, J., & Waldorf, D. (1992). Sisters are doin' it for themselves: A Black female gang in San Francisco. *Gang Journal, 1*, 57–72.

Leadbeater, B., & Way, N. (Eds.). (1996). *Urban girls: Resisting stereotypes, creating identities.* New York: New York University Press.

Lee, V. E., Croninger, R. G., Linn, E., & Chen, X. (1996). The culture of sexual harassment in secondary schools. *American Educational Research Journal, 33*, 383–417.

Lesko, N. (2000). *Masculinities at school.* Thousand Oaks, CA: Sage.

Lever, J. (1976). Sex differences in the games children play. *Social Problems, 23*, 478–487.

MacKinnon, C. (1979). *Sexual harassment of working women: A case of sex discrimination.* New Haven, CT: Yale University Press.

MacKinnon, C. (2001). *Sex equality.* New York: Foundation Press.

Males, M. (2003). *Girls' arrest rates in three California counties.* Unpublished manuscript.

Males, M., & Shorter, A. (2001). *To cage and serve.* Unpublished manuscript.

Merten, D. (1997). The meaning of meanness: Popularity, competition, and conflict among junior high school girls. *Sociology of Education, 70*, 175–191.

Messner, M. A. (1990). Boyhood, organized sports and the construction of masculinities. *Journal of Contemporary Ethnography, 18*, 416–444.

Miller, S. (2004). *Sugar and spice and everything nice? The paradox of women's violence in relationships.* New Brunswick, NJ: Rutgers University Press.

Morris, M. (2002, June). Black girls on lockdown. *Essence*, p. 186.

Nansel, T. R., Overpeck, M., Pilla, R. S., Ruan, W. J., Simons-Morton, B., & Scheidt, P. (2001). Bullying behavior among U.S. youth: Prevalence and association with psychosocial adjustment. *Journal of the American Medical Association, 285*, 2094–2100.

National Research Council and Institute of Medicine. (2003). *Deadly lessons: Understanding lethal school violence.* Washington, DC: National Academy Press.

O'Connor, K. (1980). *Women's organizations' use of the courts.* Lexington, MA: Lexington Books.

Ohye, B., & Henderson Daniel, J. (1999). The "other" adolescent girls: Who are they? In N. Johnson, M. Robert, & J. Worell (Eds.), *Beyond appearance: A new look at adolescent girls* (pp. 115–129). Washington, DC: American Psychological Association.

Olweus, D. (1993). *Bullying at school.* Cambridge, MA: Blackwell.

Olweus, D. (2001). *Olweus' core program against bullying and antisocial behavior: A teachers' handbook. Version III.* Clemson, SC: Olweus Bullying Prevention Program.

Olweus, D., Limber, S., & Mihalic, S. (1999). *Blueprints for violence prevention: Bullying prevention program*. Golden, CO: Venture.

Orenstein, P. (1994). *Schoolgirls: Young women, self-esteem and the confidence gap*. New York: Doubleday.

Perlstein, D. (1998). Saying the unsaid: Girl killing and the curriculum. *Journal of Curriculum and Supervision, 14*(1), 88–104.

Phillips, L. (2000). *Flirting with danger: Young women's reflections on sexuality and domination*. New York: New York University Press.

Pleck, J. (1981). *The myth of masculinity*. Cambridge, MA: MIT Press.

Pollak, O. (1961). *The criminality of women*. New York: A. S. Barnes.

Pollock, J. M. (1999). *Criminal women*. Cincinnati: Anderson.

Rennison, C., & Rand, M. R. (2003). *Criminal victimization, 2002*. Washington, DC: Government Printing Office.

Robinson, R. (1990). *Violations of girlhood: A qualitative study of female delinquents and children in need of services in Massachusetts*. Unpublished doctoral dissertation, Brandeis University, Boston.

Russ, H. (2004, February). The war on catfights. *City Limits*, pp. 19–22.

Ryan, J. (2003, September 5). Girl gang stirs up false gender issue. Data show no surge in female violence. *San Francisco Chronicle*, p. A23.

Savoie, J. (1999). Youth violent crime. *Canadian Centre for Justice Statistics: Juristat, 19*(13).

Schwartz, R., & Rieser, L. (2001). Zero tolerance as mandatory sentencing. In W. Ayers, B. Dorhn, & R. Ayers (Eds.), *Zero tolerance* (pp. 126–135). New York: New Press.

Shakeshaft, C., Barber, E., Hergenrother, M. A., Johnson, Y., Mandel, L., & Sawyer, J. (1995). Peer harassment in schools. In J. L. Curcio & P. F. First (Eds.), *Journal for a just and caring education* (pp. 30–44). Thousand Oaks, CA: Corwin Press.

Shakeshaft, C., Barber, E., Hergenrother, M. A., Johnson, Y., Mandel, L., & Sawyer, J. (1997). Boys call me cow. *Educational Leadership, 55*(2), 22–25.

Shakeshaft, C., & Mandel, L. (2000). Heterosexism in middle schools. In N. Lesko (Ed.), *Masculinities at school* (pp. 75–103). Thousand Oaks, CA: Sage.

Silverman, J. G., Raj, A., & Clements, K. (2004). Dating violence and associated sexual risk and pregnancy among adolescent girls in the United States. *Pediatrics, 114*, 220–225.

Silverman, J. G., Raj, A., Mucci, L. A., & Hathaway, J. E. (2001). Dating violence against adolescent girls and associated substance use, unhealthy weight control, sexual risk behavior, pregnancy, and suicidality. *Journal of the American Medical Association, 286*, 572–579.

Simpkins, S. B., Hirsch, A. E., Horvat, E., & Moss, M. (2004). The school to prison pipeline for girls: The role of physical and sexual abuse. *Journal of Children's Legal Rights, 24*(4), 56–72.

Smart, C. (1976). *Women, crime and criminality: A feminist critique*. London: Routledge.

Snyder, H. N., & Sickmund, M. (1999). *Juvenile offenders and victims: 1999 national report* (NCJ 178257). Washington, DC: U.S. Department of Justice, Office of Justice Programs, Office of Juvenile Justice and Delinquency Prevention.

Spivak, H., & Prothrow-Smith, D. (2001). The need to address bullying—An important component of violence prevention. *Journal of the American Medical Association, 285*, 2131–2132.

Stahl, A. (2003). *Delinquency cases in juvenile courts*. Washington, DC: U.S. Department of Justice.

Steffensmeier, D. J., & Steffensmeier, R. H. (1980). Trends in female delinquency: An examination of arrest, juvenile court, self-report, and field data. *Criminology, 18*, 62–85.

Stein, N. (1981). *Sexual harassment of high school students: Preliminary research results*. Unpublished manuscript, Massachusetts Department of Education, Boston.

Stein, N. (1992). *Secrets in public: Sexual harassment in public (and private) schools* (Working Paper 256). Wellesley, MA: Wellesley College Center for Research on Women.

Stein, N. (1993a). It happens here, too: Sexual harassment and child sexual abuse in elementary and secondary schools. In S. K. Biklen & D. Pollard (Eds.), *Gender and education: 92nd yearbook of the National Society for the Study of Education* (pp. 191–203). Chicago: University of Chicago Press.

Stein, N. (1993b). No laughing matter: Sexual harassment in K–12 schools. In E. Buchwald, P. R. Fletcher, & M. Roth (Eds.), *Transforming a rape culture* (pp. 311–331). Minneapolis, MN: Milkweed.

Stein, N. (1995). Sexual harassment in K–12 schools: The public performance of gendered violence. *Harvard Educational Review, 65*, 145–162.

Stein, N. (1999). *Classrooms and courtrooms: Facing sexual harassment in K–12 schools*. New York: Teacher's College Press.

Stein, N. (2001a). Sexual harassment meets zero tolerance: Life in K–12 schools. In W. Ayers, B. Dohrn, & R. Ayers (Eds.), *Zero tolerance: Resisting the drive for punishment in our schools* (pp. 130–137). New York: New Press.

Stein, N. (2001b). What a difference a discipline makes: Bullying research and future directions (introduction). *Journal of Emotional Abuse, 2*(2/3), 1–5.

Stein, N. (2003). Bullying or sexual harassment? The missing discourse of rights in an era of zero tolerance. *Arizona Law Review, 45*, 783–799.

Stein, N., Tolman, D., Porche, M., & Spencer, R. (2002). Gender safety: A new concept for safer and more equitable schools. *Journal of School Safety, 1*(2), 35–50.

Thornberry, T. R., & Krohn, M. D. (2000). The self-report method for measuring delinquency and crime. In *Criminal justice: Measurement and analysis of crime and justice* (Vol. 4, pp. 33–83). Retrieved October 14, 2004, from http://www .ojp.uddog.gov/NIJ/criminal_justice2000/ Vol4_2000.html

Thorne, B. (1989). Girls and boys together . . . but mostly apart: Gender arrangements in elementary school. In M. S. Kimmel & M. A. Messner (Eds.), *Men's lives* (pp. 61–73). Needham Heights, MA: Allyn & Bacon.

Thorne, B. (1993). *Gender play: Girls and boys in school.* New Brunswick, NJ: Rutgers University Press.

Tolman, D. L. (2002). *Dilemmas of desire.* Cambridge, MA: Harvard University Press.

Tolman, D. L., Spencer, R., Rosen-Reynoso, M., & Porche, M. V. (2003). Sowing the seeds of violence in heterosexual relationships: Early adolescents narrate compulsory heterosexuality. *Journal of Social Issues, 59*, 159–178.

Villarruel, F. S., Walker, N. E., Minifee, P., Rivera-Vázquez, O., Peterson, S., & Perry, K. (2002). *¿Dónde está la justicia? A call to action on behalf of Latino and Latina youth in the U.S. justice system.* East Lansing: Michigan State University, Institute for Children, Youth, and Families, Building Blocks for Youth.

Vossekuil, B., Fein, R., Reddy, M., Borum, R., & Modzeleski, W. (2002). *Final report and findings of the Safe School Initiative: Implications for the prevention of school attacks in the United States.* Washington, DC: U.S. Department of Education.

Ward, J. (2000). *The skin we're in: Teaching our children to be emotionally strong, socially smart, spiritually connected.* New York: Free Press.

Way, N. (1995). "Can't you see the courage, the strength that I have?" Listening to urban adolescent girls speak about their relationships. *Psychology of Women Quarterly, 19*, 107–128.

Whalen, C., & Whalen, B. (1985). *The longest debate: A legislative history of the 1964 Civil Rights Act.* Washington, DC: Seven Locks Press.

Chapter 3

FEMINISM IN CRIMINOLOGY

Engendering the Outlaw

DANA M. BRITTON

Criminology remains one of the most thoroughly masculinized of all social science fields; certainly, it is one of the last academic bastions in which scholars regularly restrict their studies to the activities and habits of men without feeling compelled to account for this (Rafter and Heidensohn 1995). The reason lies, at least in part, in the fact that criminology is in possession of one of the most consistently demonstrated findings in all of the social sciences: as long as statistics have been collected, they have revealed that men are considerably more likely than women to engage in activities defined as criminal. Students are thus attracted to criminology courses by the promise of studying dangerous men; so, too, have scholars been fascinated for decades by the allure of the male outlaw, "hoping perhaps that some of the romance and fascination of this role will rub off" (Chesney-Lind 1995, xii).

In this context, the phrase "feminist criminology" may well seem something of an oxymoron. However, while the vast overrepresentation of men as criminals has served some as a rationale for ignoring women, for others, it has been a point of departure for considering them. The founding of feminist criminology can be somewhat arbitrarily fixed at 1976, with the

publication of Carol Smart's *Women, Crime and Criminology: A Feminist Critique*. Though a handful of earlier works had addressed some of the general themes she raised, Smart's book brought them together in a systematic critique of the treatment (or lack thereof) of women offenders in mainstream criminology and the neglect of women's experiences as victims in an attempt to set out some directions for the new field of feminist inquiry.

Almost 25 years later, a substantial body of research has accumulated in the areas specified in Smart's pioneering work, and the field has moved considerably beyond these boundaries. As has been the case for many disciplines, however, the feminist revolution in criminology is still incomplete. Some universities do now routinely offer courses like "Women and Crime," and the Division on Women and Crime has taken its place among other specialty sections in the American Society of Criminology. Even so, these labels bespeak the marginalization of feminist criminology, which is still regarded, by and large, as something outside the mainstream. Feminist criminologists have made great strides in terms of adding women in at the margins of the discipline, but they have, as yet, been less successful in deconstructing its central frames of

Source: Britton, D. M. (2000). Feminism in criminology: Engendering the outlaw. *Annals of the American Academy of Political and Social Science, 571*(1), 57–76.

reference and theoretical and methodological assumptions (Morris and Gelsthorpe 1991).

As is the case in most areas of academic feminism, there is ongoing debate over what the aims of feminist inquiry in criminology should be and over what counts as work that can carry the name. I will not attempt to resolve this debate here. The emerging subject divisions in the field are easier to discern. Feminist criminology may be divided into work that focuses on women as criminal offenders, women as victims of crime, and women as workers in the criminal justice system. Reviews of the field generally do not include the third category, which is something of a hybrid, attracting scholars from both criminology and the sociology of work. I will focus here, however, on all three areas, attempting to give readers a very brief sense of what we know, a review of some key work and important debates, and a sense of the directions in which the field seems to be moving. I will conclude with a discussion of some of the central challenges that remain for feminist criminology.

Before moving on, a caveat is necessary. Although I have referred to the discipline thus far as if it existed as a unified set of frameworks and assumptions, this is not really the case. There are a wide variety of theoretical and methodological perspectives in criminology, and some (for example, critical, interactionist, and Marxist approaches) have been more receptive to feminism than others. My focus here, however, will be on the mainstream in criminology, which I take to be a set of theoretical and methodological frameworks and empirical studies aimed at understanding the etiology of crime (a category taken to be a given) and proposing, implementing, and evaluating methods of crime control. This kind of criminology has historically been very closely allied with state mechanisms of social control, and it is the state that provides the lion's share of research funding in these areas. Therefore, while one might accurately say that there are a variety of criminologies currently extant, mainstream criminology is clearly hegemonic and has most thoroughly marginalized feminist research and theory. It will be my focus in the analysis to follow.

WOMEN AS OFFENDERS

Women are vastly underrepresented as criminal offenders. Of course, any data claiming to represent

the facts about crime are always the end product of an interaction between the responses of social control authorities and the behaviors of the individuals involved. Even so, there is no serious dispute among criminologists that the extant data substantially misrepresent the actual sex ratio of criminal offending. The primary source of such data, the Uniform Crime Reports (UCR) program of the Federal Bureau of Investigation (FBI), reports detailed information on eight index crimes (these are homicide, forcible rape, robbery, aggravated assault, burglary, larceny-theft, motor vehicle theft, and arson). Women composed 26 percent of those arrested for these offenses in 1997. The UCR also reports statistics for less serious offenses, which constitute the bulk of all arrests. For men and women, these offenses are consistently similar, with larceny-theft (a category largely of petty theft, including shoplifting), simple (nonaggravated) assault, drug offenses, and driving under the influence of alcohol (DUI) topping the list for women in 1997, accounting for 45 percent of women's arrests. For men, the top four offenses were drug crimes, DUI, simple assault, and larceny-theft, composing 38 percent of men's arrests (Maguire and Pastore 1999).

These data indicate that men and women are actually quite similar in terms of the offenses for which they are most often arrested and that the majority are crimes that most would view as petty, for example, larceny-theft. The most striking difference is the absolute level of men's and women's offending. Although larceny-theft accounts for 16 percent of arrests of women, men's arrest rates for this crime are almost 2.5 times higher. Data for violent offenses illustrate this pattern in much clearer detail. In 1997, women were only 16 percent of those arrested for the index offenses of homicide, forcible rape, robbery, and aggravated assault (known collectively as the index of violent crime). Men's arrest rates for homicide were 9 times higher than women's; for rape, 83 times higher; for robbery (defined as the taking or attempted taking of property by force or fear), 10 times higher; and for aggravated assault, 5 times higher. The only offenses for which women's arrests exceed men's are prostitution, for which women are 60 percent of those arrested, and running away from home (a juvenile offense), for which girls were 58 percent of those arrested in 1997.

Arrest rates vary by race as well. In 1997, whites were 63 percent of those arrested for all index offenses; African Americans were 35 percent. For violent index offenses, whites accounted for 57 percent of arrests, versus 41 percent for African Americans. The FBI does not publish arrest statistics by sex and race. We do know, however, that African American men and women are over-represented among those arrested.

Studies of unpublished UCR data and self-reports show that African American women have higher rates of arrest and participation in homicide, aggravated assault, and other index offenses than white women (Simpson and Elis 1995). For some offenses, such as larceny-theft, arrest rates for African American women most closely match those for white men (Chilton and Datesman 1987); black men's arrest rates are the highest; white women generally rank at the bottom, regardless of the offense.

This statistical picture illustrates some of the challenges facing feminist criminology. The sex ratio of offending is remarkably constant, which seems to indicate the need for theory that would account for why it is that women are so much less likely than men to offend. Indeed, this was the place that criminology, when it considered women at all, often began. Paradoxically, however, rather than being viewed as successes, women have been seen by mainstream theorists as aberrant because they do not commit crime. Newer feminist work in this vein has viewed women's conformity in a somewhat more positive light, relying, for example, on Carol Gilligan's theories of moral development to suggest that women's "ethic of care" makes them less likely to offend (Steffensmeier and Allan 1996). Even a cursory examination of the statistics on sex and race, however, reveals the dangers that can come from viewing women as a unitary category. Differences in arrest rates between African American and white women are often dramatic, and feminist criminology has only just begun to grapple with the implications of these differences (Daly and Maher 1998). Even more problematic is the almost complete lack of data about criminal offending among other racial groups, such as Asian or Hispanic women.

The first studies of women and offending that fell, at least putatively, in the realm of feminist criminology appeared in 1975, with the publication of Freda Adler's *Sisters in Crime* and Rita James Simon's *Women and Crime*. Though these books differ slightly in focus, both make the same general theoretical argument, which has come to be known as emancipation theory. Adler and Simon both contended that women's lower rates of participation in criminal activity could be explained by their confinement to domestic roles and by discrimination that limited their aspirations and opportunities (Daly and Chesney-Lind 1988). With the advent of the women's movement, the situation could be expected to change, however. Adler saw increasing participation in violent crime as inevitable as women became more like men as a result of their social and political emancipation. Simon believed that opportunities created by women's higher levels of formal labor market activity would lead to higher arrest rates for property and occupational crimes, such as fraud, larceny, and embezzlement. Adler did consider race, arguing that black women's higher rates of participation in crime could be explained by their more liberated status: "If one looks at where Black women are as criminals today, one can appreciate where white women are headed as liberated criminals in the coming years" (154).

This argument has obvious appeal for opponents of the feminist movement, but empirically, the theory has received very little support. While women's rates of violent crime have increased, in absolute terms, their rates relative to men's have not changed substantially since 1960 (Steffensmeier 1995). Contrary to popular mythology, there is simply no evidence of the large-scale existence of a new, more violent female offender (Maher 1997). Women's rates of property offending relative to men's have increased since the 1960s, but almost all of the increase has come from higher rates of arrest for larceny-theft, mostly shoplifting (Chilton and Datesman 1987). Rather than reflecting expanding opportunities, however, this increase is more likely due to women's increasing economic marginalization and changing views of women by social control authorities (Morris 1987). There is also no evidence that women with more feminist attitudes are more likely to be criminal; in fact, the opposite is true (Simpson 1989). Although there is now fairly broad consensus that Adler's and Simon's work would not fall within the purview of feminist criminology (Morris and Gelsthorpe 1991; cf. Brown 1986), these books did put women's crime on the empirical agenda for the discipline, and they were groundbreaking in their attempts to build a theory that would explain men's as well as women's crime.

In addition to documenting the levels of women's criminal offending, feminist criminologists have drawn attention to women's (and men's) treatment by police, the courts, and the prison system. Contradicting popular stereotype, studies of women's experiences with the criminal justice system have revealed that women do not benefit, at least not uniformly, from chivalry at the hands of police, prosecutors, and judges. In some instances, such as juvenile status offenses, girls are subject to much harsher treatment than boys (Chesney-Lind 1989). Some research reveals that African American women receive more negative treatment by police, are more likely to be sentenced to prison, and receive longer sentences than white women (Mann 1995), although there is still considerable debate around this issue. A series of studies (for example, Daly 1987) has shown that women who are married and have children do sometimes receive more leniency than other defendants. This effect is double edged, however; women who do not conform to traditional stereotypes of wives and mothers or who are perceived to shirk their responsibilities may be dealt with especially severely (Morris and Wilczynski 1994).

The kinds of quantitative studies reviewed here have provided some answers to the question of how women's rates of offending and treatment by the system compare to men's and, as such, are a crucial first step. This equity approach (Cain 1990) has been guided largely by liberal feminist precepts, conceptualizing gender as an independent variable and seeing men and women as essentially equal and therefore deserving of equal treatment (Daly and Maher 1998). The fundamental limitation of such a strategy is put best by Cain (1990):

> Equity studies do not enable us to pose the question whether or not even absolutely equal sentences might be unjust . . . too high or too low in themselves, or [whether] behaviour . . . should not, from some standpoints at least, be subject to penalty. A concern with equity leaves the substance of what is being equalised un-analysed. (2–3)

This kind of liberal feminist approach poses men as the criminal yardstick and equates justice with equality. Larger questions about the processes of criminalization of some acts, rather than others, and the inherent justice or injustice of the system are left unanswered. Such studies also fail to question the meanings and active construction of the categories of sex, race, and class, taking them simply as givens.

More recently, a substantial body of ethnographic and interview research has appeared that takes as its central focus the construction and meaning of such categories. This work has substantially deepened our understanding of the lives of women involved in crime. Mirroring overall trends in feminist theory, the best of this work is moving toward a nuanced and contingent conception of women's agency, one that sees women neither exclusively as victims nor as unfettered actors. Lisa Maher's richly textured ethnographic study of women involved in street-level sex and drug markets (1997) is a particularly good example. Maher convincingly demonstrates that the women she studies are not liberated drug kingpins, but nor are they mindless slaves, willing to sink to any depth of depravity to serve their addictions. Rather, they actively work within the constraints of the male-dominated informal economy, rarely controlling significant resources; they perform a range of gender-typed tasks, such as "copping" (buying) drugs for customers fearful of being arrested. While women do sometimes initiate violence, they are more likely to be the targets of victimization by police, male partners, and "tricks."

Feminist research and theorizing on women's offending has also been closely connected with activism. This has been the case on a number of fronts but has perhaps been most visible in the area of women's imprisonment. America is in the throes of an imprisonment binge—since 1990, our prison population has grown by about 6.5 percent per year. Women constitute only about 7 percent of those incarcerated, but their rates of imprisonment have been rising much faster than men's. Between 1988 and 1997, arrests for men increased by only 11 percent, and the number of men incarcerated increased by 96 percent. For women, the situation was much starker: arrests increased by 40 percent, and women's prison population increased 146 percent. This increase fell particularly heavily on Hispanic and African American women, whose rates of incarceration, respectively, are 3.5 and 8.0 times those of white women (Maguire and Pastore 1999).

Advocates for women in prison have been instrumental in bringing these facts to light and in generating public concern over women's rising rates of imprisonment. They have also brought about practical changes that have improved the lives of women inmates, including the elimination of some laws that imposed harsher (indeterminate) sentences on women, the expansion of medical services, improvements in job training and educational opportunities, and even some in-prison nurseries, such as the pioneering program at New York's Bedford Hills (Price and Sokoloff 1995). This work has also generated serious policy alternatives that take into account men's and women's different life histories (for example, women in prison are six times more likely to report prior sexual abuse than their male counterparts), the context of their offending (women are much more likely than men to be first-time offenders or to have committed only nonviolent offenses previously), and women's much lower rates of recidivism compared to men (Chesney-Lind 1996; Davis 1997).

WOMEN AS VICTIMS

As in the case of offending, women are under-represented as victims of crime, at least as victimization is measured by the statistics most widely used by criminologists. The primary source of data derives from the National Crime Victimization Survey (NCVS), conducted annually since 1973 by Census Bureau personnel for the Bureau of Justice Statistics. The NCVS is administered to approximately 101,000 individuals, who are asked questions about their crime victimization. NCVS data consistently show that men are more likely to be victimized by all kinds of violent crime than are women, except rape and sexual assault. Men's overall rate of violent crime victimization in 1997 was 45.8 (per 1,000 population aged 12 years or older); women's was 33.0. Data on homicide, collected by the FBI, show that men are three times as likely to be victims.

NCVS data also indicate that African Americans and Hispanics are more likely to be victims of violent crime than whites and that the young and those with lower incomes also have higher rates of victimization. Unlike the UCR, the NCVS does publish victimization statistics that are disaggregated by sex and race combined, and the dramatic differences they reveal again demonstrate the danger of treating women (or men) as a unitary category. For homicide, white

women have the lowest rates of victimization; African American women's rates are about four times higher, and African American women are more likely even than white men to be victims. African American men's rates of homicide victimization—eight times higher than those of white men—starkly testify to an epidemic level of violence, as does the persistent finding that for violent crimes other than homicide, African American men are about one and a half times as likely to be victims as white men. Among women, African Americans are generally much more likely than whites to be victims of all kinds of violent crime; generally, their rates of victimization most closely match white men's rather than white women's.

Feminist criminology has perhaps made its greatest impact on mainstream criminology in the area of women's victimization. The realm in which this has happened, however, has been somewhat limited, as the literature has generally focused on the kinds of offenses of which women are most likely to be victims. As the foregoing data suggest, rape has been a central concern and so, too, has intimate violence. NCVS data indicate that, although women's levels of violent victimization are lower than men's overall, their victimization is much more likely to be personal; from 1992 to 1996, women were five to eight times more likely than men to be victimized by intimates (Maguire and Pastore 1999). Though there is little question that women face specifically gendered violence of this kind, concentrating only on these offenses has had the effect of highlighting the differences between men and women as victims and excludes an analysis of the ways in which other kinds of victimization (which account for far more incidents overall) may be gendered (Chesney-Lind 1995). Even so, feminist research in these areas has clearly been influential; mainstream criminology texts now invariably include sections on rape and intimate violence, and many discuss feminist empirical work and theory.

Unlike studies of female offenders, which did exist before feminist criminology drew attention to them in the 1970s, there simply was no comparable research in mainstream criminology on women's experiences of victimization or on the crimes that disproportionately affect women. A rare exception is Menachem Amir's *Patterns in Forcible Rape* (1971). Although this was one of the first attempts to untangle the dimensions along which rape offending varies (for example, sex, race, class, circumstances), the study paid no attention to the experiences of the victims themselves. The effect of this omission becomes particularly clear in Amir's introduction (or perhaps official legitimation) of the concept of "victim-precipitated" rape, which he claimed accounted for about 19 percent of the cases in his study:

> [Victim-precipitated rape occurs in] those rape situations in which the victim actually, or so it was deemed, agreed to sexual relations but retracted before the actual act or did not react strongly enough when the suggestion was made by the offender(s). The term applies also to cases in risky situations marred with sexuality, especially when she uses what could be interpreted as indecency of language and gestures, or constitutes what could be taken as an invitation to sexual relations. (266)

Feminist critics, both within and outside criminology, quickly charged that this notion clearly placed criminology in collusion with the rapist, who can apparently claim sexual access whenever he deems that his victim has aroused him (Schwendinger and Schwendinger 1983).

The first influential feminist studies of women's victimization appeared during the 1970s and focused on wife battering and rape. Susan Brownmiller's work (1975), in particular, is a deft synthesis of mainstream criminological research on rape offenders (including Amir's study) with a radical feminist perspective that views rape as the sine qua non of men's control of women under patriarchy. Both in content and in timing, these early feminist accounts posed a powerful challenge even to radical criminology, which was rising to prominence during the 1970s. At the heart of the radical perspective was a view of crime as resistance to class and race domination (Taylor, Walton, and Young 1973) and a conceptualization of the offender as the "rogue male" using the only resources available to him in fighting an unjust system. Radical criminologists were caught off guard by the rising tide of radical feminist research on the experiences of women who disproportionately suffered at the hands of such outlaws (Gelsthorpe and Morris 1988). Roger Matthews and Jock Young, two leading British radical criminologists, have admitted that feminist research convinced them of "the limits of the romantic

conception of crime and the criminal" (Matthews and Young 1986, 2). Subsequently, radical criminology has taken a more "realist" turn, attempting to come to terms with women's victimization as well as the fact that the poor and working classes are disproportionately the victims of crime (DeKeseredy 1996).

Unlike research on women's offending, which has been guided largely by liberal feminist ideas and methodologies, women's victimization has been a central issue for radical feminists. The relationship with mainstream criminology has been an awkward one, complicated both by radical feminism's antipositivist assumptions and by its advocacy of social change. Modern mainstream criminology, born at the turn of the twentieth century, is also called the positivist school. To oversimplify, this means that most traditional criminologists have used the tools of the scientific method, such as the social survey and statistical methodology, to document what has been conceptualized as a universe of preexisting social categories. Such inquiry has been framed as value neutral, and it posits the discovery of facts about the social world as an eventual goal. In criminology, scholars have gone about measuring crime and victimization as if these behaviors were readily apparent, uncontested, and invariant in their meaning across social groups. The equity studies discussed previously are examples of this approach, and some of its limitations have already been noted.

Radical feminists take this critique one step further. Radical feminist accounts, like Brownmiller's, have argued that violence against women cannot simply be equated with the victimization of men but, rather, that it takes on a different meaning in the context of a social system in which men are dominant over women. Thus women's violence against men is not the same as men's violence against women. Radical feminists have also pointed to the role of social institutions (such as the criminal justice system and the family) and social norms around sexuality and violence in working together to erase and normalize women's victimization. As a result, victims of rape and battery are often persuaded that such things are either normal or justified, and their victimization may not be apparent, even to themselves. This stance clearly renders any mere quantification of experiences of victimization necessarily incomplete. In addition, radical feminists have argued for the use of research as a tool for social change, a position also at odds with mainstream criminology.

Fault lines have formed around a number of issues, but the ongoing debate over statistics on women's victimization is a particularly apposite case. As noted earlier, the NCVS serves as the primary source of victimization data used by criminologists. Yet before 1992, this instrument did not query sample respondents specifically about rape or sexual assault, asking instead only whether they had been "beaten up" or attacked in other ways. Nor did the survey specifically attempt to measure victimization in the home, inquiring only whether "anyone" had committed violence against the respondent. An extensive redesign process, prompted in part by criticisms from feminist advocacy groups (although general methodological criticisms had also been raised by others), led to the inclusion of questions specifically about rape as well as an item addressing victimization in the home. After the redesign, overall estimates of personal victimization increased by 44 percent, but rape and sexual assault victimization rates increased by 157 percent. The new instrument also produced a 72 percent increase in women's reporting that they had been victimized by intimates, and a 155 percent increase in reports of victimization by other relatives (Bachman and Saltzman 1995). There is little doubt that the statistical picture has become a more accurate one.

Even so, criminology has remained resistant to the implications of radical feminism's assumption that women may not see violence against them in terms of standard legal categories, such as those used in the NCVS. Much feminist empirical work on women's victimization has employed substantive definitions of these acts, asking respondents in general terms if they, for example, have had sex against their will due to force, threat of force, or incapacity to consent. Such studies typically yield higher prevalence estimates than those reflected in official statistics. For example, while 14.0 percent of the ever-married women in Russell's sample (1982) reported incidents of victimization by their husbands that fit the legal definition of rape, only 0.9 percent of these women mentioned these experiences when asked directly if they had ever been the victim of a rape or an attempted rape. Such research has been the subject of a considerable backlash from critics, however, who typically rely on official statistics,

such as the UCR and NCVS, to assert that feminists have vastly inflated the extent of women's victimization.

A second area of dispute has arisen around the radical feminist assumption that any analysis of victimization is incomplete without an understanding of the patriarchal context that shapes the meaning of these acts (Hanmer and Maynard 1987). The implication of this critique is that any simple count of events, no matter how accurate, will necessarily fail to tell the whole story. Perhaps the best example of this controversy is the debate over statistics on rates of partner or spousal violence, which has crystallized recently around the mutual combat hypothesis. Briefly, this notion arose from research employing an instrument (the Conflict Tactics Scale) that directs respondents to count instances of their own use of a wide spectrum of physically aggressive techniques against their partners during marital or relationship conflicts (Straus, Gelles, and Steinmetz 1980). Surprisingly, studies using this instrument indicate that women are just as likely to use physical violence as men. This result has been offered as a fundamental challenge to feminist constructions of marital violence as a problem experienced primarily by women in the patriarchal context of marriage. Calls for attention to the problem of battered husbands have followed, and the mutual combat hypothesis has achieved wide cultural and disciplinary currency. Criminology texts now largely refer to "partner" or "spousal" violence; I recently reviewed a criminology textbook-in-development that began the section on violence in marriage by framing the problem as one of mutual combat.

Feminist critics have responded that the context in which violence is experienced is crucial. Women are much more likely than men to use violence in self-defense, more likely to be injured by acts of intimate violence directed against them, more likely to feel seriously threatened by it, less likely to be able to effectively defend themselves, and less likely to have the resources to leave violent relationships (Nazroo 1995; for a review, see Gelles and Loeske 1993). Again, this controversy illustrates the uneasy relationship between criminology's positivist tradition and the antipositivist implications of the assumptions that undergird radical feminist research and theorizing on women's experiences of violence. A similar controversy exists in research on fear of crime, an area in which women's much higher rates of expressed fear are seemingly unaccounted for by their lower rates of victimization. Pioneering work by Elizabeth Stanko (1990) and others, however, has revealed that much of women's victimization is hidden (that is, not accounted for by official statistics), routine, and socially legitimated (Madriz 1997) and that women have ample reason to express high levels of fear.

As in the case of women offenders, activism both within and outside the discipline has been instrumental in framing women's victimization as a legitimate social problem and in making concrete changes in the criminal justice system. Presumptive arrest policies regarding domestic violence incidents, now in place in the majority of U.S. jurisdictions, were prompted in large part by empirical research conducted by criminologists (Sherman and Berk 1984). While such a strategy represents an important symbolic step, indicating that such violence is finally being taken more seriously by the system, subsequent research (Sherman 1992) indicates that such policies are not working as well as their proponents had hoped, and in some cases, they appear to increase the chances of repeat violence. Debate and research within criminology continue to be influential in shaping policy in this area. Other significant legal and political changes include revisions in laws defining rape or sexual assault; the passage of "rape shield" laws, which do not allow the discussion of victims' sexual histories in court; and the recent passage of the Violence Against Women Act, which defines gender-based victimization as a hate crime and allocates increased funds for battered women's shelters, rape crisis centers, and policing and research efforts directed to reducing the number of crimes against women.

WOMEN AS WORKERS

During the last 25 years, increasing numbers of women have entered criminal justice occupations. Most research to date has addressed women's experiences in policing, prison work, and law, and these will be my focus here. Before the 1970s, few women were employed in any of these jobs. A variety of factors eased women's entry. As has been the case with most male-dominated occupations, legislative change and legal pressure have been most influential; Title VII and the Equal Employment Opportunity Act formally opened all of these occupations to women. Title DC was also important for women in law, as it struck down policies that had either barred them from law schools entirely or kept their numbers to a minimum. Even so, administrators, coworkers, and clients did not immediately welcome women. Lawsuits challenging recruitment and promotion practices, among other things, were necessary to fully open the doors for women's entry (Martin and Jurik 1996).

Women have also benefited from demographic changes. The sheer number of people employed in all of these jobs has increased dramatically over the last two decades, and women have filled the gap as the supply of male workers has not been adequate to meet the rising demand. This effect has been particularly dramatic in prison work. Between 1983 and 1995, the number of staff in prisons and jails increased 187 percent, but the number of female staff almost quadrupled, increasing by 372 percent (American Correctional Association 1984; Maguire and Pastore 1999). Additional factors, specific to law, policing, and prison work, have also contributed to women's increasing representation in these fields. By 1998, women constituted 12 percent of all police officers, 24 percent of all prison officers, and 34 percent of all attorneys (Bureau of Labor Statistics 1999).

Increasing access has not necessarily meant equal rewards. There is a considerable wage gap in each occupation; women's incomes in policing are only 86 percent of those of their male counterparts; in prison work, 89 percent; and in law, 70 percent. The relatively smaller gaps in policing and prison work are undoubtedly due to the fact that the employer in these cases is the government, a labor market sector in which recruiting and promotion practices are at least somewhat formalized. Law, on the other hand, is practiced in highly diverse settings, each with its own set of employment practices and its own reward structure. Regardless, women in all three occupations are likely to be found at the lowest rungs of their respective occupational ladders. In policing, for example, women are 16 percent of municipal officers but only 7 percent of state police (National Center for Women in Policing 1999). Women in prison work continue to face blocked access to supervisory positions (Britton 1997), and women in law are concentrated in the least prestigious specialties (for example, family law and public defense) and work in the lowest-paid settings (Pierce 1995).

While there have always been women criminals and women victims, until a quarter-century ago, there was a paucity of women working in criminal justice occupations. What this means is that, although mainstream criminological research existed on police, prison workers, and attorneys prior to 1975, these studies essentially focused on "the men and their work" and lacked an analysis of gender. Subsequently, a considerable volume of literature on women in criminal justice occupations has appeared. I will not attempt to cover the literature on each occupation here (for a review, see Martin and Jurik 1996). Two clear, though sometimes overlapping, areas of research have emerged in studies of women's experiences in all three occupations, however. The first has involved a focus on difference, asking questions about how or whether women perform their jobs differently from men and about the unique gendered characteristics women bring to their work. The second line of research has contended that these jobs and the organizations in which they are performed are themselves gendered and has looked at the ways in which gendered organizational structures, ideologies, policies and practices, interactions, and worker identities assume and reinforce inequality.

Theoretical and empirical work in the first vein is in some ways a response to critics who have long argued that women, on account of their gender, do not possess the characteristics necessary for success in these heavily masculinized and male-dominated occupations. As a male attorney interviewed by Pierce (1995) put it, "I think Clarence Darrow once said women are too nice to be lawyers. I think he was right. It's not that I don't think women are bright or competent—they just don't have that *killer* instinct" (26). Similar, and usually less charitable, sentiments can be found in both popular and academic discussions of the role of women in prison work and in policing. Research from the difference perspective has attempted to turn this critique on its head, arguing that women are not the same as their male counterparts but that the gendered qualities that they bring with them are actually assets.

In some ways, this line of argument represents a return to the discourse employed by women criminal justice system reformers of the nineteenth century. Claims that women were simply inherently better able to deal with women victims, suspects, clients, and prisoners were largely successful in persuading state and local governments to hire policewomen, whose main responsibility was to deal with delinquent women and girls and to build reformatories, staffed exclusively by women, to hold women inmates (Appier 1998; Freedman 1981). The principal change is that such rhetoric is now being used to argue for the integration of women into male-dominated occupations, rather than the establishment of separate, sex-segregated jobs and institutions. Menkel-Meadow (1987), for example, argues that women bring a "different voice" to the practice of law and that women, by virtue of their socialization and experiences, will be less adversarial, more interested in substantive justice (rather than strict procedural fairness), and will ultimately seek to empower their clients, rather than themselves. Advocates for women in policing have long contended that women's supposedly superior communication skills will make them better at resolving conflicts through dialogue, rather than force, and that they will be more empathetic and effective in working with victims and suspects (Appier 1998; Martin 1997). A similar argument has been made for increasing the number of women officers in men's prisons, where their presence is held to "normalize" and "soften" the work environment (Britton 1997).

On balance, however, empirical research and experience have not been supportive of these kinds of claims. Neither policing, nor prison work, nor law have been radically transformed or even become much kinder and gentler as women have increasingly moved into these occupations. The reason lies, in part, in a factor left out of the difference equation, the gendered structure of occupations and organizations themselves. This has been the focus of the second line of research. Pierce (1995), for example, finds that the adversarial structure of the legal profession, and litigation work in particular, leaves women few options; to succeed, they must adopt the tactics of their successful male peers, developing qualities such as aggression, intimidation, and impersonality. This creates a double bind for women, as those who take on this role are usually perceived more negatively than their male counterparts. Some women do resist, but most do so at the cost of success, at least as it has been defined by others. The gendered structure of the practice of litigation leaves little room for the meaningful assertion of difference, even if women lawyers were so inclined. Further, the masculinization of these occupations and of the organizations in which they are performed means that the rewards that accrue to difference vary dramatically by sex. Britton (1997) finds that male officers in men's and women's prisons benefit from asserting their unique abilities to use physical force. Women's purportedly unique gendered abilities, such as higher levels of empathy, emotionality, and communication skills, are often seen by administrators and coworkers, particularly in men's prisons, as either dangerous or extraneous.

These kinds of findings should not be taken to mean, however, that difference is immaterial. Women in these occupations do often differ from their male counterparts, particularly in relationship to issues like balancing work and family. Research also demonstrates that many do see themselves as different, both in terms of work styles and personality. It is also clear that we can meaningfully speak of characteristics that have been more or less associated with masculinity and femininity. Whether they display these characteristics or not, research and experience tell us that individual workers will be held accountable for them. An emerging trend in research on women in criminal justice occupations (and research on women and work more generally) recognizes this but at the same time argues that organizational and occupational structures are also important. This approach is in some ways a synthesis of the two perspectives outlined earlier and contends that the crucial issue is context; some work settings are more amenable to, or at least less penalizing of, gendered characteristics associated with women workers (Britton 2000). Miller (1999), for example, finds that community policing draws on traits like empathy, a service orientation, and communication skills and that women are often drawn to the work for this reason. Ely (1995) finds that women in law firms with a higher proportion of women in positions of power are less likely to see feminine-stereotyped characteristics as impediments to success and are more flexible in their ideas about gender overall. Anleu's research (1992) indicates that women have greater career opportunities in corporate

legal departments than in private law firms, at least partly because occupational demands and domestic responsibilities are not as incompatible. Taken together, these findings suggest that while increasing the number of women in these occupations is an important step, structural changes in policing, prison, and legal organizations are also necessary to produce significant change in the direction of equality for women.

EMERGING ISSUES

Kathleen Daly and Lisa Maher (1998) divide feminist criminology into two periods. The first phase, into which much of the work previously described falls, has focused on the tasks of filling in gaps, comparison, and critique. With little knowledge about women offenders, victims, and workers in the criminal justice system available, the first chore of feminist criminology was to provide this information. Though a substantial beginning has been made, it is likely that research in these areas will continue.

The second phase is characterized by work that disrupts the existing frameworks of criminology in more fundamental ways, resulting in the growth of a body of research and theory that Maureen Cain (1990) has called "transgressive criminology." For example, some feminist criminologists have crossed the traditional division between offending and victimization. As research on women offenders accumulated, it became clear that they were usually also victims, having experienced substantial physical and verbal abuse at the hands of intimates. The "blurred boundaries" thesis argues that women's offending is intimately linked to their previous victimization; a central task for feminist criminology in the years to come will be filling in the black box (Daly 1992) that connects the two. Undoubtedly, this will require a new, more nuanced conception of women offenders that disrupts the dichotomy in which they have been seen only either as innocent victims or as hardened criminals. Some work in this vein has already appeared; Lisa Maher's research (1997), described earlier, is but one example.

This dichotomy is deeply racialized, and this presents yet another challenge for feminist criminology. There is little doubt that the face of the much-mythologized new, more dangerous, female offender is that of a woman of color and that the most innocent victims have always been white. Feminist criminology is just beginning to come to terms with this. Whatever the difficulties posed by official statistics, research and theorizing must continue to reject the essentialism inherent in treating women as a unitary category (Simpson 1989). We already know much about the ways in which race, class, and sexual inequality interweave with women's experiences as victims, offenders, and workers. The challenge for feminist criminology in the years to come will lie in formulating theory and carrying out empirical studies that prioritize all of these dimensions, rather than relegating one or more of them to the background for the sake of methodological convenience.

Given men's overrepresentation as offenders and victims, the screaming silence in criminology around the connection between masculinity and crime has always been something of a paradox. Feminist criminology has recently begun to draw attention to this issue. Messerschmidt's (1993) was one of the first significant theoretical contributions in this area; it argues that, for men who lack access to other resources, crime can serve as an alternate means of doing masculinity. More recent accounts (see Newburn and Stanko 1994 for a review) have begun to untangle the contexts in which this use of crime is more or less likely and to explore the kinds of masculinities that result. A similar line of research has very recently begun to inquire into the social construction and reproduction of gendered identities among women involved in crime. On a parallel track, studies of work in criminal justice occupations are drawing attention to the individual and organizational construction of gender among both men and women workers (Britton 1997; Miller 1999; Pierce 1995). This research represents a promising direction for the field, both because it finally acknowledges men as men and because it moves us beyond dichotomized, static, individualistic notions about gender.

Finally, one of the most important issues facing activists in the discipline during the coming years will undoubtedly lie in rethinking feminist criminology's relationship with the state. Those working on issues connected to women offenders have already recognized the perils of the liberal strategy of strict legal equality. Such policies, when imposed in an already unequal and gendered context, have almost invariably disadvantaged women. Victimization activists have been more enthusiastic about the criminal justice system as a force for change but find that even well-intentioned policies, such as presumptive arrest for domestic violence offenders, have had unanticipated negative consequences. Women in policing, prison work, and law have also found that obtaining the legal right of access to these jobs is not enough to ensure equality.

Simply creating new laws to enforce, providing more offenders to incarcerate, and allowing women to work in the system have done little to disrupt its underlying structure, which is deeply gendered and racialized. As Carol Smart (1998) notes, the turning point for feminist criminology will come in realizing that "law is not simply . . . a set of tools or rules that we can bend into a more favourable shape" (31). Smart herself, arguably one of the founding mothers of feminist criminology, has recently disavowed the project entirely, arguing instead for a deconstructionist approach that disrupts and subverts criminology's traditional categories and frames of reference (Smart 1995). Rethinking feminist criminology's relationship to the state and to the criminal justice system does not necessarily mean that feminists in the discipline (or elsewhere) should reject efforts directed toward legal change. What this critique does suggest is that in feminism's continuing encounter with criminology, conceptions of justice, rather than law, should occupy a much more central place in our thinking (Klein 1995).

REFERENCES

Adler, Freda. 1975. *Sisters in Crime: The Rise of the New Female Criminal.* New York: McGraw-Hill.

American Correctional Association. 1984. *Juvenile and Adult Correctional Departments, Institutions, Agencies and Paroling Authorities, United States and Canada.* College Park, MD: American Correctional Association.

Amir, Menachem. 1971. *Patterns in Forcible Rape.* Chicago: University of Chicago Press.

Anleu, Sharon Roach. 1992. Women in Law: Theory, Research and Practice. *Australian and New Zealand Journal of Sociology* 28(3):391–410.

Appier, Janis. 1998. *Policing Women: The Sexual Politics of Law Enforcement and the LAPD.* Philadelphia: Temple University Press.

Bachman, Ronet and Linda E. Saltzman. 1995. *Violence Against Women.* Washington, DC: Bureau of Justice Statistics.

Britton, Dana M. 1997. Gendered Organizational Logic: Policy and Practice in Men's and Women's Prisons. *Gender & Society* 11:796–818.
_____. 2000. The Epistemology of the Gendered Organization. *Gender & Society* 14(3):418–435.

Brown, Beverley. 1986. Women and Crime: The Dark Figures of Criminology. *Economy and Society* 15(3): 355–402.

Brownmiller, Susan. 1975. *Against Our Will: Men, Women, and Rape.* New York: Simon & Schuster.

Bureau of Labor Statistics. 1999. *Highlights of Women's Earnings in 1998.* Washington, DC: Government Printing Office.

Cain, Maureen. 1990. Towards Transgression: New Directions in Feminist Criminology. *International Journal of the Sociology of Law* 18:1–18.

Chesney-Lind, Meda. 1989. Girls' Crime and Women's Place: Toward a Feminist Model of Female Delinquency. *Crime and Delinquency* 35(1):5–29.
_____. 1995. Preface. In *International Feminist Perspectives in Criminology: Engendering a Discipline,* ed. Nicole Hahn Rafter and Frances Heidensohn. Philadelphia: Open University Press.
_____. 1996. Sentencing Women to Prison: Equality Without Justice. In *Race, Gender, and Class in Criminology: The Intersection,* ed. M. D. Schwartz and D. Milovanovic. New York: Garland.

Chilton, Roland and Susan K. Datesman. 1987. Gender, Race, and Crime: An Analysis of Urban Arrest Trends, 1960–1980. *Gender & Society* 1(2):152–71.

Daly, Kathleen. 1987. Discrimination in the Criminal Courts: Family, Gender, and the Problem of Equal Treatment. *Social Forces* 66(1):152–75.
_____. 1992. Women's Pathways to Felony Court: Feminist Theories of Law-breaking and Problems of Representation. *Southern California Review of Law and Women's Studies* 2:11–52.

Daly, Kathleen and Meda Chesney-Lind. 1988. Feminism and Criminology. *Justice Quarterly* 5:497–538.

Daly, Kathleen and Lisa Maher. 1998. Crossroads and Intersections: Building from Feminist Critique. In *Criminology at the Crossroads,* ed. Kathleen Daly and Lisa Maher. New York: Oxford University Press.

Davis, Angela Y. 1997. Race and Criminalization: Black Americans and the Punishment Industry. In *The House That Race Built,* ed. Wahneema Lubiano. New York: Pantheon.

DeKeseredy, Walter S. 1996. The Left-Realist Perspective on Race, Class, and Gender. In *Race, Gender, and Class in Criminology,* ed.

M. D. Schwartz and D. Milovanovic. New York: Garland.

Ely, Robin J. 1995. The Power in Demography: Women's Social Constructions of Gender Identity at Work. *Academy of Management Journal* 38(3): 589–634.

Freedman, Estelle. 1981. *Their Sister's Keepers: Women's Prison Reform in America, 1830–1930.* Ann Arbor: University of Michigan Press.

Gelles, Richard and Donileen Loeske, eds. 1993. *Current Controversies on Family Violence.* London: Sage.

Gelsthorpe, Loraine and Allison Morris. 1988. Feminism and Criminology in Britain. *British Journal of Criminology* 28(2):93–110.

Hanmer, J. and M. Maynard. 1987. *Women, Violence, and Social Control.* London: Macmillan.

Klein, Dorie. 1995. Crime Through Gender's Prism: Feminist Criminology in the United States. In *International Feminist Perspectives in Criminology: Engendering a Discipline,* ed. Nicole Hahn Rafter and Frances Heidensohn. Philadelphia: Open University Press.

Madriz, Esther. 1997. *Nothing Bad Happens to Good Girls: Fear of Crime in Women's Lives.* Berkeley: University of California Press.

Maguire, Kathleen and Ann L. Pastore. 1999. *Sourcebook of Criminal Justice Statistics.* Washington, DC: Government Printing Office. Available at http://www.albany.edu/sourcebook.

Maher, Lisa. 1997. *Sexed Work: Gender, Race, and Resistance in a Brooklyn Drug Market.* New York: Oxford University Press.

Mann, Coramae Richey. 1995. Women of Color and the Criminal Justice System. In *The Criminal Justice System and Women: Offenders, Victims, and Workers,* ed. Barbara Raffel Price and Natalie J. Sokoloff. New York: McGraw-Hill.

Martin, Patricia Y. 1997. Gender, Accounts, and Rape Processing Work. *Social Problems* 44(4):464–82.

Martin, Susan E. and Nancy C. Jurik. 1996. *Doing Justice, Doing Gender: Women in Law and Criminal Justice Occupations.* Thousand Oaks, CA: Sage.

Matthews, Roger and Jock Young. 1986. *Confronting Crime.* London: Sage.

Menkel-Meadow, Carrie. 1987. Portia in a Different Voice: Speculating on a Women's Lawyering Process. *Berkeley Women's Law Journal* 1(1): 39–63.

Messerschmidt, James W. 1993. *Masculinities and Crime.* Boston: Rowman & Littlefield.

Miller, Susan L. 1999. *Gender and Community Policing.* Boston: Northeastern University Press.

Morris, Allison. 1987. *Women, Crime, and Criminal Justice.* New York: Basil Blackwell.

Morris, Allison and Loraine Gelsthorpe. 1991. Feminist Perspectives in Criminology:

Transforming and Transgressing. *Women & Criminal Justice* 2(2):3–26.

Morris, Allison and Ania Wilczynski. 1994. Rocking the Cradle: Mothers Who Kill Their Children. In *Moving Targets: Women, Murder, and Representation,* ed. Helen Birch. Berkeley: University of California Press.

National Center for Women in Policing. 1999. *Equality Denied: The Status of Women in Policing, 1998.* Arlington, VA: Feminist Majority Foundation.

Nazroo, James. 1995. Uncovering Gender Differences in the Use of Marital Violence: The Effect of Methodology. *Sociology* 29(3):475–94.

Newburn, Tim and Elizabeth A. Stanko, eds. 1994. *Just Boys Doing Business? Men, Masculinities and Crime.* New York: Routledge.

Pierce, Jennifer. 1995. *Gender Trials: Emotional Lives in Contemporary Law Firms.* Berkeley: University of California Press.

Price, Barbara Raffel and Natalie J. Sokoloff, eds. 1995. *The Criminal Justice System and Women: Offenders, Victims, and Workers.* New York: McGraw-Hill.

Rafter, Nicole Hahn and Frances Heidensohn. 1995. Introduction: The Development of Feminist Perspectives on Crime. In *International Feminist Perspectives in Criminology: Engendering a Discipline,* ed. Nicole Hahn Rafter and Frances Heidensohn. Philadelphia: Open University Press.

Russell, Diana E. H. 1982. *Rape in Marriage.* New York: Macmillan.

Schwendinger, Julia R. and Herman Schwendinger. 1983. *Rape and Inequality.* Newbury Park, CA: Sage.

Sherman, Lawrence A. 1992. *Policing Domestic Violence.* New York: Free Press.

Sherman, Lawrence A. and Richard A. Berk. 1984. The Specific Deterrent Effects of Arrest for Domestic Violence. *American Sociological Review* 49(2): 261–92.

Simon, Rita James. 1975. *Women and Crime.* Lexington, MA: Lexington Books.

Simpson, Sally S. 1989. Feminist Theory, Crime, and Justice. *Criminology* 27: 605–31.

Simpson, Sally S. and Lori Elis. 1995. Doing Gender: Sorting out the Caste and Crime Conundrum. *Criminology* 33(1):47–81.

Smart, Carol. 1976. *Women, Crime and Criminology: A Feminist Critique.* Boston: Routledge & Kegan Paul.

————. 1995. *Law, Crime and Sexuality: Essays in Feminism.* London: Sage.

————. 1998. The Woman of Legal Discourse. In *Criminology at the Crossroads,* ed. Kathleen Daly and Lisa Maher. New York: Oxford University Press.

Stanko, Elizabeth. 1990. *Everyday Violence.* London: Pandora.

Steffensmeier, Darrell. 1995. Trends in Female Crime: It's Still a Man's World. In *The Criminal Justice System and Women,* ed. Barbara R. Price and Natalie J. Sokoloff. New York: McGraw-Hill.

Steffensmeier, Darrell and Emilie Allan. 1996. Gender and Crime: Toward a Gendered Theory of Female Offending. *Annual Review of Sociology* 22:459–88.

Straus, Murray A., Richard J. Gelles, and Suzanne Steinmetz. 1980. *Behind Closed Doors.* New York: Doubleday.

Taylor, Ian, Paul Walton, and Jock Young. 1973. *The New Criminology.* London: Routledge & Kegan Paul.

Chapter 4

AN ARGUMENT FOR BLACK FEMINIST CRIMINOLOGY

Understanding African American Women's Experiences With Intimate Partner Abuse Using an Integrated Approach

HILLARY POTTER

J ust as there are many types of feminisms and feminists, it undoubtedly follows that there are adaptations on feminist criminology and no single feminist criminology can exist (Britton, 2000; Daly & Chesney-Lind, 1988; Flavin, 1998). The impetus for proposing a Black feminist criminology (BFC) is supported by Britton's (2000) argument that traditional feminist criminology still has much work to accomplish in theorizing from intersecting identities as opposed to placing emphasis on a solitary component—such as considering gender but not race—at the forefront of and central to an analysis. Flavin (1998) expressly promoted a BFC that focuses on the specific experiences of Black individuals in the crime-processing system.[1] Although feminist criminology has its roots in mainstream feminist theories (Britton,

2000; Daly & Chesney-Lind, 1988),[2] the approach presented in this chapter, BFC, is grounded in Black feminist theory and critical race feminist theory (CRFT). To begin to understand and fully conceptualize BFC, this chapter considers intimate partner abuse against African American[3] women as an illustration of its ability to explain this transgression.

Feminist criminology has aided in a notably improved understanding of gender variations in criminal activity and victimization and of the crime-processing system's dealings with female and male victims and offenders. Feminist criminology has significantly expanded the foci within the field of criminology beyond simply exploring female criminal offending and female offenders to also examining violent acts against girls and women (Britton, 2000). Although gender is

Source: Potter, H. (2006). An argument for Black feminist criminology: Understanding African American women's experiences with intimate partner abuse using an integrated approach. *Feminist Criminology, 1*(2), 106–124.

Author's Note: The author especially wishes to thank Dr. Joanne Belknap and the anonymous reviewers for their extensive comments and support in drafting this chapter.

certainly important and crucial to considering women's (and men's) involvement in crime either as victims or as offenders, for Black women, and arguably for all women, other inequities must be considered principal, not peripheral, to the analysis of women. This includes incorporating key factors such as race and/or ethnicity, sexuality, and economic status into any examination. Daly (1997) argued that considering how gender, race, and class distinctions intersect is absolutely necessary in criminology. Because traditional feminist criminology is built on mainstream feminism, which historically placed issues of race as secondary to gender (hooks, 2000; Lewis, 1977), it is reasoned here that starting at Black feminist theory and CRFT to investigate and explain the source of and reactions to crime among African Americans will be sure to explicitly take into account Black women's positions in society, in their communities, and in their familial and intimate relationships. This proposition does not serve to devalue the remarkable work resulting from the establishment of feminist criminology or the concepts purported by and examined under this rubric. Instead, BFC extends beyond traditional feminist criminology to view African American women (and, conceivably, other women of color) from their multiple marginalized and dominated positions in society, culture, community, and families. Although the example provided here to tender a Black feminist criminological theory is on one form of victimization of African American women, it has been well documented in feminist criminology analyses that there is often a clear correlation and/or pathway between women's victimization and any ultimate criminal behavior (Belknap, 2001; Britton, 2000; Chesney-Lind & Pasko, 2004; Richie, 1996). As such, using intimate partner abuse against African American women as an illustration provides us with an example that may be applied beyond Black women's experiences with victimization into other encounters with crime and the crime-processing system.

As is demonstrated here, BFC can advance future theorizing, research, and policy making regarding battered Black women. At the outset, this chapter presents an historical overview of the attention given to the issue of intimate partner abuse by feminist activists and the problems with examining African American women's encounters with domestic abuse using theory based on White women's experiences. A comprehensive description of BFC is then provided and followed by the Black feminist and critical race feminist concepts on which it is constructed. Support for a BFC is demonstrated by evaluating African American women's experiences with and responses to intimate partner abuse and the crime-processing system's intervention in domestic violence incidents involving Black women under this model. Presented throughout this application are previous assessments on battered Black women in the works of some Black and critical race feminists. As with any new theoretical proposal, criticism of the concept is to be expected. Therefore, anticipated criticisms and potential limitations are addressed.

HISTORICAL DEVELOPMENT OF FEMINIST ADVOCACY AGAINST INTIMATE PARTNER ABUSE

An increased awareness of the problem of intimate partner abuse against women has occurred only during the past few decades. Until the 1970s, concern, advocacy, and protection for battered women by the general public and officials of the crime-processing system were tremendously lacking (Belknap, 2001; Tierney, 1982). Historians had sporadically recorded attempts of various individuals who raised public concern for these victims. However, these endeavors were largely unsuccessful until the 1970s. During this decade, there was an accelerating trend toward the criminalization of domestic violence perpetrators and an increase in the assistance afforded battered women. Feminist organizations began to highlight intimate partner violence against women as a social problem needing to be remedied (Schechter, 1982), and books written by battered women and their advocates began to appear with fervor (Belknap & Potter, 2006). In 1973, the United States saw one of its first shelters to assist wives battered by their alcoholic husbands at the Rainbow Retreat in Phoenix, Arizona (Tierney, 1982), and since this time, shelters have rapidly appeared across the country (Belknap, 2001). In addition to establishing places to harbor battered women and their children away from their male batterers, law enforcement and court intervention agents began to address woman battering more seriously with the enactment and increased enforcement of laws and sanctions relating to intimate abuse (Tierney, 1982). In 1994, President Bill Clinton signed into law the landmark Violence Against Women Act to combat violence against women by providing assistance to criminal processing agents (e.g., training), support for battered women's shelters and a national telephone "hotline," and funding for research on violence against women. The act was renewed in 2000 and provided financial support in excess of US$3 billion for 5 years. The second reauthorization of the Act was passed by both the U.S. Senate and the House of Representatives and was signed into law by President Bush in January 2006.

Along with the diligent labor of feminist activists, the battered women's movement was further assisted in its development and awareness efforts by the media's attention to the movement (Tierney, 1982). Through the mid-1970s, some popular magazines considered domestic violence to be acts of rioting and terrorism, but by the end of the decade, the term became equivalent with *wife abuse* (Tierney, 1982) and other forms of family-related interpersonal violence (Belknap, 2001). Indeed, between 1987 and 1997, the media representations of domestic violence as a serious issue were instrumental in decreasing the public's tolerance of wife abuse during this decade (Johnson & Sigler, 2000).

Although intimate partner violence has experienced increased attention by the public, researchers, and the crime-processing system, abuse among intimate partners as a social problem is still not receiving the level of attention it deserves from criminal processing agents (Erez & Belknap, 1998) and health professionals (Belknap, 2001; Rodriguez, Bauer, McLoughlin, & Grumbach, 1999). For instance, there is fairly recent evidence that police officers still respond leniently to male batterers (Fyfe, Klinger, & Flavin, 1997). That is, men who abuse their female intimate partners are arrested less often than other violent offenders. In addition, battered women's shelters continue to suffer from poor financial support and the inability to house every woman and child in need of and requesting sanctuary from their abusers (Belknap, 2001). As indicated by a survey conducted by the Center for the Advancement of Women (2003), a sizeable number of women deem that intimate

partner violence warrants continued attention. In fact, the report indicates that 92% of the women surveyed believed that domestic violence and sexual assault should be the top priority for the women's movement. Violence against women as a main concern was succeeded by the following priorities: equal pay for equal work (90%), child care (85%), reducing drug and alcohol addiction among women (72%), and keeping abortion legal (41%). This finding underlies the need that much more work is needed to improve the lives of battered women and to better address the unwarranted behavior of batterers.

It is unmistakable that with the identification of domestic violence as a social problem approximately three decades ago came an unprecedented amount of research and activism surrounding the plight of battered women. In both the research and responses to intimate partner abuse, however, cultural, racial, and ethnic distinctions among women victims of intimate partner abuse have not been afforded equal levels of consideration (Bograd, 1999; Richie, 1996, 2000). Much of the extant research and policies regard all battered women as victims with similar life experiences (Richie, 2000; C. West, 2005); yet African American women and other women of color typically have life experiences distinct from White women. The research in the 1970s was conducted with predominantly White samples and a failure to take into account how the surveys and findings might be problematic in reference to victims and offenders of color. It is regrettable that more recent investigations continue to follow this precedent. Stated alternatively, using research designed to study battered White women may not adequately explain how African American women experience and respond to intimate partner abuse. It is notable that Black women encounter the serious ramifications of racism in addition to sexism, and findings indicate they are the victims of intimate partner violence at higher rates than their White counterparts (Gelles & Straus, 1988; Hampton & Gelles, 1994; Rennison & Welchans, 2000). Basing investigations on theories that do not defer to the unique experiences of Black women may be erroneous and impractical to these women because of their prospects of encountering both racism and sexism within U.S. society.

BFC and Its Origins

The Tenets of BFC

BFC incorporates the tenets of interconnected identities, interconnected social forces, and distinct circumstances to better theorize, conduct research, and inform policy regarding criminal behavior and victimization among African Americans. (This concept may also have applicability with other groups of color and possibly with White women.) The interconnected identities to be considered among African American individuals include race and/or ethnicity, gender, sexuality, class status, national origin, and religion. Certainly, this is not a comprehensive list, as this precept allows for other identities to be included dependent on how an individual self-identifies. In U.S. society's stratified composition, occurrences of inequity are often experienced because of the spectrum of diversity within each identity and the intolerance and ignorance among some members of society. As such, various identities will be deemed of less value than others. This devaluation affects how certain individuals maneuver through life, including how they respond to events and opportunities with which they are confronted. Starting from this advantage point can help us begin to improve our explanations for the experiences of battered Black women's (a) entry into abusive relationships, (b) response to their abusers, and (c) use of systemic resources to aid in withdrawing from the relationships.

These interconnected identities are greatly shaped by larger social forces. That is, groups of individuals and society at large produce and perpetuate conflict, competition, and differences in merit between the members of society. It is not battered Black women's identities that exclusively form their perceptions and reactions but the treatment of these identities filtered down from (a) the impact of the social structure through (b) the community or culture and to (c) familial and intimate exchanges. Nevertheless, this does not necessitate a linear association in every case; instead, it serves to demonstrate and argue that a patriarchal, paternalistic, and racialized social structure affects all other institutions and interactions in society. Black women's reactions to abuse are affected by their "place" in society because of their intersecting identities. Being at the least valued end of the spectrum for both race and gender

places these women in a peculiar position not faced by Black men or White women (although Black men and White women are indeed challenged with their relative and respective dominating forces). In a similar manner, other women of color, such as Latinas, Native American women, Asian American women, and immigrant women of color, can easily be placed alongside Black women in this analysis.

Last, the characteristic of "battered woman" or "criminal offender" should not be considered an element of the identities of women victims or offenders. Being abused or having committed criminal acts are situations which women encounter or in which women become implicated, not those that are endemic of their identity. Of course, this is not to diminish the seriousness of women being victimized or of criminality among women; instead, it is to emphasize that the individuals themselves rarely recognize these characteristics as central to their identity (see Potter, 2004, for an analysis of how battered Black women do not identify as victims or survivors and how abuse is a temporary setback and an additional act of oppression in their lives). Furthermore, incorporating these distinct circumstances into Black women's identity risks pathologizing Black women victims or offenders by making these events appear normal or expected among Black women.

Black Feminist and Critical Race Feminist Origins of BFC

BFC addresses concerns in the lives of Black women that are categorized into four themes: (a) social structural oppression, (b) the Black community and culture, (c) intimate and familial relations, and (d) the Black woman as an individual. As outlined above, the first three themes are components of interconnected social forces, whereas the fourth theme considers the interconnected identities of the Black woman as affected by the societal influences. The tenets of BFC are cultivated from Black feminist theory and CRFT. In general, Black feminist theory is the theoretical perspective that places the lived experiences of Black women, including any forms of resistance to their situations, at the focal point of the analysis. It considers Black women as individuals encompassing numerous and interwoven identities. The standpoint is that Black women are frequently oppressed within both the Black community (by Black men) and society at large based on their subordinated statuses within each of these spheres and that research on Black women should be conducted based on this perspective. Although the sexist oppression in the Black community may not appear as obvious as that in larger society, and presents itself in a different form, it undeniably exists. CRFT is similar to Black feminist theory in that it also considers women of color as individuals with multiple intersecting identities where one does not eclipse another. Specifically, however, CRFT has been used to consider the devalued position of women of color in greater society as their status relates to the legal field.

Unlike many White women who enjoyed the "feminist lifestyle" because it provided them the opportunity to meet and bond with other women, Black women have always had a sense of sisterhood (hooks, 2000). Although it is often assumed that Black women did not participate in the development of feminist ideology and the practice of gender equality, it is evident that Black women have indeed been involved in liberation efforts. By reading the works of women who considered themselves to be Black feminists, or were identified as such by others, Black women have a lengthy and valiant history in the liberation movement (Guy-Sheftall, 1995; King, 1988). Their struggles can be traced back to the 1600s when African women who were captured and enslaved in the so-called New World endured multiple forms of oppression by their slave masters (Fishman, 2003; Guy-Sheftall, 1995). Many of these women made attempts to defend themselves against the inhumane treatment. Recent survey research demonstrates that Black women, even more so than White women, are discontented with women's situation in society and are in want of changes in the social world that benefit women. According to Jones and Shorter-Gooden (2003), a Gallup poll conducted in June 2002 found that 48% of Black women affirmed they were dissatisfied with the treatment of women within society as compared to 26% of White women.

Mainstream feminist theory places gender as the primary consideration in women's liberation efforts (hooks, 2000). Black women have expressed difficulty in identifying with mainstream feminist theory because of its focus on this single aspect of womanhood and because the lives and concerns of White middle-class women were placed at the forefront of the liberation efforts (Collins, 2000). Black women regularly convey that they deal not only with issues of gender inequality but with racial inequality as well (Crenshaw, 1994). It is this status, Crenshaw (1994) argued, that relegates women of color to an invisible class and pulls these women's loyalties in two directions, that is, feeling the need to either choose between being loyal to feminist ideas or being loyal to their racial or ethnic community. Patricia Hill Collins (2000), Black feminist author of *Black Feminist Thought: Knowledge, Consciousness, and the Politics of Empowerment*, distinguished Black women's experiences from those of other groups of women and also considered Black women's lives as individuals:

> On the one hand, all African-American women face similar challenges that result from living in a society that historically and routinely derogates women of African descent. Despite the fact that U.S. Black women face common challenges, this neither means that individual African-American women have all had the same experiences nor that we agree on the significance of our varying experiences. Thus, on the other hand, despite the common challenges confronting U.S. Black women as a group, diverse responses to these core themes characterize U.S. Black women's group knowledge or standpoint. (p. 25)

This collective, yet individualized, aspect of Black women's lives is an important aspect in Black feminism and when considering Black women.

Used in conjunction with Black feminist theory, CRFT is a valuable approach for studies of crime and African American women because it provides a specific application to issues of women of color involved in the crime-processing system as victims, offenders, or both. Just as with many Black feminists, most critical race feminists have not involved themselves in the mainstream feminist movement but admit that they make use of certain themes of mainstream feminism in the social sciences (Wing, 2003). Developed in the 1990s, CRFT is based in the tradition of Black feminist theory, critical legal studies, and critical race theory (Wing, 1997). People of color, White women, and others were initially attracted to critical legal studies because it challenged laws related to oppression based on race and gender (Wing, 2003). Those credited with developing critical race theory reported disillusionment with critical legal studies' exclusion of the personal and intellectual viewpoints from scholars of color and White women scholars. Accordingly, critical race theory places more focus on the role of racism and a racist and classist society in the construction of realities among people of color. Although deemed as a move toward the inclusion of all people in the analysis of social interaction and social justice, many women of color continued to feel gender was not often introduced as a concern within critical race theory discourse and consequently, CRFT was born (Wing, 1997). According to Wing (1997), CRFT, like Black feminist theory, is grounded in "antiessentialism" and intersectionality. Antiessentialism asserts that there is more than one essential voice of women.[4] Battered Black women's experience with the crime-processing system and its agents can suitably be analyzed by incorporating a CRFT viewpoint into BFC.

In summation, numerous Black feminist and critical race feminist scholars have addressed the "intersecting oppressions" of Black women. In the classic article "Double Jeopardy: To Be Black and Female," Frances Beale (1970/1995), journalist and civil rights activist, wrote of the burden of the Black woman's disadvantaged status based on gender, race, and class. Gordon's (1987) analysis identified these three conditions as Black women's "trilogy of oppression" and stated that Black women are often confronted with determining which form of oppression is most important. King (1988) advocated for the term *multiple jeopardy* to describe Black women's oppression, given that Black women often undergo even more forms of subjugation and that these categories of oppression affect Black women simultaneously (also see Cleaver, 1997; Collins, 2000; Gordon, 1987; Guy-Sheftall, 1995; Hull, Bell Scott, & Smith, 1982; Smith, 1983; Terrelonge, 1984; Wing, 1997, 2003). Wing (2003), who used the term *multiplicative identity* to capture the identity of women of color, argued that "women of color are not merely White women *plus* color or men of color *plus* gender. Instead, their identities must be multiplied together to create a holistic One when analyzing the nature of the discrimination against them" (p. 7).

Although there is increased acceptance of a variety of feminist theories, hooks (2000) has continued to question whether contemporary White women understand that their perspectives may not be indicative of all women's realities and that their views may still be racist and classist. In referring to the issues raised regarding Anita Hill's reports of sexual harassment during the U.S. Senate hearings for Clarence Thomas's confirmation to the U.S. Supreme Court, McKay (1993) wrote that White women feminists "forgot that for Black women, issues of gender are always connected to race.... Black women cannot choose between their commitment to feminism and the struggle with their men for racial justice" (p. 276). Crenshaw (1994) echoed this sentiment by maintaining that modern discussions on feminism and antiracism have disregarded how racism and sexism are interwoven and "because of their intersectional identity as both women *and* people of color within discourses that are shaped to respond to one *or* the other, the interests and experiences of women of color are frequently marginalized within both" (p. 94). Collins's (2000) theoretical approach can be applied to how investigations on the lives of battered Black women should be conducted, as evident when she established that Black feminist theory is positioned within the "matrix of domination," as opposed to being dissociated from sociostructural truths.

Intimate partner abuse has been considered by many Black feminist scholars, even if only in a portion of their work (see Collins, 2000; Cole & Guy-Sheftall, 2003; hooks, 1981a, 1981b, 1989, 2000, 2004; Richie, 1996, 2000); and although still in its youthful stage, CRFT has been specifically applied to domestic violence in the lives of women of color (see Allard, 1991; Ammons, 1995; Coker, 2003; Crenshaw, 1994; Kupenda, 1998; Rivera, 1997, 2003; Valencia-Weber & Zuni, 2003). Considering issues of both multiplicative identity and intimate partner violence, Richie (2003) argued, "We now have data that supports [*sic*] the existence of racial and ethnic differences in rates but a theoretical orientation and public policy that can't accommodate or make sense of this new understanding" (p. 203). Using Black feminist theory and CRFT as foundations in considering the issues with intimate partner abuse against African American women, as well as considering their involvement in criminal behavior, will assist in addressing this limitation and contribute to the development of BFC.

UNDERSTANDING INTIMATE PARTNER ABUSE IN THE LIVES OF BLACK WOMEN USING BFC

As established above, the four themes considered within BFC include social structural oppression, interactions within the Black community, intimate and familial relations, and the Black woman as an individual, all operating under the premise that these segments are interconnected. Each of these themes is addressed in detail here, specifically examining how BFC can assist with formulating analyses of African American women's encounters with intimate partner abuse. Use of this framework allows the connection between woman battering and structural, cultural, and familial restraints to be made.

Social Structural Oppression

Under the theme of social structural oppression, matters of institutional racism, damaging stereotypical images, sexism, and classism are routinely addressed by Black feminists and critical race feminists and incorporated for analysis. Included in the examination is the limited access to adequate education and employment as consequences of racism, sexism, and classism. As education and employment deficiencies have been found to be common among battered women (Rennison & Welchans, 2000), this area of focus by BFC considers the impact of these shortcomings on battered Black women's lives. Even for Black women who are able to attain advanced levels of education and high-status employment positions, it is unlikely they reached these junctures in their careers without facing blatant or covert racist and sexist attitudes, behaviors, and policies (see Collins, 1998; Jones & Shorter-Gooden, 2003). As a result, the sociostructural stressors of even middle- or upper-class battered Black women and how they may respond to intimate partner abuse must be assessed from this standpoint.

Concerns external to remaining in abusive relationships because of poor financial status must be considered with all battered Black women, particularly battered Black women belonging to higher socioeconomic statuses. Stigmatizing constraints forcing battered Black women to remain in abusive settings could include their resistance to engendering the controlling stereotypical image of the single, Black matriarch (Collins, 2000). Based on socially constructed perceptions of Black women, BFC scrutinizes how stereotypical images of these women affect the ways in which others respond to them. Poor responses by social services professionals and crime-processing agents to Black women's interpersonal victimization crises can be considered under the auspices of this framework. Social services used by domestic violence victims in their process of leaving abusive relationships include medical assistance, battered women's shelters, and therapeutic agents. It is regrettable that African American women are often reluctant to seek assistance via these opportunities (Crenshaw, 1994; Potter, 2004; Short et al., 2000). The barriers to using these sources may be in relation to not only the short supply of battered women's shelters and therapeutic resources in Black communities (Asbury, 1987; Sullivan & Rumptz, 1994) or known to the Black community but also the ability and lack of trust in those working in the helping professions who are not able to deliver adequate culturally competent services to African American women who have suffered abuse from their intimate partners (Ammons, 1995; Sharma, 2001; Williams & Tubbs, 2002).

The criminal-processing system also has not been swift to aid battered Black women (Ammons, 1995; Robinson & Chandek, 2000), and battered women of color report distrust in using the formal criminal-processing system to assist with their exodus from abusive relationships (Bennett, Goodman, & Dutton, 1999; Richie, 1996; Weis, 2001). A history of poor relations between criminal-processing agencies (and their representatives) and communities of color can account for these misgivings (Brice-Baker, 1994). Even with higher law enforcement reporting rates than battered White women (Bachman & Coker, 1995; Rennison & Welchans, 2000), Black women victims still express reservations with trusting authorities in the criminal-processing system. Reservations about using the crime-processing system are also said to transpire because speaking out about intimate partner violence can involve the risk of generating racial shame (Ammons, 1995; Kupenda, 1998; C. West, 2005; T. West, 1999), and Black women may be viewed as traitors to their race for adding more African American men to the system's offender population (Brice-Baker, 1994; Richie, 1996; Sorenson, 1996).[5]

A focus by BFC on this documented history of poor systemic responses allows for an examination of the way in which professionals working with battered Black women may rely on stereotypical (thus, often inaccurate) assumptions of Black women when making decisions about how to respond to them. An example of the harm of cultural insensitivity and typecasting is found in this author's in-depth interviews with a diverse sample of battered Black women (see Potter, 2004). For many of the participants, assuming the role of the Strong Black Woman, as well as being perceived as a Strong Black Woman, had policy implications for battered women's shelter and counseling services. The women who capitalized on using shelters and therapy to assist them with terminating the abusive relationships were often singled out because of their distinguishing experiences with abuse and as Black women. When the participants' experiences with intimate partner abuse were pointed out by the other clients, it tended to be done for the purposes of placing battering and abuse in a hierarchical sequence and served as a perverse source of competition for the other battered women. When the participants were singled out by counselors, it was for the seemingly innocuous purposes of benefiting the battered Black women, to highlight how they are stronger than the other women (i.e., the White women) and strong enough to get out of the relationships. Even if these assertions by other battered women and service providers were true, they often served as a detriment to battered Black women's inclination to leave abusive relationships. Undervaluing battered Black women's violent encounters because they are not in abusive relationships as long as White women or because their injuries are not (or do not appear to be) as severe as other women's essentially justifies battering to a certain degree. Furthermore, it perpetuates battered Black women's impressions that they do not need to seek alternative or supplemental assistance to their familial and personal resources.

Black Community and Black Culture

The second theme addressed by BFC, the interactions within the Black community, is based on the cultural distinctions of African Americans. The nature of relationships among Blacks is a topic scrupulously discussed by critical race and Black feminists. These discussions often include the impact of historical experiences of African Americans in the United States. Some specific subjects addressed by Black feminists (although not an exhaustive list) include issues of Black women's and Black men's roles in the Black community, the occurrence of violence within the Black community, and the role of spirituality and the Black church as a staple institution in the Black community. Such a concentration allows for each of these features to be considered in how it affects Black women's encounters with domestic abuse. For instance, if indeed Black women's role in the Black community is one of an egalitarian and independent nature, how are issues of a batterer's power and control behaviors (i.e., typical qualities among batterers) displayed in relationships among Black couples? By scrutinizing the characteristics of batterers' abusive behaviors and the motivations for battered Black women to remain in abusive relationships, a sufficient explanation can be formed to demonstrate the method in which these men are still able to assert some level of power and control over the women. Again, recent qualitative research determines that battered Black women remain in abusive relationships more so out of fear of being without companionship, being without a father or father figure for minor children, and being stigmatized as yet another single Black mother than fear of further and more perilous battering incidents or of financial independence (Potter, 2004). Such fears are certainly inherent in Black women's distinctive experiences within U.S. society and the Black community and, thus, can be better understood from a BFC viewpoint.

The role of religion and spirituality must be strongly regarded when considering African American women's experiences with abuse. The substantial impact of religious practice and spirituality in the lives of battered Black women has been solidly established (Bell & Mattis, 2000; Potter, in press; T. West, 1999). Although battered Black women rely heavily on religion and/ or spirituality, a number of clergy members have not always demonstrated the support that is expected of them by battered Black women parishioners (Potter, in press). To be sure, BFC considers the essential institutions and practices in any investigation of African Americans, crime, and violence, particularly in how they relate to preventing, controlling, or the perpetration of offending behaviors.

Familial and Intimate Relations

The intimate and familial relationships theme is the third area on which BFC concentrates. The family of origin and generational characteristics of the Black family is one of the foci here, including the embeddedness in othermothers[6] and family members outside of the immediate family unit (i.e., extended family). By considering family embeddedness as a major focal point among African Americans in an analysis of battered Black women's help-seeking behaviors, a more thorough assessment of their dependency on this custom as a resource, as opposed to relying on systemic resources, can be made. This same embeddedness can demonstrate how abuse in the family of origin and among other close family members can be a detrimental and compounding factor on the victims.

Intimate relationships of Black women and their roles within these relationships, including interracial and/or lesbian couples, are essential elements of BFC, particularly as they function in and are affected by the larger societal composition. Research on interracial battering relationships is particularly lacking, but this cross-cultural dynamic would be well served by study under the auspices of BFC in determining how the various lived experiences of the members of interracial couples may affect the relationship circumstances differently. Lesbian battering relationships among Black women can be examined from the compounding element of sexuality, especially in how this component of Black lesbians' identity is viewed by others and how the quality of the relationship is consequently affected. Lesbian relationships among Black women gained more attention within Black feminist theory when lesbian Black feminists expressed their dissatisfaction with the lack of attention heterosexual Black feminists gave lesbianism and homophobia in the Black community. As a result, Black feminists fastidiously include same-gender intimate relationships in their analyses. The implications for Black women who identify as both lesbian and battered clearly require future research (Robinson, 2003) and would prosper under a BFC investigation that necessarily considers intersectionality.

Black Woman as Individual

Last, the theme of Black women as individuals is afforded considerable examination in BFC. Although examined as an individual, the life of the Black woman is strongly connected to her location, status, and role in the social structure, the Black community, and interpersonal relationships. Within this category, issues such as mental health, sexual health, and sexuality are addressed. Inclusion of this precept allows a personal yet comprehensive view of battered Black women.

Consequently, battered Black women's personal strategies for dealing with the abuse can be analyzed under this notion. These strategies include how a battered Black woman may frame the effects of the abuse. As established, Black women face many forms of oppression, and this subjugation will undoubtedly affect a Black woman's mental fitness. It is clear that being abused by an intimate partner serves only to deteriorate a Black woman's mental health beyond the injury of the bias bestowed on countless African American women on a daily basis.

Another strategy exercised by battered women includes the use of physical force against batterers. The propensity of Black women to physically strike back against their intimate abusers has been determined to be at greater rates than battered White women's retaliation (Hampton, Gelles, & Harrop, 1989; Joseph, 1997; C. West & Rose, 2000). Although it is seen as a personal tactic among many battered Black women, considering their self-defense strategies through BFC would allow for the introduction of structural and cultural influences to be considered to begin to explain this phenomenon (see Potter, 2004, for an extended analysis on this topic).

RESPONSE TO ANTICIPATED CRITICISM

Although evidence has been presented to support the use of BFC to better understand domestic abuse and African American women, some criticism of this approach can be foreseen. To start, this theoretical contribution may be viewed as being too limiting because the examination expounded here is grounded in Black and critical race theories and focuses on Black women specifically. The claim might be made that this approach does not serve an overarching benefit to responding to and preventing intimate partner abuse. A rejoinder to this potential criticism would rationalize that because Black women are estimated to be victims of abuse at higher rates than White women, it is imperative that we make greater efforts to understand and determine how to address this concern. As Black women are also overrepresented in areas of the crime-processing system as offenders (e.g., arrests, incarceration; Belknap, 2001; Britton, 2000), a new approach for comprehending this trend should be welcomed as well. For both victim and offender status among Black women, starting at a place where Black women's historically and contemporarily situated place in society is strongly embraced will afford a more comprehensive understanding of a group disproportionately implicated in offending and victimization. Ignoring distinctions in identity and experiences based on that identity serves only to perpetuate indifference toward Black women and their plight.

BFC may also be critiqued as pathologizing Black women. By placing focus on Black women's distinctive standpoint, it may be seen as deeming Black women's victimization and criminality as something normal and endemic to their personality or genetic traits. Although there is a history within communities of color to not want to reveal the injurious behavior taking place between members of these communities—oftentimes for fear of upholding criminal stereotypes—it is imperative that more attention be given to the abuses subjected on women of color (see C. West, 2005). Exposing these concerns via a BFC demonstrates that the instances of crime and violence in the Black community are not because of a so-called acceptance of such behavior and illuminates the compelling effects of structural influences. In turn, this approach helps explain the prevalence of intimate partner abuse, how Black women experience such abuse, and the reactions by the criminal-processing system and its representatives.

A third anticipated criticism of BFC is that by examining Black women as a group, it will be assumed all Black women have the same experiences. Although Black women in U.S. society indeed encounter similar circumstances, there are numerous gradations and variations in their lived experiences. As addressed above, Black feminist theory (see Collins, 2000) and as follows, BFC, consider Black women from their collective and their individual experiences simultaneously. Stories communicated by battered Black women result in similar trends that

will aid in improving culturally competent services available to Black women. As with all battered women, their individual circumstances must always be considered in conjunction with the shared experiences of these women.

The specifying of a theory that seems to consider only Black females actually opens the field to considering gender, race, and class analyses of criminality, crime victimization, and observation of the crime-processing system. BFC highlights the need to consider intersectionality of individual identities in all crime-related concerns. Certain individuals in society are more privileged than others and social structure influences culture, families, and the individual; thus, it stands to reason that individuals other than Black women and Black men are affected by their positions in society.

As established at the outset, there can be many variations on feminist criminology. It is quite possible that there may be variations on BFC as well. Even so, this concept provides a solid starting point for placing Black women victims of intimate partner abuse at the center of analysis. As such, even if another BFC theoretical proposition leads in a different direction than that presented here, at least Black women's (and Black men's) interlocking identities will be considered central, as opposed to tangential or not at all, in relative investigations. Although there exists the potential for disapproving reactions to a BFC, such an approach to understanding abuse in African American women's intimate relationships is more desirable than disadvantageous.

CONCLUSION

Approaching issues of Black women and crime from the Black feminist and critical race feminist standpoints provides an extension to feminist criminology, which can aptly be titled *Black feminist criminology.* With increased attention given to women of color, violence, and nontraditional theoretical approaches (e.g., feminist), there is still a need to examine the experiences of "marginalized" women victims of violent crime from a combined gendered and racialized standpoint. Collins (2000) discussed at length the place of Black women scholars in the theory, research, and activism process. She argued that the continued development of Black feminist thought is imperative to the social theory discipline. This does not preclude those who are not Black women from participating in the advancement of Black feminist thought but, instead, places Black women's intellectual and activist work on Black women at the forefront of theoretical hypothesizing and investigation. It is from this stance that examinations of the lives and experiences of Black women victims and offenders should be investigated. This chapter provides an analysis of how approaching intimate partner abuse against African American women from this position may offer a more comprehensive appraisal of their experiences with and responses to their victimization. Considering the historical experiences of Black women in the United States, which have been couched in multiple forms of domination, the approach advanced in this chapter is based on a fresh standpoint that regards how African American women's lives may position them to encounter intimate partner abuse differently than women of other races and ethnicities (especially in comparison to White women).

The argument expounded here by no intention undervalues the important and noble work done by original feminist criminology and its adherents. It is the advent, subsistence, and practice of feminist criminology that makes the concept insisted on here obtainable because of feminist criminology's position that although women and girl victims and offenders have parallel life circumstances, there are variations among them based on cultural, racial, and other distinctions. Indeed, mainstream feminist theory and feminist criminology allow for a more suitable assessment of women and criminal victimization than traditional male-centered criminology, but BFC necessarily provides for Black women's multiple and interconnected identity and their position in U.S. society to be considered as a central element of any analysis. This is an appropriate theory to apply when evaluating and attempting to understand intimate partner abuse against African American women, their responses to this maltreatment, and the responses to these women by official and unofficial outlets. Black feminist theory stresses that the Black woman encompasses many components that frame her identity. These elements include the general categories of race, ethnicity, gender, class, nationality, and sexuality. Moreover, the Black woman is not one or the other at different times and places in her life but all components at all times. BFC deems that being oppressed and discriminated against based on any or all of these parts of the Black woman's identity can occur at the structural/societal level, within the Black community, and within interpersonal relationships.

Although the example presented in this chapter involves intimate partner abuse against African American women, BFC can also sufficiently assess African American women's paths into criminal offending. Many Black women, regardless of offending status, are victims of differential treatment because of their subjugated racial status. As previous feminist criminology research has discovered that most female offenders have histories of childhood abuse victimizations (Belknap, 2001; Chesney-Lind & Pasko, 2004), BFC will be sure to substantiate that Black women and girl offenders likely have similar backgrounds of being treated negatively because of their intertwined identity of gender, race, sexuality, class, and so forth. Accordingly, an analysis of African American girls' and women's lives under the rubric of BFC will consider their offending from an intersecting identities perspective using, at the least, a racialized, gendered, and classed assessment.

Just as feminist criminology has afforded a more inclusive understanding of girls' and women's experiences with offending and victimization, BFC reaches beyond feminist criminology to the specific concern with African American women's distinctive position and history of domination in U.S. society that has continued on— although in varying and changing forms—to the present day. BFC focuses on African American women's devalued societal position. BFC enables the domestic violence researcher to analyze the data with the assumption that sociostructural, cultural, and familial factors affect Black women's experiences with intimate partner abuse. Scrutinizing structural, cultural, and familial dynamics aids in critically addressing the effectiveness of formal and informal regulation of partner violence against African American women. BFC may also do well in explaining the onset of and responses to abuse and crime in the lives of other women of color, White women, and even marginalized men. Hence, it is not implausible to extend a Black feminist criminological approach to understanding crime and violence in the lives of African Americans.

NOTES

1. Consistent with Belknap (2001), in this chapter the term *processing* is used in place of *justice* when referring to law enforcement agencies and agents, court systems and their representatives, and sanctions for individuals convicted as criminal offenders. *Justice* implies that victims and offenders are treated justly and equally within the "criminal justice system," however, this is not always true, particularly with African American women.

2. In this chapter, *mainstream* feminism or feminist theory are those efforts made toward gender equality by groups of predominantly White women feminists. The choice in the use of the term *mainstream* relates to the considerable attention—both negative and positive—given to the efforts of these women, as opposed to that afforded smaller, marginalized groups of feminists.

3. Throughout this chapter, *African American* and *Black* will be used interchangeably to describe U.S. citizens of Black African descent. Although there are instances where *Black* will not be capitalized, it is done so only in direct quotes of others who do not capitalize the term. There is no set standard for whether the term is to be capitalized when referring to race.

4. Collins (2000) defined *essentialism* as the "belief that individuals or groups have inherent, unchanging characteristics rooted in biology or a self-contained culture that explain their status" (p. 299).

5. It is interesting that this author's investigation of battered Black women determined that none of the respondents were deterred from contacting the police because of the concern of criminalizing another Black male. For those who did not call the police, their reasons centered on other factors, such as maintaining a resident father for their children.

6. *Othermother* refers to a woman in the Black community who shares the responsibility of mothering children with biological mothers and may or may not be related by blood or marriage (see Collins, 2000; Troester, 1984).

REFERENCES

Allard, S. A. (1991). Rethinking battered woman syndrome: A Black feminist perspective. *UCLA Women's Law Journal, 1,* 191–207.

Ammons, L. L. (1995). Mules, madonnas, babies, bath water, racial imagery, and stereotypes: The African-American woman and the battered woman syndrome. *Wisconsin Law Review, 5,* 1003–1080.

Asbury, J. (1987). African-American women in violent relationships: An exploration of cultural differences. In R. L. Hampton (Ed.), *Violence in the Black family: Correlates and consequences* (pp. 89–105). Lexington, MA: Lexington Books.

Bachman, R., & Coker, A. L. (1995). Police involvement in domestic violence: The interactive effects of victim injury, offender's history of violence, and race. *Violence and Victims, 10,* 91–106.

Beale, F. (1995). Double jeopardy: To be Black and female. In B. Guy-Sheftall (Ed.), *Words of fire: An anthology of African-American feminist thought* (pp. 146–155). New York: New Press. (Original work published 1970)

Belknap, J. (2001). *The invisible woman: Gender, crime, and justice* (2nd ed.). Belmont, CA: Wadsworth.

Belknap, J., & Potter, H. (2006). Intimate partner abuse. In C. M. Renzetti, L. Goodstein, & S. L. Miller (Eds.), *Women, crime, and criminal justice: Original feminist readings* (2nd ed., pp. 172–188). Los Angeles: Roxbury.

Bell, C. C., & Mattis, J. (2000). The importance of cultural competence in ministering to African American victims of domestic violence. *Violence Against Women, 6,* 515–532.

Bennett, L., Goodman, L., & Dutton, M. A. (1999). Systemic obstacles to the criminal prosecution of a battering partner. *Journal of Interpersonal Violence, 14,* 761–772.

Bograd, M. (1999). Strengthening domestic violence theories: Intersections of race, class, sexual orientation, and gender. *Journal of Marital and Family Therapy, 25,* 275–289.

Brice-Baker, J. (1994). Domestic violence in African-American and African-Caribbean families. *Journal of Social Distress and Homeless, 3,* 23–38.

Britton, D. M. (2000). Feminism in criminology: Engendering the outlaw. *Annals of the American Academy of Political and Social Science, 571*(1), 57–76.

Center for the Advancement of Women. (2003). *Progress and perils: New agenda for women.* Retrieved March 21, 2004, from http://www.advancewomen.org/womens_research/progress&perils.pdf

Chesney-Lind, M., & Pasko, L. (2004). *The female offender: Girls, women, and crime* (2nd ed.). Thousand Oaks, CA: Sage.

Cleaver, K. N. (1997). Racism, civil rights, and feminism. In A. K. Wing (Ed.), *Critical race feminism: A reader* (pp. 35–43). New York: New York University Press.

Coker, D. (2003). Enhancing autonomy for battered women: Lessons from Navajo peacemaking. In A. K. Wing (Ed.), *Critical race feminism: A reader* (2nd ed., pp. 287–297). New York: New York University Press.

Cole, J. B., & Guy-Sheftall, B. (2003). *Gender talk: The struggle for women's equality in African American communities.* New York: Ballantine.

Collins, P. H. (1998). *Fighting words: Black women and the search for justice.* Minneapolis: University of Minnesota Press.

Collins, P. H. (2000). *Black feminist thought: Knowledge, consciousness, and the politics of empowerment* (2nd ed.). New York: Routledge.

Crenshaw, K. W. (1994). Mapping the margins: Intersectionality, identity politics, and violence against women of color. In M. A. Fineman & R. Mykitiuk (Eds.), *The public nature of private violence: The discovery of domestic abuse* (pp. 93–118). New York: Routledge.

Daly, K. (1997). Different ways of conceptualizing sex/gender in feminist theory and their implications for criminology. *Theoretical Criminology, 1*(1), 25–51.

Daly, K., & Chesney-Lind, M. (1988). Feminism and criminology. *Justice Quarterly, 5*(4), 499–535.

Erez, E., & Belknap, J. (1998). In their own words: Battered women's assessment of the criminal processing system's responses. *Violence and Victims, 13,* 251–268.

Fishman, L. T. (2003). "Mule-headed slave women refusing to take foolishness from anybody": A prelude to future accommodation, resistance, and criminality. In R. Muraskin (Ed.), *It's a crime: Woman and justice* (3rd ed., pp. 30–49). Upper Saddle River, NJ: Prentice Hall.

Flavin, J. (1998). Razing the wall: A feminist critique of sentencing theory, research, and policy. In J. I. Ross (Ed.), *Cutting the edge: Current perspectives in radical/critical criminology and criminal justice* (pp. 145–164). Westport, CT: Praeger.

Fyfe, J. J., Klinger, D. A., & Flavin, J. (1997). Differential police treatment of male-on-female spousal violence. *Criminology, 35,* 455–473.

Gelles, R. J., & Straus, M. A. (1988). *Intimate violence.* New York: Simon & Schuster.

Gordon, V. V. (1987). *Black women, feminism and Black liberation: Which way?* Chicago: Third World Press.

Guy-Sheftall, B. (Ed.). (1995). *Words of fire: An anthology of African-American feminist thought.* New York: New Press.

Hampton, R. L., & Gelles, R. J. (1994). Violence toward Black women in a nationally representative sample of Black families. *Journal of Comparative Family Studies, 25,* 105–119.

Hampton, R. L., Gelles, R. J., & Harrop, J. W. (1989). Is violence in Black families increasing? A comparison of 1975 and 1985 national survey rates. *Journal of Marriage and Family, 51,* 969–980.

hooks, b. (1981a). *Ain't I a woman: Black women and feminism.* Boston: South End.

hooks, b. (1981b). *Feminist theory: From margin to center.* Boston: South End.

hooks, b. (1989). *Talking back: Thinking feminist, thinking Black.* Boston: South End.

hooks, b. (2000). *Feminist theory: From margin to center* (2nd ed.). Boston: South End.

hooks, b. (2004). *The will to change: Men, masculinity, and love.* New York: Atria.

Hull, G. T., Bell Scott, P., & Smith, B. (Eds.). (1982). *All the women are White, all the Blacks are men, but some of us are brave: Black women's studies.* New York: Feminist Press.

Johnson, I. M., & Sigler, R. T. (2000). Public perceptions: The stability of the public's endorsements of the definition and criminalization of the abuse of women. *Journal of Criminal Justice, 28,* 165–179.

Jones, C., & Shorter-Gooden, K. (2003). *Shifting: The double lives of Black women in America.* New York: HarperCollins.

Joseph, J. (1997). Woman battering: A comparative analysis of Black and White women. In G. K. Kantor & J. L. Jasinski (Eds.), *Out of darkness: Contemporary perspectives on family violence* (pp. 161–169). Thousand Oaks, CA: Sage.

King, D. K. (1988). Multiple jeopardy, multiple consciousness: The context of Black feminist ideology. *Signs: Journal of Women in Culture and Society, 14,* 42–72.

Kupenda, A. M. (1998). Law, life, and literature: A critical reflection of life and literature to illuminate how laws of domestic violence, race, and class bind Black women. *Howard Law Journal, 42,* 1–26.

Lewis, D. K. (1977). A response to inequality: Black women, racism, and sexism. *Signs: Journal of Women in Culture and Society, 3,* 339–361.

McKay, N. Y. (1993). Acknowledging differences: Can women find unity through diversity? In S. M. James & A. P. A. Busia (Eds.), *Theorizing Black feminisms: The visionary pragmatism of Black women* (pp. 267–282). New York: Routledge.

Potter, H. (2004). *Intimate partner violence against African American women: The effects of social structure and Black culture on patterns of abuse.* Unpublished doctoral dissertation, University of Colorado– Boulder.

Potter, H. (in press). Battered Black women's use of religious services and spirituality for assistance in leaving abusive relationships. *Violence Against Women.*

Rennison, C. M., & Welchans, S. (2000). *Intimate partner violence.* Washington, DC: U.S. Department of Justice, Bureau of Justice Statistics.

Richie, B. E. (1996). *Compelled to crime: The gender entrapment of battered Black women.* New York: Routledge.

Richie, B. E. (2000). A Black feminist reflection on the antiviolence movement. *Signs: Journal of Women in Culture and Society, 25,* 1133–1137.

Richie, B. E. (2003). Gender entrapment and African-American women: An analysis of race, ethnicity, gender, and intimate violence. In D. F. Hawkins (Ed.), *Violent crime: Assessing race and ethnic differences* (pp. 198–210). New York: Cambridge University Press.

Rivera, J. (1997). Domestic violence against Latinas by Latino males: An analysis of race, national origin, and gender differentials. In A. K. Wing (Ed.), *Critical race feminism: A reader* (pp. 259–266). New York: New York University Press.

Rivera, J. (2003). Availability of domestic violence services for Latina survivors in New York State: Preliminary report. In A. K. Wing (Ed.), *Critical race feminism: A reader* (2nd ed., pp. 270–277). New York: New York University Press.

Robinson, A. (2003). "There's a stranger in this house": African American lesbians and domestic violence. In C. M. West (Ed.), *Violence in the lives of Black women: Battered, Black, and blue* (pp. 125–132). Binghamton, NY: Haworth.

Robinson, A. L., & Chandek, M. S. (2000). Differential police response to Black battered women. *Women and Criminal Justice, 12*(2/3), 29–61.

Rodriguez, M. A., Bauer, H. M., McLoughlin, E., & Grumbach, K. (1999). Screening and intervention for intimate partner abuse: Practices and attitudes of primary care physicians. *Journal of the American Medical Association, 28*, 468–474.

Schechter, S. (1982). *Women and male violence: The visions and struggles of the battered women's movement.* Boston: South End.

Sharma, A. (2001). Healing the wounds of domestic violence: Improving the effectiveness of feminist therapeutic interventions with immigrant and racially visible women who have been abused. *Violence Against Women, 7*, 1405–1428.

Short, L. M., McMahon, P. M., Chervin, D. D., Shelley, G. A., Lezin, N., Sloop, K. S., et al. (2000). Survivors' identification of protective factors and early warning signs for intimate partner violence. *Violence Against Women, 6*, 272–285.

Smith, B. (Ed.). (1983). *Home girls: A Black feminist anthology.* New York: Kitchen Table: Women of Color Press.

Sorenson, S. B. (1996). Violence against women: Examining ethnic differences and commonalities. *Evaluation Review, 20*, 123–145.

Sullivan, C. M., & Rumptz, M. H. (1994). Adjustment and needs of African-American women who utilized a domestic violence shelter. *Violence and Victims, 9*, 275–286.

Terrelonge, P. (1984). Feminist consciousness and Black women. In J. Freeman (Ed.), *Women: A feminist perspective* (3rd ed., pp. 557–567). Palo Alto, CA: Mayfield.

Tierney, K. J. (1982). The battered women movement and the creation of the wife beating problem. *Social Problems, 29*, 207–220.

Troester, R. R. (1984). Turbulence and tenderness: Mothers, daughters, and "othermothers" in Paule Marshall's *Brown Girl, Brownstones. Sage: A Scholarly Journal on Black Women, 1*(2), 13–16.

Valencia-Weber, G., & Zuni, C. P. (2003). Domestic violence and tribal protection of indigenous women in the United States. In A. K. Wing (Ed.), *Critical race feminism: A reader* (2nd ed., pp. 278–286). New York: New York University Press.

Violence Against Women Act of 2005, Pub. L. No. 109–162 (2006).

Weis, L. (2001). Race, gender, and critique: African-American women, White women, and domestic violence in the 1980s and 1990s. *Signs: Journal of Women in Culture and Society, 27*, 139–169.

West, C. M. (2005). Domestic violence in ethnically and racially diverse families: The "political gag order" has been lifted. In N. J. Sokoloff (Ed.), *Domestic violence at the margins: Readings on race, class, gender, and culture* (pp. 157–173). Piscataway, NJ: Rutgers University Press.

West, C. M., & Rose, S. (2000). Dating aggression among low income African American youth: An examination of gender differences and antagonistic beliefs. *Violence Against Women, 6*, 470–494.

West, T. C. (1999). *Wounds of the spirit: Black women, violence, and resistance ethics.* New York: New York University Press.

Williams, O. J., & Tubbs, C. Y. (2002). *Community insights on domestic violence among African Americans: Conversations about domestic violence and other issues affecting their community.* St. Paul, MN: Institute on Domestic Violence in the African American Community.

Wing, A. K. (Ed.). (1997). *Critical race feminism: A reader.* New York: New York University Press.

Wing, A. K. (Ed.). (2003). *Critical race feminism: A reader* (2nd ed.). New York: New York University Press.

PART II

FEMALE JUVENILE DELINQUENTS

Victimization, Delinquency, and the Juvenile Justice System

Before the mid-1960s, most formal discussions of juvenile offenders and juvenile court did not include information on girls. Today, however, female juvenile offenders are no longer invisible and have become one of the fastest growing segments of the juvenile justice system. For example, in 1975, girls represented 15 percent of juvenile arrests; thirty years later, they represented nearly 30 percent.[1] While overall delinquency rates have been declining since the late 1990s, this decline has not been equally shared by both boys and girls; over the last decade, boys' arrests for most offenses decreased while girls' arrests for robbery, theft, assaults, driving under the influence (DUI), prostitution, disorderly conduct, and vandalism have all risen.[2]

Juvenile court data also suggest a similar trend. While boys represent the majority of cases handled by juvenile courts, girls in 2004 comprised over one quarter of all delinquency cases, up 92 percent since 1985.[3] In addition, girls' adjudications over the past twenty years have risen over 300 percent, and girls have also become an increasing proportion of juveniles in custody.[4] Nationally, girls comprise a fifth of those in detention and 12 percent of those in public correctional facilities. They tend to be younger than their male counterparts and are more likely to be committed for status offenses (such as running away) or probation violations rather than criminal law violations.[5]

The readings in this section include significant research findings concerning girl offenders and their encounters with the juvenile justice system. These readings examine girls' pathways to delinquency that often include family instability and abuse, school disconnection, mental health problems, and other exposure to violence. Carla P. Davis's chapter focuses primarily on the family and shows how girls' challenges to parental authority can lead to girls' court involvement. Presenting the history of girls and the juvenile justice system, Davis details the family dynamics and processes that preceded girls' entrance to juvenile court—fights with parents over "control," a breakdown in the internal order of the family, calls to police to restore order, a re-labeling of domestic conflict as daughter-initiated assault—and the arrest, adjudication, and sentencing of the offenders.

Laurie Schaffner's work also examines the context of girls' violence, but she tackles it from a different angle. Through in-depth case file analysis, she explores the emotional, physical, and sexual trauma that girls who commit violent acts suffer. In the third reading, Joanne Belknap and Kristi Holsinger further this examination of gendered pathways to delinquency and show the importance of understanding childhood trauma in girl offenders' lives. They also examine gender differences in risk exposures and victimization histories between boys and girls.

While girls are no longer invisible in the juvenile justice system, gender-specific programming that attends to their needs is still in development. In this last chapter, Barbara Bloom and her colleagues outline what gender-specific policies and programs for girl offenders should entail. They also detail the various reasons and constraints that prevent girls from engaging in programs that do exist.

NOTES

1. Federal Bureau of Investigation (FBI). (2009). *Uniform crime reports, 2008.* Washington, DC: U.S. Government Printing Office.

2. Ibid.

3. Office of Juvenile Justice and Delinquency Prevention (OJJDP). (2006). *Juvenile offenders and victims: 2005 national report.* Washington, DC: Author.

4. Ibid.

5. Sickmund, M, Sladky, T. J., & Kang, W. (2008). *Census of juveniles in residential placement databook.* Retrieved from http://www.ojjdp.ncjrs.gov/ojstatbb/cjrp.

Chapter 5

AT-RISK GIRLS AND DELINQUENCY

Career Pathways

CARLA P. DAVIS

Before the 1974 Juvenile Justice and Delinquency Prevention (JJDP) Act, girls were arrested or detained primarily for status offenses (offenses that would not be regarded as wrongdoing if committed by an adult). Although decriminalization of status offenses should have resulted in a diminished presence of girls in the justice system, there has instead been a recent increase. More than a quarter of the youths arrested every year are girls. Delinquency cases involving girls increased by 83% between 1988 and 1997, with data indicating an increase of 106% for African American girls, 74% for Anglo girls, and 102% for girls of other races (American Bar Association and National Bar Association, 2001; Federal Bureau of Investigation [FBI], 1998). The use of detention for adolescent girls increased 65% between 1988 and 1997, with African American girls, as well as African American women, comprising nearly 50% of those in secure detention (American Bar Association and National Bar Association, 2001; Bureau of Justice Statistics, 2001, 2003).

Through ethnographic fieldwork and interviews, this chapter reveals current negotiations and practices of parents and the juvenile justice system after the deinstitutionalization of status offenses. Through examining the contexts of the girls' offenses, family conflict over issues of parental authority emerged as a salient factor underlying the girls' initial contact with the system and the construction of their recorded offenses. This chapter illustrates the ways that parental responses to challenges to their authority influence entry and movement through the system. These illustrations suggest the possibility that although the 1974 act decriminalized status offenses, challenges to parental authority are now being constructed and processed under other "official" categories of crimes or delinquencies.

Source: Davis, C. (2007). At-risk girls and delinquency: Career pathways. *Crime and Delinquency, 53*(3), 408–435.

Author's Note: The author gratefully acknowledges the contributions of Robert M. Emerson. The author is also thankful for the support and encouragement of Walter R. Allen and Vilma Ortiz.

GETTING INTO THE SYSTEM: STATUS OFFENSES AND THE SEXUAL DOUBLE STANDARD

Previous literature documents how girls in the juvenile justice system have historically been disproportionately sanctioned for status offenses (Belknap & Holsinger, 1998; Chesney-Lind & Shelden, 2004; Cohn, 1970; Datesman & Scarpitti, 1977; Gibbons & Griswold, 1957; Odem, 1995; Odem & Schlossman, 1991; Schlossman & Wallach, 1978). The phenomenon of girls entering the system through status offenses is part of the broader historical development of the creation of organizations to monitor the social and moral behavior of troubled youths who do not commit serious offenses. This evolution led to the establishment of the first juvenile court in 1899. In essence, the purpose was to distinguish delinquent from criminal behavior (Platt, 1969).

In the 19th century, with the growth of urbanization, industrialization, immigration, and increased geographic mobility, communal mechanisms of social control collapsed. An underclass emerged, labeled as poor, who were perceived as living in slums regarded as unregulated and lacking in social rules (Platt, 1969). Children of the poor were primary among those whom it was believed could benefit from rehabilitation. Most were recent immigrants, with ethnic backgrounds different from that of established American residents. In general, these children were not considered hardened offenders but instead were considered to be vagrant or wayward youths whose noncriminal behavior could be rehabilitated. They were often thought of as "incorrigible" or "beyond control" and considered to be living in environments likely to foster delinquency and criminality (Chesney-Lind & Shelden, 2004). Social reformers emphasized the temporary and reversible nature of adolescent crime and believed that delinquent children must be saved by preventing them from pursuing criminal careers. Institutions proliferated to reform the behaviors of these youths. This child-saving movement crafted a system of government that had unprecedented authority to intervene in the lives of families, and particularly in the lives of youths (Empey, 1982; Platt, 1969; Zatz, 1982).

The moral behavior of girls was of specific concern to the child savers (Belknap & Holsinger, 1998; Chesney-Lind & Shelden, 2004). As part of this reform movement, White middle-class women reformers sought to protect White, working-class girls from straying from moral paths. These middle-class women's activities revolved around monitoring the moral and sexual behaviors of working-class, particularly immigrant, girls (Chesney-Lind & Shelden, 2004; Gordon, 1988; Odem, 1995). On the basis of middle-class ideals of female sexual propriety, reformers assumed they had the authority to define appropriate behavior for working-class women and girls. Girls who did not conform to these ideals were labeled as *wayward* and deemed to be in need of control by the state in the form of juvenile courts, reformatories, and training schools (Chesney-Lind & Shelden, 2004; Odem, 1995). Black female delinquents were placed in adult institutions or sent out of state until it became practically or fiscally unfeasible to do so (Young, 1994). Research examining court practices after the court's initial inception reveals a preoccupation with girls' sexuality, as revealed in charges relating to some form of waywardness or immorality, and views contemporary status-type offense charges as buffer charges for suspected sexual activity (Chesney-Lind & Shelden, 2004; Odem, 1995; Odem & Schlossman, 1991; Schlossman & Wallach, 1978; Shelden, 1981).

Studies also document the historical pattern of parental use of the status offense category in referring their daughters to authorities for a variety of activities (Andrews & Cohn, 1974; Belknap & Holsinger, 1998; Chesney-Lind & Shelden, 2004; Ketchum, 1978; Odem & Schlossman, 1991; Teitelbaum & Gough, 1977). This, coupled with the vagueness of status offense statutes and the precedence of authorities and courts to uphold parental authority, makes the misuse of the status offense category particularly likely (Sussman, 1977). The recognition that some parents turn to the courts to enforce their authority is thought to be a primary reason for many girls' presence in the juvenile justice system (Chesney-Lind & Shelden, 2004).

After establishment of the juvenile court, the next major attempt to address noncriminal, troubled youths was in the 1960s when another reform movement attempted to redefine categorization of wayward and/or noncriminal offenders (Empey, 1973; Zatz, 1982). The result of these reform efforts was the 1974 JJDP Act. The federal government recognized a specific category of offenders—"status offenders"—and ordered measures that would remove or divert this group of juveniles away from the juvenile justice system and away from incarceration. Because historically, girls have been disproportionately sanctioned for status offenses, the immediate impact of the 1974 JJDP Act was greater for girls. Girls' institutionalization rates for status offenses fell by 44% (Krisberg & Schwartz, 1983). However, this decline in the institutionalization of status offenders leveled off between 1979 and 1982, and there is continuing concern that status offenders are not being sufficiently differentiated from delinquents and that they are still largely represented in the justice system (Arthur D. Little, Inc., 1977; Chesney-Lind & Shelden, 1998, 2004; Federle & Chesney-Lind, 1992; Schwartz, Jackson-Beeck, & Anderson, 1984; Zatz, 1982).

Previous literature suggests two opposing views for the impact of deinstitutionalization on the discretionary powers of the police, with some asserting that it has increased discretionary powers, allowing circumvention of the 1974 JJDP Act (Austin & Krisberg, 1981; Klein, 1979; Lemert, 1981), and others arguing that deinstitutionalization has weakened the discretionary powers of the police (Schwartz, 1989). Previous literature has suggested that status-type offenses are being relabeled as *criminal offenses* (Klein, 1979; Mahoney & Fenster, 1982) and that some actions constituting nonserious family conflicts have been relabeled upward as violent or assault charges (Acoca, 1999; Acoca & Dedel, 1998; Chesney-Lind & Shelden, 1998, 2004; Mayer, 1994). This is considered one reason underlying the increase in assault charges for girls, particularly a rise in the category of "other" assaults. This is particularly thought to be a significant factor in African American girls' prevalence in the system (Bartollas, 1993; Robinson, 1990). Although authorities may have historically incarcerated White immigrant working-class girls for protectionist reasons during the child-saving movement, Black and Brown girls are also likely to be detained or incarcerated because, like Black and Brown boys, they are seen as dangerous.

The findings in this chapter begin to provide evidence of the processes of relabeling status-type offenses as criminal offenses. The data illustrate how these families in their interactions with authorities have negotiated alternative methods for dealing with troublesome teenage girls since the 1974 Deinstitutionalization Act

has restrained courts from responding vigorously to status-type offenses.

THEORETICAL FRAMEWORK: THE INSANITY OF PLACE

Conflicts over parental authority form the basis on which parents eventually turn to the justice system to seek help in restoring their authority with their daughters. Although enforcing the sexual double standard is an underlying source of tension between parents and their daughters, this in itself does not explain how the girls come into contact with the system. Goffman's (1971) "The Insanity of Place" provides a useful framework for understanding the processes by which girls come in contact with the juvenile justice system. In "The Insanity of Place," Goffman examined the processes in families by which a person comes to be classified as mentally ill and committed to hospitalization. According to Goffman, the productive functioning or welfare of a family depends on family members' supporting the expected internal order of authority relationships. In supporting the internal order of a family, members know and keep their places in the family structure. When a family member fails to support the internal order by not keeping his or her expected social position in relation to others within the family, this threatens one of the fundamental elements on which family unity is based.

A breakdown in family solidarity begins when a family member, for whatever reason, feels the life that others in the family have been according him or her is no longer sufficient; thus the member makes demands for change. In response, other family members may accept these demands for change as valid and modify the structure of the family in accordance, or they may refuse to recognize the demands and attempt to maintain the existing social structure. It is the latter—when family members decide not to honor or recognize the family member's demands for change and the demanding family member's refusal to fall back to the status quo—that results in increasing tension. In this standoff, the family member may either voluntarily withdraw from the family organization or remain a part of the family. If he or she chooses to remain with the family but refuses to fall back to the status quo in family relationships, the member in effect promotes himself or herself in the family hierarchy, thus beginning his or her "manic" activity. According to Goffman (1971) the demands of the "maniac" are not necessarily bizarre in themselves but are bizarre coming from the person with respect to his or her social location in the family. At this breaking point, the stronger of the two participants may form a collaborative arrangement with a third party to control the weaker party's environment and definition of the situation.

The parents (primarily mothers) act as informal agents of control by attempting to assert authority over their daughters' actions. Rather than accepting parental authority, these girls challenge parental assertions of authority and demand the same autonomy over their actions as have the parents. The girls' promotion of themselves in the family hierarchy to that of an equal plane as their parents is disruptive to the internal organization of the family. In these instances, the parents neither physically withdraw, nor do they reconstitute the family organization to accommodate the self-assumptions of autonomy of their daughters. Instead, in attempting to restore their authority with their daughters, these parents form collaborative arrangements with the justice system to either threaten the girls into obeying parental authority or having the girls removed by detention if they do not act accordingly.

Frequently, it is the collusion of the families and the justice system that places the girls in the category of delinquent. This collusion is accentuated by racial and ethnic stereotypes of formal social control agents that contribute to perceptions of Black and Brown girls as dangerous. Although Goffman's (1971) framework provides a base for understanding these family dynamics, an understanding of this collusion is deepened when Goffman's framework is coupled with literature (Bishop & Frazier, 1992; Bridges & Steen, 1998; Gaarder, Rodriguez, & Zatz, 2004; Leiber & Stairs, 1996; Miller, 1999; Wordes, Bynum, & Corley, 1994) exploring how racial and ethnic stereotypes affect perceptions and subsequent processing by formal social control agents.

As this chapter will illustrate, tensions escalate as the girls persist in their autonomous conceptions and accompanying demands and/or actions, while their parents exercise great efforts in attempts to bring the girls back into an appropriate

relationship to them: a relationship in which their daughters keep a "child's place." It is not so much that their daughters' actions represent delinquent acts as much as that the actions are out of line with daughters' expected social position in the family. The remainder of this chapter will use Goffman's (1971) framework in examining how issues of authority are negotiated between the girls and their parent(s) or guardians and how a breakdown in these negotiations may facilitate contact, entry, and movement through the juvenile justice system. Since the 1974 Deinstitutionalization Act restrained courts from responding vigorously to status-type offenses, families in their interactions with authorities have negotiated alternative methods for dealing with troublesome teenage girls.

DATA AND METHODS

Sample Population

The data on which this chapter is based consist of field notes from 2 years of participant observations of 50 girls, periodic taped interviews with 30 of those girls during incarceration, and field notes and interviews with 7 of the 30 girls after they were released from incarceration. The data in this chapter are part of a larger study in which I examined not only the girls' pathways but also their institutional adaptation patterns while they were incarcerated. At the time I began the research, all of the girls were incarcerated in a coed public detention facility for minor offenders between the ages of 13 and 18. I gained access to this facility through a juvenile court order granting me permission to do a participant observation and interview study of all activities of the girls at the facility, after meeting with the facility's clinical director and clinical staff. The ethnic composition of the girls is predominantly African American and Latina (Salvadoran and Mexican), and they are from predominantly underprivileged to lower- and/or working-class neighborhoods. The most common charges included assault, assault and battery, assault with a deadly weapon, and prostitution.

The interviews occurred after months of having established rapport, by "hanging out" with the girls, during which time I recorded extensive field notes. The interviews were continuous and unstructured (more in the form of conversations) and primarily consisted of the girls telling me about their lives before and after they entered the system. Although I did not formally interview their parents, I was able to substantiate the girls' accounts through informal conversations with parents and probation officers and by sitting in on family group therapy sessions.

Of my sample interview population of 30 girls, 57% had family or guardian conflicts that facilitated either contact with the system (13%), movement toward detention and incarceration (34%), or both contact and movement (10%). Of the remaining 43%, 17% were girls who did not have families and came into the system from the Department of Child and Family Services (DCFS). Girls from DCFS will often move into the juvenile justice system as a result of the same types of control struggles that are faced by girls coming from families. Just as the standoff between girls and their parents often results in the parents' reliance on the justice system to help them establish authority over the actions of their daughters, the standoff between girls and foster parents or group home staff often results in foster parents' or staff reliance on the system to help them establish authority.

Of those girls who did not come into the system from DCFS, the majority lived with their mothers and stepfathers. The remaining were almost evenly divided between girls living with grandparents, girls living in two-parent homes, and girls living in single-mother homes. For simplification, I will use the term *parent* in the sense of adult guardian. The actual person may be a grandmother or other relative. For the most part, even in families that included either male parents or guardians, maintaining authority with the girls was primarily left to the female parent or guardian.

Data Analysis

In contrast to studies analyzing data through preconceived categories of preliminary literature reviews, I conducted my literature review after identifying emerging salient themes in the data. This is consistent with the purpose of grounded theory methods. I used grounded theory methods to conduct an inductive analysis of the interview and field note data. I built my theoretical analysis on what I discovered as relevant in the worlds of the girls in my study. This process involved a stage of initial coding followed by a round of focused coding. During the

stage of focused coding, I took earlier initial codes that continually reappeared in my initial coding and used these codes to sift through large amounts of data. Focused coding allowed me to create and try out categories for capturing data and begin to see the relationships and patterns between categories. These categories were part of my developing analytic framework, as I selected certain codes as having overriding significance in explaining events and processes in my data. In generating categories through focused coding, I made comparisons between girls, comparisons of data from the same girls at different points in time, and comparisons of categories in the data with other categories.

Limitations

Although some aspects of the findings in this study are consistent with findings of previous qualitative studies of girls in the juvenile system, caution should be used in generalizing beyond the sample population in this study.

PARENTAL AUTHORITY VERSUS GIRLS' AUTONOMY: "GOING OUT"

At the root of these family conflicts are struggles over control, in which the parent attempts to establish authority over the girl's actions, whereas the girl resists this authority in an attempt to gain autonomy. These struggles revolve around such issues as doing chores, going to school, seeing boys, hanging out with friends, observing curfews, and spending time talking on the phone. However, the most contentious issue in these control struggles is the girls' desire to have the freedom to "go out"—to spend time away from home. Parents (or grandparents) attempt to establish authority over their daughters' freedom to go out or spend time away from home by using varying strategies to control or restrict it, whereas the girls use various strategies to counter these restrictive measures. The following excerpts illustrate how the girls and parents negotiate going out even before they enter the juvenile justice system. Subsequent sections will illustrate how these struggles may facilitate contact and entry into the system.

One way that parents may assert their authority is by placing restrictions on their daughters' time away from home. Their daughters may respond in a variety of ways. If the internal order of the family (family solidarity) is intact, the daughters may accept this authority restricting time away from home and simply abide by these restrictions. Alternatively, children may attempt to alter the prohibition by pleading and agreeing to be back by a certain time:

> *Mara (Age 16):* Going out. Wanting to go out is a big thing in my house. Cause they'll be like, "No, you don't wanna come back at this time and da-da-da-da-da." I'll be like, "Well, why don't you let me come back at ten o'clock? I'ma be here." "No, cause it's a school night, and it's this and it's that."

At least at this point, although Mara is challenging authority by pleading to go out, she appears to be sticking to her social place in the family. She makes demands for change, which are denied by her grandparents, and she appears to acquiesce to their position, thus internal order or parental authority appears to be intact.

Alternatively, a girl may not agree to her parent's restrictions on going out but instead may choose to ignore the restrictions:

> *Cathy (Age 17):* She didn't like me going out partying . . . and she tried—convincing me not to go— . . . she would say, "Please be home by two." And I would never be home by two . . . it's not like you're gonna be home by two, you know, it's like—*two?* I leave at *twelve,* how am I gonna be back by two—you know?

In the earlier excerpt, Mara's grandmother appears to have some semblance of authority in that she denies Mara's pleads to go out, and Mara appears to accept these restrictions. However, in Cathy's scenario, a breakdown in family solidarity is evident by the mother's, rather than the daughter's, resort to pleading. With restrictive command statements not being enough, Cathy's mother resorts to pleading with her daughter not to go out. When it becomes apparent that these appeals will not be heeded, Cathy's mother attempts to set curfew limits by pleading for her to be back by 2:00 a.m. Cathy denies both the legitimacy and the feasibility of her mother's pleas and ignores both the restrictions on leaving and the 2:00 a.m. curfew. In so doing, Cathy has promoted herself in the family hierarchy by refusing to keep a child's place in that she refuses

to comply with her mother's restrictions over her time away from home.

The previous scenario illustrated the parent's resort to pleading in the case of a breakdown in the internal order of the family. When the breakdown of parental authority reaches a point where resorts to pleading are to no avail, family members may then resort to the use of physical coercion. When a parent uses physical coercion in attempting to restrict the daughter from leaving the house, the daughter may counter with physical force:

> *Monica (Age 17):* I remember one night, they [friends] came to pick me up and—I was— running down the stairs to go out the house— my aunt was blocking one door, my dad was blocking the other, and my grandma was blocking one—I said okay, you know, who do I go for—so, I went—I went to try to go through the door my grandma was at—and it ended up—I didn't hit her, but it ended up, I pushed her—out of the way—to go out there, because they're [friends] honking, I'm like, "Shit, I wanna get high, oh my god,"—next thing I know, my dad has me by my hair on the floor, "You fucking little bitch—don't you *ever* hit my mother," you know—so it was really bad—so I ended up not going out that night.

A breakdown in the functioning of the internal order of the family is signaled by the fact that Monica's parents are apparently unable to gain compliance with prohibitions on going out and thus resort to physical coercion by blocking the doors. The daughter attempts to counter with physical force, but the parent's physical force prevails. Because of physical strength, using physical force to challenge girls' attempts to go out generally only works when the challenger is a male.

When there is a breakdown in authority, physical force may prevent overt attempts of a girl to go out, but it does not address covert attempts. To counter covert attempts to go out, parents may resort to more manipulative measures in attempting to restrict their daughters from going out, such as maintaining locked doors and keeping close reign on the keys. However, the girls may counter with various strategies, as illustrated in the following scenario in which Mara's grandmother keeps all of the doors locked and carries the keys with her on a chain around her waist. Mara finds a way to remove the keys without being detected:

Mara (Age 16): I would sneak out the house . . . she [grandmother] watches movies on the floor on the mat, and she falls asleep . . . she likes holding me when she sleeps—like I'm her teddy bear . . . when she fell asleep . . . I acted like I had fallen asleep . . . I pushed the hook, and I pulled it off . . . I held the keys with me . . . I wiggled away from her . . . and she just turned back over. I had the keys and I ran to the back door, and I unlocked the door, and I came running back and I, um, I slipped them on her and . . . I'll just act like I'll turn on my T.V. in my room . . . and I'll go to the back door, and I'll just leave for like 2 or 3 hours and she won't even know I'm gone, she'll be asleep, and I'll come back—and I'll—get the keys again and lock the door, and she'll *still* be asleep.

The grandmother's practice of keeping all of the doors locked and the keys around her waist symbolizes a breakdown in the internal order and functioning of parental authority. A simple prohibitive command and honoring of that command is apparently not enough to gain the granddaughter's compliance to prohibitions on going out. The fact that the grandmother has resorted to such extreme measures indicates that she is aware that her authority is not intact and must resort to more coercive measures. However, whereas an institution is equipped to effectively exercise such surveillance measures, the family is not set up to effectively exercise coercion. Pure coercion (with no trust and legitimacy) is generally an unreliable method of maintaining control in a family and home (Goffman, 1971). In addition, covert challenges to parental authority generally do not lead to overt friction between daughters and parents as long as the measures remain undetected by the parent.

COMING INTO CONTACT WITH THE SYSTEM: CALLING POLICE TO HELP RESTORE AUTHORITY

Previous literature has suggested the phenomenon of parents calling on police to act as family disciplinarians (Joe, 1995). This section illustrates what happens when parents call police to help them restore authority. Similar to Andrews and Cohn's (1974) findings in New York, parents were likely to refer their children to the court for a variety of reasons. One way that these family conflicts over parental authority may contribute to placing girls at risk for initial contact with the juvenile justice system is when parents solicit assistance from police. When their authority is challenged and attempts to try to restore authority internally by resorting to mechanisms such as pleading, bargaining, and physical coercion have failed, these parents frequently appeal to the police as a means to restore or reestablish parental control. At least initially, the police reaction is primarily symbolic—they are constrained from and/or hesitant to react punitively by making arrests; rather, they "talk to," lecture, cajole the girls into behaving. The following scenario provides an example of how this unfolds. Mara's grandmother began calling the police to her home when Mara was 11:

Carla: What did she used to call the cops for?

Mara
(Age 15): When we wouldn't listen to her.

Carla: And she—what would she say when she called them?

Mara: My—my grandchildren aren't listening to me—they don't wanna do what I tell them—I don't want them here.

Carla: And they would come out to the house?

Mara: And they would pull us outside and just talk to us and that was it . . . Umm—maybe about 12 times. . . . The *same* ones would come. . . . They said, "We're always coming over here, your grandma's always telling us something new, or it's always the *same* thing. And you know what?—It's always something stupid, and we're tired of you guys not listening to your grandmother—they're old—your grandparents are old—they—they—they should be retired, they should be—just kicking back in rocking chairs, and you guys shouldn't be—they shouldn't be handling you, and we think we should take you away—and—" I'd be like, "No—no—no—no—I'm gonna be good, I'ma listen to my grandmother, don't take me away, I don't wanna go anywhere—"

A breakdown in family solidarity is evident by Mara and her brother not supporting the expected internal order of authority relationships. With her authority not intact, Mara's grandmother resorted to appealing to the police for assistance. The police responded by lecturing and threatening Mara and her brother with "We think we should take you away." Just as a breakdown in family solidarity may result in parents' mechanisms for asserting authority becoming more progressive, the same may be true for police techniques attempting to restore authority. When lecturing and threatening seem not to be effective, police may resort to scare tactics in attempting to restore parental authority:

> *Mara (Age 15):* They [police] were forever like, "You ain't got no fucking respect for your grandmother, and you're gonna end up in the Halls, and you don't know what it's like—people—be um—people be *raping* people, and—" . . . they were just like constantly in my face . . . cussing at me—they were *basically* trying to scare me . . . but it never worked.

Similarly, Cathy estimates that before she entered the system, her mother called the cops to the house approximately 20 times. Although the specific points of contention ranged from not washing the dishes to staying away from home for extended periods of time, her mother's overall complaint is that Cathy does not listen to her and does not follow her rules:

> *Cathy (Age 17):* She's called them before, but for stupid stuff like I didn't wash the dishes . . . I got home late . . . I didn't come home . . . total times, she's called the cops I'd say around . . . maybe 20 . . . just for incidents like I didn't come home, and—stuff like that or—you're not listening to your mom—you're not following the rules—stuff like that. . . . They would just tell me, "Well, listen to your mom, just begin—" —just like whatever—and they just wanted to leave—they were like, "Well, ma'am, . . . we have things to handle—we have things to do—you just can't be calling us for *this.*"

These excerpts illustrate how the police, at least initially, treat these calls as interpersonal problems rather than as criminal matters. However, when the police run out of patience, they may consider arresting and processing the matter as a criminal case, bringing the girl officially into the juvenile justice system. The following is an example of what happens when the police run

out of patience in these situations. In this example, Mara's family calls the cops for a third time to report her as a runaway. Whereas the first couple of times, the cops simply retrieved her and returned her home, their patience is tried the third time they receive this request, and they threaten to take her to juvenile hall:

> *Mara (Age 15):* So I was just sitting in the cop car, and I was crying—I was like, "No, I don't wanna go to the—um—juvenile hall—I don't wanna go, I don't wanna go," they were like, "Well, that's it—that's your last chance, this is your third time running away, and—um, we're sick of being called, and we're tired of all this bullshit and da-da-da-da-da," . . . my aunt comes over, and it's—you know—my aunt's sitting there *crying* to the cops, "*Please* don't take her, she'll be good, she'll be good, she'll be good." . . . "Just let her come home with me, and she'll be—you know—she'll start acting right" . . . she [aunt] convinced him, and then. . . . They let me go under the condition that I stayed at my aunt's house, and I said, "Okay."

This time when the family called to report Mara's running away, rather than doing the usual and returning her home, the police prepare (or at least feign preparation) to take her to the police station for processing. Mara's aunt's intervention once the police arrive on the scene illustrates how family may influence whether a girl enters the system in the first place by influencing police decisions about taking her in for processing. In this instance, although the aunt was the one who initially called in the police, she diverted her niece from entering the system at this time by meeting the cops on the scene and persuading them to let her niece go home with her. It also illustrates the amount of discretion that police have in determining when to cease treating a family conflict as a personal matter and to instead begin treating it as a criminal matter.

Struggles Culminating in Assault Charges: Relabeling Domestic Disputes

The previous sections of this chapter explored the types of family conflicts over parental authority and how a breakdown in family solidarity or internal order of family may lead to parents' soliciting help from outside authorities. This is often many of the girls' initial contact with the system before they actually enter it, and this section will explore how these family conflicts over authority result in the girls actually entering the system. Although Joe (1995) found that with respect to runaways, the police's net of social control does not appear to be widening, others suggest that police discretionary powers allow them to circumvent the restraints of deinstitutionalization in other circumstances (Acoca, 1999; Acoca & Dedel, 1998; Austin & Krisberg, 1981; Chesney-Lind & Shelden, 1998, 2004; Klein, 1979; Lemert, 1981; Mahoney & Fenster, 1982; Mayer, 1994). This happens when the police relabel family conflicts or domestic disputes as assaults. This section explores the process by which relabeling of family conflicts into assaults occurs.

Girls' arrests for assaults have dramatically increased since 1970 (Chesney-Lind & Shelden, 2004; FBI, 1971, 1981, 1995, 2001). The increases are greatest for two categories of assaults: aggravated assaults and "other" assaults. Arrest rates for girls for aggravated assault increased by 364% between 1970 and 1995 (Chesney-Lind & Shelden, 2004; FBI, 1971, 1981, 1995). Arrest rates for girls for "other" assaults increased by 343% between 1970 and 1995 (Chesney-Lind & Shelden 2004; FBI, 1971, 1981, 1995). One explanation offered for this increase is the possibility of "greater attention to normal adolescent fighting and/or girls fighting with parents" (Chesney-Lind & Shelden 2004, p. 11). In the past, these conflicts may have been more likely dealt with informally. Previous literature has suggested that greater attention to conflicts between girls and parents may at least partly be attributed to increased attention to domestic violence and/or changes in domestic violence laws, which encourages more active involvement of police in family conflicts (Chesney-Lind & Shelden, 1998, 2004; Gaarder et al., 2004).

Family-related assault charges often represent the highest degree of escalation in family control struggles. By the time assault charges occur, struggles over parental authority have been ongoing for some time and have reached a breaking point. By the time families reach this point, their attempts to establish authority through conventional mechanisms (routine commands and/or requests) or through less conventional methods (pleading, bargaining, or manipulation) have failed. Parents then resort to attempting to exert parental authority with coercive physical control, which is likely to be countered with similar physical resistance from the daughters. Earlier examples in this chapter described instances where parents called police to their homes to restore order and police responded by going to the homes and talking, cajoling, or threatening the girls. In situations where the girls may use physical force to counter parental attempts of controlling with physical force, both parents and police seek a restoration of order by removing and detaining the girl at least temporarily. Many girls either enter the system with assault charges or are subsequently incarcerated for these charges after having already entered the system.

There may be evidence of assault in some cases. However, in many cases, there often seems to be a lack of evidence supporting these assault charges. These instances often seem to be opportunities for parents to appeal to the juvenile justice system for assistance in their overall control struggles with their daughters. When police arrive on the scene, they are much more likely to believe the parent or guardian rather than the girl's version of what transpired. Countering coercive physical control with physical resistance presents the opportunity for parents to begin the process of having disobedience classified as "delinquent." Changing the plea from "she won't obey me" to "she assaulted me" gives police something on which to act. Many of these family assault charges seem to have one theme in common. They appear to almost always involve a parent's attempting to physically block the daughter from taking some kind of action, such as leaving the house, and a daughter's subsequent push to resist the parent's restraining action results in the parent's alleging assault. As the following passages will illustrate, it is not uncommon for family assault charges to emerge from the most contentious point underlying control struggles—a daughter's freedom to leave the house or "go out."

In the following excerpt, Renee describes what happened when she returned home to pick up some items after one of her extended periods away from home:

Renee (Age 16): So we went back to my house, and I was picking up my makeup . . .
shampoo . . . lotion. . . . And—my mom's like, "No, this isn't a motel, you're not just gonna

come in and out whenever you please, you're only *fourteen*," . . . she was really upset . . . she was trying to keep me in the house . . . and—basically I—I pushed her. I had a whole bunch of stuff in my hands, like all these bottles and stuff—and I pushed her out of my way when I was coming out of the bathroom . . . then . . . they [parents] called the police . . . "she needs to stay here," . . . "she's out of control," and he [stepfather] would not let me go anywhere . . . the police came, and I was cussing them out . . . they arrested me . . . they're like, "Well, I'm getting you for battery on your mom,"—"Battery on my mom, I didn't do anything to her"—"You pushed her, didn't you?" I'm like, "Yeah." Shit—okay, they got me for battery.

Being able to come and go as one pleases is distinctly an adult prerogative. Renee's mother suggests her frustration lies in part by Renee's not keeping a child's place in the family order when she says, "You're not just gonna come in and out whenever you please, you're only *fourteen*." In this case, it is not just that Renee is not keeping her place by coming or going as she pleases; she has returned home with concrete justification for parental attempts to police her sexual activities—a boyfriend. In attempting to prevent Renee from leaving the house again, her mother first attempts to block her, and Renee responds by pushing her out of the way. Her stepfather then intervenes to block and restrain Renee while they call the police and continues to block Renee from leaving until the police arrive. In this situation, the parents attempted to restore authority or order in the family by calling in outside authorities (police) to remove and detain Renee. This illustrates the police role or influence in defining the situation upon arriving on the scene and shows the importance of social control agents in defining what constitutes a criminal act—in this case, battery. This also challenges Joe's (1995) conclusions that the consequence of deinstitutionalization was a narrowing and restricting of police discretion and social control.

Similarly, the following excerpt also illustrates how conflict over leaving the house or going out resulted in assault charges. In this instance, a breakdown in authority relationships is symbolized by Teresa's not adhering to her mother's restrictions on going out. Consequently, Teresa's mother resorted to attempts to manipulate the situation by making it more difficult for Teresa to leave the house. Because getting dressed is a precondition of leaving the house, by placing Teresa's clothes in her (mother's) closet, Teresa's mother attempted to keep Teresa from leaving. This made it more difficult for Teresa to leave the house because Teresa would have to go through her mother to retrieve her clothes. The following illustrates what happened when Teresa attempted to retrieve some items of clothing before she left on one of her extended stays away from home:

> *Teresa (Age 16):* So, she took my clothes—she put it in . . . the closet in her room—so that I couldn't get to it. And I needed something to wear that day, so I went to—the closet—in *her* room—and I was going to get my clothes—so she walked to—over from her bed—and she tried to block me— she tried to hold the closet door closed. And then . . . she tripped over my little brother's toy that was on the floor . . . that's when she called the police . . . she said that I hit her and almost made her fall.

Teresa's mother's attempts to gain authority over Teresa's leaving the house by manipulating placement of her clothes failed and resulted in Teresa's mother resorting to coercive, physical control. However, in attempting to block Teresa from retrieving her clothes from the closet, either her mother tripped or perhaps some sort of altercation occurred, prompting her mother to trip. Either way, the event provided the opportunity for Teresa's mother to gain assistance in her overall authority struggles with Teresa by constructing Teresa's actions as being serious enough to warrant removal from the home and detention. The police had come to the house twice before in response to Teresa's mother's calls and, as with this time, indicated that they found no evidence to apprehend the daughter. It seems that the mother's persistence and suggestions that her daughter was out of control may have influenced the police to take her in for processing and incarceration in juvenile hall. In addition to describing the possible context for assault charges, this case also illustrates how the police serve as mediators in family conflicts well before the girls actually enter the system. In this case, not only was there no evidence of assault when the police appeared on the scene for the third time, but the charges were subsequently dropped because Teresa's mother did not show up in court to testify.

Although family control struggles seem to most commonly occur between parents (primarily mothers) and daughters, these struggles may also occur between the girls and older siblings:

Brenda (Age 15): I had got into it—the one—the brother [age 23] I said I don't like—one day—um—my mama had found some weed in my room—and I had got mad and then—I started cussing and stuff—and he don't like me cussing—especially with my mom right there—so like I cussed, and I ran outside—and [he] came behind me—and he was like holdin me—he threw me on the ground, and he started holdin me—like—and I started kickin him and stuff, and he was still holdin me . . . I was just kickin him so hard, and he slipped . . . he slapped me . . . he didn't mean to do it—I was just kickin him so hard, and he slipped . . . then I went to go get a knife, and then I called the police—then they end up takin *me* . . . he always big and bad like when I ain't got nothing—but if I like pick up a stick, then he wanna move back—so I picked up a knife . . . and then the police came . . . I threw the knife before they came, and my sister—let me know—she like—"The police out there," . . . I just threw 'em [knife] down—and then they came and—and they—took me.

One of the interesting dimensions of this scenario is that when the police arrived on the scene, the struggle had subsided, and there was no knife in sight:

Carla: They didn't even *see* you with the knife.

Brenda: They sho didn't—that's what—like the police—he came to court too—he said he didn't see me and um—my attorney [public defender] was telling 'em—he was like, "If she wasn't swingin the knife—it can't be assault with a deadly weapon."

That the police were ready to remove Brenda with no apparent evidence of struggle raises the question of the basis for removing Brenda from her home:

Brenda: My mom told 'em like—she need a break . . . she told 'em that um—like, "Take her cause she goin crazy." . . . At trial, my mom was telling him [judge] like—she just wanted me gone for like 2 weeks just to—give me a lesson or whatever—and she was just sayin stuff like—she wanted me home . . . she just wanted to give me a lesson—but my judge—he was like—he ain't goin for none of that—he deal with all my mama' kids—like most of 'em—they done been in here . . . he was like—"What makes you think if I release you—like you ain't gon be like them and get in trouble again?" So, he was like, "Nah—I'ma keep you."

As illustrated in previous excerpts, this particular control struggle provided an opportunity for Brenda's mother to appeal to authorities for "a break" by pleading with them to remove Brenda. Age or minor status of the girls leaves them powerless in defining what actually occurred when the police arrive on the scene. The tradition of upholding parental authority over the rights of children results in authorities nearly always accepting the parent's or guardian's definition of the situation. Although filing assault charges may be one strategy that parents or guardians use as a last resort to gain help in their overall control struggles with their daughters, in most instances, they only intend for their daughters to be gone for short periods of time, such as a short-term stay in juvenile hall to "teach her a lesson." This is particularly the case for those parents who are familiar with the way the system works. However, the above passage illustrates how sometimes this strategy may backfire. In this situation, the judge did not see authority in the home as viable and sentenced Brenda to incarceration.

Brenda's situation breaks with the general pattern of girls not being incarcerated after their first contact with the system and/or first arrest if the parent is willing to take them home. This illustrates how a judge's sentencing decision may be based not on the girl's offense but on the judge's perception of whether the internal order of the family's authority relationships is intact. In this situation, the judge's decision to incarcerate Brenda seems to evolve from a sense that Brenda's family lacks a viable authority or control structure, based on the fact that several of Brenda's siblings had previously been in this judge's court.

How Control Struggles May Shape Differential Juvenile Justice Outcomes

Not only are many girls in the system for status offenses, but also a substantial number of girls are in the system for violating court orders. Many of these acts of violations of court orders are in essence status offenses, such as running away. Previous literature suggests judges' use of violations of court orders as a technique of "bootstrapping" girls into detention (Costello & Worthington, 1981). Once a girl enters the system, control struggles are reproduced as violations of probation, and with each of these violations, punitive measures are likely to increase. Whereas going out and/or running away were not crimes before the girl entered the system, once in the system (on probation), going out, especially for extended periods of time, now becomes a violation of probation, or in other words, going out against parental prohibitions now becomes a crime.

Just as family control struggles may contribute to placing a girl at risk for entering the system, these struggles may also influence differential outcomes after she enters the system. Once the juvenile justice system becomes involved, it is not uncommon for the judge to consult with the parent before rendering a decision. A parent's input may influence whether a girl is able to come home or whether she is institutionalized after arrest. For example, if a parent stipulates to the judge that her daughter may come home if she abides by her rules, then the judge may send the girl home on house arrest. House arrest is a more severe measure than simply being placed on probation because it prohibits the girls from leaving the house for any purposes other than school. For this reason, house arrest appears to be a favorable measure for parents in their struggles to control their daughters' time spent away from home, or going out. However, this is rarely the case. Because many of the girls' entries into the justice system are predicated on family authority struggles, house arrest often fails because nothing is done to address the underlying control struggles:

Miranda (Age 14): House arrest—that couldn't even *fade* me. . . . House arrest cannot fade me, cause I would be at home, and I'm supposed to be in the house—I would *leave*—I'd just get up and *leave.*

Sentencing a girl to house arrest represents the court's attempt to reinforce parental authority by supplementing parental prohibitions with court-sanctioned prohibitions, thus the penalties for disobeying restrictions to go out are much harsher. However, what house arrest does is add another layer of authority, assuring more punitive consequences for the girls' strategies to gain more freedom away from home. Specifically, house arrest makes the girls' extended periods of time away from home crimes for which they can be incarcerated, which usually means recurrent stays of approximately 30 days in juvenile hall.

Alternatively, if a parent or guardian refuses to accept the girl back home, the judge may institutionalize her or send her to a group home:

Mara (Age 15): They said, "Okay, then we're gonna let you go on probation," and my grandmother ended up saying, "No, I don't want her home. She can't listen to me. . . . She doesn't obey me, she's always answering back . . . I don't want nothing to do with her." . . . So . . . they arrested me. They put me in a soda pad [temporary home] and gave me a couple more court dates. And my grandmother still said she didn't feel I was changing, and she didn't want me home. So, they put me in placement.

Mara's grandmother confirmed that at the court hearing, the judge was ready to release Mara home with probation, but the grandmother refused to accept her. Not yet willing to sentence her to incarceration or placement outside of the home, the judge placed her in a temporary shelter, and she was given a couple more court dates, giving the grandmother a longer time to reconsider. Only after the grandmother seemed steadfast in her decision not to accept her granddaughter home did the judge sentence her to an open placement (group home).

Although sentencing to a foster home or open placement (group home) is considered to be a viable alternative to incarceration, for many girls in the juvenile justice system, it is often the first step to eventual incarceration. Girls who are sent to foster or group homes rather than returning to their parents' homes face the same dilemmas. Control struggles are often reconstructed in foster and group homes, which are deemed community alternatives to incarceration. Not surprisingly, the girls want the same freedom of action that they wanted at home, whereas the foster parents or group home staff wish to establish authority and curtail girls' freedom:

Sabrina (Age 18): Yeah—it was two of 'em—parents [foster parents]—they were like pastors at a church. And it was just like something I wasn't used to, and it was like I couldn't be myself—you know?—I'm the type of person where I like to blast my music, I like to—smoke cigarettes, I like to—go out partying, and I like to talk on the phone—and they wasn't having it, and I didn't—like it—you know? So, my social worker made an agreement with me—"Well, this is gonna be your curfew—you do whatever you have to do on that when you're out,"—you know?—and it worked for a little bit, and then I got tired of it, and—I left [after about 6 months]. . . . I went to a group home . . . I—awoled and I never went back . . . finally turned myself in to my social worker, and she took me to *another* foster home.

Control struggles between Sabrina and her foster parents are evidenced by Sabrina's assertion that she is "the type of person where I like to blast my music, I like to—smoke cigarettes, I like to—go out partying, and I like to talk on the phone—and they wasn't having it." Sabrina's social worker attempts to ease the standoff between Sabrina and her foster parents by suggesting, if not implying, to Sabrina that in exchange for abiding by her curfew, she may do whatever she wishes during her time out or away from the home. This practice of "don't ask, don't tell" about activities while away as long as home by curfew was also a tactic some mothers used after release, which resulted in diminishing, if not eliminating, control struggles. Because of these control struggles, Sabrina went from a foster home, to a group home, to a foster home, then back to a group home.

Just as the standoff between girls and their parents often results in the parents' reliance on the justice system to help them establish authority over the actions of their daughters, the standoff between girls and group home staff often results in staff reliance on the system when there is a breakdown in authority:

Mara (Age 15): And I went to S. for my first [group home] . . . all girls. . . . And so—they were trying to get us to go to a boy's [group home] and have this dance . . . I didn't want to go. . . . And you know, I just said, "Well, if you

take me there, I swear, I'm just going to go off on everybody there, you know, and they ain't gonna like it." So they [group home] sent me to a mental hospital. And the mental hospital—I didn't want to go there . . . and I ended up staying there for 2 weeks . . . I got sent back to [group home]. And I didn't want to go back to [group home], and they [group home] ended up keeping me again, and . . . when I came back, they were trying to get me to go to school. I was like, "I'm not going to school," . . . they took me to [juvenile hall] trying to—you know—admit me in, and [juvenile hall] said they couldn't take me. . . . So they took me back to the [mental] hospital. In the hospital, I stayed there a week . . . the one I liked—the exact same one. And—I stayed there for a week, and—the [group home] came to pick me up again. I told them, "No—I'm not going back. I am *not* going back." So I refused [group home], and [juvenile hall] just came, and they picked me up right away.

As illustrated in the above scenario, group home control struggles result in girls' moving from institution to institution (often from group home to group home), with incarceration in juvenile halls in between each group home. This occurs not because the girls commit new offenses but because the same control struggles that took place between parents and daughters take place between group home staff and the girls.

After release from institutionalization, girls in the juvenile justice system are likely to return to the same family control struggles that contributed to their entering the system or being incarcerated. Their desires for autonomy are often not likely to be dampened after time spent incarcerated:

Monica (Age 17): I had just got out, so my mom was still kinda tripping, like—you know—"Oh, you're already trying to go out," and—"blah-blah—whatever." . . . So, I started getting really like—I don't know—like—just anxious—I wanted to leave the house—I started going out a lot . . . she tried to put twelve o'clock on me, but—that never happened—we would—me and my sister would pour into the house like two or three in the morning . . . my mom's like, "Well—no, I don't want you going, you have school tomorrow," you know,—this and this and that—"No, you're not gonna go,"—and I was like, "No, I *am* gonna go." I was like, "I'll be right back."—"Oh Monica, don't go,"—"No, I *am* gonna go."—

"Okay, okay, that's how you wanna play it—go ahead—go Monica," and I said, "I'm going,"—so I took off.

This illustrates how struggles over parental authority have not been modified from their pre-incarceration form. Monica's mother first attempts to exercise her authority with a direct command, "No, you're not gonna go." Monica dismisses her mother's command with "No, I *am* gonna go," to which her mother resorts to some semblance of a pleading. After realizing that this battle was lost, Monica's mother concedes—"Okay, okay, that's how you wanna play it—go ahead."

In addition, if family control struggles resume after a girl is released, she may face the constant threat that her parent may report her misbehaviors to the court or other authorities. The girls often fear that their freedom is dependent on their parents. In the following passage, Mara expresses concern that at her upcoming court date, her grandmother will tell the judge that she should not be home and they will reincarcerate her:

> Mara (Age 15): My grandma—since we've been fighting, she's been threatening me, that's she gonna tell the—um—the court that I shouldn't be home . . . so I hope she doesn't do that. Because they'll put me right back in the system . . . little things we'll argue over . . . it starts off with something little, and then it works—very big. I don't know. But every *day,* there's a fight . . . and then she ends up picking up the phone, and I end up leaving the house. Cause I don't wanna stick around . . . to see the cops if she does call'em.

In this instance, the grandmother's leverage in their arguments consists of constant threats to report Mara to either the police or to court officials at her upcoming hearing. It is debatable whether this is an effective tool to bring her granddaughter in line, but it is enough to keep Mara in a heightened sense of anxiety, which serves to exacerbate tensions.

The level of family discordance is likely to have significant consequences for the quality of life of girls after they are released, thus having consequences for whether they are successfully able to get off of probation. This is significant because most girls are reincarcerated not on the basis of new offenses but on probation violations. Because periods of incarceration are unlikely to contribute to improving the family control struggles that propelled the girls into the system, after the girls are released, these control struggles are one of the most difficult challenges with which they must contend.

DISCUSSION AND CONCLUSION

In finding that family dynamics often generate what is officially considered an offense, this research supports previous literature suggesting that some deviance is in large part the product of the response of the group, either family or community (Becker, 1963; Goffman, 1971; Lemert, 1951; Perrucci, 1974). These girls are largely classified as delinquent through their families' appeals to the justice system for help. The parents (primarily mothers or female guardians) act as informal agents of control until a breakdown in family solidarity prompts appeal to more formal measures of control. In many instances in attempting to restore their authority with their daughters, these parents form collaborative arrangements with the justice system to either threaten the girls into obeying parental authority or having the girls removed by detention if they do not act accordingly. Although nearly all families have these struggles, the mechanisms and/or options used by families depend on their social locations along hierarchies of race, ethnicity, and class. The most marginalized along these hierarchies are less likely to have resources other than appealing to police and the justice system. Furthermore, unlike those at other social locations, these families are in environments that more readily bring them in contact with police.

The system's response to these parents' pleas for help shows continuation of historical practices of state intervention into the families of children perceived to come from environments regarded as unregulated and lacking appropriate values and structure thought necessary to foster obedience, self-discipline, and hard work. Whereas in the 19th century, children of European immigrant families who had ethnic backgrounds different from those of established American residents were primarily the target population of excessive state intervention, in the 20th and 21st centuries, these demographics have shifted to children of primarily African American and Latino families. Whereas intervention in the

19th century was primarily imposed from the outside, these contemporary parents (lacking alternative familial or community resources) are themselves calling the police, thus initiating state intervention.

Although there are previous studies on how macro structural factors may converge to shape fractured emotional attachments between parents and children in impoverished African American families (Duncan, Brooks-Gunn, & Klabanov, 1994; Henriques & Manatu-Rupert, 2001; Leadbeater & Bishop, 1994; Sampson & Laub, 1994), there are no studies of how these factors may shape problematic authority relationships in these families. Simultaneous intersecting structures of race/ethnicity, class, and gender converge to place African American women and Latinas in positions of extreme powerlessness. Although the powerlessness of African American women and Latinas has been acknowledged relative to the larger society, the powerlessness of these women in their own communities and in their families has been less explored. These women have no power and are often struggling economically and emotionally just to survive.

To the extent that challenges to parental authority play an instrumental role in the girls' coming in contact and moving through the justice system, this suggests the continuing significance of status offenses (offenses that would not be considered wrongdoing if committed by an adult) in the arrest and incarceration of girls, even though the 1974 JJDP Act officially decriminalized status offenses. The findings in this chapter suggest that not only has the problem of differentiating youths whose actions are more affronts to parental and local authority than violations of law not been resolved but challenges to parental authority are now being constructed and processed under other "official" categories of crimes or delinquencies.

The family dynamics revealed in this chapter play a significant role in the girls' contact, entry, and movement through the justice system and are important not only for implications for the continuing significance of status offenses but also for subsequent program and policy planning for girls in the system. The data in this chapter suggest the extent to which families lack resources to navigate these conflicts. Certainly, the institution provides a remedy to family control struggles over "going out," by locking the girls in; however, the institution's resources and measures for ensuring discipline and obedience are not something that can be readily transferred to the family. As reflected by one mother's comments to her daughter, "Well, of course you get up and go to school here [institution], you have a whole team of people to help with that."

The girls return to the same family control struggles that existed before they entered placement. Policy and program designers should take into consideration the significance and nature of these family control struggles in facilitating girls' contact and entry into the system, and programming should be aimed at developing community resources to address these issues. Any program that does not also address the needs of the families, particularly the mothers or other female guardians, will fall woefully short because this is to whom the girls return. Although directing resources toward building programs within institutions may be expedient, the girls and their families would be better served by emphasizing and developing community, rather than institutional, programs.

REFERENCES

Acoca, L. (1999). Investing in girls: A 21st century challenge. *Juvenile Justice, 6*, 3–13.

Acoca, L., & Dedel, K. (1998). *No place to hide: Understanding and meeting the needs of girls in the California juvenile justice system.* San Francisco: National Council on Crime and Delinquency.

American Bar Association and National Bar Association Joint Report. (2001). *Justice by gender: The lack of appropriate prevention, diversion and treatment alternatives for girls in the justice system.* Washington, DC: Author.

Andrews, R., & Cohn, A. (1974). Ungovernability: The unjustifiable jurisdiction. *Yale Law Journal, 83*, 1383–1409.

Arthur D. Little, Inc. (1977). *Responses to angry youth: Cost and service impacts of the deinstitutionalization of status offenders in ten states.* Washington, DC: Author.

Austin, J., & Krisberg, B. (1981). Wider, stronger, and different nets: The dialectics of criminal justice reform. *Journal of Research in Crime and Delinquency, 18*, 165–196.

Bartollas, C. (1993). Little girls grown up: The perils of institutionalization. In C. Culliver (Ed.), *Female criminality: The state of the art* (pp. 30–47). New York: Garland.

Becker, H. (1963). *Outsiders.* New York: Free Press.

Belknap, J., & Holsinger, K. (1998). An overview of delinquent girls: How theory and practice have failed and the need for innovative changes. In *Female offenders: Critical perspectives and effective interventions* (pp. 31–64). Gaithersburg, MD: Aspen.

Bishop, D. M., & Frazier, C. (1992). Gender bias in juvenile justice processing: Implications of the JJDP Act. *Journal of Criminal Law and Criminology, 82,* 1162–1186.

Bridges, G., & Steen, S. (1998, August). Racial disparities in official assessments of juvenile offenders: Attributional stereotypes as mediating mechanisms. *American Sociological Review, 63,* 554–570.

Bureau of Justice Statistics. (2001). *Prisoners in 2000.* Washington, DC: U.S. Department of Justice.

Bureau of Justice Statistics. (2003). *Prisoners in 2000.* Washington, DC: U.S. Department of Justice.

Chesney-Lind, M., & Shelden, R. (1998). *Girls, delinquency, and juvenile justice.* Belmont, CA: Wadsworth.

Chesney-Lind, M., & Shelden, R. (2004). *Girls, delinquency, and juvenile justice* (3rd ed.). Belmont, CA: Wadsworth.

Cohn, Y. (1970). Criteria for the probation officer's recommendations to the juvenile court. In P. G. Garbedian & D. C. Gibbons (Eds.), *Becoming delinquent* (pp. 66–80). Chicago: Aldine.

Costello, J., & Worthington, N. L. (1981). Incarcerating status offenders: Attempts to circumvent the Juvenile Justice and Delinquency Prevention Act. *Harvard Civil Rights-Civil Liberties Law Review, 16,* 41–81.

Datesman, S., & Scarpitti, F. (1977). Unequal protection for males and females in the juvenile court. In T. N. Ferdinand (Ed.), *Juvenile delinquency: Little brother grows up* (pp. 45–62). Beverly Hills, CA: Sage.

Duncan, G. J., Brooks-Gunn, J., & Klabanov, P. K. (1994). Economic deprivation and early childhood development. *Childhood Development, 65,* 296–318.

Empey, L. T. (1973). Juvenile justice reform: Diversion, due process and deinstitutionalization. In L. E. Ohlin (Ed.), *Prisoners in America* (pp. 13–48). Englewood Cliffs, NJ: Prentice Hall.

Empey, L. T. (1982). *American delinquency.* Homewood, IL: Dorsey.

Federal Bureau of Investigation. (1971). *Uniform crime reports: Crime in the United States.* Washington, DC: U.S. Department of Justice.

Federal Bureau of Investigation. (1981). *Uniform crime reports: Crime in the United States.* Washington, DC: U.S. Department of Justice.

Federal Bureau of Investigation. (1995). *Uniform crime reports: Crime in the United States.* Washington, DC: U.S. Department of Justice.

Federal Bureau of Investigation. (1998). *Uniform crime reports: Crime in the United States.* Washington, DC: U.S. Department of Justice.

Federal Bureau of Investigation. (2001). *Uniform crime reports: Crime in the United States.* Washington, DC: U.S. Department of Justice.

Federle, K. H., & Chesney-Lind, M. (1992). Special issues in juvenile justice: Gender, race, and ethnicity. In I. M. Schwartz (Ed.), *Juvenile justice and public policy: Toward a national agenda* (pp. 165–195). Indianapolis, IN: Macmillan.

Gaarder, E., Rodriguez, N., & Zatz, M. (2004). Criers, liars, and manipulators: Probation officers' views of girls. *Justice Quarterly, 21*(3), 547–578.

Gibbons, D., & Griswold, M. J. (1957). Sex differences among juvenile court referrals. *Sociology and Social Research, 42,* 106–110.

Goffman, E. (1971). The insanity of place. In *Relations in public* (pp. 335–390). New York: Harper & Row.

Gordon, L. (1988). *Heroes in their own lives.* New York: Viking.

Henriques, Z., & Manatu-Rupert, N. (2001). Living on the outside: Women before, during, and after imprisonment. *The Prison Journal, 81*(1), 6–19.

Joe, K. A. (1995). The dynamics of running away, deinstitutionalization policies and the police. *Juvenile and Family Court Journal, 46*(3), 43–55.

Ketchum, O. (1978). Why jurisdiction over status offenders should be eliminated from juvenile courts. In R. Allinson (Ed.), *Status offenders and the juvenile justice system* (pp. 33–56). Hackensack, NJ: National Council on Crime and Delinquency.

Klein, M. (1979). Deinstitutionalization and diversion of juvenile offenders: A litany of impediments. In N. Morris & M. Torry (Eds.), *Crime and justice* (pp. 145–201). Chicago: University of Chicago Press.

Krisberg, B., & Schwartz, I. (1983). Re-thinking juvenile justice. *Crime & Delinquency, 29,* 381–397.

Leadbeater, B. J., & Bishop, S. J. (1994). Predictors of behavioral problems in preschool children of inner-city Afro-American and Puerto Rican adolescent mothers. *Child Development, 65,* 638–648.

Leiber, M. J., & Stairs, J. (1996). Race, contexts, and the use of intake diversion. *Journal of Research in Crime and Delinquency, 36,* 76–78.

Lemert, E. (1981). Diversion in juvenile justice: What hath been wrought. *Journal of Research in Crime and Delinquency, 18,* 34–46.

Lemert, E. M. (1951). *Social pathology: A systematic approach to the theory of sociopathic behavior.* New York: McGraw-Hill.

Mahoney, A., & Fenster, C. (1982). Female delinquents in a suburban court. In N. Hahn & E. Stanko (Eds.), *Judge, lawyer, victim, thief: Woman, gender roles and criminal justice* (pp. 26–42). Boston: Northeastern University Press.

Mayer, J. (1994, August). *Girls in the Maryland juvenile justice system: Findings of the female population taskforce.* Paper presented at the Gender Specifics Services Training, Minneapolis, MN.

Miller, J. (1999). An examination of disposition decision-making for delinquent girls. In M. D. Schwartz & D. Milovanovic (Eds.), *Race, gender and class in criminology: The intersections* (pp. 219–246). New York: Garland.

Odem, M. (1995). *Delinquent daughters: Protecting and policing adolescent female sexuality in the United States, 1885–1920.* Chapel Hill: University of North Carolina Press.

Odem, M. E., & Schlossman, S. (1991). Guardians of virtue: The juvenile court and female delinquency in early 20th century Los Angeles. *Crime & Delinquency, 37,* 186–203.

Perrucci, R. (1974). *Circle of madness.* Englewood Cliffs, NJ: Prentice Hall.

Platt, A. (1969). *The child savers.* Chicago: University of Chicago Press.

Robinson, R. (1990). *Violations of girlhood: A qualitative study of female delinquents and children in need of services in Massachusetts.* Unpublished doctoral dissertation, Brandeis University, Waltham, MA.

Sampson, R. J., & Laub, J. H. (1994). Urban poverty and the family context of delinquency: A new look at structure and process in a classic study. *Child Development, 65,* 538.

Schlossman, S., & Wallach, S. (1978). The crime of precocious sexuality: Female delinquency in the Progressive Era. *Harvard Educational Review, 48,* 65–94.

Schwartz, I. (1989). *(In)justice for juveniles: Rethinking the best interests of the child.* Lexington, MA: D. C. Heath.

Schwartz, I., Jackson-Beeck, M., & Anderson, R. (1984). The hidden system of juvenile control. *Crime & Delinquency, 30,* 371–385.

Shelden, R. G. (1981). Sex discrimination in the juvenile justice system: Memphis, Tennessee, 1900–1917. In M. Q. Warren (Ed.), *Comparing male and female offenders* (pp. 88–102). Beverly Hills, CA: Sage.

Sussman, A. (1977). Sex-based discrimination and the PINS jurisdiction. In L. E. Teitelbaum & A. R. Gough (Eds.), *Beyond control: Status offenders in the juvenile court.* Cambridge, MA: Ballinger.

Teitelbaum, L., & Gough, A. (1977). *Beyond control: Status offenders in the juvenile court.* Cambridge, MA: Ballinger.

Wordes, M., Bynum, T., & Corley, C. (1994, May). Locking up youth: The impact of race on detention decisions. *Journal of Research in Crime and Delinquency, 31,* 149–165.

Young, V. D. (1994). Race and gender in the establishment of juvenile institutions: The case of the South. *The Prison Journal, 732,* 244–265.

Zatz, J. (1982). Problems and issues in deinstitutionalization: Historical overview and current attitudes. In *Neither angels nor thieves: Studies in deinstitutionalization of status offenders* (pp. 55–72). Washington, DC: National Academy Press.

Chapter 6

VIOLENCE AGAINST GIRLS PROVOKES GIRLS' VIOLENCE

From Private Injury to Public Harm

LAURIE SCHAFFNER

Hidden in accounts of the rise in girls' arrests for violent offenses lies an alarming and undertheorized trend. A disproportionate number of girls come into the juvenile system with family histories of physical and sexual violence and emotional neglect. This link between childhood victimization and later juvenile offending has been confirmed by research in a variety of academic disciplines and by practitioners in social work, sociology, public health, and criminology (Belknap & Holsinger, 1998; Miller, 2001; Owen, Bloom, & Covington, 2003).

Some studies now estimate that more than 90% of girls in the juvenile legal system have histories of sexual, physical, or emotional abuse (Acoca & Dedel, 1998). Compared to sexual abuse reported by approximately 7% of teenage girls in general, this figure is staggering (Moore, Winquist Nord, & Peterson, 1989). In a 1995 national study, about 20% of women reported that at some time in their lives they had been forced by a man to have intercourse (Abma, Chandra, Mosher, Peterson, & Piccinino, 1997). One nationwide study conducted by the American Correctional Association (1990) of girls in juvenile correctional facilities found that 61% of girls had been physically abused and 54% had been sexually abused. In a nationwide study of adult women in the criminal justice system, researchers found that almost 68% of incarcerated women reported being violently victimized as young girls (Acoca & Austin, 1996). So among the population of court-involved girls, we find a disproportionate representation of girls who are also victims of abuse.

According to a comparative longitudinal study, abused and neglected girls are nearly twice as likely to be arrested as juveniles (Widom,

Source: Schaffner, L. (2007). Violence against girls provokes girls' violence: From private injury to public harm. *Violence Against Women, 13*(12), 1229–1248.

Author's Note: This chapter draws from ideas developed in my book *Girls in Trouble With the Law* (Rutgers University Press, 2006). The research was supported in part by a Woodrow Wilson Fellowship for Children's Health, as well as the Great Cities Institute at the University of Illinois at Chicago. I would like to thank the young women who shared the stories of their lives for this project. The chapter is dedicated to the memory of Esther Madriz, "*Que descanse en paz.*"

2000). Researchers find that children exposed to multiple forms of family violence report more than twice the rate of youth violence as those from nonviolent families (Thornberry, 1994). At the Harvard School of Public Health, scholars studied the connection between delinquency and depression and found that 82% of girls suffering depression committed crimes against persons, compared to 42% of other girls in their study (Obeidallah & Earls, 1999). These data reveal that similar to young men, young women express depression and distress as aggression (Campbell, 1994; Lamb, 1999). Understanding this link between coercion, injury, emotions, and subsequent female delinquency becomes salient as the prevalence of abuse and its chronic and long-term effects are more widely known to health specialists and as arrest and detention rates for girls remain at unprecedented levels.

To apprehend the complete ramifications of the experiences of abuse, they must be contextualized. For example, poverty and socioeconomic class status influence girls' outcomes differentially because of a lack of opportunities and diminished decisional avenues available to less advantaged young women. Poor girls of color are more vulnerable to predation by local idle older men, less likely to be protected by the law, and lack access to resources to heal from previous trauma (Levine, 2003; Rogers Park Young Women's Action Team, 2003; Veysey, 2003). For these reasons, it becomes relatively meaningless to think about abuse on its own, separated from its racial, gendered, and sexist content and meaning.

This point cannot be overemphasized: Violence against women animates women's violence. It is time we unmask the now rather flatly coined term *abuse* and reinvigorate it as the traumatic ground that provides explanatory links in girls' pasts, presents, and futures. The social consequences of the emotional injuries that girls in trouble with the law have sustained have been inadequately theorized, partially because these topics are so segregated by disciplinary boundaries. Important features of their trauma have not been afforded the primacy they deserve when working to understand the distinct experiences of court-involved girls, for it is precisely at the location of injury that the psychic and structural are inexorably intertwined. A sociology of emotion allows us to theorize how the social is imbibed, mapped onto the body, in

psychological ways. The abuse and harm of young girls comes to be seen as a process, not an event. And although this harm may take place in the private sphere, as individual or personal events altering girls' very sense of self, it contributes to drastic public behaviors with social consequences. The injuries sustained, invisible to the (social scientist's) eye, cannot be understood as simply phenomenological events to be recorded or analyzed as variables. This harm must be articulated and theorized to be apprehended. These human experiences are not uniform, regardless of age, race, or gender, and especially not, as this chapter illuminates, for low-income girls of color in troubled urban communities. We hear in their accounts how court-involved young women worked through these processes of injury in their adolescence and find that some of that emotional work involved aggression.

A correlation can be drawn between young women's early experiences of harm and exploitation and later problems with juvenile authorities (Acoca, 1998; Thornberry, 1994; Widom, 2000). The research presented in this chapter introduces a sociological link that articulates a deep intersectionality among sexual and violent experiences as embedded locations where structural damages, such as sexism and racism, are heaped upon the emotional life of individuals. Listening to young women who are being adjudicated delinquent illuminates that it is impossible to comprehend girls' offenses without considering their prior victimization, but not in deterministically causal or quantitatively measurable ways. To theorize girls' offending, we must consider the distinct significance of the experiences of this harm for unprotected girls, often low-income minorities, who are then punished for coping mechanisms they deploy in response to their victimization.

Young women in the juvenile legal system report enduring prior trauma that was sustained, chronic, and acute. Whereas for boys, abuse goes against what they are taught to expect from their gender position of superiority, abuse of girls confirms their place in the gender hierarchy. A distinct process needs to be enacted for girls to heal and to achieve a sense of safety and psychological integrity. The social forces of gender influence how childhood abuse is processed emotionally and how recovery occurs. This chapter argues several related points. Sexual violence is fundamentally gendered and racialized, experienced differently by different girls. Abuse plays a special role in the lives of many girls who come to the attention of authorities. This role must be theorized because its meaning cannot be determined empirically. Girls' agentic aggression, contextualized, can then be seen for what it is: a coping strategy to survive within an increasingly violent culture. This theoretical process allows us to broaden the definition of community violence and capture more accurate accounts of sexual, gendered, and physical violence in girls' lives because the violence girls experience in so-called private is deeply interrelated to the community experience of public harm.

Two interrelated factors will be highlighted. First, in studies of girls who were being adjudicated delinquent from the 1990s to the present, reports indicate that they witnessed and were the victims of inordinately high rates of what is termed domestic and community violence. Second, there has been an alarming increase in girls' offenses for violent crime. Although quantitative data have not consistently yielded statistical significance linking these factors causally, interviews with young women reveal an undeniable connection between their having been harmed earlier in their lives and later court involvement, often for violent offending.

This chapter draws from a larger study of court-involved girls conducted between 1994 and 2004 (Schaffner, 2006). Interviews were gathered from girls who were being adjudicated delinquent in the juvenile legal system in 22 facilities across the United States. A total of 42 adults who worked with young women were interviewed as well. Interviews were life history in nature, included open-ended questions, and often lasted 2 hours. Of the 100 young women discussed in this chapter, 37% were African American, 35% Latina, 4% Asian, 3% Native American, and 8% biracial. Girls ranged in age from 13 to 18 years. Participant observation ethnography was also conducted in various agencies and other settings frequented by adolescent girls.

After a brief review of research regarding child abuse and violence in the lives of youth, including an outline of studies of the quantity of violence and the social consequences of the abuse, the chapter proceeds in the following manner. First, I highlight two different contexts where girls' violence led them to come into the

juvenile legal system: lesbian battery and fighting back from sexual harassment. Second, I present a discussion of how witnessing violence is learning violence. I conclude with recommendations for future research.

LITERATURE REVIEW: REVISITING THE TERM *ABUSE*

Child abuse—its study, measurement, prevention, and treatment, and the punishment of offenders—has become a veritable cottage industry. Social work, law, public health, psychiatry, psychology, and criminology have developed definitions, coursework, even diplomas. Legal experts and government officials make their cases and win elections by focusing on attendant popular moral outrage. Meanwhile, young women across the United States are quietly dying from it. In the course of this research, I found it increasingly disturbing to hear from everyone—from Oprah Winfrey to both Presidents Bush—about prostitution, trafficking, and child abuse, while defenseless young women continue to be punished for defense mechanisms that they deploy in response to the onslaught against them.

The Amount of Harm

Family researchers and social service providers consider violence against children one of the most serious social problems of our times. According to a special report investigating violence among family members and intimate partners, more than 1,550,000 incidents of family violence were reported between 1996 and 2001 (Federal Bureau of Investigation, 2003). An estimated 906,000 children were determined to be victims of child abuse or neglect in 2003. More than 60% experienced neglect, almost 19% were physically abused, 10% were sexually abused, and 5% were emotionally maltreated (National Clearinghouse on Child Abuse and Neglect Information, 2005). Even though the rates of victimization in the national population declined between 1990 and 2003, the rate of 12.4 children per 1,000 is unacceptably high. In a national study, 33% of high school youth reported having been in at least one physical fight during the preceding year. Seventeen percent of students reported that they had carried a weapon. In 2003, one out of nine (12%) high school girls reported having been raped at some point in their lives (Centers for Disease Control and Prevention, 2004).

In one U.S. study, 8% of women reported their first intercourse to be nonvoluntary (Abma et al., 1997). Of all Americans who do report episodes of nonvoluntary sexual intercourse, women were more likely than men to report having had this experience, with just under one half of all nonvoluntary experiences among women occurring before age 14 (Moore et al., 1989). Numerous national reports indicate that sexual offenses against children are widespread (Finkelhor, 1994; Moore et al., 1989; Runtz & Briere, 1986; Stock, Bell, Boyer, & Connell, 1997). It is now generally known that girls are sexually abused and raped more often than boys (Finkelhor & Baron, 1986). Most abuse (90%) is committed by men and by persons known to the child (70%–90%) (Finkelhor, 1994). Indeed, one scholar frames sexual coercion of girls and women as so prevalent as to be a kind of a new norm (Schur, 1989). The victims of one in four persons incarcerated for sexual assault in the United States were the assaulters' own children or their stepchildren. Convicted violent sexual assault offenders revealed that more than 75% of their victims were younger than 18. Almost 85% of their victims were females (Greenfield, 1997). These data point to a crisis of violence in the everyday lives of U.S. youth.

As girls in general were disproportionately victims of abuse, so too were girls in trouble with the law. In a recent report of girls in the California juvenile correctional system, 92% reported experiencing sexual, physical, or emotional abuse; many reported combinations of multiple forms of abuse and experiencing abuse on multiple occasions (Acoca, 1998). Of the participants in my study, 53% had experienced physical injury, 53% sexual injury, and 71% reported that they had been neglected emotionally (Schaffner, 2006).

The Price of Harm

Abuse of girls takes its toll in many alarming ways: from psychological problems ranging from depression to suicide, to problems with the criminal justice system resulting in incarceration. Almost 68% of adult women in the U.S. criminal justice system reported having been beaten, abused, molested, or burned when they were young girls (Acoca & Austin, 1996). Survivors of sexual injury develop common psychological effects such as depression, anxiety, low self-esteem, loss of trust, and difficulty establishing intimacy (Herman, 1992; Powers & Jaklitsch, 1989). Researchers note a variety of problems: complex posttraumatic stress disorder, feelings of hopelessness, feelings of angry aggression, disassociative behaviors, self-mutilation, and suicide attempts are common for survivors of sexual abuse (Briere & Elliott, 1994; Herman, 1992; Holden, Geffner, & Jouriles, 1998). Substance dependency has been linked to sexual abuse (Briere & Elliott, 1994). Girls may also become pregnant as a result of the abuse, with some obtaining an abortion and others giving birth. Bulimia, anorexia, eating disorders, and self-loathing related to being overweight and underweight also manifest among adolescent girls as responses to abuse or emotional neglect (Acoca & Dedel, 1998).

Many girls being adjudicated delinquent are not formally diagnosed. For some, their emotional conditions are not recognized by parents or authorities as the results of sexual victimization (Powers & Jaklitsch, 1989). Adults sometimes characterize these kinds of female troubles as part of "teenage angst" or "raging hormones." Probation officers are known to consider girls in trouble as "liars" and "manipulators" (Gaarder, Rodriguez, & Zatz, 2004). Socioeconomic differences exist as well. Compared to privileged girls, poor girls are less likely to be seen by medical and mental health personnel. Girls from no-income and low-income families have less access than middle-class girls to the most highly skilled therapists and their careful guidance through psychopharmaceuticals (Duncan, Yeung, Brooks-Gunn, & Smith, 1998). Girls report feeling that nobody was listening or taking the time to notice and proactively help them (Apter, 1990; Bernardez, 1991).

Studies suggest a correlation between early injury and female trouble behavior such as psychological disturbances and juvenile delinquency (Goldman, 1987; Herman, 1992; Runtz & Briere, 1986). In one study of homeless youth, 75% of female adolescent prostitutes had been sexually abused (Deisher & Rogers, 1991). The authors noted that another study revealed that of runaways in Southern California, 36% left home because of physical or sexual abuse and 44% ran from other severe long-term problems. Nearly all the street youth whom we have seen in our clinics have histories of significant abuse and neglect, and well over half have been involved in intermittent or full-time prostitution. (Deisher & Rogers, 1991, p. 501)

Owen and Bloom's (1997) study of young women in the California Youth Authority found that 85% indicated some type of abuse in their lives. It is possible that for injured girls, subsequent decisions they made seemed to them to actually "solve" their sexual abuse problem or heal prior hurt and injury (Runtz & Briere, 1986; Schaffner, 1997).

The choices that harmed girls made in response to their injuries may have led them to the attention of juvenile authorities. Often living in a fast "culture of urgency" moment, their impetuous or numbed solutions may lead to involvement in aggressive and violent situations. Young women report that they often find themselves in situations where they need to protect themselves physically, or they get so angered at being injured that they fight back (Wolfe & Tucker, 1998). Others report feeling generally demoralized and debased, so they "jus' go off and do things." It is often at this point that girls come to the attention of the juvenile legal system. Thus, it is plausible that many young women involved in behaviors that draw attention from juvenile corrections may be fleeing, and otherwise responding to, childhood sexual and physical injury.

FINDINGS: GIRL FIGHTS IN DIFFERENT SETTINGS

Among commentators who notice the rise in girls' arrests for violent offenses, disagreement remains as to why. Is it the case that girls are actually more violent than ever before (Putallaz & Bierman, 2004)? Alternative explanations include that decreases in chivalry on the part of police officers and judges draw girls into the system at higher rates, that violent offenses by girls are so few that any increase in numbers creates huge gains in proportions, that mandatory

arrests for intimate violence increase girls' chances for arrest at the scenes of domestic disputes, that police categorize girls' fights as more serious assaults, and that the media have jumped onto a bandwagon of sensationalizing an increase in rates of violence among girls (Artz, 1998; Chesney-Lind, 2004). Whatever the reasons, we do a grave disservice not to notice, contextualize, and analyze the system response to experiences of young women who are being adjudicated delinquent for violent offenses. The current judicial penalization of gender transgression is important because it profoundly affects young women's developmental courses and life trajectories. When young women are treated with disrespect and aggression, they learn to respond with it.

Context One: Cora Winfield Confronting Homophobia

During fieldwork in a juvenile detention facility, I met Cora Winfield, a 15-year-old raised in a White East Coast working-class family by a proud Irish father and U.S.-born mother.[1] In detention for aggravated assault, Cora explained to me that "I don't how else to say it. I get drunk and kick my girlfriend's ass just like my dad gets drunk and kicks my mom's." Her management of her adolescent knowledge of her homosexuality was complicated by the homophobia and misogyny in her family of origin. Expressing a disturbing self-hatred, Cora talked to me about how she wasn't going to "stay gay."

> I ain't gonna be gay my whole life, you know . . . I can't take it. I probably won't stay gay. Hidin', pretendin', gettin' hassled all the time at school or even just hangin' out—I can't take it. I'm always stressin' over where the next fight is gonna go down. I'm sick of being called "lezzie." I kick it fine with my homeys. They just treat me like another lil' dude anyways. I don't know . . .

Cora was lanky and long-legged, slim and tall. Her dirty blonde hair, bobbed straight and tucked behind her ears, fell forward onto her cheeks as she hung her head and talked. I found hers to be a particularly disturbing confession, given the high rate of suicide attempts among queer youth. In a 1989 report on teen suicide, the U.S. Department of Health and Human Services concluded that 30% of teen suicides were among lesbian and gay youth and that these were largely the result of antigay attitudes within the society. In other words, these deaths were preventable (Owens, 1998). When Cora said she was not going to be gay her whole life, I hoped she did not intend it as a statement of suicidal ideation.

There is no safe space in the dominant culture for girls to explore same-sex desire: Rarely are girls given open social permission to explore lesbian sexuality and identity as a normative option (Fontaine & Hammond, 1996; Weston, 1991; Zemsky, 1998). Sexual diversity manifests in various ways among troubled girls. Gendered norms of beauty, especially for butch girls, as well as norms toward heterosexuality can impede psychological and emotional development of queer and questioning girls by tagging them with the label *deviant*. Confusingly, even though a hypersexualization of adolescence in the West since the 1960s included a sense of entitlement to explore sexualities (Rubin, 1990), for young women caught exploring same-sex desire, extreme forms of social exclusion and marginalization can result.

At the turn of the 21st century, a tension exists in the dominant Western culture between an increased sense of entitlement to sexual rights, a heightened homophobia and heteronormativity, and a hypersexualization of youth culture. What is historically new about attention to cases of homophobia and same-sex desire among children in trouble with the law is that for the first time in the history of modern sexuality, it is possible for youth to adopt identity categories such as lesbian, gay, transgender, bisexual, questioning, or queer (D'Emilio, 1983; Herdt, 1989). Thus, uneducated, confused, and unprepared families—and sociolegal and delinquency systems—have meager experience in raising gay children, processing their cases, and, most important, protecting their human and civil rights.

According to various studies, approximately 10% to 15% of the U.S. population is estimated to be predominantly homosexual. Fontaine and Hammond (1996) estimate that if 10% of the population was gay or lesbian, it would mean that one in every five families has a gay or lesbian child. Others have estimated the homosexual population to be lower, from 2% to 4% (Michael, Gagnon, Laumann, & Kolata, 1994), which nonetheless translates into an estimate that from 4% to 8% of American families could include a gay or lesbian child. Yet queer girls are invisible and often isolated, dealing alone with social stigma and cultural rejection (Braverman & Strasburger, 1993; Remafedi & Blum, 1986).

Homophobia includes feelings of confusion, disgust, anger, hatred, or fear of people who are homosexual. In my research, descriptions of events surrounding homophobic feelings—which girls expressed toward each other and toward themselves—was a pattern that emerged from listening to the accounts of girls' troubles and their behaviors of anger- and aggression-related offending. In an ominous development for queer and questioning young women who struggle simultaneously with their sexuality, self-love, and a need to avoid juvenile corrections, homophobia was on the rise in schools, and gay bashing among youth was widespread in the United States (Brooke, 1998; D'Augelli & Dark, 1995; Kurwa, 1998; Sullivan, 1998). In a recent poll of thousands of the highest achieving American high school students, almost half admitted prejudice against gays and lesbians (Ness, 1998). Ten percent of girls reported "being called lesbian" in a national survey of sexual harassment in schools (American Association of University Women, 2001).

An achievement of a sexual identity is a complex developmental process during puberty and adolescence (Braverman & Strasburger, 1993). In contemporary Western culture, a society-wide and cross-cultural homophobia provokes a disproportionate number of lesbian and gay teens into inordinate emotional struggle. Those who work with gay and lesbian teen populations report that these youth describe feelings of self-hatred, withdrawal, and anger that seem to lead them to indulge in alcohol and other drugs as a way to hide from their problems or attempt to fit in with peers (Fleisher & Fillman, 1995).

Researchers find that this unique population drops out of school, runs away from home, lives without shelter, and self-medicates with street drugs and alcohol at high rates (D'Augelli, 1998; Fleisher & Fillman, 1995). Some queer teenagers—especially young women with butch demeanors, such as Cora Winfield—report that they suffer such vilification at home or in school that they are forced out onto the streets. Government agencies estimate that approximately 25% of gay and lesbian youth are forced to flee homophobia from their families and schools and that from a quarter to a third of the runaway, homeless, and street youth population are gay or lesbian (Los Angeles County

Task Force on Runaway and Homeless Youth, 1988; U.S. Department of Health and Human Services, 1989).

Others note that teenagers living on the street are forced into survival sex, the sex trade, and the street economy in order to live (Pfeffer, 1997; Yates, Mackenzie, Pennbridge, & Swofford, 1991). In a study of U.S. adolescents living in the street economy, Yates and colleagues (1991) found that youth involved in prostitution were more than 5 times as likely to report homosexual or bisexual identities.

In the United States, runaway, homeless, and street youth then come to the attention of the state (juvenile authorities and emergency rooms) in disproportionate numbers (Kruks, 1991; Scholinski, 1997). In addition, the *Diagnostic and Statistical Manual* diagnoses of "Sexual Dysfunctions" and "Gender Identity Disorders" provide pathways to psychiatric wards and other juvenile "correctional" systems (American Psychiatric Association, 1994; Herdt, 1989; Hunter, 1990; Kennedy, 1991).

Data on the number of lesbian, bisexual, and questioning female youth in U.S. juvenile correctional facilities are difficult to obtain. Given the widespread stigma attached to coming out and identifying as gay, many young women do not openly identify as lesbian or queer even as they pursue sexual experiences and deep emotional relationships with other females. Despite the absence of systematic data, anecdotal information confirms the reality that homophobia in the lives of queer teenage girls can be a challenge that often includes traversing a juvenile corrections system.

Homophobia affects girls in juvenile corrections in different ways (Curtin, 2002; Dang, 1997; see also Owens, 1998). One young woman testified that when she was locked in detention, she was "never given a roommate because she was a lesbian" and that "special showering arrangements were made to prevent her from showering with other girls" (Dang, 1997, p. 17). One girl told her story of living in a group home: "I prepared myself to get in a fight the very first night when I went downstairs later that night for dinner." This young woman had been driven out of her house by her homophobic mother, but the girls in the group home finally accepted her (Foster Care Youth United, 1994). Findings from one Human Rights Commission report found that "many youth who enter the juvenile justice system for hate-related crimes have committed crimes *against* [italics added] LGBTQQ [lesbian, gay,

bisexual, transgendered, queer, and questioning] people" (Dang, 1997, p. 17).

Battery between lesbian couples is another hidden problem among girls in trouble (Lobel, 1986; Scherzer, 1998). Three young women from my study (of the nine who talked about their lesbian relationships) revealed that they had beat up their girlfriends/lovers. For example, they said,

> I was involved with a hooker—she was bisexual. I was always buyin' her things but we fought a lot. I beat her up off crystal so I got an ADW off that. (Claudia Sereno, 16 years old, Los Angeles, possession and sale of marijuana)

> I beat my girl 'cause she ran away with Miguel. First we left him, but then he started buggin' her. Then we fought. I beat her bad. (Leslie Rollins, 15 years old, Marin County, CA, simple assault)

Lesbian, bisexual, and questioning girls may be victimized by violence perpetrated by males or females when they strike out in anger and fear towards each other (Pastor, McCormick, & Fine, 1996; Way, 1996). Thus, the effects of homophobia, both on queer girls who are victims of violence and on those girls who perpetrate violence, must be taken into account when theorizing girls' offending behaviors.

Cora Winfield learned her anger and physical fighting at home and spent a lot of time in public facilities because of it. She turned her discomfort with her own sexuality aggressively outward, resulting in her getting into emotional and legal trouble. Cora talked about her situation, her fears, and her father:

> My father is some bigwig in his company and he thinks he owns the whole damn world! He thinks he can push me and my mom around. If he had any idea about me and my girl he will kill me. And now he's gonna find out because they're gonna tell him I'm in here on a DV [domestic violence] charge. Like they're gonna tell him I beat up my girlfriend—not just some girl. Shit! I am so totally fucked! I hate this stupid life. I ain't never heard anyone had it so bad as me. I cannot always be like this. This is the worst! I super need me a cold one [beer] just to get through today. . . .

One advantage Cora enjoyed at the time of our interview was luck—luck to be in a location where service providers could identify and locate community support for her. In the particular facility where she was detained, her well-trained gender-aware public defender put Cora in contact with a local queer youth center to assist Cora with her feelings and her case. Countless other teens around the world go through the agonies of adolescence—as well as "corrections"—feeling hopeless, angry, fearful, and sad, but with no such access to a supportive community.

Despite the sexualization of the adolescent female, mainstream American culture and law lag in the recognition of homosexuality and lesbian desire as legitimate experiences. These institutions and systems fail to acknowledge that being gay is about more than just sex, that homophobia has a devastating impact upon young people struggling to form their sense of self, and that elimination of prejudice is essential to fair treatment in the juvenile justice system (Owens, 1998). State response to gender transgressions such as "intimate violence" of gay and lesbian youth demands inclusion in any contemporary theory of girls' violence.

Context Two: Mylen Cruz's Fight Back Against "Sexual Harassment"

Mylen Cruz's story illustrates her attempt to manage misogyny and sexual harassment—an attempt that went terribly awry. Mylen grew up in Northern California, in a semihomeless situation with her mother and younger brother. She moved from home to home, in other people's houses, staying with relatives and her mother's boyfriends. Mylen Cruz was Filipina American, 16 years old, and in detention for attempted murder.

> Mommy was always totally stressing. I mean, it got me worried all the damn time. Was there food? Did Eddie [her little brother] need shoes? Where we gonna live next? I seen my mom get beat out on the corner—hell, *I* got beat out on the corner. . . . It was always some crazy shit goin' on. I din't get to have any kind of childhood, like, um, be a little girl and all—uh uh, no how.
>
> In the schools I went to, you hadda be bad if you were goin' to make it. Is jus' like that. I'm not no bad-ass but I ain't take shit offa nobody. Especially no boy gonna disrespect me like that! You got to come at me correct if you want some of this. He jus' all, "hey wassup, girl" and all that.

Mylen talked about how Jackson, her assailant, had approached her. She required young men to approach her with respect and decency. According to Mylen, Jackson had basically just sidled up to her and started teasing her in a threatening way, putting his hands all over her body.

> I was in the office at my school and this boy come up to me to fuck with me. He was all, "I'ma get me some of this shit, man." He all started to touch my butt! He thought we gonna be kickin' it or some shit! We got into a violent fight. I did a violent act. I don't know. I was mad. I couldn't deal, I couldn't hold it. I'm not a killer but I would be able to do it. I hoped he wouldn't die but . . . I wasn't scared to come to Juvey.

She said that first she froze, and then she was overcome by her feelings:

> See I had this little knife in my bag that I always carry with me. So he's all touchin' me and tryin' to feel me up and um, and first I couldn't believe it. I was just like, you know, stuck there or something. Then, I just got it out my bag and started swingin' it at him. I went crazy!—I really did. I jus' felt it sooo mad and like felt all hot and I don't know . . . and I jus' . . . I don't know how, I just did it.

"He got stabbed," she said, oddly passive in her language. It was as if Mylen could not process her own actions, that *she* had stabbed him.

In her file, I read that her mother was often homeless with Mylen and her little brother. I asked her about her family.

> Mommy is there for me sometimes. She's always busy 'cause she has a lot of problems: the rent, money. We used to be close but her stress affects me. I never ran away, but we always got evicted. Out in the shelters, well, it's crazy. They's some crazy motherfuckers out there.

Mylen described a situation in which her family was staying with another family and her mother "had to serve him [the other family's father] coffee and take a lot of shit like she was the slave." Mylen said she hated school and knew she shouldn't have gone that day. "I knew I was gonna go off on somebody eventually." Mylen was very upset at this point in our conversation and started crying. She said she felt like so many things were wrong with her life, she couldn't figure out how to begin to fix it.

Mylen's situation—fighting off a possible rapist—was not framed as self-defense. She was actually being adjudicated in adult court for attempted homicide. Factors such as being subjected to cruelty during an unprotected childhood and witnessing her mother (her only caregiver) receive consistent maltreatment must be taken into account when adjudicating girls as perpetrators of violence.

DISCUSSION: WITNESSING VIOLENCE IS LEARNING VIOLENCE

In academic and public discourse, community violence is represented, in the main, by facts and accounts of guys in gangs with guns. Definitions of community violence need to be broadened to include what girls see, face, and deal with in everyday life at home, at school, and out on the streets (Garbarino, Dubrow, Kostelny, & Pardo, 1992; Holden et al., 1998; Osofsky, 1997; Zimring, 1998). Recognizing the gravity of witnessing violence and its long-term impact on the life course and development of healthy children will fuel the reinvigoration of state response to perpetration of gender and sexual violence and revive community, school, and family recognition of gender violence as dangerous and destructive.

Not until blood was spilled or police were called could the young women in my study "see" the community and family violence surrounding them. Whereas 53% of the young women reported being physically or sexually injured directly, when asked if they had ever witnessed their parents or other combinations of family and household members in physical battle, 71% of the young women in this project answered in the affirmative. However, when asked if they had ever witnessed abuse or if they felt that there was violence in their homes, only a small portion framed abuse and fights as violence. A relationship between witnessing violence and subsequent offending was certainly suggested by these findings, but it was as if young women did not see it, and if they did, it was not that bad, according to them.

Research in psychology reveals, however, that abuse and subsequent anger may result in aggressive behavior:

Feelings of rage and murderous revenge fantasies are normal responses to abusive treatment. Like abused adults, abused children are often rageful and sometimes aggressive. They often lack verbal and social skills for resolving conflict, and they approach problems with the expectation of

hostile attack. The abused child's predictable difficulties in modulating anger further strengthen her conviction of inner badness. Each hostile encounter convinces her she is indeed a hateful person. If, as is common, she tends to displace her anger far from its dangerous source and to discharge it unfairly on those who did not provoke it, her self-condemnation is aggravated still further. (Herman, 1992, p. 104)

At first, young women expressed no discord with the chaos and violence they reported witnessing. Upon follow-up questions that signaled to the girls that I thought it was crucial, they began to unfurl details of powerful events that had made up just four- or five-word phrases in their files (and lives): "gfa [grandfather] raped her mo [mother] in her room one night"; "was kidnapped and forced to watch pornographic sex acts before being released"; or "was raped with a gun inserted into her vagina." Upon prompts from me such as "So, how do you feel about what happened that night?" or "What do you think that means to you now?" girls reported feeling frozen with fear, terrified at seeing their mothers and siblings being hurt and unable to do anything to stop it, and panicked when recalling harm. Of course, who can know how much of our discussion was prompted by my very questioning? Even so, that to become disturbed about violent mistreatment would need provocation was interesting in itself.

Some girls explored the idea that exposure to trauma was linked to their current troubles. A few insisted there was no connection whatsoever. Others seemed disassociated from the terror while recounting it. But many more appeared a little bored by telling their stories over and over to yet another social worker, which I believe is how I was often perceived. For example, one young woman related an account of watching her mother get raped by some men who stopped to "help" them when they had a flat tire on a Colorado highway one night. Yet there was a way that she repeated the story in such a monotonous tone, as if, "Oh well, this is what happened." She knew it was an extraordinary experience, but I got the sense from her that it had become so normalized in a way, made into a notation in her file, that she did not seem to think it was of much importance or that out of the ordinary anymore. Children are now considered "invisible victims" of domestic and community violence:

More than half of the police calls in many communities are for domestic disturbances, many of which are witnessed by children. Countless numbers of children whom one never hears about, and for whom the police do not receive calls, are exposed to physical and verbal abuse between their parents or caretakers several times a week. (Osofsky, 1998, p. 97)

The girls' accounts in my research exemplify why definitions of community violence need to be broadened to include what youths (including girls) experience.

Court-involved girls revealed that they witnessed an inordinate amount of violence on a regular, routine basis. They talked about seeing brothers, friends, cousins, fathers, and boyfriends being kicked, beaten, punched, knifed, shot, and killed. In interviews, young women reported witnessing their mothers being devalued and hurt physically by fathers, stepfathers, and boyfriends. Well over half of the girls in my sample reported witnessing physical, sexual, or emotional abuse of others. Almost every girl had accounts to relate regarding this. Most recounted multiple events. Many intertwined tales of abuse and mistreatment among the regular stories of their daily lives:

My mom drinks 2 cups of vodka every day. My dad was arrested for beating on my mom. They have 6 kids, but only my brother is my real brother. I used to put my head under my pillow when I was little so I wouldn't hear my brother cry when he got hit. (Ilsa Davis, 14 years old, simple assault)

My best friend's brother hanged himself. I found him there. . . . I'm stressin' now because my friend Benito got killed in Bayview and they wouldn't let me go to the *funeraria*. See what happened is, um, *chiflaron y salio mucha gente. Luego lo mataron* [They whistled and a bunch of people came out of the house and then they killed Benito]. (Claudia Sereno, 16 years old, arrested for assault, relating various events strung together)

I got cut off Home Detention 'cause I didn't go to school. I need to stay at my boyfriend's [apartment] 'cause he lives nearby my school and I can just go from there. My mom's always goin' to jail.

   For what?

   For partyin'—I don't know what you call it. She freaked out because my cousin got shot so my brother shot the people who shot him and then *he* got shot. Me and my mom aren't getting along ever since my brother died. I probably want to go to NA for crank [Narcotics Anonymous for taking speed]—I been doin' like 6 lines a day to forget about my problems. (Cheyanne McDerby, 17 years old, probation violation)

My daddy gets in jail a lot for drinking. I run away from home because it is loud and noisy there—the music—it's hard to concentrate. I've run from placements and hospitals, too! My mom and her boyfriend hit each other and hit me too. They give me bloody lips. But I went to a hospital for cutting my arm. [File reads: "Body covered with scars from cutting herself."] (Sasha Rudnik, 15 years old, CA PC 245 assault with a deadly weapon)

I came to consider the young women in this population as unnoticed, mute witnesses of frontline violence in day-to-day urban life. Girls in my study reported living in worlds tainted daily by aggression and assault. Many adolescents experience power struggles with siblings and parents, but for these girls common household conflicts, such as not being able to use the telephone or go out with friends, or discussions over their chores, turned into physically violent disputes.

For some people in some situations, violence becomes normalized, even utilized, as an emotional strategy and a psychological response to troubles and frustrations (see Dougherty, 1998; Scheper-Hughes, 1992; Stein, Katz, Madriz, & Shick, 1997; van der Kolk & Greenberg, 1987). A certain routinization of violence in girls' everyday lives was embedded in their decision making. Girls interspersed accounts about throwing coffee cans, seeing their mothers get hit, and whacking folks on the head in the street all in one breath. They called it "goin' off"—meaning losing one's temper, letting frustrations build up, and then pouring it out in violent expressions, as if that were how things just were. The social logic to these expressions of anger was that, unfortunately, they were a normal and natural part of day-to-day interactions.

Data from my interviews and observations indicated that factors such as witnessing sexual and physical trauma were salient when interpreting girls' violent offenses. It is impossible to understand girls' troubles with juvenile authorities without contextualizing them within the violence they suffer, including listening to fighting and watching brutal assaults.

My dad was an abusive alcoholic and the divorce helped him straighten up. But since their divorce when I was 11, all went downhill from there for me. I grew up in a bad household, I seen my dad pound on my mom. I can't blame it on my mom and dad but ever since my mom and dad got their divorce I haven't got through it yet. I never thought it could happen to our family. Now I'm in here for jumping this girl and beatin' on her—I stole her chain, too. It's jus' all bad for me. (Doris Montoya, 14 years old, assault and battery)

I even had to call the police on my own dad. He used to fight with my mom, with my uncle, even our neighbors! Fights: my dad taught me, "If someone hits you then hit them back!" I don't know how many times he's been in jail for assault and battery! He taught me how to fight pretty good, well, not that good [laughs]. I lost the fight I'm in here for. (Joanne Billingsly, 15 years old, assault and battery on school grounds)

In accounts from court-involved girls' everyday lives, some girls were able to relate aggression and anger, and their parents' marital discord, to their offending behaviors.

Yet mainstream criminology fails to capture the ways girls growing up in homes where there was wife beating responded by being aggressive themselves (see, for example, Siegel, 2005). Studies cannot prove that witnessing or being victimized by brutality in childhood directly caused later offending behaviors, nor can they predict which witness will become an offender. Yet plausible links among factors such as exposure to violence, girls' anger, and subsequent offenses, especially girls' involvement in violent crimes, became easy to verify by hearing the voices of girls who were locked up for violent offenses.

CONCLUSION: FROM PRIVATE HARM TO PUBLIC INJURY

Children are born into families where they learn their culture and family history, values, and how to love and work. We know that young people gravitate to safe and loving places in which to grow up. As one group of feminist scholars found in their work with urban girls,

"Homeplaces" can be broadly defined to include comforting, safe spaces in institutions such as schools or in social groups such as clubs, social movements, or gangs. Listening to young women's critiques of schooling, domestic spaces, gender relations, racial hierarchies, and social violence, we have learned that homeplaces, broadly defined, can also become constricting places from which they often try to break free. (Pastor et al., 1996, p. 15)

Cora's and Mylen's experiences typify how families can simultaneously offer girls and young women love, care, nurturing, and encouragement—and also violence, incest, neglect, abuse, and homophobia.

When we dig deeper in court-involved girls' accounts, we see how their private anguish affects us as a public. In their families, friendships, neighborhoods, and schools, young women were provoked to astonishing levels of aggressive assaults. Their injuries were connected to their sexual misconduct as well. Young women who were sexually exploited and witnessed violence in their daily lives came to the attention of juvenile correctional systems with psychiatric diagnoses of "oppositional defiant conduct disorders" and probation conditions regarding "disorderly conduct." The explanatory power of listening to their narratives revealed neither a simple structural determinism from being poor or discriminated against nor facile psychosexual dysfunction or pathology. Instead, girls' involvement in juvenile corrections resulted from interplay between these forces and others, mediated by a less protective culture and more punitive social stance.

This study raises important questions for further research about the relationship between violence and female offending. For example, some gender scholars find that the anger that girls express through violence is framed as more a "relational" anger than boys' anger (Crick et al., 2001; Crick & Grotpeter, 1995). More thought needs to attend to exactly what happens to these analyses as we challenge essentialist or binary characterizations (see, for example, Butler, 2004). Much needed is comparative research into how masculinities are adopted into the socialization of court-involved girls' identities and the role of emotionality in the lives of boys in trouble with the law. Yet empirical data provided here yield glimpses of typologies and symbolic meanings of the emotion work beneath accounts of juvenile offending, lending insight into the connections among sexual and violent victimization and the state's interventions into gender transgressions.

NOTE

1. All names, descriptions, locations, details of cases, exact situations, charges, job titles, and any other identifying features have been altered to protect project participants' anonymity and confidentiality. This research was conducted with informed consent and under the guidelines of university human subjects review.

REFERENCES

Abma, J. C., Chandra, A., Mosher, W. D., Peterson, L., & Piccinino, L. (1997). *Fertility, family planning, and women's health: New data From the 1995 National Survey of Family Growth.* Hyattsville, MD: National Center for Health Statistics.

Acoca, L. (1998). Outside/inside: The violation of American girls at home, on the streets, and in the juvenile justice system. *Crime and Delinquency, 44,* 561–589.

Acoca, L., & Austin, J. (1996). *The crisis: Women in prison.* San Francisco: National Council on Crime and Delinquency, the Women Offender Sentencing Study and Alternative Sentencing Recommendations Project.

Acoca, L., & Dedel, K. (1998). *No place to hide: Understanding and meeting the needs of girls in the California Juvenile Justice System.* San Francisco: National Council on Crime and Delinquency.

American Association of University Women. (2001). *Hostile hallways: The AAUW survey of sexual harassment in America's schools.* Washington, DC: Author.

American Correctional Association. (1990). *The female offender: What does the future hold?* Washington, DC: St. Mary's Press.

American Psychiatric Association. (1994). *Diagnostic and statistical manual of mental disorders* (4th ed.). Washington, DC: Author.

Apter, T. (1990). *Altered loves: Mothers and daughters during adolescence.* New York: Fawcett Columbine.

Artz, S. (1998). *Sex, power, and the violent school girl.* New York: Teacher's College Press.

Belknap, J., & Holsinger, K. (1998). An overview of delinquent girls: How theory and practice have failed and the need for innovative changes. In R. Zaplin (Ed.), *Female offenders: Critical perspectives and effective interventions* (pp. 31–64). Gaithersburg, MD: Aspen.

Bernardez, T. (1991). Adolescent resistance and the maladies of women: Notes from the underground. In C. Gilligan, A. G. Rogers, & D. L. Tolman (Eds.), *Women, girls, and psychotherapy* (pp. 213–222). New York: Haworth.

Braverman, P., & Strasburger, V. (1993). Adolescent sexual activity. *Clinical Pediatrics, 32*(11), 658–668.

Briere, J. N., & Elliott, D. M. (1994). Immediate and long-term impacts of child sexual abuse. In *The future of children: Sexual abuse of children* (Vol. 4, No. 2, pp. 54–69). Los Altos, CA: David and Lucile Packard Foundation.

Brooke, J. (1998, October 14). Homophobia often found in schools, data shows. *New York Times,* p. A19.

Butler, J. (2004). *Undoing gender.* New York: Routledge.

Campbell, A. (1994). *Men, women, and aggression.* New York: Basic Books.

Centers for Disease Control and Prevention. (2004). *Youth risk behavior surveillance, United States, 2003.* Washington, DC: U.S. Department of Health and Human Services.

Chesney-Lind, M. (2004). *Girls and violence: Is the gender gap closing?* (Applied Research Forum). Available from Violence Against Women Net, a project of the National Resource Center on Domestic Violence: http://www.vawnet.org

Crick, N., & Grotpeter, J. (1995). Relational aggression, gender, and social-psychological adjustment. *Child Development, 66,* 710–722.

Crick, N., Nelson, D., Morales, J., Cullerton-Sen, C., Casas, J., & Hickman, S. (2001). Relational victimization in childhood and adolescence: I hurt you through the grapevine. In J. Juvonen & S. Graham (Eds.), *Peer harassment in school: The plight of the vulnerable and victimized* (pp. 196–214). New York: Guilford.

Curtin, M. (2002). Lesbian and bisexual girls in the juvenile justice system. *Child and Adolescent Social Work Journal, 19,* 285–301.

Dang, Q. H. (1997). *Investigation into the needs of lesbian, gay, bisexual, transgender, queer, and questioning youth.* San Francisco: Human Rights Commission City and County of San Francisco.

D'Augelli, A. (1998). Developmental implications of victimization of lesbian, gay, and bisexual youths. In G. Herek (Ed.), *Stigma and sexual orientation* (pp. 187–210). Thousand Oaks, CA: Sage.

D'Augelli, A., & Dark, L. (1995). Lesbian, gay, and bisexual youths. In L. Eron, J. Gentry, & P. Schlegel (Eds.), *Reason to hope: A psychosocial perspective on violence and youth* (pp. 177–196). Washington, DC: American Psychological Association.

Deisher, R., & Rogers, W. (1991). The medical care of street youth. *Journal of Adolescent Health, 12,* 500–503.

D'Emilio, J. (1983). Capitalism and gay identity. In A. Snitow, C. Stansell, & S. Thompson (Eds.), *Powers of desire* (pp. 100–113). New York: Monthly Review Press.

Dougherty, J. (1998). Female offenders and childhood maltreatment: Understanding the connections. In R. Zaplin (Ed.), *Female offenders: Critical perspectives and effective interventions* (pp. 227–244). Gaithersburg, MD: Aspen.

Duncan, G. J., Yeung, W. J., Brooks-Gunn, J., & Smith, J. R. (1998). How much does childhood poverty affect the life chances of children? *American Sociological Review, 63,* 406–423.

Federal Bureau of Investigation. (2003). *Crime in the United States, 2001.* Washington, DC: U.S. Department of Justice.

Finkelhor, D. (1994). Current information on the scope and nature of child sexual abuse. In *The future of children: Sexual abuse of children* (Vol. 4, No. 2, pp. 31–53). Los Altos, CA: David and Lucile Packard Foundation.

Finkelhor, D., & Baron, L. (1986). Risk factors for child sexual abuse. *Journal of Interpersonal Violence, 1,* 43–71.

Fleisher, J., & Fillman, J. (1995, January/February). Lesbian and gay youth: Treatment issues. *The Counselor,* pp. 27–28.

Fontaine, J., & Hammond, N. (1996). Counseling issues with gay and lesbian adolescents. *Adolescence, 31,* 817–830.

Foster Care Youth United. (1994). *Interview with "Sandra," a lesbian in the system.* New York: Youth Communications, Inc.

Gaarder, E., Rodriguez, N., & Zatz, M. (2004). Criers, liars, and manipulators: Probation officers' views of girls. *Justice Quarterly, 21,* 547–578.

Garbarino, J., Dubrow, N., Kostelny, K., & Pardo, C. (1992). *Children in danger: Coping with consequences of community violence.* San Francisco: Jossey-Bass.

Goldman, M. (1987). Prostitution, economic exchange, and the unconscious. In J. Rabow, G. Platt, & M. Goldman (Eds.), *Advances in psychoanalytic sociology* (pp. 187–209). Malabar, FL: Krieger.

Greenfield, L. (1997). *Sex offenses and offenders: An analysis of data on rape and sexual assault.* Washington, DC: U.S. Department of Justice, Bureau of Justice Statistics.

Herdt, G. (Ed.). (1989). *Gay and lesbian youth.* New York: Harrington Park Press.

Herman, J. (1992). *Trauma and recovery.* New York: Basic Books.

Holden, G., Geffner, R., & Jouriles, E. (Eds.). (1998). *Children exposed to marital violence: Theory, research, and applied issues.* Washington, DC: American Psychological Association.

Hunter, J. (1990). Violence against lesbian and gay male youths. *Journal of Interpersonal Violence, 5,* 295–300.

Kennedy, M. (1991). Homeless and runaway youth mental health issues: No access to the system. *Journal of Adolescent Health, 12,* 576–579.

Kruks, G. (1991). Gay and lesbian homeless/street youth: Special issues and concerns. *Journal of Adolescent Health, 12,* 515–518.

Kurwa, N. (1998, May 19). Do schools condone harassment of gay students? *San Francisco Examiner,* p. D7.

Lamb, S. (Ed.). (1999). *New versions of victims: Feminists struggle with the concept.* New York: New York University Press.

Levine, K. (2003). *Prosecution, politics and pregnancy: Enforcing statutory rape in California.* Unpublished doctoral dissertation, University of California, Berkeley.

Lobel, K. (Ed.). (1986). *Naming the violence: Speaking out about lesbian battering.* Denver, CO: National Coalition Against Domestic Violence, Lesbian Task Force.

Los Angeles County Task Force on Runaway and Homeless Youth. (1988). *Report and recommendations of the task force.* Los Angeles: City and County of Los Angeles.

Michael, R., Gagnon, J., Laumann, E., & Kolata, G. (1994). *Sex in America: A definitive survey.* Boston: Little, Brown.

Miller, J. (2001). *One of the guys: Girls, gangs, and gender.* New York: Oxford University Press.

Moore, K. A., Winquist Nord, C., & Peterson, J. L. (1989). Nonvoluntary sexual activity among adolescents. *Family Planning Perspectives, 21,* 110–114.

National Clearinghouse on Child Abuse and Neglect Information. (2005). *Childhood maltreatment 2003.* Washington, DC: U.S. Department of Health and Human Services.

Ness, C. (1998, November 12). Gay bias rising among top students. *San Francisco Examiner,* p. A1.

Obeidallah, D., & Earls, F. (1999). *Adolescent girls: The role of depression in the development of delinquency.* Washington, DC: U.S. Department of Justice, National Institute of Justice.

Osofsky, J. (Ed.). (1997). *Children in a violent society.* New York: Guilford.

Osofsky, J. (1998). Children as invisible victims of domestic and community violence. In G. Holden, R. Geffner, & E. Jouriles (Eds.), *Children exposed to marital violence: Theory, research, and applied issues* (pp. 95–120). Washington, DC: American Psychological Association.

Owen, B., & Bloom, B. (1997). *Profiling the needs of young female offenders: Final report to the executive staff of the California Youth Authority.* Washington, DC: U.S. Department of Justice, National Institute of Justice.

Owen, B., Bloom, B., & Covington, S. (2003). *Gender-responsive strategies: Research, practice, and guiding principles for women offenders.* Washington, DC: U.S. Department of Justice, National Institute of Corrections.

Owens, R. (1998). *Queer kids: The challenges and promise for lesbian, gay, and bisexual youth.* New York: Haworth.

Pastor, J., McCormick, J., & Fine, M. (1996). Makin' homes: An urban girl thing. In B. R. Leadbeater & N. Way (Eds.), *Urban girls* (pp. 15–34). New York: New York University Press.

Pfeffer, R. (1997). *Surviving the streets: Girls living on their own.* New York: Garland.

Powers, J., & Jaklitsch, B. (1989). *Understanding survivors of abuse: Stories of homeless and runaway adolescents.* Lexington, MA: Lexington Books.

Putallaz, M., & Bierman, K. (Eds.). (2004). *Aggression, antisocial behavior, and violence among girls.* New York: Guilford.

Remafedi, G., & Blum, R. (1986). Working with gay and lesbian adolescents. *Pediatric Annals, 15,* 773–783.

Rogers Park Young Women's Action Team. (2003). *"Hey cutie, can I get your digits?" A report about the street harassment of girls in Rogers Park.* Chicago: Friends of Battered Women and Their Children.

Rubin, L. (1990). *Erotic wars: What happened to the sexual revolution?* New York: HarperPerennial.

Runtz, M., & Briere, J. (1986). Adolescent "acting out" and childhood history of sexual abuse. *Journal of Interpersonal Violence, 1,* 326–334.

Schaffner, L. (1997). Families on probation: Court-ordered parenting skills classes for parents of juvenile offenders. *Crime and Delinquency, 43,* 412–437.

Schaffner, L. (2006). *Girls in trouble with the law.* New Brunswick, NJ: Rutgers University Press.

Scheper-Hughes, N. (1992). *Death without weeping: The violence of everyday life in Brazil.* Berkeley: University of California Press.

Scherzer, T. (1998). Domestic violence in lesbian relationships: Findings of the Lesbian Relationships Research Project. In C. Ponticelli (Ed.), *Gateways to improving lesbian health and health care* (pp. 29–47). New York: Haworth.

Scholinski, D. (1997). *The last time I wore a dress.* New York: Riverhead Books.

Schur, E. (1989). *The Americanization of sex.* Philadelphia: Temple University Press.

Siegel, L. (2005). *Criminology: The core* (2nd ed.). Belmont, CA: Thomson Wadsworth.

Stein, N., Katz, S., Madriz, E., & Shick, S. (Eds.). (1997). Losing a generation: Probing the myths and realities of youth and violence [Special issue]. *Social Justice, 24*(4).

Stock, J., Bell, M., Boyer, D., & Connell, F. (1997). Adolescent pregnancy and sexual risk-taking among sexually abused girls. *Family Planning Perspectives, 29,* 200–203.

Sullivan, K. (1998, July 26). Gay youths struggle in personal hell. *Sunday San Francisco Examiner and Chronicle,* pp. D1, D4.

Thornberry, T. (1994). *Violent families and violent youths* (Fact Sheet No. 21). Washington, DC: Office of Juvenile Justice and Delinquency Prevention.

U.S. Department of Health and Human Services. (1989). *Report of the Secretary's Task Force on Youth Suicide: Vol. 3. Prevention and interventions in youth suicide.* Rockville, MD: Author.

van der Kolk, B., & Greenberg, M. (1987). The psychobiology of the trauma response: Hyperarousal, constriction, and addiction to traumatic re-exposure. In B. van der Kolk (Ed.), *Psychological trauma* (pp. 63–88). Washington, DC: American Psychiatric Press.

Veysey, B. (2003). *Adolescent girls with mental health disorders involved with the juvenile justice system.* Washington, DC: National Center for Mental Health and Juvenile Justice. Retrieved from www.ncmhjj.com

Way, N. (1996). Between experiences of betrayal and desire: Close friendships among urban adolescents. In B. R. Leadbeater & N. Way (Eds.), *Urban girls* (pp. 173–182). New York: New York University Press.

Weston, K. (1991). *Families we choose: Lesbians, gays, kinship.* New York: Columbia University Press.

Widom, C. S. (2000, January). Childhood victimization: Early adversity, later psychopathology. *National Institute of Juvenile Justice Journal,* pp. 3–9.

Wolfe, L., & Tucker, J. (1998). *Report of the Summit on Girls and Violence.* Washington, DC: Center for Women Policy Studies.

Yates, G., Mackenzie, R., Pennbridge, J., & Swofford, A. (1991). A risk profile comparison of homeless youth involved in prostitution and homeless youth not involved. *Journal of Adolescent Health, 12,* 545–548.

Zemsky, B. (1991). Coming out against all odds: Resistance in the life of a young lesbian. *Women and Therapy, 11,* 185–200.

Zimring, F. (1998). *American youth violence.* New York: Oxford University Press.

Chapter 7

THE GENDERED NATURE OF RISK FACTORS FOR DELINQUENCY

JOANNE BELKNAP AND KRISTI HOLSINGER

O ne of the greatest limitations of existing criminological research is the low priority given to the role of gender in the etiology of offending. In 1982, Eileen Leonard wrote, "Despite the endless volumes written to account for it, sex, the most powerful variable regarding crime, has been virtually ignored" (p. xi). Early theories on delinquency and crime either fail to include girls (and women) or if included, theorize about them in sexist and stereotypical ways (Burman, Batchelor, & Brown, 2001). It is notable that mainstream criminology still tends to ignore the importance of gender and how events perceived as risks for offending, such as poor school and family experiences, may be gendered. The ramifications of the traditionally male-centered approaches to understanding delinquency not only involve ignorance about what causes girls' delinquency but also threaten the appropriateness of systemic intervention with and treatment responses to girls. Since the early 1990s, government agencies have increasingly called for "gender-specific" approaches in intervening with and treating delinquent girls. The purpose of this chapter is to merge what has been learned from applications of various theoretical approaches to understand how characteristics and experiences often associated with gender may or may not be gendered among a delinquent population. More specifically, this study is based on the most comprehensive data including girl and boy delinquents' childhood traumas. We surveyed 163 girls and 281 boys incarcerated in Ohio in 1998 about their family, school and peers, victimization, and mental health histories and experiences to examine how risk factors may be gendered and the implications for gender-specific services.

Source: Belknap, J., & Holsinger, K. (2006). The gendered nature of risk factors for delinquency. *Feminist Criminology, 1*(1), 48–71.

Authors' Note: The authors are listed alphabetically and contributed equally to this chapter. We thank the Office of Criminal Justice Services in Columbus, Ohio, for partial funding of this project, and Tony Flores and Jennifer Sutherland for help in data collection. We are also grateful to Janet Jacobs and Scott Menard at the University of Colorado for advice on this chapter. Any mistakes or shortcomings are those by the authors. Finally, we are in debt to the girls and boys who took the time and energy to complete our survey.

THEORETICAL PERSPECTIVES EXPLAINING DELINQUENCY

In 1979, Cernkovich and Giordano wrote, "The development of accurate theory continues to suffer because some scholars rush to print with the causes of delinquency before they know what it is they should be explaining" (p. 144). It is notable that "malestream" criminological theories have questionable applicability to girls' offending largely because they were developed to understand boys' delinquency and even then, almost always fail to explain the role of gender in boys' lives (e.g., masculinity). This work has a long legacy of affecting how girls' offending is both explained and officially processed. Three more recent perspectives (generalized strain theories [GSTs], the life-course perspective, and feminist pathways and cycle of violence theories), outlined in this section, were chosen, as each offers more promising avenues to accurately theorize about the etiology of crime and delinquency, how it may be gendered, and how responses to delinquent youth might be improved.

General Strain Theory (GST)

GST was designed to explain how frustration because of unequal legitimate access to culturally agreed-on goals is an important explanation for offending (e.g., Cohen, 1955; Merton, 1949). The focus was on economic strains, and the applications were almost exclusively on middle- and working-class boys. Faith (1993) critiqued this theory from a gender perspective, pointing out that relative to boys and men, girls and women commit far less crime and they "constitute the most impoverished group of every Western Society" (p. 107). GST has also been criticized for omitting some of the major strains in youths' lives, such as abuse, sexism, racism, and other traumas (Belknap, 2001).

Some scholars have argued that the gender gap in offending is best explained by Agnew's (1992) revised GST, which acknowledges a wider variety of strain sources and allows for diverse adaptations to strains (Broidy & Agnew, 1997; Hoffman & Su, 1997). Rather than a narrow focus on the failure of the lower class to achieve monetary success, GST outlines three major social-psychological sources of strain—the failure to achieve positively valued goals, the loss of positively valued stimuli, and the presentation of negative stimuli. Another compelling aspect of GST is that it allows individuals' goals to be varied based on gender, racial, and class differences (Broidy, 2001). Thus, strains can be examined as artifacts of a gendered society and allow for gendered socialization to shape both the strains experienced and individuals' responses to them. Broidy and Agnew (1997) concluded, among other findings, that girls are more likely than boys to be the targets of sexual, emotional, and physical abuse. Girls are more concerned than boys about establishing and maintaining close relationships, whereas boys are more strained than girls about external achievements, particularly material success. Although two studies find few gender differences regarding the impact of stressful life events on delinquency (Hoffman & Su, 1997; Mazerolle, 1998), it is remarkable that they do not include any measure of abuse victimization among the stressful life events. Sharp and her colleagues' (Sharp, Brewster, & Love, 2005; Sharp, Terling-Watt, Atkins, & Gilliam, 2001) tests of GST suggest a complex interaction of variables in understanding the gendered nature of delinquent (and deviant) responses to strain. A study of college students by Sharp et al. (2005) reports that although both women and men respond to strain by being angry, women are more likely than men to also respond to strain with additional, more internalized negative emotions, which might mediate their likelihood of subsequent delinquent behaviors. Sharp et al. suggested that this complex gendered difference in responding to strain potentially explains the gendered gap in offending.

The Life-Course Perspective

The life-course perspective examines human development and views problem behaviors as age associated because of patterns in developmental stages (Laub & Lauritsen, 1993; Loeber & Le Blanc, 1990; Sampson & Laub, 1990). This perspective advocates the need to study important transitions in an individual's life, as these transitions affect offending, and to identify causal factors that occur before and, thus, may influence behavioral development (Loeber & Le Blanc, 1990; Sampson & Laub, 1992). As noted by Pollock (1999) and Belknap (2001), however, the bulk of the life-course studies focus on males (e.g., Laub & Sampson, 1993; Loeber, 1996;

Moffitt, 1990, 1993; Nagin, Farrington, & Moffitt, 1995; Piquero, Brame, Mazerolle, & Haapanen, 2003; Piquero, MacDonald, & Parker, 2002; Stattin & Magnusson, 1991). One longitudinal study including girls that compares the separate and combined effects of parental psychiatric disorders and supportive parent-child communications finds that low parental support has a greater effect on boys' deviance than girls' (R. Johnson, Su, Gerstein, Shin, & Hoffman, 1995).

Feminist Pathways and Cycle of Violence Perspectives

Feminist research claims not only that to truly understand delinquency, the differences between girls' and boys' experiences and "realities" must be examined (Holsinger, 2000) but also that patriarchy must be central to the study of causes of delinquency (Daly & Chesney-Lind, 1988). Within this perspective, the variables leading to problem behavior may be attributed to a variety of sources—socialized gender roles, structural oppression, vulnerability to abuse from males, and female responses to male domination. In other words, girls' and boys' trajectories into delinquency may be partially gender specific— with gender differences in developmental processes, resulting problem behaviors, and social and official responses to troubling (and other) behaviors. Unlike the GST or life-course perspective, the feminist pathways approach to understanding the causes of illegal behavior emphasizes childhood abuses as significant risks for subsequent delinquency. Studies on delinquent girls and incarcerated women report abuse victimizations much higher than the general population of women and girls (e.g., Arnold, 1990; Browne, Miller, & Maguin, 1999; Chesney-Lind & Rodriguez, 1983; Daly, 1992; Gaarder & Belknap, 2002; Gilfus, 1992). Moreover, the research conducting gender comparisons of childhood abuse and neglect routinely reports abuse and neglect are more common, start earlier, and last longer for girls (e.g., Artz & Riecken, 1994; Chesney-Lind, 1989; Dembo, Williams, Wothke, Schmeidler, & Brown, 1992; McClellan, Farabee, & Crouch, 1997; Miller, Trapani, Fejes-Mendoza, Eggleston, & Dwiggins, 1995). Moreover, girls' *reactions* to abuse are relevant. For example, girls' running away from a sexually abusive home is often officially tagged as offending behavior (Gilfus, 1992).

Regarding mental health, a review of literature on adolescent female development reports that girls experience greater depression, more suicide attempts, and a decrease in self-concept, whereas boys report improved self-concept and self-esteem (Miller et al., 1995). The delinquent girls interviewed in one study reported very few, if any, positive attributes associated with being female, accepting as inevitable the routine sex discrimination, lack of respect, sexual double standards, sexual harassment, and abuse they experienced (Artz, 1998). Although these girls described themselves as "tough," they conveyed a strong sense of personal worthlessness that they hoped to change through male approval (i.e., in their relationships with boys and men).

Consistent with the feminist pathways research is Cathy Spatz Widom and her colleagues' work on the cycle of violence. Widom (1989) and Rivera and Widom (1990) compared subsequent delinquency and adult offending histories of individuals with and without formal records of childhood abuse and neglect victimizations. Overall, childhood victimizations, including neglect, placed individuals at risk for both delinquency and adult offending (Widom, 1989). It is notable that abused and neglected girls were more likely than non–abused/neglected girls for violent delinquency offense arrests, whereas abused and neglected boys were no more likely to have violent delinquency offense arrests than non–abused/neglected boys (Rivera & Widom, 1990).

METHOD

As part of the Office of Juvenile Justice and Delinquency Prevention Act of 1992 to assess the gender-specific needs of girls, the authors conducted two phases of research in Ohio. Phase I was a statewide focus group study of girls and professionals who work with them (Belknap, Holsinger, & Dunn, 1997). Phase II, the source of the data for this chapter, was a survey of incarcerated girls and boys. The primary goal of this study was to broaden the scope of youthful risks hypothesized in both mainstream and feminist criminology to increase the likelihood of delinquent behavior and determine whether these risk factors were gendered among delinquent youth. Unlike the vast majority of tests of GST, life-course, and feminist pathways perspectives, which include only one sex in the sample, or the cycle of violence studies that rely on officially reported childhood victimizations, this study included both girls and boys and drew on *self-reported* childhood abuses (a more valid measure than official reports), as well as the youths' reports on their families, schools, and mental health.

Sample

In Ohio, institutionalized delinquent girls are held in 1 of 2 Department of Youth Services (DYS) girls' facilities (the majority in Scioto Village and a small population in The Freedom Center). All the girls housed in these 2 institutions were included in the sample ($n = 163$) and all completed usable surveys. Adjudicated delinquent boys are held in 1 of 10 DYS boys' facilities. Given the lack of feasibility in surveying all the boys, the Department of Research in DYS drew a random sample of 350 boys from the most recent list of admissions for DYS institutions. Of the boys randomly selected, 83% were provided with the opportunity to take the survey, and 89% of these were completed and usable. Results are based on 281 surveys completed by incarcerated boys (or 80% of those sampled) and 163 girls (100% response rate).

Measurement Instrument and Data Collection

Unlike much of the research on delinquent youth drawn from official reports, this was a "youth-centered" design (see Morrill, Yalda, Adelman, Musheno, & Bejarano, 2000), permitting the youth to directly report their own experiences (and pilot-tested on youth who gave their feedback). The 15-page measurement instrument was the result of what was learned in the focus groups in Phase I and an extensive review of research on delinquency etiology, processing, and treatment. We used the qualitative data gleaned from the focus groups to make survey items. For example, in our focus groups, the girls reported many childhood traumas as life events leading to their delinquent behavior that were not in the literature (e.g., a parent's death, abandonment by a parent, and witnessing abuse). The self-esteem items were adopted from Rosenberg (1989).[1]

A release form was used to verify voluntary participation from the youth and to convey the goals of the survey, assuring them of confidentiality and anonymity. The youth were informed that the survey would require approximately 60 minutes to complete. The cooperation of the youth was impressive, particularly given the survey length. Notably, the boys had more questions, required more assistance, and took longer to complete the survey than the girls, whereas the girls were more likely than the boys to seem to "enjoy" taking the survey and thank the research staff for conducting the study. (Typically, the girls took about 45 minutes and the boys took close to 90 minutes to complete the survey.) Finally, we structured the data collection so that youth who did not want to take the survey could sit and "doodle" on their surveys while the rest of the youth completed them, and everyone was given their own blank manila envelope to put the surveys in when they were completed. These were collected directly by the research staff (no institutional staff members were involved in data collection). Thus, we believe the environment was one in which it was safe for youth to write honest answers, including self-disclosure about abuse, family, school and peer, mental health, and offending histories.

Limitations

The major shortcoming of this study is that there is no comparison between delinquent and nondelinquent youth—we sampled only institutionalized delinquents. The state would not allow us a comparison group of nondelinquents. However, given the frequent assumptions that boys' primary childhood stressors are economic in nature and that girls and boys have unique stressors, these data allow for the much-needed examination of the gendered nature of childhood experiences with family, abuse, school and peer, and mental health *among delinquent youth*. This approach is also valid for examining the gender-specific needs of delinquent youth.

Another concern is temporal order. Given that these data were not collected prospectively, it is difficult to tell the sequencing of events. For example, did the abuse precede or follow the delinquency? This is why we directly asked the youth if they believe their abuse was related to their subsequent delinquency. Another concern is whether the youth told the truth, particularly about victimization. In this regard, we believe the data collection method (as described above) allowed a safe environment to complete the survey anonymously and confidentially. Finally, we did not have reliable scale items for many of our items, given that we were basing a significant portion of the survey items on the qualitative findings from our focus groups and the qualitative interview research from incarcerated women.

FINDINGS

The findings are divided into five sections. The first section describes the sample and the following four reflect areas identified by theories as potentially influential to gender and delinquency: abuse victimization, family, self-esteem/mental health, and school experiences. Tables 7.1 through 7.5 report (bivariate) gender comparisons. In addition, to account for whether the gender effects were "direct" or changed when controlling for race, age, and sexual identity, multivariate logistic regression analyses were conducted. The appendix presents the 10 cases where the gender became nonsignificant when controlling for race, age, and sexual identity, as well as the 2 cases where gender went from being nonsignificant to significant when controlling for these variables.

Demographic Characteristics

The sample, reported in Table 7.1, was almost half White (46%) and about two fifths (41%) African American, with the remaining 13% of the sample describing themselves as Native American, Latino/a, Puerto Rican, Spanish, Asian American, South African, or Biracial. Although youth of color are disproportionately represented in this sample of incarcerated youth by a large margin, there were no significant *gender* differences in the racial representation in the sample. The sample ranged in age from 12 to 20 years old with a mean age of 16.35 years. Girls, however, were significantly younger than the boys; approximately one third of the girls and one fifth of the boys were 15 years old or younger ($t = 4.77$, $p \le .001$). This is consistent with a significant amount of research claiming younger girls receive harsher sentences because of the paternalistic nature of the courts (Belknap, 2001).

The life-course perspective purports that adolescent development and transitions are crucial to identify to understand youth behaviors. The

existing empirical applications of life-course, GST, and cycle of violence approaches never mention sexual identity, and when addressed in the pathways research, it is done so only in passing. C. Johnson and K. Johnson's (2000) careful review of high-risk behaviors among lesbian/gay adolescents provides compelling arguments for including sexual identity in research on delinquency. They emphasized the isolation from family, peers, and mainstream culture often experienced by youth coming to terms with a lesbian/gay identity. Moreover, lesbian, gay, and bisexual youth appear to be at an increased risk of sexual and physical abuse compared to their straight counterparts (D'Augelli & Dark, 1994). In the current study, there were strong significant differences between girls and boys regarding self-reported sexual identity (see Table 7.1). Heterosexual identities were reported by 95% of the boys and 73% of the girls. Girls (22.4%) were 6 times as likely as boys (3.6%) to identify as bisexual and 3 times (4.6%) as likely as boys (1.6%) to identify as lesbian/gay ($\chi^2 = 39.85$, $p \le .001$). With these data, it is difficult to determine whether boys are less likely to report gay or bisexual identities or if it is an identity that places girls, but not boys, at increased risk of marginalization and delinquency. Perhaps lesbian and bisexual girls are more stigmatized as "masculine" and, thus, "delinquent" (Robson, 1992) relative to their gay and bisexual male counterparts and heterosexual female counterparts.

Finally, Table 7.1 reports on the intimate/romantic relationship status, children, and pregnancies as reported by the youth. Although girls and boys were indistinguishable in terms of relationship status (whether they were single, dating, or married), girls were significantly more likely to be involved with partners older than themselves compared to boys (not reported in the tables). The extent to which relationships with older boys (and in some cases, men) should also be examined as a gendered pathway for girls' involvement in crime and delinquency needs to be addressed in future research. Boys reported themselves as the father to more children than girls reported giving birth to, but girls, not surprisingly given society's gender roles, reported more actual parenting/custody than the boys. The girls were asked to report on their pregnancy histories. Almost two thirds (64.5%) had never been pregnant, one fifth (20.9%) had been pregnant once, almost one tenth (8.9%)

Table 7.1 Youths' Demographic Characteristics

Variable	n	Girls Percentage	Girls (n)	Boys Percentage	Boys (n)	Total Percentage	Total (n)	Test Statistic
Sex	444	36.7	(163)	63.3	(281)			3.05
Race	441							
African American		36.2	(59)	43.9	(122)	41.0	(181)	
White		47.9	(78)	44.2	(123)	45.6	(201)	
Other[a]		16.0	(26)	11.9	(33)	13.4	(59)	
Age[b]	444							4.77***
12 to 13		6.1	(10)	1.8	(5)	3.4	(15)	
14 to 15		26.4	(43)	17.8	(50)	20.9	(93)	
16 to 17		55.2	(90)	57.7	(162)	56.8	(252)	
18 to 20		12.3	(20)	22.8	(64)	18.9	(84)	
Sexual identity	404							39.85***
Heterosexual		73.0	(111)	94.8	(239)	86.6	(350)	
Lesbian/gay		4.6	(7)	1.6	(4)	2.7	(11)	
Bisexual		22.4	(34)	3.6	(9)	10.6	(43)	
Relationship status	436							4.57
Single		20.4	(33)	20.8	(57)	20.6	(90)	
Boy/girlfriend		74.1	(120)	77.4	(332)	76.1	(332)	
Married/common-law		5.6	(9)	1.8	(5)	3.2	(14)	
Children	412							12.78***
Yes		13.8	(22)	29.0	(73)	23.1	(95)	
No		86.3	(138)	71.0	(179)	76.9	(317)	
Pregnancy history[c]	158							
Never		64.5	(102)					
Once		20.9	(33)					
Twice		8.9	(14)					
Three or more		5.7	(9)					

Note: Chi-square tests were used for all variables except age, in which case a *t* test was used.

a. This category includes Native American, Latino/a, Puerto Rican, Spanish, Asian, South African, and Biracial.

b. The girls' mean age was 15.94, and the boys' mean age was 16.59 years old.

c. This question was asked only of the girls. Of the 158 girls who reported a pregnancy, 27.8% (*n* = 44) reported experiencing a miscarriage and 5.7% (*n* = 9) reported having an abortion.

***p ≤ .001.

had been pregnant twice, and about one twentieth (5.7%) had been pregnant three or more times. Of the girls who reported a pregnancy, more than one quarter (27.8%) reported experiencing a miscarriage and about one twentieth (5.7%) reported having an abortion.

Abuse Histories

Table 7.2 summarizes the direct effects of gender on self-reported abuse victimizations. There are two overwhelming patterns in this table. First, for virtually every abuse variable, girls reported experiencing significantly greater amounts of abuse. Second, although lower, boys' rates of reported abuse are still extremely high. Regarding verbal abuse, two thirds of girls and more than half of the boys reported experiencing verbal abuse from a family member ($\chi^2 = 5.60, p \leq .05$). More than half the girls and one third of the boys reported verbal abuse from someone outside of the family ($\chi^2 = 20.83, p \leq .001$). Physical abuse included a wide range of behaviors: spanking or slapping, pushing or grabbing, having something thrown at you, kicking or hitting, beating, choking, burning, or having weapons used or threatened to be used against you. Three quarters of the girls and almost two thirds of the boys reported physical abuse perpetrated by a family member ($\chi^2 = 6.23, p \leq .05$). Two thirds of the girls and more than one third of the boys reported physical abuse by a non–family member ($\chi^2 = 34.20, p \leq .001$). More than three fifths of the girls and more than two fifths of the boys reported physical abuse repeated with time ($\chi^2 = 14.45, p \leq .001$).

"Unwanted sexual contact" was used to measure all types of sexual abuse that involved physical contact. Almost three fifths of the girls and almost one fifth of the boys reported sexual abuse by anyone (family or non–family member; $\chi^2 = 75.73, p \leq .001$). Close to one quarter of the girls and about 1 in 12 boys reported sexual abuse by a family member ($\chi^2 = 17.45, p \leq .001$). More than half of the girls and about 1 in 7 boys reported sexual abuse from a non–family member ($\chi^2 = 77.10, p \leq .001$). Close to half of the girls and about 1 in 7 boys reported sexual abuse that was repeated with time ($\chi^2 = 42.70, p \leq .001$). Regarding the number of sexual abusers, almost half of the girls and about one sixth of the boys reported one or two different sexual abusers. Almost one eighth of the girls and about 3% of the boys reported having three or more different sexual abusers ($t = -8.55$,

$p \leq .001$). Stated alternatively regarding the sexual abuse data, of the almost three fifths of the girls who reported any sexual abuse, almost two fifths experienced sexual abuse by a family member, about nine tenths experienced sexual abuse perpetrated by a non–family member, and many of these girls had more than one abuser. In a similar manner, of the almost one fifth of boys who reported any sexual abuse, almost half reported family member–perpetrated sexual abuse and three quarters reported sexual abuse from a non–family member.

Habermas and Bluck (2000) reported that most adolescents are adept at assessing the causal ordering of important events in their lives. In the focus groups of Phase I, we asked the girls whether they could identify events that "caused" or led to their offenses. Many of the girls reported abusive and other traumatic experiences. When probed further, they explained an understanding of the sequencing or causal nature of the trauma-to-offending link. Although a fair amount of research indicates a high correlation between female delinquency and a history of physical and sexual abuse, research comparing males and females on the link between abuse and subsequent delinquency is underdeveloped. To our knowledge, no one has asked this question of youth in previous quantitative research, but given the pathways research suggestions of this link and the manner it was verbalized in our focus groups, we included this item on the survey. When asked about whether they viewed the abuses they experienced as leading to their trouble with offending, more than half of the girls and two fifths of the boys believed their victimizations had influenced their subsequent offending ($\chi^2 = 13.05, p \leq .001$; see Table 7.2).

Turning to a rarely asked form of abuse, the youth were asked if they had *witnessed* any family members being verbally, physically, or sexually abused by another family member. Half of the girls and more than two fifths of the boys witnessed verbal abuse ($\chi^2 = 7.93, p \leq .01$), half of the girls and almost one third of the boys witnessed physical abuse ($\chi^2 = 15.04, p \leq .001$), and girls (12%) were twice as likely as boys (6%) to report witnessing someone else's sexual abuse ($\chi^2 = 5.23, p \leq .05$).

When controlling for race, age, and sexual identity, four of the gender differences in abuse victimizations became nonsignificant: verbal and physical abuse from family and witnessing verbal and physical abuse (see the appendix).

| Table 7.2 | Delinquent Youths' Abuse History |

Variable	n	Girls		Boys		Total		Test Statistic
		Percentage	(n)	Percentage	(n)	Percentage	(n)	
Verbal abuse from family[a]	444	66.3	(154)	54.8	(262)	59.0	(262)	5.60*
Verbal abuse from others[b]	444	55.2	(90)	33.1	(93)	41.2	(183)	20.83***
Physical abuse from family	444	74.8	(122)	63.3	(178)	67.6	(300)	6.23*
Physical abuse from others	444	65.0	(106)	36.3	(102)	46.8	(208)	34.20***
Physical abuse repeated with time	379	62.9	(101)	42.8	(101)	50.4	(191)	14.45***
Sexual abuse from anyone[c]	444	58.9	(96)	18.5	(52)	33.3	(148)	75.73***
Sexual abuse from a family member	444	22.7	(37)	8.5	(24)	13.7	(61)	17.45***
Sexual abuse from others	444	52.8	(86)	13.9	(39)	28.2	(125)	77.10***
Sexual abuse repeated with time	343	45.8	(65)	13.9	(28)	27.1	(93)	42.70***
Total number of sexual abusers[d]	444							−8.55***
None		41.1	(67)	81.5	(229)	66.7	(296)	
1 to 2		47.2	(77)	16.0	(45)	27.5	(122)	
3+		11.7	(19)	2.5	(7)	5.8	(26)	
Abuse led to getting in trouble	310	55.8	(78)	40.1	(73)	48.7	(151)	13.05***
Witnessed verbal abuse	444	49.1	(91)	42.0	(118)	47.1	(209)	7.93**
Witnessed physical abuse	444	49.1	(80)	30.6	(86)	37.4	(166)	15.04***
Witnessed sexual abuse	444	12.3	(20)	6.0	(17)	8.3	(37)	5.23*

a. This category includes father, stepfather, mother, stepmother, brother, or sister.

b. This category includes boyfriend, girlfriend, spouse, friend, stranger, or anyone else.

c. This category includes sexual abuse from family or others.

d. Where interval-level data are used and means are reported, significance is based on t tests. The mean number of sexual abusers for girls was 1.14 and for boys was 0.29.

*$p \le .05$. **$p \le .01$. ***$p \le .001$.

However, physical abuse from family remained borderline significant for gender ($p \le .054$). In the case of witnessing sexual abuse, none of the independent variables were significantly related. For the remaining variables, race was significant: White youth were more likely than youth of color to report experiencing family verbal abuse, family physical abuse, and witnessing family verbal abuse.

Relationships With Parents and Family History

All of the theoretical perspectives included in this chapter suggest youths' experiences with their parents/guardians and family are important in examining delinquency risks. It is notable that more than 10% of the sample reported that at least one of their parents had died, about two thirds reported that at least one parent had been incarcerated, and about 7% reported a parent institutionalized in a mental hospital. Although there were no gender differences in these variables (a deceased parent, an incarcerated parent, and a parent in a mental hospital), girls (56%) were significantly more likely than boys (45%) to report desertion or abandonment by a parent ($\chi^2 = 11.33$, $p \le .001$). In some ways this may be more troubling to a child than a parent who dies or is incarcerated or institutionalized in a mental hospital, because the deserting parent is choosing to not be with her or his child. It also suggests that parenting daughters is viewed as less important, less of a responsibility, than parenting sons. In support of this interpretation, studies find that sons provide greater marital stability than daughters as fathers may be more involved and invested in their sons' (than daughters') lives (Dahl & Moretti, 2003; Morgan, Lye, & Condran, 1988).

There were no gender differences when the youth were asked whether they were raised by at least one of their parents; almost nine tenths of the youth reported this (see Table 7.3). When asked to report people other than parents who had helped raise them, girls (47%) were more likely than boys (36%) to report that others had participated in raising them. There were no significant differences in girls' (15%) and boys' (19%) reports that they were the first person in their family incarcerated. However, girls (14%) were significantly more likely than boys (9%) to report that they would rather be living in the delinquent institution than living at home ($\chi^2 = 8.68$, $p \le .01$). This suggests worse home experiences for delinquent girls relative to delinquent boys, as suggested in previous research (e.g., Moore, 1999), or even that girls could commit offenses as a means to be taken out of their homes.

Two items were asked to assess general relationships with fathers and mothers. There were no gender differences in reports on the youths' general relationships with their fathers, with about one quarter of both boys and girls reporting they did not have a relationship and another one quarter of both boys and girls reporting the relationship with their father was "great." About 13% of both girls and boys reported "poor" relationships with their fathers, and almost 3 in 10 reported their relationships with their fathers were "OK." On the other hand, these delinquent youth reported gendered evaluations of their general relationships with their mothers. Boys and girls did not differ much in the frequency of reporting relationships with their mothers as

"poor" or nonexistent, but boys (59%) were more likely than girls (41%) to describe the maternal relationship as "great" ($\chi^2 = 12.55$, $p \le .01$).

When multivariate analyses were conducted, the only family variables where previously gendered relationships became nonsignificant were for whether the youth was raised by others and the individual's relationship with her or his mother (see the appendix). In the multivariate analysis, none of the independent variables (gender, race, age, and sexual identity) were significantly related to whether the youth was raised by others. It is notable that lesbian/gay/bisexual youth reported worse relationships with their mothers than straight youth ($p \le .01$).

Mental Health and Self-Esteem Histories

Table 7.4 presents a summary of the items on mental health and self-esteem variables, areas of frequent gender differences in research on youth. In all four measures of mental health, girls reported a significantly higher likelihood of mental health problems. Girls (54%) were more likely than boys (46%) to report purposefully hurting or harming themselves ($\chi^2 = 19.55$, $p \le .001$). When asked to elaborate on how they hurt themselves, girls (43%) were more than twice as likely as boys (19%) to indicate that they had cut or burned their bodies ($\chi^2 = 30.92$, $p \le .001$). Finally, not only were girls (52%) more likely than boys (28.5%) to report thinking about committing suicide (suicide ideation; $\chi^2 = 22.34$, $p \le .001$) but also girls (46%) were more than twice as likely as boys (19%) to report that they had tried committing suicide ($\chi^2 = 31.19$, $p \le .001$).

The measures of self-esteem included 10 statements written with Likert-type responses, 4 of which indicated no gender differences (see Table 7.4). The youth were very likely to agree with positive self-esteem statements about "having good qualities" (93%), "doing things as well as most people" (90%), "feeling OK about myself" (87%), being "a person of worth" (86%), and being "satisfied with myself" (77%). Yet a sizeable majority of the youth also agreed with the negative self-esteem statement "I wish I could have more self-respect" (62%), almost half (45%) agreed that they "felt useless at times," and more than one third (35%) reported "at times, I think I am no good at all." Almost one quarter (23%) agreed with the statement "I do not have much to be proud of" and 15% agreed with the statement "I am a failure."

| Table 7.3 | Youths' Parent and Family History |

Variable	n	Girls Percentage	(n)	Boys Percentage	(n)	Total Percentage	(n)	Test Statistic
Deserted by a parent	411	55.7	(83)	38.2	(100)	44.5	(183)	11.83***
Parent in a mental hospital	436	7.5	(12)	6.5	(18)	6.9	(30)	0.15
Death of a parent	444	12.3	(20)	10.3	(29)	11.0	(49)	0.40
Raised by parents[a]	437	86.4	(247)	89.8	(247)	88.6	(387)	1.16
Raised by others[b]	437	46.9	(76)	30.2	(83)	36.4	(159)	12.33***
Rather be here than at home	438	14.1	(23)	5.8	(16)	8.9	(39)	8.68**
First person in family incarcerated	425	15.7	(25)	21.8	(58)	19.5	(83)	2.34
Parent incarcerated	425	69.2	(110)	62.4	(166)	64.9	(276)	2.01
Relationship with dad	427							4.89
Don't have one		25.5	(41)	30.1	(80)	28.3	(121)	
Poor		16.1	(26)	11.7	(31)	13.3	(57)	
OK		32.9	(53)	26.7	(71)	29.0	(124)	
Great		25.5	(41)	31.6	(84)	29.3	(125)	
Relationship with mom	429							12.55**
Don't have one		9.4	(15)	7.1	(19)	7.9	(34)	
Poor		6.9	(11)	5.6	(15)	6.1	(26)	
OK		42.5	(68)	28.6	(77)	33.8	(145)	
Great		41.3	(66)	58.7	(158)	52.2	(224)	

a. Youth being raised by parents includes youth being raised by at least one parent or their mother and father living together.

b. This category includes all others that were reported as raising the respondent. The most frequently mentioned others were grandparents, siblings, aunts, uncles, foster parents, and group homes. **$p \leq .01$. ***$p \leq .001$.

With the exception of the fairly moderate self-esteem question about feeling "OK about myself," all the gender differences in reported self-esteem had to do with endorsement of the negative self-esteem items. Thus, there were no significant gender differences for any of the statements about high self-esteem, which were highly endorsed by all youth (ranging from 77% to 99% agreement). However, for the one "mediocre" self-esteem item, "I feel OK about myself," boys (89%) were more likely than girls (81.5%) to agree ($\chi^2 = 5.84$, $p \leq .05$), and for all of the low self-esteem statements, the girls were significantly more likely to agree with these than the boys. More specific, girls were more likely than

boys to agree with the items "I wish I could have more self-respect" (72% of girls and 56% of boys, $\chi^2 = 11.00$, $p \leq .001$), "I feel useless at times" (51% of girls and 41% of boys, $\chi^2 = 4.22$, $p \leq .05$), "at times, I think I'm no good at all" (45% of girls and 29% of boys, $\chi^2 = 11.94$, $p \leq .001$), and "I am a failure" (21% of girls and 12% of boys, $\chi^2 = 5.93$, $p \leq .05$).

Regarding the multivariate analyses, when gender, race, age, and sexual identity were controlled, the effect of gender became nonsignificant in two analyses on self-esteem. Although gender was no longer a predictor of "not much to be proud of" and "feel useless at times," sexual identity was related to both, and in both cases lesbian/gay/bisexual

Table 7.4	Youths' Mental Health and Self-Esteem

Variable	n	Girls		Boys		Total		Test Statistic
		Percentage	(n)	Percentage	(n)	Percentage	(n)	
Mental health								
Purposely harmed self	425	54.1	(86)	32.3	(86)	40.5	(172)	19.55**
Cut or burned self	444	42.9	(70)	18.5	(52)	27.5	(122)	30.92***
Thought about suicide	428	51.9	(82)	28.5	(77)	37.1	(159)	23.34***
Tried suicide	428	46.3	(74)	19.0	(51)	29.1	(125)	31.19***
Self-esteem[a]								
I am a person of worth	435	84.0	(136)	87.2	(238)	86.0	(374)	0.88
I have good qualities	440	90.2	(147)	94.9	(263)	93.2	(410)	3.66
I do things as well as most people	443	88.3	(144)	91.1	(255)	90.1	(399)	0.86
I am satisfied with myself	431	72.2	(117)	79.6	(214)	76.8	(331)	3.05
I am a failure	439	21.0	(34)	12.3	(34)	15.5	(68)	5.93*
I do not have much to be proud of	440	28.4	(46)	20.1	(56)	23.2	(102)	3.91*
I feel OK about myself	441	81.5	(132)	89.6	(250)	86.6	(382)	5.84*
I wish I could have more self-respect	437	71.8	(117)	55.8	(153)	61.8	(270)	11.00***
I feel useless at times	435	51.3	(82)	41.1	(113)	44.8	(195)	4.22*
At times, I think I am no good at all	438	45.4	(74)	29.1	(80)	35.2	(154)	11.94***

a. This is the percentage of the sample who *agree* or *strongly agree* with this statement. Respondents could also mark *disagree* or *strongly disagree*. *$p \leq .05$. **$p \leq .01$. ***$p \leq .001$.

youth were more likely to report agreeing with these negative self-esteems ($p \leq .01$ in both cases). In addition, race was related to reports of feeling useless, with White youth more likely to report agreeing with this item ($p \leq .001$).

School and Peer Experiences

The life-course perspective emphasizes school experiences and delinquency as potentially influencing each other (e.g., Laub & Lauritsen, 1993), and some of the feminist pathways research interviewing incarcerated women reports extremely alienating childhood school experiences as risk factors for offending (e.g., Arnold, 1990; Gilfus, 1992). Other scholars have noted the

potential or real significance of peer relationships regarding youths' risks of offending; some in terms of the life course (e.g., Laub & Lauritsen, 1993) and some addressing whether, and perhaps how, peer relationships and their effects on offending might be gendered (e.g., Bottcher, 2001; Heimer & DeCoster, 1999; Messerschmidt, 2000; Nagasawa, Qian, & Wong, 2000). In the current study, there were few gender differences in youths' self-reported school experiences and no differences in their self-reported peer experiences (see Table 7.5). Evaluations of the overall educational experience were quite positive and not gendered. More than half the sample (54%) reported the school experience as "good," one third (34%) as "adequate," and about one eighth (12%) as "poor."

There were also no gender differences in the (high) rates in which they reported getting in trouble at school (almost half reported "usually" or "always" getting in trouble) or in their reports of being suspended (24%), expelled (22%), or repeating a grade (66%). Regarding the youths' self-reported peer experiences, there were no gender differences, with 93% of youth reporting friends use alcohol and or drugs, 84% reporting friends are involved in crime, 67% reporting that friends stay out of trouble, and 24% reporting they are currently gang members (see Table 7.5).

The only significant gender differences in the youths' reports of their school and peer experiences are related to whether and why they dropped out of or quit school. Girls (41%) were significantly more likely than boys (31%) to report ever dropping out of or quitting school ($\chi^2 = 4.35$, $p \leq .05$). Girls were more than twice as likely as boys to report they dropped out of or quit school because they "could not keep up" at school (42% of girls and 19% of boys, $\chi^2 = 9.32$, $p \leq .01$) and because they had "left home" (48% of girls and 23% of boys, $\chi^2 = 11.80$, $p \leq .001$). These findings are notable for a number of reasons, including research indicating the devaluing of girls' education and the high rates of girls running away from home because of sexual abuse. In addition, in this study, girls were more than 3 times as likely as boys to report that they dropped out of or quit school because "no one cared if I learned or attended" (12% of girls and 3% of boys, $\chi^2 = 4.20$, $p \leq .05$) and "nobody liked me at school" (12% of girls and 3% of boys, $\chi^2 = 4.20$, $p \leq .05$).

Without accounting for gender differences, the top four reasons youth reported for dropping out of school were "trouble with the law" (67%), "I left home" (33%), "I could not keep up at school" (29%), and "conflict with teachers" (25%). That "trouble with the law" is by far the most frequently given reason by both boys and girls for quitting or dropping out of school is consistent with the life-course perspective, which contends that schools are major institutions in children's lives (see Farrington, 1994), that a child being expelled or skipping school affects delinquency, and that delinquency can affect going to school. Some of the less commonly reported reasons for dropping out of or quitting school, in order of frequency, which were not gendered, were "family moved a lot" (9%), "pregnancy-related reasons" (for boys because their girlfriends were pregnant) (8%), "I had to

work to help my family earn money" (7%), "transportation problems" (3%), and "health problems" (2%). It is interesting that there were no significant differences between boys' and girls' rates of listing pregnancy as a reason for dropping out of or quitting school.

Although gender became nonsignificant for two reasons listed for leaving school (no one cared and nobody liked me) when race, age, and sexual identity were controlled, two reasons not gendered in the direct (bivariate) analyses became gendered. More specific, there were no direct gender effects in reporting leaving school because of pregnancy or trouble with the law until race, age, and sexual identity were controlled: In the multivariate analyses, girls were more likely than boys to report leaving school because of a pregnancy and because of trouble with the law ($p \leq .01$ in both cases). Age was also related to both of these reasons, and in both cases older youth were more likely to report leaving because of pregnancies and because of trouble with the law ($p \leq .01$ in both cases). Given that the peer variables were never significantly gendered (as reported in Table 7.5) and that when the peer variables were added to the multivariate logistic regressions they were never gendered, they were not included in the final multivariate analyses presented in the appendix. Perhaps that peer variables were never gendered is consistent with Bottcher's (2001) claim that youths' daily activities are all manifestations of male dominance. For example, Bottcher found "that high-risk families usher boys out of their homes and into crime. Conversely, the most troubled of these families almost force girls out" (p. 922). One could speculate that although girls' and boys' self-reports of peer experiences are not gendered in terms of rates, boys' peer experiences are more likely than girls' peer experiences to result in the type of offending more likely to "land" them in a delinquent institution.

DISCUSSION

This study highlights the need to broaden the identification and inclusion of strains in youths' lives that may be linked to delinquency. The findings are important for not only theory but also prevention of and responses to delinquency. Furthermore, the findings reported herein attest

Table 7.5	Youths' School and Peer Experiences

Variable	n	Girls		Boys		Total		Test Statistic
		Percentage	(n)	Percentage	(n)	Percentage	(n)	
Educational experience	442							0.18
Poor		12.9	(21)	12.2	(34)	12.4	(55)	
Adequate		32.5	(53)	34.4	(96)	33.7	(149)	
Good		54.6	(89)	53.4	(149)	53.8	(238)	
Got in trouble at school	444							1.21
Never		9.8	(16)	8.9	(25)	9.2	(41)	
Sometimes		42.3	(69)	45.6	(128)	44.4	(197)	
Usually		22.1	(36)	23.8	(67)	23.2	(103)	
Always		25.8	(42)	21.7	(61)	23.2	(103)	
Ever suspended	389	27.8	(52)	21.8	(52)	24.2	(94)	1.79
Ever expelled	389	25.2	(38)	20.2	(48)	22.1	(86)	1.34
Repeated a grade	429	63.9	(101)	67.2	(182)	66.0	(283)	0.47
Ever dropped out or quit	444	41.1	(67)	31.3	(88)	34.9	(155)	4.35*
Reasons dropped out or quit[a]	155							
Pregnancy-related reason		9.0	(6)	6.8	(6)	7.7	(12)	0.24
Trouble with the law		71.6	(48)	63.6	(56)	67.1	(104)	1.10
Could not keep up at school		41.8	(28)	19.3	(17)	29.0	(45)	9.32**
Family moved a lot		7.5	(5)	10.2	(9)	9.0	(14)	0.35
I left home		47.8	(32)	21.6	(19)	32.9	(51)	11.80***
Conflict with teachers		23.9	(16)	25.0	(22)	24.5	(38)	0.03
No one cared if I learned or attended		11.9	(8)	3.4	(3)	7.1	(11)	4.20*
Nobody liked me at school		11.9	(8)	3.4	(3)	7.1	(11)	4.20*
I had to work to help my family earn money		6.0	(4)	8.0	(7)	7.1	(11)	0.23
Transportation problems		4.5	(3)	1.1	(1)	2.6	(4)	1.69
Health problems		1.5	(1)	2.3	(2)	1.9	(3)	0.12
Peer variables								
Friends use drugs/alcohol	431	93.7	(149)	93.0	(253)	93.3	(402)	0.08
Friends involved in crime	430	81.1	(129)	85.6	(232)	84.0	(361)	1.49
Friends stay out of trouble	429	62.9	(100)	69.6	(188)	67.1	(288)	2.06
Currently a gang member	427	22.6	(35)	24.6	(67)	23.9	(102)	0.23

a. These analyses were conducted only on the 155 youths who reported dropping out of or quitting school. Respondents were to report as many/all reasons they dropped out of school; thus an individual could report more than one reason and the reasons do not total 100.0%. *$p \leq .05$. **$p \leq .01$. ***$p \leq .001$.

to not only important gender issues but also how gender intersects with race, sexual identity, and sometimes age to explain delinquency risk factors. The most overwhelming patterns reported in these data concern abuse victimization. Although girls reported higher rates of abuse victimization, boys' reported rates were also alarmingly high. Moreover, almost half of the youth believed the abuse was related to their subsequent delinquency, and girls were significantly more likely than boys to report this. Prior to controlling for race, age, and sexual identity, girls reported higher rates of all abuses than boys. The gender differences were particularly strong for the items measuring sexual abuse.

There are four implications of the abuse victimization findings. First, mainstream theories should incorporate what has been learned from feminist pathways theory in assessing the role of abuse events as delinquency risks for both girls and boys. More specifically, the pathways approach to delinquency risk factors appears to provide the most support for determining not only girls' risks but also boys' risks. Unlike the GST and life-course approaches, the pathways approach specifically advances the need to identify childhood traumas as precursors to delinquency (and adult offending). These findings emphasize the need to expand our definitions of childhood traumas (e.g., broadening definitions of abuse victimization, including desertion by a parent, a parent in a mental hospital) not only for girls but for boys as well. In sum, the findings from this study are more consistent with the pathways approach than the GST or life-course approaches as they are currently articulated and most commonly tested.

The second implication from the victimization findings is that improved intervention responses to abused children (girls and boys) are not only the morally appropriate actions but also crucial in deterring delinquency. Sadly, the devaluation of the lives of both juvenile delinquents and nondelinquent abused children from more economically disadvantaged homes appears to have become status quo in the United States. The ramifications of underfunded or nonexistent governmental programs means not only a serious threat to children's well-being but also the likelihood of an increase in delinquency.

In a similar manner, the third implication from the high victimization findings among these delinquent youth is that abuse treatment programs must be high in quality and availability in both girls' and boys' delinquency facilities. Thus, although the second implication reported better intervention for childhood abuses prior to delinquency, we must also attend to better programming for youth already caught up in the system. This provides the most promise for these youth to lead nonoffending lives when leaving the institutions.

Finally, the victimization findings emphasize the importance of accounting for intersecting oppressions and identities when assessing gender differences. In this study, when the combined impacts of gender, race, age, and sexual identity were examined, race appeared to mediate the impact of gender for experiencing verbal abuse, physical abuse, and witnessing verbal abuse in delinquent youths' families: These three abuses were all more common in White than other homes.

The other set of variables, which were most consistently gendered, included those measuring mental health in terms of harming oneself. Girls always reported higher levels than boys of physically harming themselves and contemplating and attempting suicide. Five of the nine items measuring the youths' self-esteem were also gendered, with girls reporting lower self-esteem on all five. However, in the two cases where gender became nonsignificant when controlling for other demographic characteristics, a lesbian/gay/bisexual identity became the predominant predictor of low self-esteem (feeling useless and having nothing to be proud of). Thus, although the literature on gender-specific programming for delinquent girls frequently addresses low self-esteem as a girl problem, we found that aspects of self-esteem are also prevalent among boys and are particularly acute for lesbian/gay/bisexual youth. Research and programs must address and understand why and how these variables are gendered and related to sexual identity. For example, delinquent girls' self-esteem programs might need to be quite different than those for delinquent boys, and both should include a healthy and nonheterosexist approach to sexuality.

This study is consistent with the GST, life-course, and pathways research concerning findings about nonabuse family history, although the nonabuse family history variables were rarely gendered (see Table 7.3). Of the youth, 7% reported a parent in a mental hospital and 11%

reported that at least one of their parents was dead. Almost two thirds reported that at least one of their parents had been incarcerated, whereas only one fifth reported they were the first person in their family incarcerated. The two gender differences regarding families were telling: Girls were far more likely than boys to report abandonment by a parent and twice as likely as boys to report that they would rather be in the juvenile delinquency facility than at home. The former indicates parents valuing sons over daughters. It is notable that two family variables that were gendered before controlling for race, age, and sexual identity were nonsignificant in this multivariate analysis. In one case, being raised by someone other than a parent was not significantly related to any of these control variables. In the other case, the only predictor of delinquent youths' relationships with their mothers was sexual identity: Lesbian/gay/bisexual youth reported significantly worse relationships with their mothers (and inclusion of this variable relegated gender to a nonsignificant predictor).

In summary, this study emphasizes the importance of both broadening our definitions of risk factors for delinquent youth and including girls and boys in these studies to truly assess gender-specific needs. Overall, the findings are supportive of the GST, life-course, pathways/feminist, and cycle of violence perspectives but emphasize the need to broaden what is included under strains, traumas, and significant life events. For GSTs to have relevance, it is clear that abusive experiences, mental health reports, and sexual identity must be included, along with better indicators of school experiences, particularly reasons for dropping out. Although the GST and life-course perspectives broaden the range of the delinquency risk factors identified in more traditional theories, the findings herein are most consistent with the feminist pathways perspective and suggest the importance of including "life events" reported in pathways research on offending women and girls in analyses of boys (and men). The feminist pathways approach not only offers a better understanding of offending girls' and women's risk factors and needs for intervention and treatment but also provides a better understanding for boys' and men's risk factors and intervention needs. The findings also stress the necessity of investigating intersecting oppressions and, unique to this study, verify the need to examine sexual identity in future research on delinquency.

NOTE

1. The survey items used for this chapter, although strongly influenced by existing qualitative and quantitative studies' findings, were most heavily influenced by the findings from our focus groups in the Phase I study (Belknap, Holsinger, & Dunn, 1997). Thus, we developed the survey items used in this chapter, with the exception of the self-esteem items that are from Rosenberg (1989).

Appendix Logistic Regression Models Where the Significance of Sex/Gender Changed When Controlling for the Impact of Race, Age, and Sexual Identity

Dependent Variable	Sex/Gender		Race		Age		Sexual Identity		Model Chi-Square
	Coefficient	SE	Coefficient	SE	Coefficient	SE	Coefficient	SE	
Abuse									
Verbal abuse from family	.325	.236	.621**	.214	.016	.078	.489	.351	14.479**
Physical abuse from family	.427	.254	.899***	.231	.048	.083	.614	.393	24.004***
Witness verbal abuse	.377	.228	.792***	.208	-.012	.077	.588	.328	24.257***
Witness sexual abuse	.587	.386	.604	.365	-.004	.154	.524	.464	8.021
Parent history									
Raised by others	-1.902	1.198	-1.869	1.172	-.606	.439	.335	1.199	7.104
Relationship with mom	-.148	.331	.220	.302	-.155	.113	-.835*	.386	9.046
Self-esteem									
Not much to be proud of	-.329	.269	-.256	.247	-.035	.091	-.946**	.334	14.108**
Feel useless at times	-.135	.234	-.842***	.213	-.089	.079	-1.060**	.340	29.525***
(Why left) school									
Pregnancy related	2.014*	.810	-.415	.746	.895**	.294	-1.351	1.136	14.833**
Trouble with law	.581*	.273	-.323	.251	.318**	.097	.441	.342	20.985***
No one cared	1.609	.834	.498	.667	-.190	.237	.512	.746	8.444
Nobody liked me	1.401	.777	2.536*	1.075	.398	.277	.543	.772	15.209**

Note: Regarding the independent variables, gender was coded 0 = boys and 1 = girls, age was coded as a ratio variable, race was coded 0 = youth of color and 1 = White, and sexual identity was coded 0 = heterosexual/straight and 1 = gay/lesbian/bisexual. Regarding the dependent variables, except for the self-esteem items, these were measured 0 = no and 1 = yes. The self-esteem items were collapsed into *agree* and *disagree.* For the items that are negatively worded (I don't have much to be proud of, I feel useless at times), 0 indicates agreement with the statements or low self-esteem and 1 indicates disagreement or higher self-esteem. For self-esteem questions that are positively worded (I have good qualities, I am satisfied with myself, etc.), 1 = agree, 2 = disagree. Thus, for the self-esteem items, a high score represents higher self-esteem. The independent variables were checked for multicollinearity problems; none existed. *p ≤ .05. **p ≤ .01. ***p ≤ .001

REFERENCES

Agnew, R. (1992). Foundation for a general theory of crime and delinquency. *Criminology, 30*, 47–87.

Arnold, R. A. (1990). Women of color: Processes of victimization and criminalization of Black women. *Social Justice, 17*, 153–166.

Artz, S. (1998). *Sex, power, and the violent school girl.* Toronto, Ontario, Canada: Trifolium Books.

Artz, S., & Riecken, T. (1994). *The survey of student life: In a study of violence among adolescent female students in a suburban school district.* Unpublished report, British Columbia Ministry of Education, Education Research Unit, Canada.

Belknap, J. (2001). *The invisible woman: Gender, crime, and justice* (2nd ed.). Cincinnati, OH: Wadsworth.

Belknap, J., Holsinger, K., & Dunn, M. (1997). Understanding incarcerated girls: The results of a focus group study. *The Prison Journal, 77*, 381–404.

Bottcher, J. (2001). Social practices of gender: How gender relates to delinquency in the everyday lives of high-risk youth. *Criminology, 39*, 893–931.

Broidy, L. M. (2001). A test of general strain theory. *Criminology, 39*, 9–36.

Broidy, L. M., & Agnew, R. (1997). Gender and crime: A general strain theory perspective. *Journal of Research in Crime and Delinquency, 34*, 275–306.

Browne, A., Miller, B., & Maguin, E. (1999). Prevalence and severity of lifetime physical and sexual victimization among incarcerated women. *International Journal of Law and Psychiatry, 22*, 301–322.

Burman, M. J., Batchelor, S. A., & Brown, J. A. (2001). Researching girls and violence. *British Journal of Criminology, 41*, 443–459.

Cernkovich, S., & Giordano, P. (1979). A comparative analysis of male and female delinquency. *Sociological Quarterly, 20*, 131–145.

Chesney-Lind, M. (1989). Girls' crime and woman's place: Toward a feminist model of female delinquency. *Crime & Delinquency, 35*, 5–29.

Chesney-Lind, M., & Rodriguez, N. (1983). Women under lock and key. *The Prison Journal, 3*, 47–65.

Cohen, A. K. (1955). *Delinquent boys: The culture of the gang.* New York: Free Press.

Dahl, G., & Moretti, E. (2003). *The demand for sons: Evidence from divorce, fertility and shotgun marriage.* Cambridge, MA: National Bureau of Economic Research. Retrieved from http://gsbwww.uchicago.edu/labor/dahl.pdf

Daly, K. (1992). A women's pathway to felony court. *Review of Law and Women's Studies, 2*, 11–52.

Daly, K., & Chesney-Lind, M. (1988). Feminism and criminology. *Justice Quarterly, 5*, 497–535.

D'Augelli, A. R., & Dark, L. J. (1994). Lesbian, gay, and bisexual youths. In L. D. Eron, J. H. Gentry, & P. Schlegal (Eds.), *Reason to hope: A psychological perspective on violence and youth* (pp. 177–196). Washington DC: American Psychological Association.

Dembo, R., Williams, L., Wothke, W., Schmeidler, J., & Brown, C. H. (1992). The role of family factors, physical abuse, and sexual victimization experiences in high-risk youths' alcohol and other drug use and delinquency: A longitudinal model. *Violence and Victims, 7*, 245–266.

Faith, K. (1993). *Unruly women: The politics of confinement and resistance.* Vancouver, British Columbia, Canada: Press Gang.

Farrington, D. P. (1994). Human development and criminal careers. In M. Maguire, R. Morgan, & R. Reiner (Eds.), *The Oxford handbook of criminology* (pp. 511–584). New York: Oxford University Press.

Gaarder, E., & Belknap, J. (2002). Tenuous borders: Girls transferred to adult court. *Criminology, 40*(3), 481–517.

Gilfus, M. E. (1992). From victims to survivors to offenders: Women's routes of entry and immersion into street crime. *Women & Criminal Justice, 4*, 63–90.

Habermas, T., & Bluck, S. (2000). Getting a life: The emergence of the life story in adolescence. *Psychological Bulletin, 126*, 748–769.

Heimer, K., & DeCoster, S. (1999). The gendering of violent delinquency. *Criminology, 37*, 277–318.

Hoffman, J. P., & Su, S. S. (1997). The conditional effects of stress on delinquency and drug use: A strain theory assessment of sex differences. *Journal of Research in Crime and Delinquency, 34*, 46–78.

Holsinger, K. (2000). Feminist perspectives on female offending: Examining real girls' lives. *Women & Criminal Justice, 12*(1), 23–51.

Johnson, C. C., & Johnson, K. A. (2000). High-risk behavior among gay adolescents: Implications for treatment and support. *Adolescence, 35*, 619–637.

Johnson, R. A., Su, S. S., Gerstein, D. R., Shin, H.-C., & Hoffmann, J. P. (1995). Parental influences on deviant behavior in early adolescence: A longitudinal response analysis of age-and gender-differentiated effects. *Journal of Quantitative Criminology, 11*, 167–193.

Laub, J. H., & Lauritsen, J. L. (1993). Violent criminal behavior over the life course: A review of the longitudinal and comparative research. *Violence and Victims, 8*, 235–252.

Laub, J. H., & Sampson, R. J. (1993). Turning points in the life course: Why change matters to the study of crime. *Criminology, 31*, 301–325.

Leonard, E. (1982). *Women, crime and society.* New York: Longman.

Loeber, R. (1996). Developmental continuity, change, and pathways in male juvenile problem behavior. In J. D. Hawkins (Ed.), *Delinquency and crime* (pp. 1–28). New York: Cambridge University Press.

Loeber, R., & Le Blanc, M. (1990). Toward a developmental criminology. In M. Tonry & N. Morris (Eds.), *Crime and justice: A review of the research* (pp. 375–473). Chicago: University of Chicago Press.

Mazerolle, P. (1998). Gender, general strain, and delinquency: An empirical examination. *Justice Quarterly, 15,* 65–91.

McClellan, D. S., Farabee, D., & Crouch, B. M. (1997). Early victimization, drug use and criminality: A comparison of male and female prisoners. *Criminal Justice and Behavior, 24,* 455–476.

Merton, R. K. (1949). *Social theory and social structure.* Glencoe, IL: Free Press.

Messerschmidt, J. W. (2000). *Nine lives: Adolescent masculinities, the body, and violence.* Boulder, CO: Westview.

Miller, D., Trapani, C., Fejes-Mendoza, K., Eggleston, C., & Dwiggins, D. (1995). Adolescent female offenders: Unique considerations. *Adolescence, 30,* 429–435.

Moffitt, T. E. (1990). Juvenile delinquency and attention deficit disorder: Boys' development trajectories from age 3 to age 15. *Child Development, 61,* 893–910.

Moffitt, T. E. (1993). Adolescence-limited and life-course persistent antisocial behavior: A developmental taxonomy. *Psychological Review, 100,* 674–701.

Moore, J. W. (1999). Gang members' families. In M. Chesney-Lind & J. M. Hagedorn (Eds.), *Female gangs in America: Essays on girls, gangs and gender* (pp. 159–176). Chicago: Lakeview Press.

Morgan, S. P., Lye, D. N., & Condran, G. A. (1988). Sons, daughters, and the risk of marital disruption. *American Journal of Sociology, 94,* 110–129.

Morrill, C., Yalda, C., Adelman, M., Musheno, M., & Bejarano, C. (2000). Telling tales in school: Youth culture and conflict narratives. *Law & Society Review, 34,* 521–566.

Nagasawa, R., Qian, Z., & Wong, P. (2000). Social control theory as a theory of conformity: The case of Asian/Pacific drug and alcohol nonuse. *Sociological Perspectives, 43,* 581–603.

Nagin, D., Farrington, D. P., & Moffitt, T. E. (1995). Life-course trajectories of different types of offenders. *Criminology, 33,* 111–138.

Office of Juvenile Justice and Delinquency Prevention Act of 1992, Pub. L. No. 102–586, § 8(c)(1), 106 Stat. 5036.

Piquero, A. R., Brame, R., Mazerolle, P., & Haapanen, R. (2003). Crime in emerging adulthood. *Criminology, 40,* 137–169.

Piquero, A. R., MacDonald, J. M., & Parker, K. F. (2002). Race, local life circumstances, and criminal activity. *Social Science Quarterly, 83,* 654–670.

Pollock, J. M. (1999). *Criminal women.* Cincinnati, OH: Anderson.

Rivera, B., & Widom, C. S. (1990). Childhood victimization and violent offending. *Violence and Victims, 5,* 19–35.

Robson, R. (1992). *Lesbian (out)law: Survival under the rule of law.* Ithaca, NY: Firebrand.

Rosenberg, M. (1989). *Society and the adolescent self-image* (Rev. ed.). Middletown, CT: Wesleyan University Press.

Sampson, R. J., & Laub, J. H. (1990). Crime and deviance over the life course: The salience of adult social bonds. *American Sociological Review, 55,* 609–627.

Sampson, R. J., & Laub, J. H. (1992). Crime and deviance in the life course. *Annual Review of Sociology, 18,* 63–84.

Sharp, S. F., Brewster, D. R., & Love, S. R. (2005). Disentangling strain, personal attributes, affective response and deviance: A gendered analysis. *Deviant Behavior, 26,* 122–157.

Sharp, S. F., Terling-Watt, T. L., Atkins, L. A., & Gilliam, J. T. (2001). Purging behavior in a sample of college females: A research note on general strain theory and female deviance. *Deviant Behavior, 22,* 171–188.

Stattin, H., & Magnusson, D. (1991). Stability and change in criminal behaviour up to age 30. *The British Journal of Criminology, 31*(4), 327–346.

Widom, C. S. (1989). The cycle of violence. *Science, 244,* 160–166.

Chapter 8

MOVING TOWARD JUSTICE FOR FEMALE JUVENILE OFFENDERS IN THE NEW MILLENNIUM

Modeling Gender-Specific Policies and Programs

BARBARA BLOOM, BARBARA OWEN,
ELIZABETH PIPER DESCHENES, AND JILL ROSENBAUM

Until recently, girls and young women have been largely overlooked in the development of juvenile justice policy and programs and few resources have been directed at them (Chesney-Lind & Shelden, 1998). With the increase in the number of female offenders committing violent and property index crimes between 1992 and 1996, the Office of Juvenile Justice and Delinquency Prevention (OJJDP) increased federal support to state and local efforts to address the issue of gender-specific services for girls (Budnick & Shields-Fletcher, 1998). The experiences of several states are described in the OJJDP publication *Female Juvenile Offenders: A Status of the States Report* (Community Research Associates, 1998). Training and technical assistance on the best practices are being offered by Greene, Peters & Associates (1998). In at least one state, gender-specific programs are being developed and implemented with funding from the Bureau of Justice Assistance. OJJDP has sponsored the Safe-Futures demonstration program for at-risk girls and female offenders. Despite the importance of these federal efforts, they remain limited in scope and it is up to the states to take action.

Moving toward justice for female juvenile offenders in the new millennium means that states must invest additional resources, conduct an assessment of the problem, and implement new policies. The common challenges facing states include a growing number of female juvenile offenders committing more serious crimes and resulting in a greater number of juveniles in

Source: Bloom, B., Owen, B., Deschenes, E. P., & Rosenbaum, J. (2002). Moving toward justice for female juvenile offenders in the new millennium: Modeling gender-specific policies and programs. *Journal of Contemporary Criminal Justice, 18*(1), 37–56.

Authors' Note: This research was supported by Grant No. 96-JF-FX-0006 from the California Office of Criminal Justice Planning (OCJP). The opinions, findings, and conclusions in this chapter are those of the authors and not necessarily those of the OCJP.

custody, a limited understanding of what works for girls, a demand for comprehensive needs assessments that identify gaps in the provision of services for girls, the need to develop and implement gender-specific services and programs designed to meet the unique needs of girls, and the competition for scarce resources in implementing these programs and policies (Budnick & Shields-Fletcher, 1998).

Even though advances have been made toward the goal of improving the status of juvenile justice for young women, there remains a paucity of programs and there is a need to seek solutions through federal, state, and local legislation (Acoca, 1999). This chapter presents a brief overview of national and state efforts to address gender-specific programming for young women in the juvenile justice system and summarizes findings from an assessment in the state of California that was conducted in 1997 and 1998 (Owen, Bloom, Deschenes, & Rosenbaum, 1998). This assessment included a review of the literature, a snapshot of trends in female juvenile offending and a profile of the offender, a review of federal and state policy initiatives, a series of interviews and focus groups with female youth and professionals serving this population, and a statewide survey of representatives of various agencies and programs.

NATIONAL EFFORTS

In 1992, as part of the reauthorization of the Juvenile Justice and Delinquency Prevention (JJDP) Act of 1974, the following language was added:

> to develop and adopt policies to prohibit gender bias in placement and treatment and establishing programs to ensure female youth have access to the full range of health and mental health services, treatment for physical or sexual assault and abuse, self-defense instruction, education in parenting, education in general, and other training and vocational services. (Community Research Associates, 1998, p. 6)

The amendment, known as the Challenge Activity E component, required all states applying for federal formula grant dollars to examine their juvenile justice systems, identify gaps in services to juvenile female offenders, and plan for providing needed gender-specific services for the prevention and treatment of juvenile delinquency.

According to a review of the literature by the Evaluation and Training Institute (1996), additional work needs to be done if the JJDP Act is to be responsive to the realities of young women involved in the juvenile justice system. For example, the language of some of the legislation is not gender-neutral. Some of the recommended programs or services continue to be oriented toward young men. There are no specific directives on how the increased services for young women will be developed and/ or funded. Many of the policies that are written specifically for young women focus on pregnancy-related issues with no recognition of other gender-specific needs. There remains a strong emphasis on placement of girls in a facility close to home, which ignores the fact that many young women have been physically or sexually abused at home and consequently family reunification services may not be beneficial. There is a failure to address the need for culturally competent services. There are requirements for juveniles to attend treatment programs or other mental health services without consideration as to whether the services are gender-specific. In sum, there are many areas for improvement.

Since the passage of the Challenge Activity E component in 1992, most of the progress on a national level has focused on program planning and training for practitioners as well as policy development, with little attention to research and evaluation. The first national training workshop on girls in the juvenile justice system was hosted by the American Correctional Association in 1994. The workshop included training on developmental differences between boys and girls and their implications for services, as well as models of gender-sensitive programming.

A second training workshop for practitioners working with girls in institutional settings was held by the National Institute of Corrections in 1995. At the same time OJJDP awarded funds to Girls, Inc. for a national symposium on girls' issues. The National Girls' Caucus, which is an advocacy group initiated by the Practical and Cultural Educational (PACE) Center for Girls, Inc., held a national roundtable in 1994 to address issues of policy, programming, and service delivery for at-risk girls. A report on the roundtable by Raviora (1999) contends that gender-specific programming should focus on some of the societal problems that challenge at-risk girls. These include the death or loss of a family member due to violence, sexual and physical abuse, domestic violence, high-risk sexual behavior, the incarceration of close family members, gang involvement, the use of alcohol or tobacco and other drugs, and adolescent health issues.

In 1997, OJJDP awarded a 3-year grant to Greene, Peters & Associates to identify "promising programs" for juvenile girls throughout the United States and to develop curricula and implement training for practitioners working with girls involved in the juvenile justice system. One product is the report entitled *Guiding Principles for Promising Female Programming* (1998), which focuses on structural issues and programmatic elements. In developing a program, Greene, Peters & Associates suggested that attention should be paid to organization and management, which includes cooperation, respect, and good communication skills; diversity of staff and training in female development as well as risk factors and cultural sensitivity; and individualizing the intake and reentry process. Specific programmatic elements include education, skills training, and elements that promote positive development such as problem solving, relationship building, culturally relevant activities, career opportunities, health services, mentoring, community involvement, positive peer relationships, and family involvement. Specific treatment concerns such as prenatal or postpartum care, parenting and health care for babies, and substance abuse are also mentioned.

For several years, the OJJDP's Special Emphasis Division has offered grants to local jurisdictions for the development of gender-specific programs for female offenders. The Comprehensive Community-Based Services for At-Risk Girls and Adjudicated Juvenile Female Offenders is part of OJJDP's Safe-Futures program. Community Research Associates (1998) provides support to national organizations working to address the needs of girls, disseminate information to states, and develop resource materials for individuals interested in the issue.

STATE EFFORTS

The OJJDP reports a high level of interest among states in the Challenge Activity E component, but it is clear that there is much to be done to meet this challenge. During 1997, 24 states embarked on such efforts (Chesney-Lind, 1997). The examination by Community Research Associates (1998) of girls' service needs within the juvenile justice system provided examples of some states that have developed unique approaches to addressing the needs of female juvenile offenders within their jurisdictions by using funding from the OJJDP.

Colorado and Delaware have established statewide committees to address the issues of girls and young women in the juvenile justice system, develop gender-specific services, and distribute federal formula grant dollars. Technical assistance to develop staff-secure cottages for girls or train staff in secure facilities has been requested in Colorado, Delaware, and Iowa.

The Florida Female Initiative of 1994 coordinated the Florida Department of Juvenile Justice, state and private programs, and one staff member from each juvenile justice district to advocate for high-risk girls in their areas. In addition, Florida is home to PACE, which provides nonresidential, community-based education programs designed to prevent juvenile delinquency.

In Maryland, the Female Population Task Force has identified program components for gender-specific services for girls, including community-based residential treatment facilities as a means for diverting young women out of the justice system, and has requested technical assistance to work with a committee to redesign the programming at the Cheltenham Young Women's Facility. Baltimore has a specially trained unit of nine probation officers that serve all the female cases.

In Milwaukee, Wisconsin, the Continuum of Care for Girls project is a multiphase, court-ordered program teaching vocational and educational skills, providing drug and alcohol treatment, and providing the opportunities for gradual reintegration of participants into mainstream society. The program includes community-based residential treatment facilities as a means for diverting young women out of the justice system.

Minnesota and Oregon have been at the forefront of the movement for several years, working to address the needs of girls and women in the juvenile and criminal justice system. State legislation in Minnesota mandates equity in services. The Office of Planning for Female Offenders works with the Adolescent Female Subcommittee Advisory Task Force to expand parity of program funding, develop a continuum of care throughout the state, and create a Center for Adolescent Female Development and Studies. Oregon's House Bill 3576 mandates all state agencies to develop plans ensuring equal access for all services and calls for the strict monitoring of implementation of improved services for young women in the areas of teen pregnancy, physical and sexual abuse, alcohol and drug abuse, and services for runaway and homeless girls.

CURRENT STUDY

In California, the Office of Criminal Justice Planning (OCJP) has addressed the needs of girls and young women at-risk or currently involved in the juvenile justice system through the governor's State Advisory Group (SAG). In 1993, SAG convened a task force of researchers, policy makers, program providers, and youth advocates to determine the nature of this problem and develop research strategies to obtain the data necessary to make informed policy decisions. To identify gender-specific responses for at-risk girls and young women, OCJP contracted with researchers from the California State University system to develop a series of reports to address these issues, which are summarized in the final report (Owen et al., 1998). The researchers conducted an overview of the literature, reviewed federal and state policy initiatives, conducted a survey of officials from various state agencies, and conducted a series of interviews and focus groups with female youth and professionals serving this population.

Legislative Review

In 1998, California passed Senate Bill 1657 creating the Juvenile Female Offender Intervention Program, which would award competitive grants to counties to develop intervention programs designed to reduce juvenile crime committed by female offenders as specified. The bill would authorize the Board of Corrections to award up to $500,000 to counties that (a) develop and implement a comprehensive, multiagency plan that provides for a continuum of responses to juvenile crime and delinquency committed by female offenders; and (b) demonstrate a collaborative and integrated approach for implementing a system of swift, certain, and graduated responses targeted to meet the unique needs of at-risk female youth and female juvenile offenders. Unfortunately, Senate Bill 1657 was not signed by the governor.

Collaborations between agencies and jurisdictions (e.g., mental health, education, and family and children's services) present additional possibilities for a more holistic approach to juvenile justice issues. The Juvenile Crime Enforcement and Accountability Challenge Grant Program (S. 1760, 1997) provided $50 million to eligible counties for the purpose of reducing juvenile crime and delinquency. Grants were awarded by the Board of Corrections to (a) develop and implement a comprehensive multiagency plan that provides for a continuum of responses to juvenile crime and delinquency and (b) demonstrate a collaborative and integrated approach for implementing graduated responses for at-risk youth and juvenile offenders. Subsequent to this legislation, the Board of Corrections awarded grants totaling $45.7 million to 16 counties to implement their local action plans. Three county local action plans (Alameda, San Diego, and San Francisco) included provisions for services to at-risk girls and female juvenile offenders.

Other state legislation, compiled by the California Task Force to Review Juvenile Crime and the Juvenile Justice Response (1996), provided for policy and program opportunities that can be used to develop and expand gender-specific services. Assembly Bill 3220 (1995) established the Repeat Offender Prevention Project to provide comprehensive social services for wards 15 years or younger who are at risk of becoming chronic juvenile offenders. Senate Bill 1763 (1995) requires the California Youth Authority (CYA) to develop a 5-year plan with strategies for treatment and housing of CYA wards. Other legislation (Assembly Bill 2189, 1997) encourages the use of innovation and experimentation in the operation of juvenile detention facilities. Senate Bill 604 (1996) authorizes funding for educational, vocational, and special education services for young offenders. The use of collaboratives to develop peer teen courts (Assembly Bill 3324, 1995) and the establishment of a pilot project for intensive wraparound services to children in foster care (Assembly Bill 2297, 1997) provide opportunities for an interdisciplinary approach to the needs of at-risk youth, especially if implemented with a gender-specific focus.

Survey and Focus Group Methodology

Quantitative and qualitative data collection techniques were used in this study. A cross-sectional survey was designed to obtain data on the types of services available to girls and young women at risk of involvement or already involved in California's juvenile justice system and to learn more about problems that are faced by various providers. Focus groups and interviews were conducted with probation officers, program staff, and program participants in 11 counties.

The survey was distributed via mail to probation chiefs, detention supervisors, juvenile court judges, commissioners, and referees in each of the 58 counties and to 387 program providers in November 1997. Probation officers for each county were identified based on the Juvenile Challenge Grant Contact List. Names of detention supervisors were obtained through a directory of criminal justice agencies. The list of judges, commissioners, and referees was obtained from the Judicial Council of California. Several sources were used to create a list of agencies that provide services to girls and young women. One source was information provided by the Juvenile Justice Coordinating Councils in each county and another was the mailing list maintained by the Office of Criminal Justice Planning. One follow-up contact was made via telephone or fax approximately 1 month following the initial mail-out. The response rate varied by type of respondent, with the highest rate among chief probation officers (71%), a moderate rate for detention supervisors (38%), and a low rate (17%) for the judges and programs. Overall, there was at least 1 survey returned from 53 out of the 58 counties in the state.

The survey included questions related to risk and protective factors for young women and men and program needs in terms of barriers to treatment and suggestions for system change.[1] Program providers were asked additional questions about their program, such as target population, program characteristics, demographic characteristics of staff and clients, and program information. Data were analyzed using SPSS with various techniques, including frequency distributions, cross-tabulations, t tests of means, and analysis of variance. Most of the results included in this chapter represent the overall descriptive statistics.[2]

Project staff conducted interviews and focus groups with a wide range of individuals, including probation officers, program staff, and girls and young women in 11 counties between August and December 1997. The counties were purposively selected to be representative of geographical location, urban or rural characteristics, or program reputation or interest. The focus group interview lasted between 60 and 90 minutes, and questions addressed the following areas: factors contributing to delinquency and other risk behavior, types of problems experienced by girls and young women, types of help and services needed, obstacles in seeking help, program gaps and barriers, and effective program elements.

STUDY FINDINGS

The research results are divided into two sections. The first section summarizes the findings from the two data collection efforts and literature review and provides information for a basic understanding of at-risk girls and young women that is necessary to program development. Many of these findings parallel the conclusions made by Acoca (1999) and support the need for gender-specific programs. The second section provides recommendations for policy and program change within the state of California, which can be generalized to other states.

Table 8.1	Rank Order of Risk and Protective Factors by Survey Respondents	
	Mean Score	
	Risk Factor	*Protective Factor*
Family issues	1.82	1.71
Individual problems	2.07	2.13
Peer group	3.09	3.31
School-related problems	3.25	3.22
Community	4.34	4.19

Research Results

Family problems, victimization, violence, and drugs are critical factors that contribute significantly to female involvement in juvenile offending. Survey and focus group respondents alike indicated that the family is the primary risk and protective factor (see Table 8.1). As shown in Table 8.2 and as reported in the focus groups, family issues include conflicts and lack of communication within the family, parents who are ill-equipped or unprepared, and a range of problems presented by the parents themselves. Survey respondents indicated that positive family communication, along with rules and structure within the family, are primary protective factors (see Table 8.3).

Individual experiences and problems are second in importance in determining the risks and needs of females (see Table 8.1). The lack of self-esteem is a primary problem displayed by many delinquent girls (see Table 8.2). Second, substance abuse is often a sign of other problems that lead to risky behavior. Sexual, physical, and emotional abuse are significant factors in producing risky and delinquent behavior among girls and young women. As mentioned in the focus groups, the effect of abuse is long lasting and creates problems with running away, emotional adjustments, trust and secrecy, future sexuality, and other risky behaviors. Gang involvement and fighting with peers contribute to delinquency for a significant number of girls and young women. According to survey respondents, creating a positive self-image and helping youth with skills related to problem solving, conflict resolution, and relationship building are among the primary protective factors for young women (see Table 8.3).

School difficulties and negative attitudes toward school contribute to truancy, dropping out, and other early warning signs of delinquency (see Table 8.2). Girls and young women at risk of future delinquency and those currently in programs reported that they lack a range of academic and social skills. Girls may also lack basic information about the world of work and planning for the future. Focus group respondents identified schools as a prime opportunity for early intervention in the lives of girls and young women but noted that they are often ill-equipped to deal with the high-risk student. Survey respondents indicated parental involvement in schooling is an important protective factor (see Table 8.3). According to focus group participants, there are few after-school and other recreational programs and activities designed for girls and young women. Girls and young women desire programs that promote active involvement in addressing their problems and needs.

Peer groups and the community are important settings for delinquency prevention. Survey respondents noted the availability of drugs and peer use of substances as important risk factors (see Table 8.2). Positive peer influences and community service were identified as important protective factors (see Table 8.3). Overall, it appears that girls and young women have multiple service needs.

Table 8.2	Risk Factors and Common Problems Identified by Survey Respondents (N = 167)	
		%
Family		
Family conflict		95.8
Family management problems		89.8
Parent or sibling history of criminal or violent behavior		88.7
Parental attitudes favorable to involvement in problem behavior		69.9
Individual		
Lack of self-esteem		95.8
Substance abuse		92.2
Sexual abuse		88.6
Emotional abuse		88.0
Sexual activity or awareness		88.0
Delinquency		86.7
Homeless or runaway youth		84.9
Pregnancy		81.9
Suicidal tendencies		80.1
Physical abuse		78.3
Gang involvement		77.1
Developmental or learning disabilities		74.1
Severe trauma or emotional disturbance		73.5
Eating disorders		64.5
School		
Discipline problems		91.0
Truancy		88.0
Academic failure		84.9
Dropout		72.5
Peer group		
Friends who engage in alcohol or drug use		90.4
Friends who engage in delinquency		89.2
Friends with favorable attitudes toward problem behavior		74.7
Community and other		
Availability of drugs		90.4
Values favorable toward problem behavior		71.1
Low neighborhood attachment, lack of community organization		69.9
Extreme economic deprivation		64.5
Lack of safe or adequate housing		59.6
Availability of firearms		52.4
Immigration problems		48.8

Table 8.3	Protective Factors Identified by Survey Respondents ($N = 167$)	
		%
Family		
Positive family communication		97.6
Rules and structure within family		89.8
Parent involvement in schooling		89.2
High level of love and support within the family		88.6
Ongoing relationship with caring adult other than parent		75.3
Lack of family stress		72.9
Individual		
Positive self-image or self-worth		97.6
Problem-solving skills		91.6
Positive values (integrity, honesty, responsibility)		89.8
Conflict-resolution skills		88.6
Social skills or competence		84.3
Relationship-building skills		83.7
Ability to express opinions, values, perspectives		78.9
Resistance skills		75.9
Ability to express range of feelings		75.9
Sense of personal safety		74.1
Ability to empathize with others		72.9
Spiritual values		61.4
School		
School engagement or bonding to school		81.2
Youth involvement in creative activities		79.5
Youth involvement in sports, athletic activities		77.7
Caring school climate		77.1
Rules and structure in school environment		74.1
Peer group		
Positive peer influences		89.2
Community and other		
Youth performing community service		73.5
Nonviolent and caring neighborhood		70.5
Community valuing youth		70.5
High expectations for youth by adults		62.7

The types of services provided by the 67 programs that responded to the survey are displayed in Table 8.4.[3] Some services are provided within the agency, whereas other services are referrals, depending on the type of program (residential or community-based outpatient).[4] The majority of programs include individual, family, and group counseling, as well as specific skills training such as education, life skills, and anger management. About half of the agencies provide individual counseling for substance abuse and more than half refer clients to 12-step groups. Programs are as likely to provide services as to make referrals for various types of general services. Focus group interviews suggested that few programs address the serious problem of victimization or provide needed services for prevention or treatment of substance abuse. Health services are inadequate across the board. In particular, pregnant and parenting teens are neglected in terms of comprehensive health programs and services. Focus group participants suggested that special attention should be given to prevention and education programs concerning pregnancy and sexually transmitted diseases.

There is a multitude of barriers to program services for girls and young women. Even though funding was identified as the most serious barrier confronted by programs, girls and young women confront many individual barriers in seeking help and treatment for their problems (see Table 8.5). Focus group interviews documented that these barriers include distrust and fear, lack of knowledge about services, teen attitudes and resistance, lack of personal contact with staff, transportation and lack of service accessibility, domestic responsibility, difficulty in making and accessing referrals, and cultural and immigration issues. In addition, racial, ethnic, gender, and economic discrimination may contribute to decreased opportunity, disparities in treatment, gender bias, and lack of program parity, although these were not identified as serious problems by survey respondents.

Survey respondents made many suggestions for program change (see Table 8.6) and indicated ways in which OCJP can help facilitate change (see Table 8.7). For example, the majority of respondents indicated that they want more information about what works for girls. Half of the respondents indicated a need to identify the best practices and provide program models. Additional resources and funding were

Table 8.4   Types of Services Provided for Female Clients by Programs ($N = 167$)

	% Provide	% Refer	% Provide or Refer
Counseling			
Individual	65.6	11.5	14.8
Family	57.4	19.7	13.1
Peer support group (coed)	54.1	18.0	3.3
Peer support group (single gender)	67.2	14.8	1.6
Skills training			
Education/tutoring	50.8	31.1	8.2
General Equivalency Diploma (GED)	23.0	55.7	0.0
Vocational	21.3	52.5	1.6
Victim awareness	37.7	34.4	1.6
Life skills	60.7	18.0	4.9
Anger management	63.9	21.3	1.6
Grief management	44.3	34.4	0.0
Parenting skills (clients)	49.2	23.0	1.6
Family planning (sex education)	44.3	34.4	4.9
Substance abuse treatment			
Individual counseling	50.8	21.3	6.6
Group counseling (coed)	41.0	26.2	1.6
Group counseling (single gender)	42.6	26.2	1.6
12-step groups	19.7	55.7	1.6
Residential or inpatient	13.1	54.1	0.0
Sober living home	11.5	42.6	1.6
Detoxification	3.3	60.7	0.0
General services			
Recreational activities	57.4	32.8	4.9
Mentoring	49.2	24.6	4.9
Food/clothing	42.6	36.1	4.9
Transportation	42.6	34.4	4.9
Housing	29.5	47.5	1.6
Foster care	18.0	47.5	1.6
Independent living	18.0	47.5	1.6
Temporary shelter	14.8	49.2	1.6
Medical and/or dental care	19.7	60.7	0.0
Child care	13.1	50.8	3.3

Note: Row percentages do not sum to 100%, as the responses that were left blank were not included in the table.

Table 8.5	Barriers to Program Services by Survey Respondents ($N = 167$)		
	% Not a Problem	*% Somewhat a Problem*	*% Serious Problem*
Administrative barriers			
Funding/resources	14.5	27.7	57.9
Transportation	33.3	42.8	23.9
Staffing	33.3	44.9	21.8
Access/waiting list	36.7	43.0	20.3
Geographic location	36.7	46.8	16.5
Appointment hours	50.6	44.8	4.5
Individual barriers			
Support system	7.0	49.0	43.9
Lure of the streets	13.0	48.7	38.3
Motivation	10.3	56.4	33.3
Peer resistance	15.7	53.6	30.7
Family resistance	10.6	66.6	23.1
Acceptance of program rules	21.0	56.1	22.9
Lack of information	26.1	52.9	20.9
Cultural	30.6	58.0	11.5
Gender bias	52.3	37.4	10.3
Language	36.3	56.1	7.6
Sexual orientation	49.7	45.2	5.2
Economic barriers			
Employment	16.9	42.9	40.3
Education	24.0	37.0	39.0
Program cost	24.8	41.8	33.3
Social environmental barriers			
Childcare	30.9	44.3	24.8
Housing	29.4	51.0	19.6
Shelter	33.6	48.0	18.4
Treatment barriers			
Mental health issues	23.2	44.5	32.3
Medical issues	34.4	53.6	11.9
Disability	48.6	45.3	6.1

also high on the list. Improvements in communication and collaboration along with workshops, training, and staff development were among the primary areas targeted for change.

In focus group interviews, respondents indicated that the juvenile justice system does not identify and address the needs of girls and young women in policy and program development. Most female delinquents continue to commit relatively minor offenses, which suggests a need for prevention and intervention programs rather than increased secure institutions. Female

Table 8.6	Suggestions for Program Change by Survey Respondents ($N = 167$)
	%
Improved or more information about what works for girls	72.3
Additional resources	54.8
Reallocation of existing resources	30.1
Better fit between funding criteria and characteristics of girls	34.9
Improved intra-agency communication/collaboration	40.4
Improved inter-agency communication/collaboration	38.6
Modified or new service delivery models	36.7
Improved client information systems	35.5
Enhanced public information efforts	35.5
Improved or more clarification of measurable outcomes	26.5
Improved/different opportunities for staff or management training	29.5
Less bureaucratic and/or administrative red tape	30.1
Changes in state laws or administrative rules	22.9
Organizational or managerial restructuring	12.7
Written policies or procedures	10.8
Lowered resistance to working with girls	18.1

Table 8.7	Ways to Facilitate Change Suggested by Survey Respondents ($N = 167$)
	%
Provide program funding	81.3
Conduct training	63.3
Provide program models	56.6
Identify best practices	54.2
Conduct workshops	54.2
Increase curriculum or program development	50.6
Promote staff development	48.8
Provide funding for program evaluation	47.0
Enhance public information efforts	41.0
Provide funding for program monitoring	39.2

youth rarely participate in program development or case management planning. Program managers lack information about available models and program effectiveness and see that funding for gender-appropriate programs is critically inadequate. Graduated sanctions and a continuum of care are not available to girls and young women in most counties. This includes front-end prevention and back-end aftercare programs. There are few linkages across and within programs. Meeting the needs of girls and young women requires specialized staffing and training, particularly in terms of relationship and communication skills, gender differences in delinquency, substance abuse education, the role of abuse, developmental stages of female adolescence, and available programs and appropriate placements and limitations.

Recommendations

The findings from this statewide assessment and review of current policy support the need for gender-appropriate policies and programs. The following recommendations are drawn from statements made by the focus group and survey respondents, as well as analysis of the scientific and applied literature. To date, California lacks any organized state office, task force, or policy division devoted solely to the needs of female adolescents or delinquents.

Analyzing the standards for services and program development utilized by several other states in the public and private sector can provide California with the necessary references to move forward. A comprehensive effort should be undertaken to ensure an eventual parity between services for young men and women. Policy development must involve decision makers from all aspects of the community, the juvenile justice system, and girls and young women.

Even though the following recommendations were developed specifically for the state of California, they may be useful to policy makers in other states.

- County and state decision makers should develop specific policies aimed at addressing the needs of girls and young women.

- Funding should be targeted to address the needs of girls and young women at the state and county level.

- To meet the multifaceted needs of girls and young women, collaborative efforts in policy, grant development, and program planning should be encouraged.

- Girls and young women require a continuum of care that incorporates graduated sanctions and addresses prevention, intervention, intermediate sanctions, appropriate custodial settings, transitional housing, and aftercare.

- Community-based program opportunities must be developed to address these gender-specific needs and problems, such as abuse, teen pregnancy, running away, substance abuse, and family conflicts.

- Schools and school-based prevention programs should develop a more focused and collaborative approach in addressing the needs of girls and young women.

- Programs at all levels should provide family-focused services that include the family, when appropriate, in addressing the problems that lead to delinquency. Family-focused services involve the family in assessment, case management, service delivery, and aftercare.

- Counties need to develop substance abuse programming for female adolescents including day treatment, clinical treatment, and residential programming.

- Local jurisdictions should increase services to female detention populations. These services include education, mental and physical health care, recreation, substance abuse treatment, and release planning.

- Health care services at all levels need to be provided in the community and detention settings. Programs that provide health education, clinical health services, and services addressing teen pregnancy and parenting should be developed and expanded.

- Staff at all levels of the juvenile justice and school systems should be provided with training and education concerning gender-specific issues such as adolescent development, sexual exploitation, awareness of family backgrounds, trust and emotional issues, relationship needs, and strategies and techniques for working with girls and young women.

- Programs and services to teen runaways should be implemented in every community.

- Academic and applied research on at-risk and delinquent female youth should be conducted.

Inquiry into the causes of female delinquency, population descriptions and needs assessments, offense patterns and trends, and effectiveness-of-program models could provide useful data toward the development of effective policies and programs.

In sum, effective programming for girls and women should be shaped by and tailored to their unique situations and problems. To do this, a theoretical approach to treatment that is gender-sensitive and addresses the realities of girls' lives must be developed (Bloom, 1997). Appropriate services for girls and young women must have multiple components that address the complex issues that adolescent girls face. These services consist of educational opportunities, employment and vocational training, placement options, and mental and physical health services, all of which must be delivered in a culturally appropriate manner. Bloom (1997) discusses the need to incorporate the concept of the female sense of self, which manifests and develops differently in female-specific groups as opposed to coed groups. She describes how the unique needs and issues of women and girls can be addressed in a safe, trusting, and supportive girl-focused environment.

Conclusion

Even though girls and young women represent a minority within the juvenile justice system, there is little justification for the overall lack of policy, program, and research attention given to this neglected population, and there is a general consensus that federal, state, and local strategies should invest in programs and policies for girls. The review of the literature and data collected in this study point to three conclusions. First, the research shows that the needs of girls and young women facing involvement in the juvenile justice system are tied to specific, identifiable risk factors. These risk factors include such personal factors as family issues; sexual, physical, and emotional abuse; and inadequate academic and social skills. Although this study did not focus on the effect of social risk factors such as racism, sexism, and economic discrimination, these too must be understood in any discussion of female delinquency. Running away, truancy, early sexual behavior, substance abuse, and other predelinquent behaviors are related to these initial risk factors.

Second, girls and young women have been largely ignored in the development of policy and programs. The juvenile justice system is ill-equipped to deal with the risks and needs of girls and young women. The critical lack of early identification and assessment opportunities is aggravated by the scarcity of appropriate and effective community-based prevention and early intervention strategies. Inadequate planning and funding, the absence of a continuum of care, and the general lack of gender-appropriate programs, placement, detention, and aftercare services is further evidence of this inattention. Even though more rigorous evaluation and monitoring efforts are required, the basic elements and gender-appropriate interventions have been articulated through research and best practices. These elements are based on the developmental, psychological, social, educational, and cultural characteristics of girls and young women and the need to provide collaborative and comprehensive services to female youth and their families in a continuum of care.

Finally, it is clear that some states, like Minnesota and Oregon, have invested in gender-specific programming and policies and are leading the way. In comparison, other states have only begun to address the issue in conducting an assessment of the problem. Even though the Challenge Activity E amendment to the JJDP Act of 1974 has provided the initial momentum toward shaping the policies and programs for the new millennium, there is still a long way to go to achieve justice for female juvenile offenders.

Notes

1. Risk factors are those factors that increase the risk of delinquency or place youth at greater risk for system intervention. Protective factors act to prevent delinquency or problem behaviors.

2. The full report (Owen, Bloom, Deschenes, & Rosenbaum, 1998), which includes more detailed analyses, is available from the Office of Criminal Justice Planning. Some of the results have been reported in journal articles.

3. The most common type of program responding to the survey was a delinquency prevention program; some were group treatment homes and others were counseling centers.

4. In response to the types of services provided, in those cases where survey respondents checked both

"provide" and "refer," the response is indicated as "provide or refer." If no box was checked, the percentage is unknown but is not reported in the table.

References

Acoca, L. (1999). Investing in girls: A 21st century strategy. *Juvenile Justice, 6*(1), 3–13.

Assembly Bill 2189, Poochigian, Chap. 100 (1997).

Assembly Bill 2297, Cunneen, Chap. 274 (1997).

Assembly Bill 3220, Connolly, Chap. 730 (1995).

Assembly Bill 3324, Connolly, Chap. 607 (1995).

Bloom, B. (1997, September). *Defining "gender-specific": What does it mean and why is it important?* Paper presented at the National Institute of Corrections' Intermediate Sanctions for Women Offenders National Project Meeting, Longmont, CO.

Budnick, K. J., & Shields-Fletcher, E. (1998). *What about girls?* (OJJDP Fact Sheet No. 84). Washington, DC: U.S. Department of Justice, Office of Justice Programs, Office of Juvenile Justice and Delinquency Prevention.

California Task Force to Review Juvenile Crime and the Juvenile Justice Response. (1996). *Final report.* Sacramento: State of California.

Chesney-Lind, M. (1997). *What about girls? Hidden victims of congressional juvenile crime control.* Hawaii: University of Hawaii at Manoa, Women's Studies Program.

Chesney-Lind, M., & Shelden, R. G. (1998). *Girls, delinquency and juvenile justice.* Belmont, CA: West/Wadsworth.

Community Research Associates. (1998). *Female juvenile offenders: A status of the states report.* Washington, DC: U.S. Department of Justice, Office of Justice Programs, Office of Juvenile Justice and Delinquency Prevention.

Evaluation and Training Institute. (1996). *Study of gender-specific services: Initial review of the literature.* Sacramento, CA: Office of Criminal Justice Planning.

Greene, Peters & Associates. (1998). *Guiding principles for promising female programming: An inventory of best practices.* Washington, DC: U.S. Department of Justice, Office of Justice Programs, Office of Juvenile Justice and Delinquency Prevention.

Owen, B., Bloom, B., Deschenes, E. P., & Rosenbaum, J. (1998). *Modeling gender-specific services in juvenile justice: Policy and program recommendations.* Final report submitted to the Office of Criminal Justice Planning, Sacramento, CA.

Raviora, L. (1999). National girls' caucus. *Juvenile Justice, 6*(1), 21–28.

S. 604, Rosenthal, Chap. 72 (1996).

S. 1760, Lockyer, Chap. 133 (1997).

S. 1763, Wright, Chap. 905 (1995).

PART III

THE WOMAN OFFENDER

Women's Experiences With Drugs, Crime, and Violence

Similar to its role in girls' lives, gender matters in women's lives and profoundly shapes the choices and situations in which they are likely to be swept up by the criminal justice system. There are important connections between girls' problems and women's crime—connections often obscured by approaches that consider *delinquency* and *crime* to be separate and distinct topics. Serious problems during childhood and adolescence often set the stage for women's entry into crime, from youth homelessness and abuse to drug use and survival sex to, ultimately, more serious offending. Understanding women's crime requires a critical and sensitive awareness of the discrimination and victimization women experience in their lives and the impact of their economic marginalization on their criminal activity.

The readings in this section seek to comprehend women's crime within the context of their lives—lives that must often negotiate a social world that is unfair to women, to people of color, and to those with low income, limited job skills, and a lack of formal education. Using a self-help perspective, Elicka S. L. Peterson explains two important phenomena: why women who are abused commit homicide against their intimate partners and why these women do not commit more homicide. She demonstrates how women who feel socially isolated and have little belief in the law's ability to help them may resort to violent self-help in order to end an abusive relationship. Even when abused, however, women generally have less-forgiving attitudes toward lethal violence and fear the criminal sanctions that would sever those relationships they hold dear to them.

In the second chapter, Priscilla Pyett and Deborah Warr continue to look at the context of women's criminal offending and illustrate the myriad routines women use to survive the health and physical risks of sex work. The authors find that age, sex work experience, confidence, and other social problems (such as homelessness, drug use, and lack of social support) affect their ability to control sexual encounters with their clients.

The last two readings in this section focus on the impact of drug use in women's lives and its relation to criminal activity. Showing how essential women are in the illicit drug economy, Tammy L. Anderson illustrates how women play important roles and perform four core activities: (1) providing housing and sustenance, (2) purchasing drugs, (3) subsidizing male dependency, and (4) participating in drug sales. Anderson provides a unique and hopeful argument about women's power and agency in drug trafficking: While women suffer numerous consequences from their interactions in the drug world, the agency they have, the empowerment they experience, and the roles they fulfill may also help them accumulate forms of capital that could serve them in future, more legitimate endeavors.

Taking a less hopeful and more critical stance on drugs in women's lives, Stephanie R. Bush-Baskette takes a broader look at the war on drugs and its effect on women drug users. She explains how women were easy targets of the war on drugs because of a long history of drug use by women in the general population. She also maintains that due to policy that intentionally targeted African American women, the war on drugs led to an imprisonment boom for this population. The next section will further explore girls' and women's incarceration.

Chapter 9

MURDER AS SELF-HELP

Women and Intimate Partner Homicide

ELICKA S. L. PETERSON

Compared to men, women commit a very small number of homicides. As such, little scholarly attention has been afforded to homicide committed by women, particularly in terms of theory. We do know that the vast majority of female-perpetrated homicides occur in the home (Goetting, 1987; Mann, 1990,1996), most are against intimates (Browne & Williams, 1993; Edwards, 1984; Goetting, 1988; Mann, 1990, 1996), and often involve no advance planning (Goetting, 1987). Frequently, these killings occur in reaction to long-term abuse (Browne, 1987; Goetting, 1987).

Understanding the conditions that explain why women commit far fewer homicides could provide insight into why men commit far more. Assumptions about vast biological differences between men and women rooted in early, and largely discounted, research on female criminality are probably responsible for an enduring belief that a greater understanding of female criminality would not advance an understanding of male criminality (for an overview, see Klein, 1973). Although biology would suggest limited malleability in terms of reducing criminality, many social factors are in fact amenable to

manipulation. Devoting attention to female-perpetrated homicide is, of course, warranted by the devastating consequences for those involved. In addition to the loss of the victim's life, the victim's family, the larger society, the perpetrator, and possibly her children—a fact with broad implications for future generations—are all deeply damaged by the homicidal event.

Much of the early scholarly attention afforded female criminality was rooted in either biology or notions about feminine gender roles (for an overview, see Rasche, 1989). In terms of explanatory models, Simpson (1991) examined the neo-Marxian theory of Colvin and Pauly, the power-control theory of Hagan, Simpson, and Gillis, and the socialist-feminist theory of Messerschmidt, all developed in the 1980s. Although she found them promising as starting points for understanding the reality of female criminality, she noted their failure to incorporate gender, social class, and race as divergent systems of control and domination.

Ogle, Maier-Katkin, and Bernard (1995) provide an elegant explanation for the homicidal behavior of women linked to the interplay of

Source: Peterson, E. (1999). Murder as self-help: Women and intimate partner homicide. *Homicide Studies, 3*(1), 30–46.

Author's Note: I am grateful to Scott Decker, Jody Miller, Rick Rosenfeld, Richard Wright, and several anonymous reviewers for their insightful comments on an earlier version of this chapter. I also thank Rick Rabe for his technical assistance.

strain proposed by Agnew, overcontrolled personality proposed by Megargee, and a high level of chronic arousal in the lives of the "truly disadvantaged" proposed by Bernard. However, this theory does not specifically address the interaction of race and the role of formal social control. The societal definition of, and reaction to, deviance are crucial elements in a discussion of female-perpetrated homicide but are noticeably absent from the literature, except as a paradigm separate from the causes of criminality (for an overview of formal reactions to the deviancy of women, see Birch, 1994; Chesney-Lind, 1997).

In this chapter, I adapt Donald Black's self-help framework to explain female-perpetrated homicide in an intimate context, a context accounting for the vast majority of murders committed by women. The resulting perspective encompasses Simpson's (1991) discussion of gender, race, and social class in an explanation that also accounts for the impact of formal social control on the homicidal behavior of women against intimates and why women kill less often than men. Indeed, the self-help perspective has even broader application, encompassing many financially motivated homicide by women and much of the homicides committed by men, particularly men with low status. Its scope is limited here to female homicide because of the pressing need for such an explanation and because it is particularly well-suited for the task, given the depressing effect of gender on social status.

Self-Help and Female-Perpetrated Intimate Partner Homicide

Illegal Justice

The foundation for this gender-specific model is found in a framework general enough to explain conflict management in almost any context—Black's (1983, 1993) self-help theory of crime. Grounded in moralism, in that one or both of the participants has defined the conflict in terms of being wronged, criminality motivated by self-help is best viewed as an illegal attempt to exact justice (for an excellent discussion of moralism in the context of homicide, see Katz, 1988). Crime takes the form of social control in

this moral context: Perpetrators view their own actions as a response to deviant acts committed against them. In this manner, the perpetrators view themselves as victims in the conflict, regardless of whether they would be so-defined legally (Black, 1993). This justice-seeking behavior is prevalent in cases of murder. In the United States, approximately 70% of criminal homicides arise from a conflict defined as moralistic in character (Maxfield, 1989).

The conflict resolution component to female-perpetrated homicide is unmistakable, particularly in the case of killing an abusive partner, which is certainly akin to removing the problem of domestic violence from the homicide perpetrator's life. In conflicts involving intimate relationships, Black (1993) asserts that the principals often "find that legal officials are relatively unconcerned about their conflicts, particularly if they occur in private and do not disturb anyone else. In all these settings neglected by law, crimes of self-help are comparatively common" (p. 40).

Thus, dissatisfaction with criminal justice responses to domestic violence leads to the creation of a lawless location in social space. The exact prevalence of the multitude of transgressions serious enough to trigger a self-help response is unknown, but research offers sobering statistics on the incidence of child and spousal abuse, incest, and extramarital affairs (Brownmiller, 1975; Chesney-Lind, 1997). Alcohol use, germane to the victim (46.7%) or perpetrator (35.6%) in many homicides (Mann, 1996), exacerbates these problems in terms of lowered inhibitions about retaliating and increased precipitation by the victim (Wolfgang, 1958).

Grant and Curry (1993) found that women incarcerated for killing male intimates were more socially isolated and perceived that they were in greater danger than women who sought refuge in a shelter. It is possible that incarcerated homicide offenders report a greater sense of fear *post facto* as a conscious or unconscious way of rationalizing their use of lethal violence. Findings from studies relying on the retrospective perceptions of incarcerated offenders, therefore, must be treated with caution. Social isolation is discussed in greater detail below, but in terms of a greater perception of danger in an abusive situation it is intuitively reasonable that women who feel more isolated might be more likely to resort to lethal self-help.

The Accessibility of Law

Another important element in this framework is access to legal forms of social control. According to Black (1993), reliance on either law or self-help depends largely on the principals involved in the conflict, with four identifiable patterns emerging (see Table 9.1 for an overview). The roles of women and men in fatal disputes are evaluated by Black in this context. "First, law may be relatively unavailable both to those with grievances and to those who are the objects of self-help, as when people of low status and people who are intimate have conflicts with one another" (p. 41).

This pattern, which is central to the current discussion, explains the reliance on self-help in most female-perpetrated homicides (see Decker, 1993, for an overview of victim-offender relationships). As roughly 80% of female-perpetrated homicides involve the murder of an intimate partner (Browne & Williams, 1993), this first category is crucial to our understanding of women who kill. Further, modern homicide is concentrated in the lower classes (Cooney, 1997) and is a largely intraracial phenomenon (Maguire & Pastore, 1997), which adds further to the number of perpetrators and victims assigned to this category through low status.

The second pattern described by Black (1993) is one in which "[l]aw may be relatively unavailable to those with grievances in comparison to those who have offended them" (p. 41). This pattern describes the legal remedies available to women in comparison to men. Much has been written about the failure of criminal justice in protecting victims of domestic abuse, but this is only part of a wider legal inequality that encompasses everything from the enforcement of child support payments to the half-hearted enforcement of protection orders (see, for example, Browne, 1987; Schafran, 1990). The message women receive is clear: There is little protection in law. For women of color and lower socioeconomic status, this message is even clearer, although a smaller gap exists between their access to legal remedies and the access of similarly situated men.

The third pattern plays less of a role in female-perpetrated homicide, illustrating a grievance against a social inferior: "Law is readily available to them but not to those against whom they might employ self-help. In this situation, the aggrieved party seemingly has a choice of law or self-help" (Black, 1993, p. 41).

The fourth pattern, illustrating a grievance among equals, also plays a smaller role in the context of female-perpetrated homicide. In this situation, self-help is rarely invoked: "[Law] is readily available to both those with grievances and those who have offended them . . . this is seen when people of high status and people who are strangers have conflicts with one another" (Black, 1993, p. 41).

Although the third and fourth patterns are less evident in female-perpetrated homicide, they do offer a contrast against which women can evaluate their own inequality in access to legal remedies. This point of comparison is sharp, and women are further reminded of their unequal access to legal help in the wake of homicide. Women are far less likely than men to successfully argue self-defense, although empirical

Table 9.1   The Accessibility of Law in Relation to the Social Status of Disputants

	Level of Status		
Pattern	Offender	Victim	Remedy
(1) Law relatively unavailable to both parties	Low	Low	Self-help
(2) Law relatively unavailable to the victim compared to the offender	High	Low	Self-help
(3) Law relatively unavailable to the offender but not to the victim	Low	High	Either law or self-help
(4) Law readily available to both parties	High	High	Law

evidence suggests that the situations in which women kill more often justify this rejoinder (Birch, 1994; Gauthier & Bankston, 1997; Gillespie, 1989; Heidensohn, 1995).

THE ROLE OF STATUS IN SOCIAL SPACE

Black (1976, 1993) asserts that social life exists in a multidimensional space that is defined by human interaction. Dimensions of social space are defined as vertical, horizontal and radial, symbolic or cultural, and normative. According to Black, these highly variable locations explain and predict human behaviors that characterize social life. They also are useful in explaining variations in female-perpetrated homicide. The theory of self-help predicts a strong, negative correlation between self-help homicide and a firm footing in each dimension of social space. Black's sociological typology yields a better understanding of the relationship between race, social class, gender, and homicide than previous unidimensional perspectives, so it will be discussed here in some detail.

Vertical Status

"A vertical dimension of social space is present when there is an uneven distribution of wealth, or social stratification" (Black, 1993, p. 159). Cooney (1997) employed income and accumulated wealth as indicators of vertical status (as per Black, 1976) and found that "measures of economic deprivation consistently emerge as one of the strongest predictors of aggregate rates of homicide" (p. 383). Specific to lower status women, dependence on government aid or their intimate partner and the number of dependent children might well be added to these constructs. In the United States, women and their children are easily the largest aggregate of poor people (National Center for Children in Poverty, 1987).

As mentioned earlier, research consistently shows that homicide offenders are concentrated at the lower end of the socioeconomic spectrum (Goetting, 1995; Gordon, 1976; Green & Wakefield, 1979; Mann, 1996; Wolfgang, 1958). Given the fact that women earn far less than men and that homicides perpetrated by women are almost always intraclass and intraracial, it is a fair assumption that female homicide perpetrators are at least as economically disadvantaged as male perpetrators and perhaps more so (see Flowers, 1987; Jones, 1996; Ogle et al., 1995). As such, low vertical status is related to self-help homicide with particular applicability to female offenders.

Horizontal and Radial Status

Black (1993) describes the horizontal social space as one that "arises from the distribution of people in relation to each other. . . . It includes any division of labor, or differentiation, and also the pattern by which people participate in social life" (p. 160). Horizontal and radial status refer to one's level of integration and participation in social life. More participation brings an individual or group closer to the center of social life, whereas less puts them closer to the periphery. Although Cooney (1997) used employment and marital status as measures of radial status, for women—particularly abused women—marriage might actually have a negative impact on horizontal and radial status. This is mainly due to the intimidation and shame experienced in an abusive marriage, which often inhibits women from cultivating and maintaining social bonds (Browne, 1995; Friedman & Shulman, 1990).

Grant and Curry's (1993) comparison of abused women who sought refuge in shelters with women who killed their abusive intimate partners revealed that women "incarcerated for killing their male partners appear to be more socially isolated from the mainstream" (p. 73) than their counterparts in shelters. Another significant difference between the two groups was that women who had killed intimates were much more likely to report a greater perception of danger in the domestic situation than women who did not resort to lethal violence. Although, as suggested earlier, this heightened perception of danger may represent post facto rationalization, it may also be related to the real increased social isolation of the women who killed their partners (Friedman & Shulman, 1990). Thus, as women become isolated owing to their low radial status, their perception of available help in the larger social world decreases, increasing the likelihood that they will resort to lethal self-help as an alternative.

In a wider sense, American women, particularly women of color and lower socioeconomic status, live in a society built on the premise of male superiority. Women have a long history of legal (for an overview, see Chesney-Lind, 1997), economic (Bernard, 1990), and social marginalization (Faludi, 1991) in this country, which has resulted in far lower horizontal and radial statuses than men experience, especially for non-White and lower-class women (Davis-Adeshoté, 1995). The culture of poverty is not the mainstream culture in the United States (Herzog, 1966), but a disproportionate number of women call this marginal location in social life "home."

Cooney (1997) also incorporates youth as an indicator of low radial status, but in the case of women, particularly those in abusive relationships, a curvilinear relationship may exist between age and status. Grant and Curry (1993) found that the average age in their sample of women incarcerated for killing their abusers was 34.5 years, compared to 28.6 years in the sample of abused women who fled to shelters. In response to this finding, they suggest that "[a]ge may be another form of social distance that may separate older women from the shelter alternative" (p. 81).

Symbolic or Cultural Status

Cooney (1997) describes cultural status as measurable "by the amount of education received and participation in the culture of the majority (conventionality)" (p. 385). In general, female homicide perpetrators and their victims have low cultural status. Membership in racial and ethnic minorities is a strong indicator of cultural marginalization (Davis-Adeshoté, 1995) for which the empirical tie to homicide, especially for African Americans at the aggregate level, has been firmly established (see Rosenfeld, 1986). The educational attainment of most female homicide offenders is low (Mann, 1996). However, an education in mainstream culture could actually serve to promote an awareness of a lack of cultural representation for members of marginalized groups (Herzog, 1966).

In the case of female homicide offenders, Black's (1993) definition of low cultural or symbolic status is perhaps best represented by the awareness and participation measures to include a lack of cultural representation or, more specifically, a lack of positive cultural representation. For example, African American women have long been marginalized in the cultural realm through the proliferation of such images as servants, prostitutes, welfare "queens," and,

more recently, by the myth of the violent crime wave of Black female "gangstas" (Chesney-Lind, 1993; Miller, 1998).

White women receive more representation in the mainstream culture but do so in roles in which "men are always the subjects and women the objects in the male-centric universe" (de Bouvoir, as quoted in Ogle et al., 1995, p. 177). In general, "widespread cultural messages imply that males are rational, moral, mature, independent, and assertive and that females are irrational, immoral, emotional, dependent, and submissive" (Ogle et al., 1995, p. 177). Women are sexualized by art, the popular media, and the law (Faludi, 1991; Friedan, 1983). Black men are arguably the only marginalized group more vilified in the popular culture (see Gibbs, 1988), but, in general, their status as males still affords more social currency than that of Black women.

Normative Status

Normative status represents the "capacity for social control—authority . . . [and the] respectability of individuals and groups: the degree to which they have been subjected to social control in the past" (Black, 1993, p. 161). Low normative status is a powerful indicator of homicidal behavior in men (Wolfgang, 1958). For women, Mann's (1996) study of female-perpetrated homicide shows that "almost half of the women arrested for killing sexual intimates had prior arrest records" (p. 146), although on average, this past history was characterized as violent in only 34% of cases (p. 144).

Lower status in social life often precipitates more frequent contact with the law, because society defines its boundaries through the social control of the people most likely to cross them (Erikson, 1966)—those on the periphery of social life. Women who kill are also frequently the subjects of formal social control outside of the criminal justice realm. For example, social services constrain recipients of government aid in a variety of ways, from designating who can and cannot live in a household to determining where that household is located. In terms of the past control of women, disparity in the handling of youths in the juvenile justice system often places girls under more restrictive control than boys, frequently for lesser offenses (Chesney-Lind, 1997). Thus, female homicide perpetrators are likely to have low normative status, which contributes more generally to a greater perception on the part of women than men of blocked access to legal remedies.

PERCEPTIONS ABOUT THE ACCESSIBILITY OF FORMAL SOCIAL CONTROL

A perceived or actual inaccessibility to formal social control is central to Black's (1993) theory of self-help. Cooney (1997) contends that "some groups occupy a stateless location in social space" (p. 393). The law almost invariably defines violence employed in handling a conflict as a crime, but low-status individuals are often reluctant to invoke legal remedies for three reasons. First, they may be more likely to see formal social control as working against them, rather than for them. Second, they may be more likely to define grievances in such a way that gives them no legal right to invoke the law. Finally, they may be more likely to believe that legal intervention would provide a less satisfactory result, due to a more punitive definition of justice (Markowitz & Felson, 1998).

Much of this reluctance is not only the product of the disputants' low social status but also of the high status of criminal justice practitioners. Black (1993) argues that the higher the status of these officials, relative to that of disputants, the more repressive their response to disputants. Lower-status disputants react to this repressive action with antagonism and disdain for the law. These negative views coalesce to form an aversion for legal means of conflict resolution (for a complete description of this process, see Cooney, 1997).

A variety of gender-specific factors could affect perceptions of the availability of law in the case of female homicide perpetrators. The highly publicized plights of abused women receiving little help from the justice system have led to a widespread perception that the police and courts are impotent in the arena of domestic violence (Birch, 1994; Jones, 1996). Arrest figures indicate that an appreciable percentage of women who eventually kill their intimate partner have had previous experience on the wrong side of the law, which almost certainly results in a conception of law as oppressor rather than helper. Women socialized in a patriarchal environment might also believe that a grievance brought by a woman against a man will likely not be resolved to her satisfaction because it will be handled by a predominantly male system. Additionally, a long history of disparity in the courts in the handling of women's cases might also influence a woman's decision to opt for self-help (see Gillespie, 1989).

Although research specific to the perceptions of law held by female homicide perpetrators has yet to be conducted, Grant and Curry's (1993) more general study indicates a reluctance on the part of women who kill abusive intimates to seek legal help in their predicament, relative to women who sought refuge in shelters, indicating a perception of legal remedies as unavailable to them.

This insight appears to have been gained either intuitively or is based on considerable direct experience with legal officials. Grant and Curry (1993) found that a much higher proportion of the women in their sample who had resorted to lethal violence either had never called the police to intervene in a domestic violence episode or had called the police eight or more times, compared to their counterparts in shelters. The absence of calls might indicate that the female homicide perpetrators never considered that formal intervention would help; in contrast, women who had called repeatedly may have felt they had, in Grant and Curry's words, "exhausted the viability of that option" (p. 81).

Women who commit self-help homicide, then, have substantial reason to believe that their experience with formal social control will be unsatisfactory. Further research is needed to determine the extent to which perceptions of blocked access result in heavier reliance on violent self-help.

WHY WOMEN DO NOT COMMIT MORE HOMICIDE

Given the low status of women, and the related perception that legal remedies are not a viable option in the resolution of a conflict, a compelling question emerges: Why don't women kill more often? This question is generally framed as relative to the homicidal behavior of men. I suggest that the answer is linked to the relationship between social status and the availability of law, coupled with a more restrictive definition of situations warranting lethal self-help.

First, women have a paradoxical relationship with the law. As such, definitions unfavorable to their seeking legal assistance with a conflict might also serve to inhibit the application of self-help. Their perception that the formal response to a homicidal resolution might be worse than the problem they were trying to resolve in the first place is not unfounded. There is evidence to suggest that women who murder intimates receive harsher punishments than men who murder their intimates (Mann, 1996). Not surprising, this increased punitiveness against women who kill their intimates is more pronounced in the case of African American women (Daly, 1989).

Exacerbating the fear of prison time is the fact that many women have children, whose fate would then be placed in the hands of the formal system as well. With children to consider, the definitions favorable to lethal self-help are weighed against higher stakes than the woman's fate alone and may fail to tip the balance. Playing into this possibility is evidence that women are more relational in character than men (Lerner, 1980). A greater propensity to consider the impact of their crime on others would serve as a control mechanism inhibiting greater use of lethal violence by women.

Second, women define fewer situations as warranting a self-help response. The socialization of gender roles places less emphasis on a competitive "win-lose" definition of self for women, compared to men. In this context, it is easier for women to extract themselves from situations that more often escalate to lethal violence when men are involved, such as reactions to behavior defined as defiant or disrespectful (Decker, 1996; Katz, 1988). With less at stake in terms of promoting a tough reputation, women can avoid defining many conflicts in a manner requiring either violent redress or a loss of status. Indeed, their relatively low status might render most conflicts steeped in the defense of honor beyond rational consideration (for a perspective on the importance of honor in male homicidal behavior, see the article by Kenneth Polk [1999]).

In summary, several factors operate to reduce the likelihood of female homicide offending. A more forgiving designation of motives worth killing for, coupled with a fear of criminal sanctions that would interrupt and significantly damage relationships held dearer to women, lead fewer women to consider homicide as an alternative to legal social control.

DISCUSSION AND CONCLUSION

Black's self-help theory provides a sound framework for studying the lethal violence of women. Although Black (1993) asserts that biological characteristics are not synonymous with social status, he does admit that biological characteristics, such as race and sex, are useful as "crude indicators" (p. 162) of one's position in social space. My designation of their utility is stronger. Factors such as race, gender, and poverty each profoundly influence the location of individuals and groups in Black's social dimensions.

My earlier reference to uncovering a greater understanding of male homicide perpetrators through a better understanding of similarly situated women is noteworthy here. When intimates kill, it is often in the context of an abusive relationship. When women are murdered, they are likely to be killed by their husbands or boyfriends (Friedman & Shulman, 1990). When women kill, they are more likely to kill their sexual intimates than persons in any other relational category (Mann, 1996). These facts imply that, in households where someone has engaged in lethal violence, the roles of victim and perpetrator might well have been reversed, if not for the violent end to the conflict.

Whereas women might be more likely to engage in self-help related to fear or actual survival in an intimate context, men might be more likely to engage in a kind of self-help related to a perception that violence is necessary to establish or maintain control in the relationship. In both scenarios, it is possible for the offender to assume a righteous posture in resolving the problem as they have defined it, even if that resolution is lethal (Katz, 1988). Through the relationship among homicide, abuse, and self-help, the dynamics in which many men kill their intimate partners can be explored from a different angle.

The response of the criminal justice system to female homicide perpetrators can also be examined from the perspective of this grounded theoretical model. Of particular interest is the role of such response in reinforcing perceptions that justice is unavailable through legal remedies, which leads to increased violence as a self-help response. The chivalry hypothesis might hold in some circumstances, but for women in domestic violence situations, the law is likely perceived as anything but a chivalrous entity.

Cooney's (1997) call for cross-cultural and historical criminological research on violence is echoed here as well. Are women who kill in the United States distinctive in some important way? Have women always been more likely to kill their sexual intimates? Empirical evidence is needed to assess whether the current relationship between women and lethal violence is a modern phenomenon or one that has remained relatively stable over time. As women have in almost every society held roles defined as subordinate to men, with even fewer legal avenues available for recourse, it seems plausible that this relationship might represent an enduring historical condition. However, this pattern may well be changing. Recent findings on the decline of intimate homicide suggest that as women are afforded more options, they are less likely to resort to lethal self-help (Dugan, Nagin, & Rosenfeld, 1997; Rosenfeld, 1997).

Black's (1983, 1993) theoretical perspective emphasizes the contextual legitimacy of formal and informal modes of social control. The varying degrees of reliance on both, in relation to the illuminating effects of race, gender, and social class suggested by Simpson (1991), warrant further investigation, as does the importance of motive and perceptions of access to legal remedies. This research would best be conducted using quantitative and qualitative techniques to assess the theory in terms of wider patterns of female homicide, in addition to the more subtle distinctions in perceptions related to alternatives and inhibitions. The scope of this perspective is not restricted to women or to the crime of intimate partner homicide. Black (1983) argues that it can be applied in almost any context. In narrowing the focus to female-perpetrated homicide against intimates, however, we would not necessarily be limiting the wider utility of the theory of self-help as we achieve a better understanding of this particular social problem.

References

Bernard, T. J. (1990). Angry aggression among the truly disadvantaged. *Criminology, 28,* 73–95.

Birch, H. (Ed.). (1994). *Moving targets: Women, murder and representation.* Berkeley: University of California Press.

Black, D. (1976). *The behavior of law.* San Diego: Academic Press.

Black, D. (1983). Crime as social control. *American Sociological Review, 48,* 34–45.

Black, D. (1993). *The social structure of right and wrong.* San Diego: Academic Press.

Browne, A. (1987). *When battered women kill.* New York: Free Press.

Browne, A. (1995). Fear and the perception of alternatives: Asking "why women don't leave" is the wrong question. In B. R. Price & M. Sokoloff (Eds.), *The criminal justice system and women* (2nd ed., pp. 228–245). New York: McGraw-Hill.

Browne, A., & Williams, K. R. (1993). Gender, intimacy, and lethal violence: Trends from 1976 through 1987. *Gender and Society, 7,* 78–98.

Brownmiller, S. (1975). *Against our will: Men, women, and rape.* New York: Ballantine.

Chesney-Lind, M. (1993). Girls, gangs and violence: Anatomy of a backlash. *Humanity & Society, 17,* 321–344.

Chesney-Lind, M. (1997). *The female offender: Girls, women, and crime.* Thousand Oaks, CA: Sage.

Cooney, M. (1997). The decline of elite homicide. *Criminology, 35,* 381–407.

Daly, K. (1989). Neither conflict nor labeling nor paternalism will suffice: Intersections of race, ethnicity, gender, and family in criminal court decisions. *Crime & Delinquency, 35,* 136–168.

Davis-Adeshoté, J. (1995). *Black survival in White America: From past history to the next century.* Orange, NJ: Bryant & Dillon.

Decker, S. H. (1993). Exploring the victim-offender relationships in homicide: The role of individual and event characteristics. *Justice Quarterly, 10,* 585–612.

Decker, S. H. (1996). Deviant homicide: A new look at the role of motives in victim-offender relationships. *Journal of Research in Crime and Delinquency, 33,* 427–449.

Dugan, L., Nagin, D., & Rosenfeld, R. (1997). *Explaining the decline in intimate partner homicide: The effects of changing domesticity, women's status, and domestic violence resources* (Working paper No. 2). Pittsburgh, PA: Carnegie Mellon University, National Consortium on Violence Research.

Edwards, S. (1984). *Women on trial.* Manchester, UK: Manchester University Press.

Erikson, K. T. (1966). *Wayward puritans: A study in the sociology of deviance.* New York: John Wiley.

Faludi, S. (1991). *Backlash: The undeclared war against American women.* New York: Crown.

Flowers, R. B. (1987). *Women and criminality: The woman as victim, offender, and practitioner.* New York: Greenwood.

Friedan, B. (1983). *The feminine mystique.* New York: Norton.

Friedman, L. N., & Shulman, M. (1990). Domestic violence: The criminal justice response. In A. J. Lurigio, W. G. Skogan, & R. C. Davis (Eds.), *Victims of crime: Problems, policies, and programs* (pp. 87–103). Newbury Park, CA: Sage.

Gauthier, D. K., & Bankston, W. B. (1997). Gender equality and the sex ratio of intimate killing. *Criminology, 35,* 577–600.

Gibbs, J. T. (Ed.). (1988). *Young, Black, and male in America: An endangered species.* Westport, CT: Auburn House.

Gillespie, C. K. (1989). *Justifiable homicide: Battered women, self defense, and the law.* Columbus: Ohio State University Press.

Goetting, A. (1987). Homicidal wives: A profile. *Journal of Family Issues, 8,* 332–341.

Goetting, A. (1988). Patterns of homicide among women. *Journal of Interpersonal Violence, 3,* 3–20.

Goetting, A. (1995). *Homicide in families and other special populations.* New York: Springer.

Gordon, D. M. (1976). Class and the economics of crime. In W. J. Chambliss & M. Mankoff (Eds.), *Whose law? What order? A conflict approach to criminology* (pp. 193–214). New York: John Wiley.

Grant, B., & Curry, G. D. (1993). Women murderers and victims of abuse in a southern state. *American Journal of Criminal Justice, 17,* 73–83.

Green, E., & Wakefield, R. P. (1979). Patterns of middle and upper class homicide. *Journal of Criminal Law and Criminology, 70,* 172–181.

Heidensohn, F. M. (with Silvestri, F.). (1995). *Women and crime* (2nd ed.). New York: New York University Press.

Herzog, E. (1966). Is there a culture of poverty? In H. H. Meissner (Ed.), *Poverty in the affluent society* (pp. 92–102). New York: Harper & Row.

Jones, A. (1996). *Women who kill.* Boston: Beacon.

Katz, J. (1988). *Seductions of crime: Moral and sensual attractions in doing evil.* New York: Basic Books.

Klein, D. (1973). The etiology of female crime: A review of the literature. *Issues in Criminology, 8,* 3–30.

Lerner, H. G. (1980). Internal prohibitions against female anger. *American Journal of Psychoanalysis, 40,* 137–147.

Maguire, K., & Pastore, A. L. (Eds.). (1997). *Sourcebook of criminal justice statistics—1996.* Washington, DC: Government Printing Office.

Mann, C. R. (1990). Black female homicides in the United States. *Journal of Interpersonal Violence, 5,* 176–201.

Mann, C. R. (1996). *When women kill.* Albany: State University of New York Press.

Markowitz, F. E., & Felson, R. E. (1998). Social-demographic differences in attitudes and violence. *Criminology, 36,* 117–138.

Maxfield, M. G. (1989). Circumstances in Supplemental Homicide Reports: Variety and validity. *Criminology, 27,* 671–695.

Miller, J. (1998). Up it up: Gender and the accomplishment of street robbery. *Criminology, 36,* 37–66.

National Center for Children in Poverty. (1987). *Household statistics on families and poverty rate.* New York: Columbia University Press.

Ogle, R. S., Maier-Katkin, D., & Bernard, T. J. (1995). A theory of homicidal behavior among women. *Criminology, 33,* 173–193.

Polk, K. (1999). Males and honor contest violence. *Homicide Studies, 3,* 6–29.

Rasche, C. (1989). Early models for contemporary thought on domestic violence and women who kill their mates: A review of the literature from 1895–1970. *Women and Criminal Justice, 1,* 31–53.

Rosenfeld, R. (1986). Urban crime rates: Effects of inequality, welfare dependency, region, and race. In J. M. Byrne & R. J. Sampson (Eds.), *The social ecology of crime* (pp. 116–130). New York/Berlin: Springer-Verlag.

Rosenfeld, R. (1997). Changing relationships between men and women: A note on the decline of intimate partner homicide. *Homicide Studies, 1,* 72–83.

Schafran, L. H. (1990). Overwhelming evidence of gender bias in the courts. In B. F. Price & N. J. Sokoloff (Eds.), *The criminal justice system and women* (pp. 333–342). New York: McGraw-Hill.

Simpson, S. S. (1991). Caste, class, and violent crime: Explaining differences in female offending. *Criminology, 29,* 115–135.

Wolfgang, M. E. (1958). *Patterns in criminal homicide.* Philadelphia: University of Pennsylvania Press.

Chapter 10

WOMEN AT RISK IN SEX WORK

Strategies for Survival

PRISCILLA PYETT AND DEBORAH WARR

In the last decade a considerable body of research has examined non-use of condoms among sex workers as a major risk factor in relation to sexually transmissible diseases (STDs) and, more particularly, HIV/AIDS. Female sex workers in Europe, the United Kingdom, the United States and in Australia have reported high rates of condom use with clients, while their use of condoms with private partners is reportedly much lower (Campbell 1991; Day and Ward 1990; Dorfman et al. 1992; Estebanez et al. 1993; Harcourt and Philpot 1990; McKeganey and Barnard 1996; Pyett et al. 1996a, 1996b; Vanwesenbeeck et al. 1993). Surprisingly few studies have examined other health and safety risks faced by women engaged in sex work. Furthermore, researchers have rarely investigated variations in the strategies adopted by sex workers to overcome problems associated with their work and social circumstances. Such problems may include their health, drug use and housing needs, as well as difficulties with clients and with private partners. The risks associated with sex work may be mediated by a range of circumstances in the women's lives. As Vanwesenbeeck et al. (1993) pointed out, the degree of control an individual is able to exert over their own or others' behaviour is likely to be significantly affected by factors such as the age of the sex worker, the legal context of sex work, and whether engaging in sex work or in a particular sexual service is voluntary or not.

Source: Pyett, P., & Warr, D. (1999). Women at risk in sex work: Strategies for survival. *Journal of Sociology, 35*(2), 183–197.

Authors' Note: This study would not have been possible without the cooperation of the Prostitutes' Collective of Victoria (PCV), Melbourne Youth Support Services, Hanover Women's Services and the Young People's Health Service (a Functional Unit of the Centre for Adolescent Health). We thank the women who formed the Critical Reference Group for their interest, enthusiasm and commitment: Alison Arnot-Bradshaw, Sarah Fair, Dona Macik, Deb Mayson, Jocelyn Snow, Leonie Tehan and Jane Treleaven. We also thank the 24 women who agreed to participate in this study, for giving their time and for sharing the often distressing details of their personal lives. The study was conducted at the Australian Research Centre in Sex, Health and Society at La Trobe University and supported by a grant from the Public Health Research and Development Committee of the National Health and Medical Research Council of Australia.

The legal context of sex work is different in each Australian state and territory (Neave 1994). Victorian law provides for the licensing of brothels and escort agencies, and for women to register as private sex workers, but all forms of street work and unlicensed sex work remain subject to criminal sanctions *(Prostitution Control Act 1995).* Although condom use is mandatory for all sex services in licensed brothels, according to the Prostitutes' Collective of Victoria (PCV), not all brothel managers adhere strictly to regulations (personal communication). However, a recent survey of female prostitutes in Victoria found high levels of reported condom use with clients, low rates of reported STD infection and no reported cases of HIV (Pyett et al. 1996a, 1996b). The main risk factors identified in that survey were injecting drug use and non-condom use with private partners. Together these findings represent potential risks for some female sex workers, particularly if the women's private partners are themselves injecting drug users who share needles or have unprotected sex with other partners, as has been found in other studies (Campbell 1995; Day and Ward 1990; Harcourt and Philpot 1990; Matthews 1990). The Victorian survey recruited a large number of women working in the legal brothels, but the methodology was less suited to reaching women who worked on the streets or in other illegal sectors of the sex industry (Pyett et al. 1996a, 1996b). Representatives of the PCV expressed concern that some of these women would be more vulnerable to risk and less able to exert control over the sexual encounter with the client (personal communication). In order to explore issues of safe sex and risk management among women in some of these different contexts, we chose to conduct a small-scale qualitative study in Melbourne.

METHODOLOGY

In collaboration with the PCV we established a Critical Reference Group composed of women who had some association with the sex industry, either as current or past sex workers, or as health educators or outreach workers in the field. These eight women provided advice during the planning phase, recruited and interviewed participants and assisted with the interpretation of findings.

In-depth interviews were conducted with a purposively selected sample of 24 women who were perceived as potentially vulnerable to risk because they were young, inexperienced, homeless, drug or alcohol dependent, or working in illegal brothels or on the street. The interviewers used a series of open-ended questions to address three broad areas: work, health and private life. 'Work' covered mode of sex work (street, brothel, escort or private), how the women went through their service, how they had learned to work safely, what support they received from management and other workers, how they went about using condoms and what difficulties they encountered using condoms, worries they had about working, how they dealt with stress, and what their plans were for the future. The second section focused on general health, difficulties with maintaining health (such as nutrition, lifestyle factors, access to health services), sexual health history, responsibility for the care of other people (children, partner), support from family and friends, and how they managed relaxation. 'Private life' referred to issues such as disclosure of sex work to friends and family, difficulties experienced in personal relationships as a result of sex work, issues around using condoms with private partners, and problems with child care.

Women were paid $50 for participating in an interview which lasted between 20 minutes and one hour. All interviews were tape-recorded and transcribed verbatim. Transcripts were manually coded and analysed by both researchers using content and thematic analysis (Patton 1990; Silverman 1993). Themes were initially drawn from the literature in accordance with the aims of the study: work experience, condom use with clients, condom use and relationships with private partners, drug use, STDs and other health issues. Additional themes emerged from the interviews themselves: experience of violence and threats to physical safety, risk management strategies, social isolation and attitudes to private sexual relationships. Findings relating to HIV risk and to the women's private relationships have been reported elsewhere (Pyett and Warr 1997; Warr and Pyett 1999). In this chapter we describe the risks faced by these women and explore the strategies they employed to avoid or manage risk. Any details that might identify the women have been altered and pseudonyms have been used for all participants.

THE SAMPLE

The women were aged between 14 and 47 years with an average age of 28 years. A quarter of the women had started sex work before the age of 16, while three women were over 30 when they started.[1] Women had been in the sex industry for as little as three months to as long as 16 years. Financial hardship was the main reason given for entering the sex industry. Half of the women were involved in street work and half worked in legal brothels, in 'massage parlours' (which function as illegal brothels)[2] or in escort agencies. We found it useful to categorise these two groups as 'street' or 'brothel' workers, and a number of differences between these two groups emerged (see Table 10.1).

Almost all the street workers and half of the brothel workers reported current or recent injecting drug use. In only a few cases did heavy drug use precede the woman becoming involved in sex work. Two-thirds of the street workers were currently homeless or without stable accommodation. Most women spoke about the difficulties associated with maintaining a private sexual relationship while engaging in sex work, and only one street worker and four brothel workers were in live-in relationships. About half the women in each group had children but most of the street workers had lost custody of their children. More than half of the street workers and only one brothel worker volunteered information about physical or sexual abuse they had experienced during childhood or while in state care. For most of the street workers, and a small number of brothel workers, daily life was characterised by profound social isolation which was most evident in the absence of family, friends or any personal support network around them. Women working in brothels reported only limited support from other workers, while street workers reported an almost total absence of support from other workers other than the outreach worker from the PCV. Many of the street workers nominated a health or welfare service provider as the only person to whom they could turn for support.

RISKS TO HEALTH AND SAFETY

As reported elsewhere (Pyett and Warr 1997), all of the women in this study were determined to use condoms for sexual intercourse with clients and most were extremely reluctant to perform oral sex without a condom. However, client resistance, whether in the form of threats or enticements, was a continual obstacle to be overcome by negotiation in the sexual encounter. Physical assault and difficulties with enforcing condom use were reported much more frequently by street workers than by brothel workers. In some licensed brothels where, although in

Table 10.1	Comparison Between 'Street' and 'Brothel' Workers		
	Street n = 12	Brothel n = 12	Whole Sample n = 24
Mean age	24.1	31.8	28
Age range	14–36	19–47	14–47
Mean age started in sex industry	17.1	24.8	19.6
Mean years in sex industry	7.2	6.4	6.8
No. of women who have had children	7	6	13
No. of women who have lost custody	5	1	6
No. of women with drug issues	10	5	15
No. of women homeless or without stable accommodation	8	1	9
No. of women reporting childhood abuse	7	1	8

contravention of the law, management did not insist on condom use for all services, women experienced competition from other workers and considerable pressure from clients. It is evident from the data described below that youth, inexperience and the effects of alcohol and other drugs contributed to the difficulties faced by women attempting to enforce condom use.

Although the majority of private relationships described by the women in this study were irregular or casual (Warr and Pyett 1999), and women were often aware of their partners having sexual relationships with other women, only two women reported regular condom use with their private partners. A number of women also reported regularly engaging in unprotected sex with their drug dealers whom they knew to be involved in sexual relationships with other women at the same time. Several street workers revealed that they had at times shared needles with partners, with drug dealers or with their dealers' girlfriends.

All of the women who had engaged in street sex work had been exposed to frequent and considerable risks of violence from clients and had experienced at least one serious assault. At the same time, women tended to blame themselves and were extremely reluctant to report assaults to the police for fear of incurring penalties for prostitution-related offences or for non-payment of previous fines. Many of the women recounted horrific instances of violence from which they had barely escaped only to stagger home afterwards and recover as best they could. Marie was only 16 when she was attacked by a client who was a taxi driver:

> So, he had my hair and he was grabbing it and I was just trying to get out the door and I just let him pull part of my hair out and I just got out . . . and asked people for a lift because he hopped out too and they're going 'Get back in and pay your fare' and I was crying and everything, you know, and I had a red mark on my neck because he tried to strangle me with my scarf.

The fear of violence was ever-present in the working lives of street workers:

> Well I've been attacked a couple of times. I worry about it all the time. (32-year-old with 15 years experience in the sex industry)

> You never know what they're going to do, if you're going to be alive after the job. (14-year-old with less than one year in the sex industry)

> I hope I don't end up being killed or dead. (29-year-old with 10 years' experience in the sex industry)

> [When I was working on the street] I went through phases like if I'd get raped or something I'd be more paranoid for a while after that because I'd know, even if I didn't want to, I'd have to do it [sex work]. (19-year-old with 4 years' experience in the sex industry)

Most of the women working in legal brothels, on the other hand, reported feeling safe. Only one claimed to have experienced a violent incident while working. Brothel workers' security was enhanced by supportive management, firm policies relating to condom use and to the price, duration and type of service, by the existence of alarm systems, the proximity to other workers and the right to legal protection. By contrast, in the 'massage parlours,' although sexual services were limited to body massage and 'hand relief,' women worked in an environment where there was a perpetual threat of police raids and a constant potential for rape.

Brothel workers reported fewer health problems than street workers and the most serious health problems were associated with heavy drug use by street workers. A number of women had acquired STDs from private partners, including one street worker who reported that she was HIV positive. Only one woman reported that she had acquired an STD through sex work and this had occurred when she was very inexperienced. Other health problems included Hepatitis B and C, serious liver and kidney problems, dental problems attributed to drug use, skin problems, loss of appetite, multiple miscarriages and amenorrhoea.

APPROACHES TO RISK MANAGEMENT

Personal strategies for dealing with risky situations have been elsewhere termed 'risk management strategies' (Loxley and Ovenden 1995). Such strategies incorporate some sort of active management of sexual or other practices to reduce the risks of unsafe sex or unsafe injecting drug use, and can reflect varying degrees of efficacy from ensuring complete safety to limited risk reduction. We identified five different approaches to risk management among the women in this study. Since this was a small sample of purposively selected women, it is clear that the results cannot be extrapolated to sex workers in general. However, we believe these findings enhance our understanding of the diversity of approaches to risk management that are adopted by sex workers.

Risk Reduction in a Protected Environment

Four women had chosen to work in a legal brothel and were clear about their reasons for staying in sex work. These women were older (25–47 years) and saw their work as part of broader life plans. One was new to sex work, while the others had been in the sex industry for over ten years. They usually enjoyed the work and the company of other sex workers, and two of the women expressed a wish that they had started sex work earlier. None of these women were injecting drug users, although one had used heroin until a few years previously. Three women were supporting children and their lives were bounded by the routines associated with child care and school. Only one woman was living with a partner. The others preferred not to have a private relationship while engaging in sex work. As Frances explained:

> If you're not in the mood for sex that night [your partner will say] 'Oh did you get enough at work?' [or] 'Did you have a good run at work?' I've been woken up in the middle of the night with a hand between my legs and you just feel like 'Please, just give me a break!'

These women were able to outline firm guidelines for the services they would and would not provide and to describe strategies they employed to enforce condom use with all clients. For example, Frances described how she lost 'a lot of clients' because she insisted on using condoms and how she had 'seen girls paid in drugs and not money' but had never taken 'that option,' even when she had been using heroin herself.

It was apparent that these women maintained strict boundaries between themselves and their clients. Irene enjoyed 'the showing off' and knowing that she was sexually attractive to clients but was clear about her role as a service provider:

> The man is coming in and paying for a service. You are getting paid to look after someone and if you don't like it, well then, don't be there because the client will want his money back.

Reflecting on their experiences in sex work, these women asserted confidence in their ability to manage difficult circumstances, using expressions such as 'I'm a survivor,' 'I've learned to cope' and 'I never, ever do anything I feel uncomfortable with.' Their relatively good health and absence of reported STDs were indicative of effective risk management.

Working With Limited Control in a Protected Environment

The other five brothel workers were much less clear about their reasons for working in the sex industry, their choice of work environment and their strategies for managing risk. The women were of similar ages (30–42 years) to the women described above, had been involved for a similar length of time in sex work (18 months to 12 years), and worked in licensed brothels, but these women were unable to articulate how they overcame client resistance. All of these women were current or recent users of heroin and, although some had tried to give up, it was not clear that any had been completely successful. The consumption of alcohol and use of illicit drugs are illegal in brothels in Victoria, and most licensed brothels do not employ known drug users or tolerate drug use on the premises. Women who cannot conceal their drug use are forced to seek work in the minority of brothels where the management may be willing to overlook some regulations (PCV, personal communication).

Drug dependence severely limited these women's choices and their capacity to control the sexual encounter. Annette described herself as a 'daredevil' who relied on 'common sense' but saw herself as 'luckily unscathed' by her experiences in sex work. Annette admitted that the effects of alcohol and other drugs rendered her 'totally disempowered,' 'extremely vulnerable' and 'easily manipulated':

Basically I would let the client run the show rather than me run the show . . . There were times where I felt—where I was not in power in the room. I was actually—I think sometimes that even if you're not particularly fond of something or you don't like the way the client's handling you, you just shut up anyway because you don't want the client to go out and complain . . . but you just go through [with] it because it's your job.

Annette said there were times she was in the room with clients when she was 'almost collapsing.' Several other women acknowledged that they had difficulty in coping with sex work without heroin. Ellie said she used more on nights when she was working and Sophie said she used heroin daily:

I can't work without it, I just can't. I mean, I've dried out and come back to work but I can't work without it.

Numerous health problems, including serious effects of sustained drug use, were reported by these women and in two cases the interviewers expressed dismay at the women's poor state of health. Work was experienced as stressful and could 'drag you down.' Ellie complained about unwanted 'groping' from 'enthusiastic' clients:

I particularly hate the clients that want to make you cum and . . . they're unaware of their strength and very fumbling and it's all very gross [and they ask] 'Have you cum with my magic finger—digging into you there?'

Val worked in a licensed brothel where the management illegally encouraged some workers to provide sex without a condom. Because of her age (42) and dissatisfaction with her appearance, Val felt she was less likely to attract clients but saw herself as having no option but to put up with this unsatisfactory situation:

There's no way known they're going to stay with me, they're going to stay with the girl who doesn't use condoms and it's unfair, very unfair.

Only two of these women had male partners, and private relationships were largely regarded as difficult or impossible to manage with sex work. Sophie expressed a belief shared by a number of these women: 'I don't believe a guy

can love you and expect that you can work. I don't think you can love a guy and do this.' She also explained, 'I don't need the pressure of having to perform in my own bed—it's my haven.'

Risk Avoidance in a Less Protected Environment

The three women who were working in 'massage parlours' or escort agencies were less protected by the law than women working in licensed brothels.[3] These women had nevertheless made choices in an attempt to avoid risks of violence or of being coerced into acts of unprotected sex.

Leah had been assaulted and raped on several occasions when she worked on the street and acknowledged that heavy drug use had contributed to her inability to maintain safe sex practices. In order to help curtail her drug habit, Leah had chosen to work with an escort agency where the management would not tolerate drug use from employees. It was also important to Leah that the agency provided good security measures:

With this agency I work for, the drivers are pretty good . . . and also I take the phone in and I've got a push dial so I've just got to press redial. The driver waits outside—he stays there. A lot of other agencies they drive off.

Leah described the agency management as 'very much girl-oriented,' allowing the workers to choose what services they would provide and to refuse a booking with any client about whom they felt uncomfortable. Without such security measures, escort workers can be extremely vulnerable to demanding or violent clients.

The two women who had chosen to work in 'massage parlours' were avoiding the requirement to provide 'full sex' and thereby avoiding the risk of having unprotected sex with a client. However, the close body contact involved in nude massage and body 'slides' left these women extremely vulnerable to unwanted sexual advances and rape. The women were acutely aware of the absence of legal protection and, because it is illegal to have condoms on the premises of a massage parlour, any enforced act of sexual intercourse would be unprotected. Afraid of the police, the clients and the management, these women felt they had little real control over the sexual encounter with the client, as illustrated in Pat's account:

> Sometimes they want to touch. I can't say no all the time, otherwise I'm not going to get work. I have to sometimes . . . I've only gotten scared like a couple of times, not many times, where I thought that my life was being threatened.

These two women were aged 25 and 35 years and had been in the sex industry between five and six years. These women had low self-esteem and were less able to maintain the boundaries between sex, work and private relationships. Beth said she liked to have a massage herself for relaxation but her partner wanted to exchange services, providing massage in return for erotic stimulation. As she explained:

> The guy I live with is involved with the [massage] industry and he's qualified but he always wants a little bit of a look so he can give it to me cheaper. So it's like work while I'm doing it. I can't just totally relax.

Active Risk Management in a Risky Environment

Four of the street workers were able to outline specific routines and practices or 'active risk management strategies.' These women were all over 25 years of age, had been in the sex industry for over ten years and were likely to be intermittent rather than regular heroin users. They were clear that they chose to work on the streets because they felt more in control of their working hours and choice of clients, and were able to keep all their earnings. None of these women was currently living with a partner and their private relationships were characterised by episodes of violence or jail for either the woman or her boyfriend. While some of these women acknowledged the difficulties associated with their private relationships, others held on to remarkably optimistic and romantic views of their partners. Cheryl commented that her boyfriend 'thought he could handle' her working but they both found it 'hard.' Kylie still loved the man she had met as a client some four years previously and was hopeful of re-establishing their relationship even though she had been deeply hurt by his repeated episodes of overt infidelity and by his failure to visit her during her recent period of imprisonment.

All of these women reported multiple health problems that were typically associated with their drug use and irregular lifestyles. They reported little or no support from family or friends. Nevertheless, the women had developed their own strategies for survival on the street. Risk management was characterised by the woman taking command of the encounter by clearly stating what she was prepared to do and where it would take place (well lighted and familiar streets or hotels). These women had established routines which included persuading the client that he needed to use a condom and checking the client for signs of STDs. For example, Yvonne explained:

> I always check them out for herpes, for cuts, for warts, for lice . . . I've had a couple of clients who have said to me 'I'm lovely and clean' and I've gone down and had a look and . . . it was disgusting and I've just said 'See you later' and I've told them to go and wash and said 'You're a pig!' There was one guy who just looked at me and I jumped out of the car. I haven't had a problem with it.

Even among these women whom we have identified as active risk managers there seemed to be a stoic acceptance that a certain amount of violence was part of the job. Women even tended to blame themselves for being too 'greedy' or missing signs of an impending attack. Several women expressed relief that they had been assaulted only once or twice. Strategies to reduce risk included avoiding cars with more than one man in them, avoiding hire cars or cars with interstate registration plates and finding an opportunity to check inside the car for hidden weapons. Kylie explained how she would take note of a car's make and colour and devise a rhyme to memorise the number plate. She would check the inside of the car thoroughly, beginning with the door handle to make sure it opened from the inside:

> I always put my fingerprints on as many places as I can in the car. Most men that pick me up have car steering wheel locks and lots of them have it behind the passenger front seat and I prefer to move it. I say 'No offence' [and] put it behind their seat 'cause I feel it's harder for them to grab it than [if it's] just behind my seat. If they've got a blanket or a jacket on the car back seat I lift it

up. I explain I'm just looking out for my own safety mak[ing] sure there's nothing under there [that's] dangerous. And as we're driving I always—I don't let the driver know, but I'm always very careful—I watch their right hand because I've had men put their right hand down beside their seat under where I can't see what they're grabbing. If they're going to grab something to hurt me and if they don't go where I say—where to go—then I'm out of the car.

For these street workers, active risk management meant that their working hours were characterised by high levels of stress and vigilance.

Working Without Strategies in a Risky Environment

Street workers we have identified as working without strategies reported the most serious health problems, including HIV. These eight women could give no account of how they would enforce safe sex practices. Their personal situations were characterised by multiple difficulties, such as homelessness, social isolation, heavy drug use and a history of physical or sexual abuse in childhood. They were younger and had begun sex work at a younger age than other women in the study, although some had already worked for ten years. These women tended to talk in terms of a 'sixth sense' that offered little practical demonstration of how they were able to deal with client resistance to condoms. Indeed, the women acknowledged that their instincts sometimes left them vulnerable to risk. Most of these women had been persuaded to have unprotected oral sex with clients. Almost all of these women needed large amounts of money to support drug habits and many acknowledged that they could lose control of the sexual encounter when seriously affected by drugs, or 'savagely on the nod,' as one woman put it. Paula insisted that 'everything's got to be with a condom' but she also admitted that she 'could be asleep for forty-five minutes' and 'wake up dreaming about traffic lights.'

The very young women who had been working on the streets for only a year or less had few skills for actively managing the paid sexual encounter. Too young to be employed in a licensed brothel or to hire a hotel room, these young women had no choice but to work on the streets. According to their own reports, all

decisions upon entering the client's car were left up to him. Their knowledge of STDs was inaccurate and gathered haphazardly from other workers. Marie, for example, was prepared to provide oral sex without a condom if the client looked 'quite young' and 'clean.'

Although all of these street workers had suffered violent assaults from clients, none had developed any strategies to reduce risk. Paula believed that 'safety is you've just got to keep your head strong' but admitted that when she was 'smacked off her head . . . anything could happen, ten guys could come into the room and you're just not in control.' Joy said she 'just hoped for the best' and Karen used her 'sixth sense':

> Working for yourself, there's not a great deal you can do [about safety] but normally I can suss out whether I'm going to have trouble with them, generally I suss out if I should take them back to my room to do the job.

The younger women were more passive with clients. For example, Marie was happy if she and the client were able to 'meet halfway in agreement,' while 14-year-old Tina routinely got into the car and asked the man his name. The interviewer asked if she 'jumped straight in' and Tina replied:

> Yeah . . . and I ask them what they like to do and how they want me to do stuff and what they like and what they don't like.

Relying on hope and fatalism did not protect these women from finding sexual encounters enormously scary, as illustrated in this exchange with Tina:

> T: Because you're not sure whether they going to— like—hurt you or they're going to rape you and bloody kill you or something.
>
> I: The clients?
>
> T: Yeah, like they're going—just keep going, keep going and keep going—and they— they're going to kill you or throw you out and you're stuck with someone and—it's scary . . .
>
> I: So what sorts of things do you think you do to help you not to be so scared—or is there nothing?

T: I just try and relax, but it's hard because you're always uptight thinking 'Oh no, they're going—what's going to happen to me? They're not going to kill me or something!' But you just try and just lay back and relax and stuff, but it's hard.

To deal with her fears of being found 'half dead,' another of the very young women was taking up to four 'relaxing pills' a night that had been prescribed by a doctor.

DISCUSSION

The aim of this study was to identify women who were particularly vulnerable to risks in sex work and to examine their strategies for managing such risk. This was a small study and we would be wary of generalising to the wider population of sex workers. However, the risks faced by the women in our study were similar to those reported in a number of studies from other Western countries (Benson and Matthews 1995; Day and Ward 1990; Green et al. 1993; McKeganey and Barnard 1996; Vanwesenbeeck et al. 1993; Weiner 1996). Non-use of condoms with private partners was clearly a risk for these women. Their reasons for engaging in unprotected sex in casual, irregular and unstable relationships requires further investigation (see Warr and Pyett 1999). The findings from this study also provide further evidence that the specific context of sex work is an important determinant of risk behaviour (Harcourt 1994; Jackson et al. 1992; Perkins 1994; Vanwesenbeeck et al. 1993). Legal brothels clearly provided the safest environment for sex workers, although some women were unable to maintain control of the sexual encounter when severely affected by drugs. The level of support provided by brothel managers contributed to the women's safety in regard to both sexual health and physical assault. Street workers were at much greater risk of coercion, threats and physical assault by clients, had suffered more violence and experienced much poorer health, usually associated with drug use. However, women's choice of work environment was itself constrained by their age, drug dependence and capacity to manage the routine working hours of brothel employment. We found that the degree of control individual women were able to exert during sexual encounters with clients was affected not only by the legal context of sex work but also by the age, experience, self-esteem and self-confidence of the women and by their drug use at the time of the encounter.

While the legal context and organisation of sex work differs significantly between Australia and the Netherlands, our findings support the conclusions reached by Vanwesenbeeck et al. (1993) in their study of condom use among female sex workers. In the Dutch study, women who were 'consistent condom users' worked mostly in the organised sex industry, had positive and professional attitudes to their work and detached and business-like relationships with clients. These women could be seen to lead fairly structured lives, had chosen sex work for the high level of income they could earn, were confident in the efficacy of condoms and not worried about acquiring HIV infection themselves. By contrast, those least likely to use condoms with clients were younger women who worked in the less protected environment of the 'windows' or on the streets. They had negative attitudes to sex work and saw no alternative in the short term; many were drug users and most had experienced violence and past abuse. Like the young women in our study, they expressed fatalistic attitudes and feelings of powerlessness in relation to clients and their fear of AIDS (Vanwesenbeeck et al. 1993).

Vanwesenbeeck et al. (1993) concluded that work location clearly impacts on risk-taking but is itself determined by other factors. In our study it was apparent that women who had more experience and had developed specific routines and active risk management strategies were better able to protect their sexual health and to avoid physical violence than those whose passive acceptance of risk was managed only by hope, fear, fatalism or relaxing pills. Brothel and street workers who were older, had made clear choices about how and where they worked, could outline specific routines and practices to avoid risk, and were confident of their ability to avoid or manage difficult situations. However, it appeared that street workers were prepared to accept violence as a condition of working in an illegal and socially marginalised occupation. The brothel and street workers whom we have identified as having very limited strategies for avoiding or managing risk were vulnerable because their youth, inexperience or drug dependence meant that they had little control over the risks they encountered. Those most at risk were the very young women who passively accepted the client's control of the sexual encounter, and the women who relied on their own fallible instincts for survival in the face of not infrequent episodes of client coercion and violence. While the value of experience and practice wisdom should not be underestimated, the findings from this study suggest that reliance on 'gut instinct' or 'sixth sense' is neither reliable nor sufficient as a means of protection from the levels of risk and violence to which street workers are exposed.

CONCLUSION

The implications of the findings from this study suggest that legislators and policy-makers need to reconsider the detrimental consequences for some female sex workers of maintaining legal sanctions against prostitution, particularly street prostitution where women are least able to protect themselves from client violence or demands for unsafe sex. Decriminalisation of all forms of prostitution would increase sex workers' autonomy and capacity to protect themselves. By enabling sex workers to report violence to police, clients would be deterred from threatening and assaulting them. Decriminalisation may also reduce the stigma of prostitution which contributes to sex workers' low self-esteem. In the meantime, health education strategies need to take into account the variations in the personal circumstances of different groups of women engaging in sex work. It is apparent that more comprehensive and creative interventions are called for (Benson and Matthews 1995; Weiner 1996). For some women in this study, problems associated with homelessness, drug use and extreme social isolation far outweighed most of the risks associated with sex work. In addition to seeking ways to improve these women's strategies for survival in a harsh environment, it is important to address the needs these women have for stable and reliable accommodation, for support in reducing their drug dependence and for access to alternative sources of income.

NOTES

1. In reporting results of this study, numbers are provided only where specific information was elicited from all participants.

2. There are other types of illegal brothels operating in Victoria but none of these were accessed in this study.

3. Escort agencies have been able to register to operate legally with the Prostitution Control Board in Victoria since 1995, but at the time of this study escort work was still subject to criminal sanctions.

REFERENCES

Benson, C. and R. Matthews (1995) 'Street Prostitution: Ten Facts in Search of a Policy' *International Journal of the Sociology of the Law* 23: 395–415.

Campbell, C. (1991) 'Prostitution, AIDS, and Preventive Health Behaviour' *Social Science and Medicine* 32(12): 1367–78.

Campbell, C. (1995) 'Male Gender Roles and Sexuality: Implications for Women's AIDS Risk and Prevention' *Social Science and Medicine* 41(2): 197–210.

Day, S. and H. Ward (1990) 'The Praed Street Project: A Cohort of Prostitute Women in London' in M.A. Plant (ed) *AIDS, Drugs and Prostitution* London: Routledge: 61–75.

Dorfman, L., P. Derish and J. Cohen (1992) 'Hey Girlfriend: An Evaluation of AIDS Prevention Among Women in the Sex Industry' *Health Education Quarterly* 19(1): 25–40.

Estebanez, P., K. Fitch and R. Najera (1993) 'HIV and Female Sex Workers' *Bulletin of the World Health Organisation* 71(3/4): 397–412.

Green, S.T., D.J. Goldberg, P.R. Christie, M. Frischer, A. Thomson, S.V. Carr and A. Taylor (1993) 'Female Streetworker-Prostitutes in Glasgow: A Descriptive Study of their Lifestyle' *AIDS Care* 5(3): 321–35.

Harcourt, C. (1994) 'Prostitution and Public Health in the Era of AIDS' in R. Perkins, G. Prestage, R. Sharpe and F. Lovejoy (eds) *Sex Work and Sex Workers in Australia* Sydney: University of New South Wales Press: 203–24.

Harcourt, C. and R. Philpot (1990) 'Female Prostitutes, AIDS, Drugs, and Alcohol in New South Wales' in M. A. Plant (ed) *AIDS, Drugs and Prostitution* London: Routledge: 132–58.

Jackson, L., A. Highcrest and R. A. Coates (1992) 'Varied Potential Risks of HIV Infection Among Prostitutes' *Social Science and Medicine* 35: 281–6.

Loxley, W. and C. Ovenden (1995) '"It's the Same Risk Isn't It?": Needle Sharing, Unsafe Sex, Intoxication and Risk of HIV in a Western Australian Group of Young Injecting Drug Users' in *HIV, AIDS and Society 1995: Social Science: From Theory to Practice* Proceedings of the 3rd HIV, AIDS and Society Conference Sydney: Macquarie University: 62–73.

Matthews, L. (1990) 'Outreach Work with Female Prostitutes in Liverpool' in M.A. Plant (ed) *AIDS, Drugs and Prostitution* London: Routledge: 76–87.

McKeganey, N. and M. Barnard (1996) *Sex Work on the Streets: Prostitutes and Their Clients* Buckingham: Open University Press.

Neave, M. (1994) 'Prostitution Laws in Australia: Past History and Current Trends' in R. Perkins, G. Prestage, R. Sharp and F. Lovejoy (eds) *Sex Work and Sex Workers in Australia* Sydney: University of New South Wales Press: 67–99.

Patton, M. Q. (1990) *Qualitative Evaluation and Research Methods* (second edition) London: Sage.

Perkins, R. (1994) 'Female Prostitution' in R. Perkins, G. Prestage, R. Sharpe and F. Lovejoy (eds) *Sex Work and Sex Workers in Australia* Sydney: University of New South Wales Press: 143–73.

Pyett, P. M., B. R. Haste and J. Snow (1996a) 'Risk Practices for HIV Infection and Other STDs Amongst Female Prostitutes Working in Legalized Brothels' *AIDS Care* 8(1): 85–94.

Pyett, P. M., B. R. Haste and J. Snow (1996b) 'Who Works in the Sex Industry? A Profile of Female Prostitutes in Victoria' *Australian and New Zealand Journal of Public Health* 20(3): 431–3.

Pyett, P. and D. Warr (1997) 'Vulnerability on the Streets: Female Sex Workers and HIV ' Risk' *AIDS Care* 9(5): 439–547.

Silverman, D. (1993) *Interpreting Qualitative Data: Methods for Analysing Talk, Text and Interaction* London: Sage.

Vanwesenbeeck, I., R. De Graaf, G. Van Zessen, C. J. Straver and J.H. Visser (1993) 'Condom Use by Prostitutes: Behavior, Factors and Considerations' *Journal of Psychology and Human Sexuality* 6: 69–91.

Warr, D. and P. Pyett (1999) 'Difficult Relations: Sex Work, Love and Intimacy' *Sociology of Health & Illness* 21(3): 290–309.

Weiner, A. (1996) 'Understanding the Social Needs of Streetwalking Prostitutes' *Social Work* 41(1): 97–105.

Chapter 11

DIMENSIONS OF WOMEN'S POWER IN THE ILLICIT DRUG ECONOMY

TAMMY L. ANDERSON

INTRODUCTION

The purpose of this chapter is to advance our understanding of the gendered social and economic organization of the illicit drug world by articulating several often overlooked dimensions of women's power. I develop the argument that women routinely perform four core activities (e.g. providing housing and other sustenance needs, purchasing drugs, subsidizing male dependency and participating in drug sales) that show not only their power in and contributions to the illicit drug world but also how the organization of this social world is fundamentally gendered. Thus, I offer an alternative to the leading 'pathology and powerlessness' narrative in the drugs and crime discourse, especially as this discourse relates to women. In addition, developing this view promises new directions for social policy and related research.

Understanding Power

The argument to be presented here requires a particular and broadened definition of power.

Power has traditionally been defined as entailing dominance and control over others (Connell, 1987), that is, as a possession one does or does not have, or can or cannot obtain. Some (Allen, 1999) have called this 'power-over.' This definition of power is also structurally oriented, viewing power as something unequally distributed in society, especially by gender, race/ethnicity and class. Indeed, discourse on problems related to the illicit drug world often presupposes a 'power-over' definition. Furthermore, a dualistic construction of hegemonic masculinity and femininity (Connell, 1987) has often also been taken for granted, one wherein men's dominance over women is seen as predominant in the organization and routine activities of the illicit drug economy.

Feminist concepts of 'dominance and control' have tended to be more complex, and ought to be mentioned given this chapter's overall purposes. For example, some feminist theories have focused on the transformative and relational character of power (Allen, 1999) rather than on its expression in relationships of dominance and subordination. Power is transformative when it is oriented

Source: Anderson, T. (2005). Dimensions of women's power in the illicit drug economy. *Theoretical Criminology,* 9(4), 371–400.

toward accomplishment and change; its relational nature pertains to usefulness for the self as well as others (e.g. for children, loved ones or a more communal entity). In order to envision women's experiences with this more transformative and relational concept, one must also define 'power' in the sense of competency and ability to achieve desired ends. Feminists have often referred to this 'power-to' as 'empowerment' (Hartsock, 1985; Allen, 1999), an idea that is nested in connections to others. Of course, prior to these usages, Foucault (1979, 1990) also famously distinguished between 'power over' and 'power to' in expanding our understanding of how both operate in modern society.

The organization of the drug world features multiple types of power that are interdependent in character. At a bare minimum, these include structural features of power (i.e. possession of resources, domination and control) as well as relational or transformative features of power (i.e. empowerment of the self and others). However, an effect of gender has been to skew the possession and utilization of these types of power. In general, men have been able to exercise more structural power while women frequently utilize power in relational and transformative senses that involve 'empowerment' (defined here as the ability and competence to influence and achieve desired outcomes) and 'agency' (defined here as the ability to benefit others as well as the self,[1] and in terms of actions that bring about these outcomes).

A point to be developed is that men's greater possession of structural power (i.e. 'power-over') in drug markets is, to a considerable extent, made possible by women's agency and the types of relational or transformative power (i.e. 'power-to' and 'empowerment') they wield. In other words, *women's more relational power assists males' accumulation of structural power and is, therefore, fundamental to 'successful' (i.e. stable and lasting) illicit drug world organization.* Therefore, men's and women's powers are interdependent.

Many women, especially minority and lower-class women living in inner-city neighborhoods, regularly use agency on their own and others' behalf in ways that are both relational and autonomous. For example, single mothers who attempt to care for children and run the household have historically and increasingly exercised agency by the above definition as they face large-scale economic changes that have decimated

legitimate work opportunities in urban areas and punitive social policies that have institutionalized large numbers of men (and also, though in fewer numbers, other women). Thus, the assumption that males active in the inner-city drug economy are the predominant ones with power and status effectively obscures a more gender-intertwined reality where women share power (by a more complex definition of this term) and accrue capital from their own exercising of agency. More precisely, then, empowerment in the sense of ability and competency to operate in the drug world are patterned by gender into routine interactions. Men and women share some experiences but differ in other, important ways; again, the roles and undertakings of each are interdependent and facilitate the drug world's existence. Therefore, a fuller understanding of the gendered organization of power in the illicit drug economy is possible through analyzing the connection between women's activities and the various forms of capital they produce for themselves and others.

SHIFTING THE NARRATIVE

This chapter's objective counters much of the sociological literature on women, drugs and crime which, to date, has told a surprisingly traditional tale about women 'deviants,' especially drug users. A repetitive narrative has emphasized themes of dysfunction, dependence, exploitation and victimization, whereas references to agency and power rarely appear (Zerai and Banks, 2002). A recent piece by Evans et al. provides a typical example:

> Women still occupy marginal positions within drugs markets and this has increased their risk of victimization. Women get into drugs because of experience with abuse and violent trauma early in life. Men lead them into drugs. They are still forced to rely largely on prostitution for economic gain and when they do engage in other crimes, such as stealing, it is always in partnership with a male leader. Furthermore, when women are able to gain access to the dominant drug market, it is through their boyfriends or husbands. Women's participation in the informal drug economy, in terms of drug sales and distribution, is contingent upon their link to men in their lives. (2002: 488)

Reports like this come from both male and female scholars studying women's experiences in the illicit drug economy (Rosenbaum, 1981; Bourgois and Dunlap, 1993; Inciardi et al., 1993; Maher, 1997; Sterk, 1999; Sommers et al., 2000; CASA, 2003). The few empowerment-related stories that analysts do tell often end in failure or other negative outcomes, keeping them consistent with the pathology narrative. For example, some have concluded that women's infiltration of drug selling is controlled and exploited by men. They are relegated to high-risk, low-paying jobs, or are manipulated into turning over criminal profits to men or the products men sell (Inciardi et al., 1993; Sommers et al., 2000; Cross et al., 2001). Ultimately, women fail at these activities because they become addicted to drugs and do not realize any positive outcomes or experiences. Thus, they return to prostitution where they defile their essence as women (Ettorre, 1992).

This raises another concern about the voyeuristic nature of the discourse on women in the illicit drug economy involving sexual objectification as another form of pathology and powerlessness. For example, the voluminous literature on prostitution and drugs details the 'sexual' activities and consequences of women sex workers (see, for example, Inciardi et al., 1993; McCoy and Inciardi, 1995; Inciardi and Surrat, 2001), prioritizing them as the critical focal point for social science and policy research. Equal treatment of their power and agency in broader respects are absent, an observation discussed in more detail later.

What makes this pathology and powerlessness narrative even more compelling is that women's fall from grace into drug use is considered even more tragic than men's. A recent report by CASA highlights this notion:

Females experience physical, psychological and social consequences from smoking, drinking and using drugs, many of which are different from or more severe than those experienced by male substance users. For instance, at the same levels of use, females are more likely to become dependent on tobacco and more intoxicated from drinking than males and are more vulnerable to alcohol-induced brain damage and other substance-related problems than males. Females with substance use disorders are likelier than males to have co-occurring mood or anxiety disorders. (2003: 17)

This chapter, then, offers an alternative view to women's experience in today's illicit drug world by suggesting that women's agency is fundamental to the social and economic organization of the drug world and earns them various forms of capital among their similarly situated peers. This more 'empowerment' oriented narrative does not deny the victim-centered version told by past and present scholars; of course, women do suffer abuse and varied forms of discrimination that have led them to participate in the drug world. Moreover, while several routine activities performed by women illustrate their significance and centrality in illicit drug world organization, they also expose women to abuse, neglect, victimization and social penalty. Still, my point is that the situation is not quite as simple as it has been made out to be: 'victimization' and 'empowerment' can be, and often are, interrelated.

Moreover, adding this level of complexity may have notable policy repercussions. For while scholars and policy makers discuss the consequences to society of the illicit drug world and participation within it, those directly involved often hold a different or competing view. While women's contributions in the illicit drug world may not be recognized as legitimate in conventional society, they may be perceived as valuable indeed from within the illicit drug economy. This point is supported by research on criminal success (McCarthy and Hagan, 2001), which shows that both males and females gain confidence and identity empowerment from being able to exercise some level of independence in the drug world. It is, therefore, imperative to understand the nature and form of such perceived empowerment in order to promote offender re-integration and combat the social ills related to drug abuse. To date, then, the absence of scholarship on women's economic contributions in the illicit drug world hinders a more comprehensive understanding of this important dynamic. This chapter seeks to address that shortcoming.

THEORETICAL ASSUMPTIONS AND OPERATING PREMISES

I begin by stating several premises on which this chapter is based that flow from the character of the illicit drug economy. First, the perspective offered here derives from research on inner-city, street-level illicit drug markets that are dominated by the sale of heroin, crack, cocaine and marijuana. By extension, observations to be made about gender, power, agency and capital may be limited to the extent that this type of market differs dramatically from others. For example, inner-city, street-level markets are most often located in impoverished areas, characterized by physical environment deterioration, high residential turnover and ethnic heterogeneity (large populations from ethnic and racial minority groups) and low informal social control and community efficacy (Harrell and Peterson, 1992; E. Anderson, 1999). Obviously, then, the distribution and nature of power in drug market organization and the agency demonstrated by participants therein likely differs from what occurs in suburban white, middle-class settings where different drugs tend to be marketed (e.g. ecstasy, ketamine, powder cocaine).

Second, I am presuming a particular historical framework. The ideas presented here should be placed in the larger context of a voluminous literature on the illicit drug economy of the late 1970s through the mid-1990s, a period when heroin use escalated after years of stability and the crack cocaine epidemic stormed the urban landscape. It was during this time that theory and research about drug market organization, the drugs–crime connection and drug-related social consequences itself exploded (see White and Gorman, 2000 for a thorough review). At present, though, many scholars are arguing that the crack epidemic has 'subsided' and government agencies (ONDCP, 2002, 2003) seem more concerned about other drugs and crime problems (e.g. club drug use, Oxycontin diversion and blunt smoking) that may impact the same communities hit by crack cocaine and heroin. These impressions of change have also been conveyed through media coverage. But while crack cocaine and heroin therefore receive less public attention than before, the criminal justice system still processes a considerable number of cocaine, marijuana and heroin offenders, especially in inner cities (see ONDCP, 2004a, 2004b, 2004c). In addition, given the cyclical history of cocaine use in the USA and the persistence of heroin use, theoretical observations about the marketing of these substances remain highly salient. Finally, even if crack and heroin were to disappear from the urban landscape, inner-city drug marketing would continue to thrive absent major economic renewal (Wilson, 1996; Marable, 2000; Sassen, 2002; Wallerstein, 2004).

Third, focusing on gender in this chapter does not amount to denying that, overall, drug sales are still 'dominated' by men. Men are more often sellers than women, and they typically occupy more economically lucrative or higher status roles in the illicit drug economy. As already stated, men therefore possess a disproportionate share of structural power in the illicit drug world. Fewer women (although more so now than in earlier periods) participate directly in sales and distribution and when they do so, they are congregated in lower-status positions.

But it is at this point where this argument diverges from a good deal of prior research that, due to its reliance on dominance and control definitions of power, has neglected vital 'behind-the-scenes' action where women play important roles in facilitating drug deals or making the market thrive. This agency empowers themselves and others in a relational sense even if it does often earn them a more powerful position in the drug market hierarchy defined in structural terms. For this reason, the following paragraphs expand on women's 'supporting roles' in drug marketing endeavors (e.g. as middle-men/women, cookers/baggers) and on their 'parallel industry' activities (e.g. sex work) that feed the drug economy with necessary money capital and an ever-expanding consumer base. The purpose of this elaboration is to show that women's power in the illicit drug economy comes from their use of agency in performing such 'supporting roles' that are fundamental to illicit drug world organization. Without these supporting roles, the performance of direct marketing activities and the growth and persistence of the drug market overall could not occur.

It should be noted that in recent debates about gender and the family, some feminist scholars have been suspicious of such performances of 'supporting roles'; these roles can be seen as manifestations of sexism, reflecting household divisions wherein dependent females are subordinated to independent, dominant males. Moreover, feminist critics have held, these roles neutralize women's sense of agency, defining them in 'other' oriented terms. Feminists have also shown that a woman's domestic agency permits the accumulation of more structural forms of power by her husband and children, while keeping her relatively powerless (see Allen, 1999 for a review). But, while valuable, these critiques may not fully encompass the complexity of women's experiences in illicit drug markets. Alternatively, I suggest in the following that the 'supporting' functions that women perform are not exclusively relational, nor are they primarily intended or performed for men's benefit. This is especially so for female-headed homes in the African-American and Latino communities. Rather, these functions may be performed for the women themselves and their families; they comprise exercises of both autonomous and relational agency (Allen, 1999) that have social value. While it is true that women's agency does not earn them a more structurally recognized position of power in the illicit drug market, less recognized is that their agency may empower them to better excel in future conventional (i.e. legal) activities than their male counterparts. This point is discussed further later.

One last point that deserves reiteration: again, by elaborating upon dimensions of women's power in the illicit drug economy, I am not saying that women always experience empowerment nor that victimization (personal, economic and legal) does not occur. Women active in the illicit drug world regularly suffer exploitation and victimization at the hands of other participants and are subject to social controls via punitive drug laws seeking to stamp out the trade. Scholars have done well in documenting their plight and mobilizing resources on their behalf. Nevertheless, women, like men, persist in risky activities. Therefore, it is important to recognize that successful re-integration of drug offenders may require more knowledge about the satisfactions, not only the pains, that people obtain from drug world participation so that we can counterbalance both with meaningful and conventional alternatives during criminal justice and other interventions.

FOUR DIMENSIONS OF WOMEN'S ECONOMIC POWER

Women routinely perform several core activities (e.g. providing housing and other sustenance needs, purchasing and selling drugs and subsidizing male dependency) that are fundamental to the social and economic organization of the illicit drug world. These involve exercises of empowerment and agency that can satisfy women's needs and those of their families, while simultaneously securing the organization of the illicit drug economy. Moreover, the contributions

about to be detailed earn women important forms of capital that can arguably assist them in establishing more conventional lifestyles in the future. Themes of responsibility, risk-management and stability permeate these activities, making resultant forms of capital more reliable and transferable than the high-risk activities or more unstable capital their male counterparts amass.

Capital

Four types of capital are relevant to this discussion. These are financial capital (tangible forms of material wealth such as money, credit, investment and assets), human capital (degrees, education, skills, training and experience), social capital (benefits from relationships individuals have with or resources they get from others) and personal capital (the desire for wealth, risk-taking propensity, willingness to cooperate and competence; see McCarthy and Hagan, 2001). Capital, in any form, must be reliable and stable in order for its benefits to accrue. Uncertainty and unpredictability reduce its value. In the following sections, I discuss four dimensions of women's power in the illicit drug economy, which produces various types of capital valuable both in the illicit drug world and outside it in more conventional activities. Furthermore, the capital accrued by women is often more reliable and stable than that of their male counterparts, which acts to empower them further.[2]

Women's Control of the Household

The first dimension of women's power in the illicit drug economy pertains to the housing that non-drug-using women and, at times, drug-using women, provide to members of inner-city drug worlds. Providing housing and/or controlling the household is one example of how women contribute resources to the illicit drug economy while at the same time keeping themselves, and their families, anchored in conventional society. Thus, it is an example of both empowerment and relational and autonomous agency that benefits the illicit drug world (and, by extension, its perpetuation within conventional society).

For example, Dunlap et al. (2000) discussed the role of grandmothers in providing housing to drug-using family members. This shows the power, capital and importance of older women's contributions not only to the lives of others but also to the stability and solidarity of families in an institutional sense. Additional work by Hardesty and Black (1999), Murphy and Rosenbaum (1999) and Sterk (1999) also reminds us that women, including those living in inner-city drug markets, remain committed to the responsibilities of running the household despite considerable risk (e.g. victimization or financial exploitation) and consequence (arrest or dislocation).

Dunlap et al. (2000) did not, however, discuss the provision of housing as a form of empowerment for women. In fact, few researchers[3] have taken such a perspective. I hope to show how women's control of the household (i.e. securing and maintaining its physical structure as well as furnishing basic sustenance and social support that make a 'home' for its residents) is fundamental to the economic and social organization of the drug world and, consequently, returns precious forms of capital to participants in that world.

To begin, research on inner cities consistently shows high concentrations of female-headed households with grandmothers, mothers and other female relatives securing and maintaining residences for family members (McNeil, 1998). Both non-using and using women are more likely today than ever before to be financially responsible for the costs of the household. For example, using US Census data, McNeil (1998) showed that female-headed households with children and no spouse grew dramatically between 1969 and 1996, precisely the same period when illicit drug use became an 'epidemic' and rose to national prominence. Older non-using grandmothers typically provide shelter in inner-city, drug-infested neighborhoods (Wilson, 1993; Maher et al., 1996; E. Anderson, 1999; Dunlap et al., 2000). According to the US Census (Casper, 1996), single females over 65 years of age are more than twice as likely than their male counterparts to run households nationally.

A perusal of ethnographies (e.g. Hamid, 1990, 1992; Bourgois, 1995; Dunlap and Johnson, 1996; Anderson, 1999; Sterk, 1999; Dunlap et al., 2000) on the illicit drug world provides consistent evidence that both male and female drug users and sellers often reside in both nuclear and extended family households controlled by women. In fact, drug-involved family members remain in or return to older female relatives' homes well into adulthood (see, for example, T. Anderson et al., 2002). According to Laidler and Hunt, 'It is the mother who they define as the primary caregiver and nurturer in the family. It is the mother who they look to for shelter, care, affection, support, discipline, guidance, and structure' (2001: 665).

Women have been able to retain control of the household despite considerable financial challenges. This is due, in large part, to their qualification for rental support (e.g. Section 8 housing vouchers or other public housing assistance), purchasing of homes via assistance programs (especially common in the past) and their subsequent commitment to paying household rent or mortgages. Most importantly, however, it is an outcome of their continued commitment to the family (see Dunlap and Johnson, 1996; Maher et al., 1996; Hardesty and Black, 1999; Dunlap et al., 2000, 2002 for examples).

Housing provisions are critical to the accumulation of capital not only for household heads but also for dependents living therein. Moreover, while analogies between the two realms do not always hold, this aspect of the analysis does apply both to people living in 'convention' and in illicit drug worlds. Recently, Bratt (2002) specified the value that housing affords to all individuals. Women's maintenance of the household provides safety, sustenance needs, a sense of identity (and therefore empowerment), accessibility to employment and educational opportunities and job search networks to household members. All are examples of social, human and personal capital. In turn, female heads gain social and personal capital for themselves by demonstrating considerable commitment to household responsibility and stability. Their agency empowers their own futures and those dependent on them.

This is especially the case for poor African American and Latino families that have historically provided needed assistance, child rearing and care for household members. According to Hill, 'It [housing] is perhaps the most enduring cultural strength that has enhanced the functioning of Black families since their days in Africa' (1998: 21). The Black family protects members from life obstacles and provides needed support that is unavailable in major social institutions (Hill, 1993; McAdoo, 1997; Nobles, 1997). Dunlap et al. add that:

Helping someone meet their own basic needs frees them to find and implement hopefully lasting solutions to their problems. When their efforts are rewarded, the pool of demands shrinks while resources become more abundant, thus buttressing everyone's eventual access to resources, thus reducing the salience of stress for all members. (2000: 153)

Housing and Drug Market Success

While sociologists have previously acknowledged the contributions women make to household sustenance, few have considered the centrality of this provision to the economic and social maintenance of the illicit drug world. For example, the opportunity to attain a powerful position in the drug trade and to accumulate financial capital by young males is facilitated, one could argue, by women's control of the household and responsibilities for basic sustenance needs.

Private residences enable dealers to bring the product to market (a place to prepare and package product and store commodities and supplies—see Wilson, 1993 and Maher, 1997). In addition, the re-designed ADAM survey shows that in major US cities, on average, more than 60 percent of arrestees made their last drug purchase indoors (ADAM, 2002), suggesting the importance of residential properties as a place of sale. Moreover, housing reduces the 'costs' of business by guarding against law enforcement or other social control agencies (e.g. police must obtain search warrants to enter private residences) and victimization (see also Jacobs, 1999 for more on this point). Finally, housing provides a consistent or stable way to contact the dealer, that is, to locate someone for a potential transaction or business deal. While cell phones and pagers are also used for communication, having a secure residence enables one to always be located by customers or associates.

To summarize, women's autonomous and relational agency in providing housing and sustenance needs for themselves and others helps earn important forms of capital for themselves and their dependents. It also assists in organizing the drug world, enabling both men and women to engage in drug selling. Dealers are able to eschew the financial demands of complete independence and responsibility that setting up and running a conventional business

would require, thus promoting their attainment of structural power positions in the market. Such independence calls for much more capital than most dealers typically possess (see Bourgois, 1995; Jacobs, 1999).

While numerous social, economic and political factors have positioned women as the predominant heads of households in the inner city, late 20th century anti-drug policies threaten to invalidate these exercises of positive agency and destabilize neighborhoods. Consider, for example, landlord–tenant, anti-drug policies that evict household owners or heads for drug arrests (*Daily Business Review*, 2002). This provides a powerful example of how power and consequence coexist for women in the illicit drug world. When housing tenure is lost, families are often disrupted and members may 'double up' with others, contributing to crowding and a host of other problems (Anderson et al., 2002). This is especially the case with public housing, which is often boarded up and sits empty until a qualified tenant can be located. Such houses may remain unoccupied for a long while since public housing support has increasingly dwindled. Abandoned homes and residential transition, researchers[4] have found, contribute to illicit activity and other social problems. Therefore, the female-controlled household may be a lesser evil (and in many respects a socially valuable entity) than the outcome of increasingly punitive war on drugs policies.

Women Drug Users' Purchasing Power

While control of households is also a dimension of power that non-using women exercise, this section elaborates directly on the economic power of drug-using women. For a second critical dimension of women's power in the illicit drug world emerges vis-à-vis spending on drugs and related products. Here, the focus is on consumer empowerment (i.e. his/her ability to raise finances for the purchase of goods and services as desired) and agency (e.g. actual spending on themselves and others), which helps stimulate both illegal and legal economies.

To begin, the capacity to consume is fundamental to the growth of capitalist economies and to personal existence within them. This principle applies to all individuals living in capitalist societies, even those engaged in illegitimate activities. In the illicit drug world, then, women's ability to generate money and subsequent spending on drugs increases dealers' profits. Furthermore, this spending expands illicit markets by providing additional and stable revenue sources, contributing thereafter through 'legal' purchases to the maintenance of the US and global mainstream economies[5] (ABT Associates, 2001). In other words, women's ability to generate and spend money is a good example of relational agency that further empowers them in attaining their desired goals and helps males achieve structural market power,[6] even if it is not intended to do so.

Women's spending on illicit drugs is typically not discussed in this fashion, although a recent study by Murphy and Arroyo (2000) has opened dialogue about the power and control women possess as consumers. Many ethnographers (Hamid, 1990, 1992; Maher, 1997; Sterk, 1999) have noted that women have considerable income to spend. Consider, for example, recent findings from large survey-based studies. They show women's drug expenditures approximate those of men or surpass them (Fagan, 1993; Lovell, 2002). Too often this point gets lost in the pathology narrative highlighting women's drug-related misery, that is, their decline into sex work where they settle for crack instead of money capital (Bourgois and Dunlap, 1993; Inciardi et al., 1993; Ratner, 1993). But the following paragraphs articulate the centrality of women's spending to the capital accumulation of male dealers, the social organization of the drug world and the economic vitality of the drug market and the larger society.

The purchasing power of the female user and addict comes from numerous avenues, many of which introduce new and stable sources of income into the market, allowing it to thrive and expand. I consider three here: sex work, social transfer payments and employment in the secondary labor market.

First, sex work engaged in by women drug users provides a constant infusion of financial capital into illicit markets. This view of women's sex work departs dramatically from the more voyeuristic literature that focuses only on their sexual activities. For example, May et al. (2000) found that the survival of drug markets is largely dependent on women sex workers. This is especially the case with crack cocaine and, to a lesser extent, heroin. Profits for male dealers can be maximized not only from the money drug-using

women sex workers spend on drugs for themselves and others, but also the money their clients spend (some of which are introduced to the drug world through the purchase of sex). Previous work on crack-abusing sex workers (e.g. Bourgois and Dunlap, 1993; Inciardi et al., 1993; Ratner, 1993) maintained most transactions were for drugs instead of cash[7] or were controlled by male pimps. Maher's (1996, 1997) study of women drug abusers in New York, Miller's (1995) work in Columbus, Ohio, and Sterk's (1999) research in Atlanta found the opposite; most sex work featured cash exchanges with women operating independently outside of 'pimping' relationships.

Sex workers bring new sources of revenue (i.e. money from outside clients) into illicit drug markets (May et al., 2000). Revenues from drug-using female sex workers are abundant and stable because of the ever-present desire for sex. They deliver new financial capital infusion into the drug world via sex-for-money exchanges (non-using johns who pay for sex and get more heavily involved in drugs). For example, men's purchase of sex transfers financial capital to women. Women drug-abusing sex workers, in turn, transfer money capital to male sellers when they buy drugs for themselves and, for example, their addicted male partners (see later for more on this point). Male dealers, subsequently, often spend their money on retail goods in displays of machismo and status (Bourgois, 1995, 1996; E. Anderson, 1999; Jacobs, 1999). Thus, women are central to the growth of the illicit and licit economies. The market is dependent on their agency, yet it disallows their accumulation of structural power. Though women also waste money on highly disposable goods, many channel monies from illegal activities into home maintenance and the sustenance needs of family members (Dunlap et al., 1997; Sterk, 1999; Sommers et al., 2000). In fact, Hardesty and Black (1999) found that women addicts are committed to simultaneously supporting their drug use and families.

Social transfer payments are a second source of stable revenue, which involves some women as customers (see Hamid, 1990, 1992; Maher, 1997; Sterk, 1999). For example, numerous studies have established that a portion of monthly social transfer payments is spent by some recipients in the illicit drug economy (see Hamid, 1990, 1992; Bourgois, 1995; Anderson et al.,

2002). Sellers compete for the very small number of compulsive crack cocaine addicts (Jacobs, 1999) at the beginning of each month (i.e. when social transfer payments are disbursed). That sellers actually 'compete' with each other for customers with social transfer payments (most of these customers being women) indicates the power customers have with this form of financial capital.

Moreover, receipt of a monthly check also allows its recipient to secure loans from dealers, who are willing to extend 'credit' in order to facilitate continuous sales and constant profit. This is an example of how financial capital also secures social capital within the drug world, while being devalued in the conventional world. However, while drug purchases with social transfer payments are problematic, numerous studies (Goldstein et al., 2000; Anderson et al., 2002) have shown that most recipients spend most, if not all, of these funds on basic sustenance needs for themselves and their families.

A third source of women's purchasing power can be found in their employment in the secondary labor market. De-industrialization and uneven international economic development in the latter part of the 20th century have worsened the financial status of inner-city males and females (see Wilson, 1996; Marable, 2000; Sassen, 2002; Wallerstein, 2004). However, women's willingness to seek and maintain employment in the secondary labor market (Browne, 1999; Browne and Kennelly, 1999) has not only assisted them in assuming family responsibilities, but has also provided them with a third source of reliable money capital available for drug purchasing. Women have had much more experience with these kinds of jobs (Reskin, 1999), using them to support themselves and their families over time. Money earned from secondary labor market employment is meager, often not enough to elevate an individual or family out of poverty.

Still, it is valuable in the drug world. It is easy to obtain such jobs because fast food restaurants and other service-sector employers have high turnover rates and low human capital requirements. For numerous reasons, many having to do with gender socialization, women are willing to seek and stay employed in them. This work commitment earns them capital (financial, human, social and personal) in the illicit drug world.

Unlike the more stable sources of revenue that women have to spend on drugs, men's financial capital is often less valuable or more problematic. For example, male drug abusers' revenue more often comes from illegal activities at greater risk of social control (e.g. major and minor theft and some violent crime). Thus, their income tends to be more sporadic even while it can, at times, be larger than women's.

Furthermore, men in the illicit drug economy have less access to social transfer payments since the advent of 1990s' welfare reform. For example, impoverished males received most of the supplemental security income benefits for the addiction disability (see Goldstein et al., 2000; Anderson et al., 2002), but these funds were abolished during 1996 welfare reform. Today, they seldom receive TANF benefits (i.e. temporary assistance to needy families) because they typically have not assumed primary responsibility for raising children (McMahon and Rounsaville, 2002). Therefore, drug sales reliant on social transfer payments today come, almost exclusively, from women.

Finally, men are reluctant to seek employment in the secondary labor market for the same reason, that is, gender socialization, women embrace it. This rings especially true for young African American males in the inner city who are routinely confronted with numerous symbolic disincentives to seek and remain employed in service-sector jobs (i.e. these jobs contradict core masculine values and identities: see Bourgois, 1995; Wilson, 1996; Anderson, 1999). However, there is some indication that this pattern may be shifting (see, for example, Bourgois, 2003) toward greater participation in the secondary labor market by inner-city minority males.

One last point about the differences between female and male purchasing power is that while research has documented that women's work in the illegal drug economy involves an effort to balance work and family priorities (e.g. relational agency), men's work is usually primarily self-serving (e.g. autonomous agency). For example, studies (Bourgois, 1995; Jacobs, 1999) have shown that male dealers seldom channel money into the household or family responsibilities, spending their revenues instead on conspicuous consumption. This practice helps perpetuate their alienation from conventional institutions (e.g. the family) and should be addressed in drug treatment and offender reintegration programs.

In sum, women are powerful economic actors, contributing stable and reliable income that facilitates growth in the illicit drug and conventional economies. At least three of their income sources—sex work, social transfer payments and secondary labor market employment—earn them financial capital that is more stable, overall, than their male counterparts' sources of funds. In their financial negotiations of the illicit drug world, women demonstrate empowerment and agency to earn important forms of capital. In fact, Murphy and Arroyo (2000) showed how women gain competence, control and power from negotiating drug sales and communicating with drug sellers. Personal capital accumulates from these risk-aversive techniques that women use to independently manage their money to maximize their own drug use and that of others, while attempting to provide for their families. The stability with which they can purchase drugs and their nonviolent and confrontational style in doing so, earns them social capital with dealers (who often compete for their sales and extend them credit) and obligation from other using friends, lovers and family.

Sometimes, no doubt, women's economic power is manipulated or exploited by others; dealers understand their value as customers and family and friends continue to rely on them as providers. Yet, while most participants in the drug world do not retain financial capital over the long term, women's experience in raising revenues for family support and drug purchasing earns them some level of independence, thereby highlighting the interplay between relational and autonomous agency among women. This experience will help them with more prosocial undertakings, including providing for themselves and others (i.e. economic independence and money management) and securing positive and fulfilling relationships.

Women Subsidize Male Dependency

A closely related third source of women's economic power is subsidizing male drug users and addicts, that is, their consumption of drugs, sustenance needs and lifestyles. Again, this is an example of relational agency because women drug users often use their economic resources to pay for drugs for themselves and their dependent male partners.

Few studies have addressed the vulnerable position of the male addict and the empowered position of the female sex worker and/or drug user in providing for him. Instead, previous work has constructed this as another form of women's powerlessness and exploitation—for example, men force women into sex work to financially support their habits (Inciardi et al., 1993). Such constructions tend to ignore the interpersonal dynamics that sustain relationships between women and men. The following paragraphs elaborate on this notion as a form of women's empowerment, beginning with brief consideration of the prevalence of women's support of men.

Consistently, both large-scale surveys and smaller ethnographic studies have shown that adult males' rates of abuse and addiction are considerably larger than females'. For instance, a recent National Household Survey of Drug Abuse (NHSDA, 2002) reported that men are twice as likely as women to abuse or be dependent on alcohol or illicit drugs. Absent official estimates of how many male sellers, users and addicts there are in the inner city, the recent ADAM (2002) data show that despite a proportionately larger pool of female arrestees for drugs, male arrestees in large urban areas were more often heavy drug users and heavy drinkers. It stands to reason, therefore, that the pool of drug-abusing and addicted men is quite large, outpacing the group of non-using male sellers.[8]

In addition, studies by Waterston (1993), Bourgois et al. (1997), Duneier (1999) and Anderson and Levy (2003) have shown just how capricious and unforgiving the world of drug sales can be to male abusers, especially those who are older. This larger pool of men is vulnerable, just like women, both in the conventional economy and within the drug world. Consequently, many may seek support from breadwinning females.

The idea of women drug users as breadwinners, who support the drug habits and lifestyles of male partners, is alien not only to the study of drugs and crime but also to the discipline of sociology. Discussions of breadwinners and financial dependency often emanate from the economic dependency model. To date, very few articles have been written about women breadwinners and even fewer about men's economic dependency on women. Brines described the pervasive bias in favor of the male breadwinner: 'Some have argued that female headed households are too few and too poor to merit conceptualization on the same terms as male household heads' (1994: 655). This omission has remained in sociology because most studies have focused on legal, mainstream economic activity among married partners. However, knowledge about economic dependency can also help explain the gendered organization of the illicit drug world.

To begin, the economic dependency model presumes a dichotomized division of labor between financial support and domestic work. Traditionally, men provide financial support for the household through paid work in the external labor market and women provide unpaid labor in the form of household maintenance and childcare. In this model, women become economically dependent on men (Brines, 1994). Alternatively, when women drug users finance men's drug use, it challenges the basic tenets of the economic dependency model by reversing women's role to that of financial head.

The notion that breadwinning women provide for dependent men also departs from early drug abuse studies of the 1960s to mid-1980s which characterized female heroin users as needing a man to support their drug consumption (File at al., 1974; File, 1976; Hser et al., 1987). The reverse is true with crack cocaine (see Hamid, 1990, 1992; Maher and Daly, 1996; Sterk, 1999). As major breadwinners and providers, women drug users (especially those involved in sex work) who support drug-addicted male partners assume the more powerful economic role while their male dependants fall into economic subordination. In short, this is a very compelling case of women's empowerment and agency that past research has neglected.

Work by Anderson (1990, 1999), Jankowski (1991), Bourgois (1995) and Jacobs (1999) has largely ignored addicted men and their economic vulnerability within the illicit drug world. However, lower-class men's economic dependence on women is likely to continue. For example, male drug abusers are likely to become dependent on others as they age. Research has shown they get shut out of the most lucrative hustles and often suffer injury and illness from their more violent and risky lifestyles (see Waterston, 1993; Bourgois et al., 1997; Anderson and Levy, 2003). To restate the point made earlier, the elimination of some forms of social welfare (SSI—see Goldstein et al., 2000) and

increased social control policies (arrest and incarceration) may also increase men's economic dependency on women. Finally, as Bourgois (1995) and Anderson (1999) noted, men's willingness to work or stay employed in many service-sector and secondary sector jobs lags behind that of women. On the contrary, women are empowered to achieve more financial independence and become the main or sole breadwinners by demonstrating responsible, risk-aversive and stable agency in each of these scenarios.

What do women obtain from supporting addicted men who contribute very little to their relationships or the household? At first glance, it would seem little and that the research cited earlier about men's financial exploitation of them might be correct. However, a closer look suggests numerous benefits for women.

To begin, when women breadwinners (those who both use and do not use drugs) support men's alcohol and drug use and sustenance needs, they secure and retain a companion in an era when men, especially minority men, are becoming a scarce commodity due to increased social control policies. This helps keep them anchored in conventional roles and identities and aids preservation of the family. Such agency, consequently, has utility in both the illicit drug world and in conventional society.

Black feminist scholars including hooks (1981, 1984) and Hill-Collins (1990) have made this point in works that trace the phenomenon back to slavery. While procuring companionship in this way is obviously problematic at one level, at another, it meets a basic human need. Moreover, the degree to which women gain personal capital from managing these relationships may promote their economic independence and enable them to secure more fulfilling relationships in the future. A woman drug user with competence and know-how (i.e. who has been empowered) in achieving economic independence may be better equipped to successfully re-enter conventional society should she be incarcerated for a criminal offense or attempt to terminate a career in drug use.

Women's Role in Drug-Dealing Activities

The last dimension of women's power involves their role in drug dealing. Over the past decade, a vigorous debate has been waged about the level and nature of women's participation in drug-dealing activities, these being the most coveted jobs in the illicit drug economy let alone a major concern of policy makers. The debate centers on structural power: how many women are involved in drug selling, where are they located in the hierarchy and are they gaining ground in relation to men? In criminology, interest in this so-called gender question in the marketing of drugs and in the organization of the drug world has escalated as the level of women's participation in sales has climbed. Women's presence in drug selling has, to date, been the only aspect of economic activity that research has considered.

There is an epistemological fallacy in focusing on structural power only, one that Harding (1986, 1991) previously identified. This focus assumes that gender is relevant only when women are noticeable enough to warrant attention to difference, failing to acknowledge that male-only contexts are gendered as well. Invariably, when I have raised this point with social problems ethnographers or criminologists, I have been told that, 'Yes, you should study the women.' But these same scholars have seldom considered using a gender-oriented framework in their research with male subjects.

Nonetheless, the application of dominance and structural power definitions in understanding the illicit drug world has underestimated gender as an organizational force. For instance, some (Bourgois and Dunlap, 1993; Wilson, 1993; Fagan, 1995; Sommers et al., 1996, 2000) have argued that the illicit drug world, especially the crack market of the 1980s and 1990s, has become an equal opportunity employer where women comprise a formidable portion of drug sellers. But, these scholars argue, women's liberation into drug sales ultimately harms them in considerable ways. This is both a modern-day extension of both Adler's (1975) and Simon's (1975) classic statements on women and crime and of the pathology and powerlessness narrative.

Another body of work (Maher and Daly, 1996; Maher, 1997; Sterk, 1999) disputes the 'liberation' point, arguing that while the 'equity' premise in drug dealing is a possibility, women have yet to realize it. This work shows no significant structural presence of women drug sellers in urban drug markets because male drug dealers employ numerous physical and rhetorical techniques, consistent with hyper-masculinity, to keep women out. Thus, women's exploitation by men and their powerlessness continue in the illicit drug world despite their progress in the mainstream economy.

Common to both literatures, though, is a tendency to focus only on structural forms of power as the leading 'narrative' for describing how gender operates. While I do not dispute that men dominate drug sales or that women occupy lower status positions in the organizational structure, attention should also be paid to the style women employ in these activities that demonstrates empowerment and agency and results in capital accumulation of all types. Again, this style can be characterized as displaying responsibility (to oneself and others), risk-avoidance and stability. I use two examples to illustrate my point, and to counter the focus on women's pathology and powerlessness that currently dominates sociological discourse and social policy.

'Style' and Empowerment

Recent scholarship has shown that women bring a unique style to drug dealing that rewards them with respectable and stable social and financial capital. Research (Dunlap et al., 1997; Jacobs and Miller, 1998) has revealed that women are more cautious than men in their drug-dealing activities. While many business models would propose such an approach would limit profits, at least two benefits—reducing the threat of arrest and victimization—lead one to conclude just the opposite.

Perhaps the clearest and most recent example of this point can be found in the work of Jacobs and Miller (1998). Their ethnography in St Louis, Missouri, detailed the risk-avoidant strategies women drug dealers used to protect themselves from arrest (thus enhancing their ability to remain in the community and available, to some extent, to family) and to reduce their victimization and that of others (an example of stabilizing often volatile drug sales).

The first tactic involves conveying a sense of normalcy in both their demeanor and physical appearance during drug transactions. This runs counter to the hyper-masculine self-image that male dealers sometimes like to convey. Jacobs and Miller (1998) found that women drug sellers often rejected the blatant form of dealing that their male counterparts favored. They reduced their risk of arrest this way by not calling attention to themselves as dealers. As such, they were able to operate undetected for a considerable period of time. Furthermore, assuming such a posture likely endeared them to others concerned about the many risks associated with drug purchasing. Jacobs and Miller observed: 'Perhaps because they face less pressure to conform to the "flash" of the street culture, females also may be more successful in channeling available discretionary income to rent and bills' (1998: 563).

Three other risk-avoidant tactics concern where and when women would sell drugs and what they often did with their supplies. First, women dealers attempted to adhere to less risky, more conventional business hours—often preferring to sell drugs during 'normal' business hours and not at all hours of the day. Doing so not only protected them from law enforcement (which is distributed differently over the course of the day/month), it also made them more available for other responsibilities (family, legitimate work, etc.). Second, women often integrate drug selling into their routine activities so as to, once again, divert law enforcement attention. For example, women in Jacobs and Miller's study (1998) often sold drugs at picnics, in parks or at other social activities. They were aware of the risk associated with open drug dealing on street corners and, consequently, shifted their venues of business. Finally, women demonstrated competence in hiding drugs in locations undetectable by others, for example on their person or at their homes.

The growing literature on female gangs is consistent with these observations and supports some of this chapter's major claims. For example, work by Brotherton (1996) and Kontos et al. (2003) shows that 'independent' female gangs are tightly bonded entities that exercise relational power in taking care of each other and their families. Principles of community and equity characterize their drug selling and other illegal activities. Adoption of a 'smartness' ethic in doing business, similar to the tactics described by Jacobs and Miller (1998), enables them to avoid confrontation, detection and social control.

The Positions Women Hold

A second illustration of women's empowerment and agency in drug sales pertains to their excelling in the roles of drug-purchasing middle-women (e.g. steerers or tout; see Furst et al., 2001). Fagan (1993, 1995), Maher (1997), Sommers et al. (2000) and Furst et al. (2001) found that when women are involved in drug dealing, they are most often middle-women. It is currently not possible to estimate how many middle-men and women currently operate in illicit drug markets or what proportion of them are women. Despite the extent of their presence, however, the middle-woman represents another important dimension of women's economic power.

To begin, middle-women are usually drug users/abusers, indigenous to inner-city drug markets, making a living and financing their drug use by purchasing drugs for less knowledgeable customers, novices or outsiders. In short, middle-men and women purchase drugs for others not familiar with the market. Their fees for this risky activity range from 25–100 percent of the base purchase or a portion of the drugs. The middle-man or woman position epitomizes the ethic of relational power discussed here insofar as agency is exerted on behalf of both the self and others.

The value of middle-men and women to the vitality of the illicit drug market cannot be over-stated. First, they play a direct role in expanding the profits of the market by ushering in new revenues and safely negotiating transactions. This produces new and stable financial capital into the illicit drug economy. Thus, they contribute in a fashion similar to the female sex worker. Second, they help neutralize the violence that can often accompany sales by replacing transactions that would otherwise be fraught with suspicion, fear and ineptitude with familiarity and competence. This earns them considerable social capital among dealers, users and even community members who are not involved in drug activities.

Furthermore, possessing confidence, knowledge and skill (i.e. personal capital) in navigating an illicit market, while eluding arrest and victimization, comprises the essence of what McCarthy and Hagan (2001) called 'criminal success.' While such capital may not be recognized in the conventional economy, it is likely to empower women and men who are situated within the inner-city's illicit drug market in varied ways.

TRANSFERRING DRUG WORLD POWER AND CAPITAL INTO CONVENTIONAL ACTIVITIES

A premise repeatedly communicated in this chapter is that calling attention to these dimensions of women's power in the illicit drug economy could aid efforts to contain drug-related social problems. In this section, I elaborate on a few general ideas that support this point. My focus is on the utility of the empowerment and agency argument to social policy, not on specific types of interventions that could redress drug-related problems.

First, by employing a 'power-to' definition instead of a 'power-over' one, we learn that empowerment and agency are about transformation (i.e. the essence of offender re-entry). When women demonstrate empowerment and agency, they are putting into practice a bringing about of change. As a result, they may be more comfortable with the transformation idea when presented with strategies to desist from drug use and criminal activity. Focusing on power-over forms, on the other hand, leaves them preoccupied with possession and loss and may disadvantage them in embracing 'change' opportunities encountered in the community and in institutions (e.g. prison). Criminal justice interventions should, therefore, acknowledge the different orientations and experiences with power and agency that men and women have experienced because of gender, and work to channel their agency into more conventional activities.

Second, the notion that illicit drug world participation and work could translate into valuable forms of capital in the conventional world or even improve the chances of escaping negative pursuits seems implausible, given the dominant narrative and current discourse. Nevertheless, I have argued that this connection exists and is important to understand. For example, women's role in providing housing not only helps organize the drug world and allows for more consistent financial capital accumulation by dealers (especially males), but it contributes to individual and family survival possibly for generations to come.

Experience and success in economically based activities, even illicit ones, furnish women with personal capital for future conventional pursuits, such as providing for themselves and their children and, perhaps, enabling them to secure more fulfilling, non-abusive relationships. Also, women's

competence as breadwinners can help ease poverty in low-income families where a second income is often absent. Consequently, cutbacks in treatment programs and social supports (e.g. cash assistance, women's shelters and violence prevention programs) and continued punitive responses (e.g. turns only toward incarceration) may impede the realization of these more pro-social goals. An approach favoring increased social support combined with treatment programs that are part of alternatives to incarceration might be a wiser course of action.

Then, too, women's identities as mothers often anchor drug users into mainstream society and provide a source of empowerment outside of drugs. Because inner-city, drug-using and -selling males are often absent in parenting and lag behind women in employment in the secondary labor market, they have fewer resources for empowerment outside of the illicit drug world. This gendered link between illegal and conventional worlds not only impacts people's lives today but, again, promises to influence the next generation.

For example, Pyke (1996) has noted that girls learn roles from watching their mothers, while boys must learn their roles from rules that structure the life of an absent male figure. This is especially relevant for poor inner-city neighborhoods fraught with illicit drug markets. Drugs, gangs and the code of the streets act as a surrogate fatherhood for detached males (Anderson, 1999). Therefore while girls can identify with a concrete example, even if it is a drug-abusing female present in their daily lives, boys embrace ideals that may or may not be present in real males.[9] Thus, girls learn roles with more interpersonal and relational skills, while males become disconnected due to identification with abstract cultural stereotypes and masculine fictions. Therefore, women's continued commitment to the family, children and household is not only critically important to the social and economic organization of the drug world, but also to future generations' well-being in the conventional world. Criminal justice efforts should be designed to preserve this for women and encourage it for males.

Third, while women gain empowerment and capital from doing for others, too often they are pressured to channel their energies into others' benefit. For example, many intervention programs seek to restore women as effective mothers or to prepare them to become effective mothers in the future. This denies women a more complete self-fulfillment or existence outside of the family. We must be careful not to channel all of women's agency and sense of empowerment into the benefit of others (fostering, perhaps, co-dependency). So many women drug users I have interviewed over the years have told me drug use was a way for them to secure something for themselves, that is, to be independent, absent any real hobbies or friends they could enjoy. Interventions should, therefore, help them find ways to use their empowerment and agency for their own fulfillment outside the world of drugs.

DISCUSSION

Many influential ethnographic texts on the drug world (Jankowski, 1991; Bourgois, 1996; Anderson, 1999 to name a few) feature story lines about men's resistance to mainstream endeavors via the dangerous, yet socially valuable expression of hyper-masculinity and dominance in the accumulation of money and sexual conquest. This power-over narrative perpetuates the idea of women's pathology and powerlessness. More importantly, however, such accounts obscure the mundane actions of people in the illicit drug world.

Simultaneously, some of the same works have taught us that markets in the informal economy (e.g. illicit drugs, criminal enterprises and street vending) are entities with operating principles (language, norms and roles) designed to preserve order and facilitate stable business practices for all involved. Instability and turmoil are undesirable. While scholarship has articulated the role men play in negotiating this order (showing that they are the most central actors and possess the most power and control), there has been less understanding about the roles women play. When we add to this the failure to use a gender framework to comprehend these phenomena, both epistemological realities and improved social policy are hindered.

I have insisted on three major theoretical points about illicit drug world organization. First, the accumulation of structural forms of power (more often held by men) requires empowerment and agency by others. Since the illicit drug world is patriarchally organized, it is

no surprise that men continue to dominate the marketing hierarchy. However, undoubtedly, men's ability to exercise this dominance depends greatly on women's empowerment and agency. The illicit drug market is best characterized as a web of social, financial and interpersonal relationships between men and women, focusing on the exchange of illicit goods. As such, drug world organization is fundamentally gendered. Future discourse and policy would be well advised to incorporate this point.

Second, the view of women as pathological, powerless and sexualized objects denies their experience both in general and, in particular, within the drug world organization. This point should raise new questions about other possible contributions of women. Here, I have focused almost exclusively on the economic side of drug-marketing activities. However, there are many other issues about experience in the drug world that could benefit from a more feminist-empowered viewpoint. These issues include questioning how women and men learn to stabilize their lives around drug use and selling; how drugs become routinized in people's lives; what benefits and consequences are entailed for those involved in and outside the drug world; and how structural power as opposed to emphases on empowerment and agency affects using careers and cessation efforts. Finally, more research needs to be done on how these different forms of power function to aid or hinder family and intimate relations where exposure to drugs and related problems are involved.

Third, I have argued that several activities routinely performed by women (providing housing, purchasing and selling drugs and subsidizing male dependency) are both fundamental to the social and economic organization of the illicit drug world and earn them various forms of capital that can aid future conventional pursuits. This crucial point is rarely made in pathology and powerlessness-oriented debates about women's involvement in the illicit drug economy. Here, alternatively, I have attempted both to 'center' women in a discussion of drug world economic and social organization and to demonstrate the value of utilizing a gender-oriented framework to study this world.

While I have not denied that women suffer numerous personal and social consequences from interaction in the illicit drug world, I have also tried to show that they accumulate important forms of capital that may serve them well in future, more legitimate pursuits. Allowing this dimension of women's economic power in the drug world broadens our understanding of women's experience beyond notions of pathology and powerlessness and helps to articulate a link between legal and illegal social worlds or deviant and mainstream contexts.

Notes

1. Empowerment and agency can and often do have a reciprocal relationship with each other. For example, task performance and other forms of agency or action are made possible by feelings and perceptions of ability and competence. Agency can also generate increased perceptions, by self and others, of empowerment. This chapter uses the term 'empowerment' to describe feelings and perceptions of ability and competence, whereas agency is used to define actions. Taken together, the terms allow for a broader conception of power that is seldom employed in drugs and crime research.

2. The argument I put forth here emanates from a critical review of current and past research on women and substance abuse. The four activities reviewed emerged from my reading of this and other literatures. I used such an approach in previous papers that offered theoretical contributions to the drugs debate (see Anderson, 1995, 1998). Like my previous work, this study does not utilize quotes from published studies. Pulling quotes selectively from published studies to support the argument I make here might be construed as a form of bias. In other words, selective use of pre-published quotes about women and drugs might compromise their authenticity due to removing them from the social context in which they were offered and reported on in their original reports. Thus, findings from extant research are incorporated here rather than re-printing selected quotes.

3. The value of women's provisions of a stable residence to the drug trade and the criminal success of its interactants was discussed by Wilson (1993) and raised again later by Maher (1997). Wilson claimed that 'the mesh between women's provision of a home base and their lack of mobility and men's lack of a home base but high mobility may be a combination that works well for a sexually integrated drug network' (1993: 188). Wilson argued that women's control of the household contributed to their criminal involvement, enabling them to reach parity with men. Thus, Wilson located the provision of housing within the traditional discourse on women deviants. Maher (1997) challenged this by showing that women have yet to reach parity with men in the drug world.

4. The literature on vacant housing, residential transition and illicit activity is considerable and is located within numerous disciplines (sociology, criminology, urban studies, etc.). It is too large to reference here.

5. US residents are estimated to have spent about $63.8 billion on illicit drugs in 2000. Approximately $400 billion per year, a significant portion of the GDP, including the United States and other countries, enters the legitimate economy via the illicit drug trade (see ABT Associates, 2001).

6. This is a good example of the reciprocal nature between empowerment and agency.

7. A recent study reported that when work is exchanged for drugs instead of cash, men and women do it with equal frequency.

8. Jacobs's (1999) ethnography in St Louis, Missouri, indicates, however, that most young male drug dealers (including crack) use drugs (i.e. often blunts [marijuana soaked in PCP, crack, etc.]) and may become more addicted to crack than they are willing to admit. Anderson and Levy's work in Chicago with older drug addicts (Anderson and Levy, 2003; Levy and Anderson, 2005) revealed that most males had commenced drug-dealing careers by not using their own supplies but that over time, they became addicted, which damaged their dealing careers.

9. The absence of fathers in the inner city is, to some extent, filled by godfathers and other positive male role models who often exact a positive influence on younger individuals. While their contributions are powerful and central, primary fatherhood remains problematic and lacking.

References

ABT Associates (2001) *What Americans Spend on Illicit Drugs: 1988–2000*. Washington, DC: Office of National Drug Control Policy.

ADAM (2002) *Drug Use and Related Matters among Adult Arrestees, 2001*. Washington, DC: Bureau of Justice Statistics, National Institute of Justice.

Adler, Freda (1975) *Sisters in Crime: The Rise of the New Female Criminal*. New York: McGraw-Hill.

Allen, Amy (1999) *The Power of Feminist Theory*. Boulder, CO: Westview Press.

Anderson, Elijah (1990) *Streetwise: Race, Class, and Change in an Urban Community*. Chicago, IL: University of Chicago Press.

Anderson, Elijah (1999) *Code of the Street*. New York: W. W. Norton.

Anderson, Tammy (1995) 'Toward a Preliminary Macro Theory of Drug Addiction,' *Deviant Behavior* 16(4): 353–72.

Anderson, Tammy L. (1998) 'A Cultural-Identity Theory of Drug Abuse,' *The Sociology of Crime, Law, and Deviance* 1: 233–62.

Anderson, Tammy L. and Judith A. Levy (2003) 'Marginality among Older Injectors in Today's Illicit Drug Economy: Assessing the Impact of Ageing,' *Addiction* 98(6): 761–70.

Anderson, Tammy L., Caitlin Shannon, Igor Schyb and Paul Goldstein (2002) 'Welfare Reform and Housing: Assessing the Impact to Substance Abusers,' *Journal of Drug Issues* 2(1): 265–96.

Bourgois, Philippe (1995) *In Search of Respect: Selling Crack in El Barrio.* New York: Cambridge University Press.

Bourgois, Philippe (1996) 'In Search of Horatio Alger: Culture and Ideology in the Crack Economy,' *Contemporary Drug Problems* 16(4): 619–49.

Bourgois, Philippe (2003) *In Search of Respect: Selling Crack in El Barrio* (2nd edn). New York: Cambridge University Press.

Bourgois, P. and E. Dunlap (1993) 'Exorcising Sex-for-Crack: An Ethnographic Perspective from Harlem,' in M. S. Ratner (ed.) *Crack Pipe as Pimp: An Ethnographic Investigation of Sex-for-Crack Exchanges*, pp. 97–132. New York: Lexington Books.

Bourgois, Philippe, Mark Lettiere and James Quesada (1997) 'Social Misery and the Sanctions of Substance Abuse: Confronting HIV Risk among Homeless Heroin Addicts in San Francisco,' *Social Problems* 44(2): 155–73.

Bratt, Rachel G. (2002) 'Housing and Family Well-Being,' *Housing Studies* 17(1): 13–26.

Brines, Julie (1994) 'Economic Dependency, Gender, and the Division of Labor at Home,' *American Journal of Sociology* 100(3): 652–88.

Brotherton, David C. (1996) '"Smartness," "Toughness," and "Autonomy": Drug Use in the Context of Gang Female Delinquency,' *Journal of Drug Issues* 26(1): 261–77.

Browne, Irene (ed.) (1999) *Latinas and African American Women at Work.* New York: Russell Sage Foundation.

Browne, Irene and Ivy Kennelly (1999) 'Stereotypes and Realities: Images of Black Women in the Labor Market,' in Irene Browne (ed.) *Latinas and African American Women at Work*, pp. 302–26. New York: Russell Sage Foundation.

CASA (2003) *The Formative Years: Pathways to Substance Abuse among Girls and Young Women Ages 8–22.* New York: National Center on Addiction and Substance Abuse, Columbia University.

Casper, Lynne M. (1996) *Who's Minding Our Preschoolers?* Current Population Reports, Housing Economic Studies. Washington, DC: US Department of Commerce, Bureau of the Census.

Connell, R. W. (1987) *Gender and Power.* Stanford, CA: Stanford University Press.

Cross, John C., Bruce D. Johnson, W. Rees Davis and Hilary James Liberty (2001) 'Supporting the Habit: Income Generation Activities of Frequent Crack Users Compared with Frequent Users of Other Hard Drugs,' *Drug and Alcohol Dependence* 64(2): 191–201.

Daily Business Review (2002) 'U.S. Supreme Court OKs Public Housing Drug Evictions,' (Miami, FL), *Daily Business Review*, 27 March, 76(201): A9.

Duneier, Mitchell (1999) *Sidewalk.* New York. Farrar, Straus & Giroux.

Dunlap, Eloise and Bruce D. Johnson (1996) 'Family and Human Resources in the Development of a Female Crack-Seller Career: Case Study of a Hidden Population,' *Journal of Drug Issues* 26(1): 175–98.

Dunlap, Eloise, Bruce D. Johnson and Lisa Maher (1997) 'Female Crack Sellers in New York City: Who They Are and What They Do,' *Women and Criminal Justice* 8(4): 25–55.

Dunlap, Eloise, Sylvie C. Tourigny and Bruce D. Johnson (2000) 'Dead Tired and Bone Weary: Grandmothers as Caregivers in Drug Affected Inner City Neighborhoods,' *Race and Society* 3(2): 143–63.

Dunlap, Eloise, Andrew Golub, Bruce D. Johnson and Wesley Damaris (2002) 'Inter-Generational Transmission of Conduct Norms for Drugs, Sexual Exploitation and Violence: A Case Study,' *British Journal of Criminology* 42(1): 1–20.

Ettorre, Elizabeth (1992) *Women and Substance Abuse.* New Brunswick, NJ: Rutgers University Press.

Evans, Rhonda D., Craig J. Forsyth and DeAnn K. Gauthier (2002) 'Gendered Pathways into and Experiences within Crack Cultures Outside of the Inner City,' *Deviant Behavior* 23(6): 483–510.

Fagan, Jeffrey A. (ed.) (1993) *The Ecology of Crime and Drug Use in Inner Cities.* New York: Social Science Research Council.

Fagan, Jeffrey (1995) 'Women's Careers in Drug Use and Drug Selling,' *Current Perspectives on Aging and the Life Cycle* 4: 155–90.

File, Karen (1976) 'Women and Drugs Revisited: Female Participation in the Cocaine Economy,' *Journal of Drug Issues* 24(2): 179–225.

File, Karen N., Thomas W. McCahill and Leonard D. Savitz (1974) 'Narcotics Involvement and Female Criminality,' *Addictive Diseases: An International Journal* 1(12): 177–88.

Foucault, Michel (1979) *Discipline and Punish: The Birth of the Prison.* New York: Vintage Books.

Foucault, Michel (1990) *The History of Sexuality.* New York: Vintage Books.

Furst, R. Terry, Richard S. Curtis, Bruce D. Johnson and Douglas S. Goldsmith (2001) 'The Rise of the Middleman/Woman in a Declining Drug Market,' *Addiction Research* 7(2): 103–28.

Goldstein, Paul, Tammy L. Anderson, Igor Schyb and James Swartz (2000) 'Modes of Adaptation to Termination of the SSI/SSDI Addiction Disability: Hustlers, Good Citizens, and Lost Souls,' *Advances in Medical Sociology* 7: 215–38.

Hamid, Ansley (1990) 'The Political Economy of Crack-Related Violence,' *Contemporary Drug Problems* 17(1): 31–78.

Hamid, Ansley (1992) 'Drugs and Patterns of Opportunity in the Innery-City: The Case of Middle-Aged, Middle-Income Cocaine Smokers,' in Adele Harrell and George Peterson (eds) *Drugs, Crime, and Social Isolation*, pp. 209–39. Washington, DC: Urban Institute Press.

Hardesty, Monica and Timothy Black (1999) 'Mothering through Addiction: A Survival Strategy among Puerto Rican Addicts,' *Qualitative Health Research* 9(5): 602–19.

Harding, Sandra (1986) *The Science Question in Feminism.* Ithaca, NY: Cornell University Press.

Harding, Sandra (1991) *Whose Science? Whose Knowledge?* Ithaca, NY: Cornell University Press.

Harrell, Adele and George Peterson (eds) (1992) *Drugs, Crime, and Social Isolation.* Washington, DC: Urban Institute Press.

Hartsock, Nancy (1985) *Money, Sex, and Power.* Boston, MA: Northeastern University Press.

Hill, R. (1993) *Research on the African American Family: A Holistic Perspective.* Westport, CT: Auburn House.

Hill, R. (1998) 'Understanding Black Family Functioning: A Holistic Perspective,' Special Issue (Comparative Perspectives on Black Family Life, vol. 1) of *Journal of Comparative Family Studies* 29(1): 15–26.

Hill-Collins, Patricia (1990) *Black Feminist Thought.* New York: Routledge.

hooks, bell (1981) *Ain't I a Woman: Black Women and Feminism.* Boston, MA: South End Press.

hooks, bell (1984) *From Margin to Center.* Boston, MA: South End Press.

Hser, Yih Ing, M. Douglas Anglin and Mary W. Booth (1987) 'Sex Differences in Addict Careers. Part 3. Addiction,' *American Journal of Drug and Alcohol Abuse* 13(3): 231–51.

Inciardi, J. A. and H. Surrat (2001) 'Drug Use, Street Crime, and Sex Trading among Cocaine-Dependent Women: Implications for Public Health and Criminal Justice Policy,' *Journal of Psychoactive Drugs* 33(4): 379–88.

Inciardi, J. A., D. Lockwood and A. Pottieger (1993) *Women and Crack Cocaine.* New York: Macmillian.

Jacobs, Bruce A. (1999) *Dealing Crack: The Social World of Streetcorner Selling.* Boston, MA: Northeastern University Press.

Jacobs, Bruce and Jody Miller (1998) 'Crack Dealing, Gender, and Arrest Avoidance,' *Social Problems* 45(4): 550–69.

Jankowski, Martin Sanchez (1991) *Islands in the Street: Gangs and American Urban Society.* Berkeley, CA: University of California Press.

Kontos, Luis, David Brotherton and Luis Barrios (eds) (2003) In *Gangs and Society: Alternative Perspectives.* New York: Columbia University Press.

Laidler, Karen Joe and Geoffrey Hunt (2001) 'Accomplishing Femininity among the Girls in the Gang,' *British Journal of Criminology* 41(4): 656–78.

Levy, Judith A. and Tammy L. Anderson (2005) 'The Drug Career of the Older Injector,' *Addiction Theory and Research* 13(2): 245–58.

Lovell, Anne M. (2002) 'Risking the Risk: The Influence of Types of Capital and Social Networks on the Injection Practices of Drug Users,' *Social Science and Medicine* 55(5): 803–21.

Maher, Lisa (1996) 'Hidden in the Light: Occupational Norms among Crack-Using, Street-Level Sex Workers,' *Journal of Drug Issues* 26(1): 143–73.

Maher, Lisa (1997) *Sexed Work: Gender, Race, and Resistance in a Brooklyn Drug Market.* London: Oxford University Press.

Maher, Lisa and Kathleen Daly (1996) 'Women in the Street-Level Drug Economy: Continuity or Change?' *Criminology* 34(4): 465–91.

Maher, Lisa, E. Dunlap, B. Johnson and A. Hamid (1996) 'Gender, Power, and Alternative Living Arrangements in the Inner-City Crack Culture,' *Journal of Research in Crime and Delinquency* 33(2): 181–205.

Marable, Manning (2000) *How Capitalism Underdeveloped Black America: Problems in Race, Political Economy, and Society.* Cambridge, MA: South End Press.

May, Tiggey, Michael Hough and Mark Edmunds (2000) 'Sex Markets and Drug Markets: Examining the Link,' *Crime Prevention and Community Safety* 2(2): 25–41.

McAdoo, H. P. (ed.) (1997) *Black Families* (3rd edn). Thousand Oaks, CA: Sage Publications.

McCarthy, Bill and John Hagan (2001) 'When Crime Pays: Capital, Competence, and Criminal Success,' *Social Forces* 79(3): 1035–59.

McCoy, Clyde and J. A. Inciardi (1995) *Sex, Drugs and the Continuing Spread of AIDS.* Los Angeles, CA: Roxbury Press.

McMahon, Thomas J. and Bruce J. Rounsaville (2002) 'Substance Abuse and Fathering: Adding Poppa to the Research Agenda,' *Addiction* 97(9): 1109–15.

McNeil, John (1998) *Changes in Median Household Income: 1969–1996.* Current Population Reports. Washington, DC: US Department of Commerce, Bureau of the Census.

Miller, Jody (1995) 'Gender and Power on the Streets: Street Prostitution in the Era of Crack Cocaine,' *Journal of Contemporary Ethnography* 23(4): 427–52.

Murphy, Sheigla and Karina Arroyo (2000) 'Women as Judicious Consumers of Drug Markets,' in Manzai Natarajan and Mike Hough (eds) *Illegal Drug Markets: From Research to Prevention*, pp. 101–20. Monsey, NY: Criminal Justice Press.

Murphy, Sheigla and Marsha Rosenbaum (1999) *Pregnant Women on Drugs*. New Brunswick, NJ: Rutgers University Press.

NHSDA (2002) *Substance Abuse or Dependence*. Washington, DC: Substance Abuse and Mental Health Services Association, Office of Applied Studies.

Nobles, W. (1997) 'African American Family Life: An Instrument of Culture,' in H. P. McAdoo (ed.) *Black Families*, pp. 83–93. Thousand Oaks, CA: Sage Publications.

ONDCP (2002) *Drug Use Trends*. Washington, DC: The White House.

ONDCP (2003) *Club Drugs: Facts and Figures*. Washington, DC. www.whitehousedrugpolicy.gov

ONDCP (2004a) *Cocaine Facts and Figures*. Washington, DC. www.whitehousedrugpolicy .com

ONDCP (2004b) *Heroin Facts and Figures*. Washington, DC. www.whitehousedrugpolicy .com

ONDCP (2004c) *Marijuana Facts and Figures*. Washington, DC. www .whitehousedrugpolicy.com

Pyke, Karen (1996) 'Class-Based Masculinities: The Interdependence of Gender, Class and Interpersonal Power,' *Gender and Society* 10(5): 527–49.

Ratner, M.S. (ed.) (1993) *Crack Pipe as Pimp: An Ethnographic Investigation of Sex-for-Crack Exchanges*. New York: Lexington Books.

Reskin, Barbara F. (1999) 'Occupational Segregation by Race and Ethnicity among Women Workers,' in Irene Browne (ed.) *Latinas and African American Women at Work*, pp. 183–206. New York: Russell Sage Foundation.

Rosenbaum, Marsha (1981) *Women on Heroin*. New Brunswick, NJ: Rutgers University Press.

Sassen, Saskia (2002) *Global Networks, Linked Cities*. New York: Routledge.

Simon, Rita J. (1975) *Women and Crime*. Lexington, MA: Lexington Books.

Sommers, Ira, Deborah Baskin and Jeffrey Fagan (1996) 'The Structural Relationship between Drug Use, Drug Dealing, and Other Income Support Activities among Women,' *Journal of Drug Issues* 26(4): 975–1006.

Sommers, Ira, Deborah Baskin and Jeffrey Fagan (2000) *Workin' Hard for the Money: The Social and Economic Lives of Women Drug Sellers*. Huntington, NY: NOVA Science Publishers.

Sterk, Claire E. (1999) *Fast Lives: Women Who Use Crack Cocaine*. Philadelphia, PA: Temple University Press.

Wallerstein, Immanuel (2004) *World-Systems Analysis: An Introduction*. Durham, NC: Duke University Press.

Waterston, Alice (1993) *Street Addicts in the Political Economy*. Philadelphia, PA: Temple University Press.

White, Helene R. and D. M. Gorman (2000) 'Dynamics of the Drug–Crime Relationship,' in Gary LaFree (ed.) *The Nature of Crime: Continuity and Change*, Criminal Justice 2000, vol. 1, pp. 151–218. Washington, DC: National Institute of Justice.

Wilson, N. K. (1993) 'Stealing and Dealing: The Drug War and Gendered Criminal Opportunity,' in C. C. Culliver (ed.) *Female Criminality: The State of the Art*, pp. 169–94. New York: Garland Publishing.

Wilson, William J. (1996) *When Work Disappears*. New York: Vintage Books.

Zerai, Assata and Rae Banks (2002) *Dehumanizing Discourse, Anti-Drug Law, and Policy in America*. Burlington, VT: Ashgate.

Chapter 12

THE WAR ON DRUGS AS A
WAR AGAINST BLACK WOMEN

STEPHANIE R. BUSH-BASKETTE

The number of Black females incarcerated for drug offenses increased by 828% between 1986 and 1991. This increase was approximately twice that of Black males (429%) and more than 3 times the increase in the number of White females (241%) (Mauer & Huling, 1995, p. 20). In Florida, Black females constituted 55.6% of the incarcerated female population in 1983. By 1993, the percentage had increased to 58.3% and by 1994, to 59.3%. In 1993, a drug offense was the primary offense of 38.9% of the Black female inmates in Florida. Drug offenses were the primary convictions for 29.5% of the incarcerated White females (Florida Department of Corrections, 1993/1994).

Although Black females generally constitute a higher percentage of the incarcerated female population than Black males do of the incarcerated male population, the Black female's presence in the criminal justice system is seldom studied. The impact of the so-called war on drugs on the incarceration of Black females is no exception. Tonry (1995), although acknowledging the apparent impact of the drug policies on Black females, chose to focus his attention on the impact of the war on drugs on the Black male. Feminist criminologists often generalize the impact of drug policies to all women and propose that "the 'war on drugs' has been translated into a war on women" (Chesney-Lind, 1995, p. 111). As such, the experiences of Black females in the criminal justice system are often ignored or marginalized. Even when criminologists attempt to place Black females at the center of their research on the processing of females by the criminal justice system, such investigations tend to be piecemeal and incomplete. The problem often derives from the lack of data sources that provide information with regard to the intersection of race and gender throughout the criminal justice process (Mann, 1995).

The purpose of this chapter is to (a) further the study of the treatment of the Black female by personnel within the criminal justice system, (b) investigate the impact of drug law violations on the incarceration of the Black female, and (c) substantiate the need to test the impact of "war on drug" initiatives on the incarceration of the Black female.

CONCEPTUAL FRAMEWORK

Although drug use had begun to decline by the early 1980s (except in the case of cocaine use,

Source: Bush-Baskette, S. (1998). War on drugs as a war against Black women. In S. Miller (Ed.), *Crime control and women: Feminist implications of criminal justice policy* (pp. 113–129). Thousand Oaks, CA: SAGE.

which declined in the mid-1980s), beginning in 1987–1988, the war against drugs focused on the arrests of low-level drug dealers and street-level drug offenses, such as possession and trafficking (Tonry, 1995). The drug war initiatives enacted by state and federal legislators included increased penalties, mandatory sentencing laws, and stricter enforcement for drug law violations. Coinciding with these drug law initiatives was an increase in the arrest and imprisonment of Black people. In 1976, Blacks constituted 22% of the arrest cases in the United States for drug abuse violations (as compared to 77% for Whites). By 1990, the percentage of arrests involving Blacks nationwide had risen to 41% and had decreased to 59% for Whites.

Although Blacks were disproportionately arrested for drug law violations, as indicated in Table 12.1, reported drug use by Blacks and Whites did not support the racially disproportionate patterns of drug arrests.

Table 12.1	U.S. Percentage of Drug Use by Race, 1990	
Type of Illicit Drug	Black	White
Marijuana	31.7	34.2
Cocaine	10.0	11.7
Hallucinogen	3.0	8.7
Heroin	1.7	0.7

Source: Adapted from Bureau of Justice Statistics (1991) and Tonry (1995).

It was only in the case of heroin that drug use by Blacks exceeded that of Whites, and then only by 1%. The drug used most prevalently by both Blacks and Whites was marijuana (31.7% for Blacks and 34.2% for Whites). Tonry proposed that the drug policies of 1987–1988 led to the increase in the racial disparity of increased incarceration for the Black male living in the inner city while having no positive impact on the drug problems in the United States (Tonry, 1995).

Some feminist criminologists posit that this war against drugs has actually been a "war against women" (Chesney-Lind, 1995; Feinman, 1994). They support their position with statistics that reveal that the increased incarceration of females coincided with the onset of the drug law initiatives. Although the incarceration rate of females has

remained somewhat constant, with only a 1.6% increase, the number of incarcerated females in state and federal prisons increased from 12,746 in 1978 to 47,691 in 1991 (Feinman, 1994). Between 1980 and 1990, there was an increase of 256% in the number of females incarcerated in state and federal institutions, as compared to an increase of 139.6% for males. Incarceration data for Florida also indicate an increase in the number of incarcerated females between 1983 and 1991. The incarcerated female population in 1983 was 1,253; by 1991, the number had more than doubled to 2,687 (Florida Department of Corrections, 1993/1994).

Most of the increase in the rate of female incarceration was for nonviolent property crime and drug offenses. An analysis of individual states indicates that the percentage of women incarcerated for violent crimes is far less than that for women incarcerated for drug offenses. In 1990, Rhode Island reported that 10% of the incarcerated female population had been convicted of violent crimes, whereas one third had been convicted of drug offenses. During the same year, in Massachusetts, 22% of incarcerated females had been convicted of violent offenses, as compared to 47% who were found guilty of drug offenses (Chesney-Lind, 1995).

Drug offenses represented the single most prevalent primary offense for female inmates in Florida in both 1993 and 1994. Of the female prisoners, 35% in 1993 and 31% in 1994 were imprisoned for a drug offense as the primary charge (Florida Department of Corrections, 1993/1994, 1994/1995). This figure does not include those women who were incarcerated for drug offenses as secondary or lower offenses.

The percentage of females who were incarcerated at the federal level for various offenses significantly shifted between 1986 and 1991, as indicated in Table 12.2.

Table 12.2	Offenses of Female Inmates in Federal Institutions, 1986 Compared With 1991 (in percentages)	
Offense Type	1986	1991
Violent	7.1	2.0
Drug	26.1	63.9
Property	28.2	6.3
Robbery	4.4	2.0

Source: Adapted from Kline (1993).

Between 1986 and 1991, the percentage of females (from 26% to 64%) incarcerated for drug-related offenses more than doubled.

National arrest data indicate that the nonviolent offense category of larceny-theft was the single most frequent arrest charge for women in 1983, 1987, and 1991. Furthermore, beginning in 1987, drug abuse violations consistently appeared in the top five crimes for which women were most frequently arrested in selected years from 1960 to 1991. Arrests for violent crimes were not prevalent enough to be included in these listings (Feinman, 1994).

Mann (1995) reports that much of the recent growth in the arrest and incarceration of women can be attributed to increased drug use and related offenses by women in "an era of harsher drug laws." In 1989, one out of every three women (33.6%) who were held in jails nationwide were charged with a drug offense. Property crimes (31.9%), public order violations (19%), and all other offenses (2.2%) followed (Mann, 1995, p. 129). In Mann's study of the criminal justice processing of women in California, Florida, and New York, she concluded that drug offenses were the third most frequent cause of arrests for women when the arrests of the three states were combined; larceny-theft and driving under the influence being the first and second most frequent arrest charges.

These studies and data support the assertion that the increase in the incarceration of women can be attributed to the policies incorporated in the war on drugs, namely, mandatory sentencing for drug offenses and mandatory sentencing for felony convictions.

A CLOSER ANALYSIS OF THE FEMALE PRISONER

The general profile of the incarcerated female has changed very little over the past 20 years. Glick and Neto (1977) conducted a study of 14 states and the federal correctional systems. From their study evolved a profile of the typical female prisoner as a woman who was (a) Black (more than 50%), (b) unmarried (80%), and (c) the mother of at least one child (75%). Over half of the women were recipients of welfare prior to their imprisonment.

In 1980, a national study was conducted of federal and state correctional facilities. As in the Glick and Neto (1977) study, the findings of the national report concluded that incarcerated females tended to be members of a minority group, young, poor, unskilled, and unmarried. Furthermore, the single most frequent reason for the imprisonment of these women was their conviction for a drug-related or economic crime (Feinman, 1994).

The American Correctional Association (1990) conducted a national survey of state correctional facilities in 1987. They reported a similar profile for the incarcerated female: 57% of the women were members of minority groups, approximately 80% were mothers, and 60% were on welfare prior to their incarceration (60.1%). The single largest crime that led to the incarceration of the female inmates was drug law violations (20%), and the reason most often provided for the commission of women inmates' current offense was their desire or need to buy drugs (25.1%).

In a recent study, Chesney-Lind (1995) discovered an increasing relationship between drugs offenses and the incarceration of women. Between 1980 and 1986, there was an *increase* in the number of women who were incarcerated for the *possession* of drugs and a *decrease* in the number of women who were incarcerated for *drug trafficking*. Her review of a 1990 Rhode Island study indicated that the number of women who were incarcerated in that state increased from 25 to 250 in a 5-year period. Of the 250 women, 33% were incarcerated for drug offenses. In Massachusetts in 1990, nearly half (47%) of the incarcerated women were imprisoned for drug offenses. In New York between 1980 and 1986, 23.3% of the incarcerated females were imprisoned for drug offenses; by 1991, this percentage had increased to 62%. In California in 1984, 17.9% of the incarcerated females were imprisoned for drug offenses; in 1989, the percentage had increased to 37.9%. Of those females who were incarcerated for drug offenses in California in 1989, 37% were held for the possession of marijuana. Chesney-Lind (1995) concludes that "mandatory sentencing for particularly drugs has affected women" (p. 112).

A drug offense was the primary offense of 38.9% of the Black females incarcerated in Florida during 1993. Drug offenses were the primary convictions for 29.5% incarcerated White females. In 1994, 34% of the incarcerated Black females had a drug offense as the primary charge, as compared to 27.2% of the White females. The second most prevalent category of offenses for Black females in 1993 was theft, forgery, fraud (15.7%); for White females, it was murder-manslaughter (26%). The second most prevalent category of charges continued to be theft, forgery, fraud (18.7%) for Black females, and murder-manslaughter (22.9%) for White females (Florida Department of Corrections, 1993/1994, 1994/1995).

Feinman (1994) summarized the increase in the incarcerated female population as follows:

> The increase from 1983 to 1991 can be attributed to the "war on drugs," mandatory sentencing for drug offenses, mandatory sentencing for second felony convictions, and more women getting involved in both the use/possession and the sale of drugs, especially the cheap, easy-to-produce "crack." (p. 47)

These studies support the hypothesis that the drug war has been a major factor in the increase of the incarceration of females. This is inferred from the increase in the number of women incarcerated for drug offenses since the early 1980s.

To summarize, it is apparent from these studies that most of the incarcerated female population are Black or members of a minority group, single mothers, and economically marginalized. Drug law violations are a major factor in the incarceration of women.

GENDER, RACE, AND CRIMINAL JUSTICE SYSTEM PRACTICES

Black women constitute a greater proportion of the incarcerated female population than do Black males of the incarcerated male population. In 1993, a total of 48,170 females were incarcerated in state correctional institutions. Of this group, Black females composed 51.06% (24,595) of the incarcerated female population; White females constituted 43.9% (21,135). The Black male constituted 49.65% of the male state prison population in 1993 (Bureau of Justice Statistics [BJS], 1995). In New Jersey, 69.37% of the incarcerated female population were Black females, as compared to Black males constituting 65.58% of the incarcerated male population. The proportions were similar for New York (58.28% Black female as compared to 54.4% Black male), Florida (59.71% Black female to 58.36% Black male), and California (34.86% Black female to 32.45% Black male; BJS, 1995). These three states were selected for the analysis because of the disproportionate representation of Black females within their respective incarcerated female populations. However, this overrepresentation of the Black female is not exclusive to these states (see Table 12.3).

Table 12.3	Female and Male Prisoners Under State and Federal Jurisdiction by Race, 12/31/92

| Region and Jurisdiction | Number (and Percentage) of Female Prisoners | | | Number (and Percentage) of Male Prisoners | | |
	Prison Population	White	Black	Prison Population	White	Black
U.S. total	55,061	25,148 (45.67)	27,292 (49.57)	891,885	406,632 (45.59)	429,278 (48.13)
Federal	6,891	4,013 (58.5)	2,697 (39.13)	82,696	52,523 (63.51)	27,472 (33.22)
State	48,170	21,135 (43.88)	24,595 (51.06)	809,189	354,109 (43.76)	401,806 (49.66)
New Jersey	1,133	338 (29.83)	786 (69.37)	22,698	6,301 (27.76)	14,885 (65.58)
New York	3,528	1,446 (41)	2,054 (58.21)	61,041	25,508 (41.78)	33,221 (54.42)
Florida	2,699	1,080 (40)	1,612 (60)	50,349	19,949 (39.62)	29,385 (58.36)
California	7,581	4,622 (61)	2,643 (34.86)	112,370	71,139 (63.30)	36,461 (32.45)

Source: Adapted from Bureau of Justice Statistics (1995).

Considering that Black females and Black males separately make up about 6% of the general population, these data indicate that both groups are disproportionately represented in the population of incarcerated individuals in all of the referenced jurisdictions.

Between 1980 and 1991, the number of Black females in state or federal prisons increased by 278%, as compared to an increase of 186% for Black males and an increase of 168% in the overall prison population. Moreover, there was an eightfold increase in the number of Black women incarcerated in state facilities between 1986 to 1991, which was the largest increase among Black, White, and Hispanic females or males, as shown in Table 12.4 (Mauer & Huling, 1995, p. 19).

Lewis (1981), in her review of the data and findings of the San Francisco jail study and Glick and Neto's national study, concluded that in the criminal justice system, racism seems to negatively affect the Black woman more than the Black man. Other researchers have concluded that Black women are treated more harshly than their White female counterparts by police officers and judges (Feinman, 1994; Mann, 1989; Odubekenon, 1992; Simpson, 1989; Young, 1986).

Based on this research and data, it would be counterintuitive to assume that the drug law initiatives have affected Black and White women similarly or that the types of drug offenses (type of drug and level of offense) for which Black and White women are arrested and convicted are the same. Research on these issues is limited. As stated earlier, it is apparent from the American Correctional Association (1990), Glick and Neto (1977), and Mann (1995) studies that the majority of the women who are incarcerated are (a) Black or a member of a minority group, (b) single mothers, and (c) economically marginalized. Drug law violations are a major factor in the incarceration of women. However, the studies do not answer these questions: (a) Are Black women disproportionately arrested for drug offenses? (b) Are Black women disproportionately incarcerated for drug offenses? (c) Are most female prisoners Black women who are incarcerated for drug offenses?

THE NEED TO INVESTIGATE THE EFFECTS OF THE DRUG WAR ON THE INCARCERATION OF BLACK FEMALES

Tonry (1995) restricted his research solely to the impact of the 1987–1988 federal drug law initiatives on the incarceration of the Black male. He explained his rationale for doing so as thus:

Racial disproportions are about as bad in women's prisons as in men's. Like men, about half of female prisoners are Black. However, women make up only 6 to 7 percent of the total number of prisoners. Because one of my central arguments is that by removing so many young Black men from their families and communities,

Table 12.4   State Prisoners Incarcerated for Drug Offenses by Race-Ethnic Origin and Sex, 1986 and 1991

	1986		1991		Percentage Increase	
Race	Male	Female	Male	Female	Male	Female
White non-Hispanic	12,868	969	26,452	3,300	106	241
Black non-Hispanic	13,974	667	73,932	6,193	429	828
Hispanic	8,484	664	35,965	2,843	324	328
Other	604	70	1,323	297	119	324
Total	35,930	2,370	137,672	12,633	283	433

Source: Mauer and Huling (1995, p. 20).

crime control policies are undermining efforts to ameliorate the conditions of life of the Black urban underclass, the focus on Black men is necessary. *The story of Black women as offenders and as prisoners is important, but it is a different story* [italics added]. (p. ix)

This researcher posits that the story of the Black female offender and prisoner is important *and* is different from that of the Black male and the White female. The imprisonment of women also has a profound effect on the family and the community, particularly because, unlike the male, most female inmates were responsible for the care of a child or children at the time of their arrest or imprisonment (American Correctional Association, 1990). Unfortunately, few criminologists have studied Black female criminality and the treatment of Black females within the criminal justice system. Furthermore, there is little understanding of the interactive effects of race and gender on the treatment of Black women within the criminal justice system. As noted by Mauer and Huling (1995) in their attempt to explain the fact that the Black female experienced the greatest increase in criminal justice control of all demographic groups studied,

Although research on women of color in the criminal justice system is limited, existing data and research suggest it is the combination of race and sex effects that is at the root of the trends which appear in our data. (p. 18)

Existing studies support Mauer and Huling's position and have found that Black females and White females are treated differently at every stage of the criminal justice system (Daly, 1987, 1989, 1994; Mann, 1989, 1995).

For at least the past two decades, researchers have consistently concluded that the Black female has experienced harsher treatment in the criminal justice system, from the decision to arrest through sentencing, than White females. Visher (1983) concluded from her observational study of arrests by police in various cities that chivalrous treatment tends not to be displayed toward the Black female. Instead, White female suspects who are older and submissive receive the preferential treatment afforded by chivalry. Simpson (1989) confirmed these findings in her review of the literature from 1984 to 1989. Police were found to extend preferential treatment to

White women as opposed to Black, married women received more lenient sentences than single women, and women with families were treated with more leniency than women who had no families. Part of the explanation for the disparity in treatment may be explained by the fact that more Black females tend to be single. Omole (1991) also found that gender statuses affected the pretrial release dispositions of federal defendants, particularly for the Black females in her sample.

Mann (1995), in a 1989 study of the female jail populations in Florida, New York, and California, confirmed that one third of these prisoners were being detained for drug offenses. When differentiated by race, 32.2% of the White females and 33.8% of the Black females were held in jail for drug offenses. Mann reports that the White female drug offenders tended to be jailed for drug trafficking, whereas the Black female drug offenders were most often detained for the lower-level offense of drug possession.

Mann (1993) noted the virtually unlimited discretion exercised by prosecutors in determining who will be charged or not charged at the very beginning of the processing of a criminal case. This unbridled discretion increases the likelihood that minorities will be "charged, overcharged, and indicted" (p. 108). Spohn, Gruhl, and Welch (1987) studied the prosecutors' rejection or dismissal of charges in felony cases in Los Angeles. Controlling for the defendants' ages, prior criminal records, seriousness of the charges, and uses of weapons, these researchers found that both White females and White males enjoyed higher rates of rejection of their charges at the initial stages, whereas the racial-ethnic minority suspects and defendants did not. They also noted that White females had a notably lower (19%) prosecution rate as compared to African American females (30%).

Foley and Rasche (1979) conducted a 16-year study in Missouri to investigate the effects of race on the sentencing of defendants. They concluded that the African American women in their study received longer (55.1 months) sentences than the White women (52.5 months) for the same crimes. They also discovered that although White women received longer sentences (182.3 months) for personal crimes than their African American counterparts (98.5 months), the latter group served more actual time for these offenses (African American women, 26.7 months; White women,

23 months). These two groups showed no significant difference in mean sentences for drug offenses; however, the African American women served more time (20.4 months compared to 13.2 months).

Kruttschnitt (1980–1981) reviewed sentencing outcomes for 1,034 female defendants in a northern California county during 1972 to 1976. She concluded that the African American female who was convicted of drug offenses or disturbing the peace was sentenced more harshly than her White counterpart. Approximately 18 years later, in 1990, Mann (1995) compared the arrest figures to the imprisonment data for women in California, New York, and Florida who were charged with major felonies (drug violations, theft, burglary, robbery). Mann found that women of color who were arrested for these crimes were sentenced to prison more often than White women with similar arrests. Furthermore, she determined that California, the state that incarcerates more women than any other state in the nation and that also has the largest incarcerated female population in the world, appears to differentiate among these women based on race. Mann pointed out that although White female felons (48.3%) were arrested more often for drug law violations, theft, and burglary, than the African American (30.5%) or Hispanic women (18.7%), the percentage who went to prison for these offenses was much less. Only 38.3% of the White females who were arrested for drug violations were incarcerated, whereas 34.1% of the African American females and 26.1% of the Hispanic American females were imprisoned for the same offenses. Unfortunately, Mann was unable to control for the prior records of the female felons in this study. She did state, however, that with such controls, she would still expect to find evidence of disparate treatment. Mann posited that it would be implausible that prior arrests could affect the three racial-ethnic groups, in the three separate states, in such a way as to explain away the disparity in sentencing (Mann, 1995, p. 129).

Mandatory imprisonment for drug offenses and for second felony convictions are integral parts of the drug law initiatives initiated by many jurisdictions (Feinman, 1994). These laws have an impact on the incarcerated female population. In Florida, the percentage of females incarcerated for drug offenses under mandatory offenders laws increased for both Black and White females between 1993 and 1994. The percentage of Black female inmates sentenced under such laws rose from 40.5% in 1993 to 54% in 1994; for White females, the increase was from 44% to 54% (Florida Department of Corrections, 1993/1994, 1994/1995). An analysis of the percentage of females sentenced under Florida's Felony Habitual Offenders statutes with drug offenses as the underlying felonies is necessary to better understand the impact of the drug law initiatives on the incarcerated female population.

Being both Black and female places Black women in two groups that are experiencing immense growth in their contact with the criminal justice system (Mauer & Huling, 1995). It has been postulated that the treatment of Black women by the criminal justice system actually mirrors the social and historical experiences of Black women in the United States. "Black women in American society have been victimized by their double status as blacks and women" (Young, 1986). Young describes the characterizations used to describe the American Black woman:

> As an Amazon . . . she is domineering, assertive and masculine. . . . *In the case of the black female offender, there is no need for the criminal justice system to protect her by keeping her out of jail or prison or by giving her shorter sentences, because she can take care of herself. She will not be harmed by these harsh dispositions* [italics added]. On the other hand, if she is a black female victim of wife-battering, there is no need to intervene, because she is inherently violent, and again capable of protecting herself. As a "sinister sapphire,". . . she is treacherous toward and contemptuous of black men, dangerous and castrating. *As a black female offender, she is deserving of harsher dispositions* [italics added]. On the other hand, if she is a black female rape victim, she is . . . vindictive and is not a believable complainant. A black female battering victim . . . deserves the violence perpetrated upon her because she precipitated it. . . . The black mammy . . . is a long-suffering paragon of patience. . . . *[As a] black female offender, this suggests that she can endure incarceration, so there is no need to focus on alternatives* [italics added]. As a seductress, then she is loose, immoral and sexually depraved. As a black female rape victim, she cannot be a legitimate victim. She precipitated her victimization and deserves the violence perpetrated against her. (p. 323)

The findings in the studies presented provide substantiation for the need to investigate the possible interactive effects of race and gender on the treatment of the Black female within the criminal justice system in general and the war on drugs specifically. The purpose of any such research should not be to debate whether the war on drugs is a war against Black females, Black males, or women in general. The goal of the research must be to develop the means and measures that will lead to more fully understanding the impact and effectiveness of these legislative initiatives on the incarceration of various groups of persons; to test the effect of the incarceration of these groups on their continued drug use and participation in violent crimes; and to evaluate the impact of these policies on the communities, families, and future employment opportunities for ex-inmates. If the analysis indicates that the differential impact on Black women or other demographic groups is not related to, and outweighed by, a reduction in drug use or violent crimes, then these policies may be deemed to be suspect.

Moreover, the need to investigate the impact of the drug war initiatives on the incarceration of the Black woman extends beyond the women themselves and includes the responsibility of and costs of using these policies to society as a whole. Specifically,

- There is an inherent responsibility for all policymakers to be aware of the effects of their initiatives; this includes determining if the policy differentially affects certain groups of the population.

- The effectiveness of all criminal justice policies to meet their stated goals should be analyzed to determine if the policy should be continued, modified, or abolished.

- Studies, as indicated earlier, have shown that female defendants and offenders are treated differently by criminal justice personnel based on the female's race. It is, therefore, important to investigate if such differential treatment is present in the impact of drug laws on the incarceration of females. If differential treatment is shown, it becomes important to determine the cause(s): increased drug use, possession, trafficking, and manufacturing by particular groups of women or harsher treatment of particular groups of women by the criminal justice system because of their race and gender.

- The majority of women who are incarcerated are mothers (approximately 80%); most of the incarcerated mothers had legal custody of their children at the time of their incarceration (72.3%); and during the incarceration of the women who were mothers, over 90% of the children were living with someone other than the child's father (American Correctional Association, 1990). It is evident that the incarceration of a woman usually affects one or more children and, at a minimum, results in the children's displacement from their homes. The incarceration of the women and the displacement of their children also affect the persons who must act as the children's caretakers during the incarceration and the persons who must pay for this care.

- Although the number of incarcerated women pales in comparison to the number of incarcerated males, the incarceration rate of females has more than tripled in the past decade (Chesney-Lind, 1995). This increase in the incarceration of females requires the facilities in which to imprison them. Nicole Hahn Rafter (1990), who is a prison historian, noted that between 1930 and 1950, only two or three female prisons were created. In the 1980s, 34 prisons for females were created. In addition to the social costs of incarcerating female offenders, there is an economic cost that is borne by the taxpayers. These costs also determine the community's ability to provide financial support for other services.

Without question, Black women have been disproportionately represented among females who are arrested, convicted, and incarcerated for drug offenses. What must now be queried is (a) if this disproportionate representation is due to race-gender effects inherent in the application of the drug law initiatives and that are operating against the Black female, and, if so found, then (b) if the costs—to individuals, communities, and society as a whole—are worth the displacement of the Black women from mainstream society to prison.

References

American Correctional Association. (1990). *The female offender: What does the future hold?* Washington, DC: St. Mary's.

Bureau of Justice Statistics. (1991). *Special report on women in prison*. Washington, DC: Government Printing Office.

Bureau of Justice Statistics. (1995). *Correctional populations in the United States, 1993*. Washington, DC: U.S. Department of Justice.

Chesney-Lind, M. (1995). Rethinking women's imprisonment: A critical examination of trends in female incarceration. In B. R. Price & N. J. Skoloff (Eds.), *The criminal justice system and women* (pp. 105–117). New York: McGraw-Hill.

Daly, K. (1987). Structure and practice of familial-based justice in the criminal court. *Law and Society Review, 21*(2), 267–290.

Daly, K. (1989). Neither conflict nor labeling nor paternalism will suffice: Intersections of race, ethnicity, gender and family in criminal court decisions. *Crime and Delinquency, 35*(1), 136–168.

Daly, K. (1994). *Gender, crime and punishment*. New Haven, CT: Yale University Press.

Feinman, C. (1994). *Women in the criminal justice system*. Westport, CT: Praeger.

Florida Department of Corrections. (1993/1994). *1993–94 annual report: The guidebook to corrections in Florida*. Tallahassee, FL: State of Florida.

Florida Department of Corrections. (1994/1995). *Florida Department of Corrections annual report: Corrections as a business*. Tallahassee, FL: State of Florida.

Foley, L. A., & Rasche, C. E. (1979). The effect of race on sentence, actual time served and final disposition of female offenders. In John A. Conley (Ed.), *Theory and research in criminal justice*. Cincinnati: Anderson.

Glick, R., & Neto, V. (1977). *National study of women's correctional programs*. Washington, DC: National Institute of Law Enforcement and Criminal Justice.

Hagan, J. (1985). Toward a structural theory of crime, race, and gender: The Canadian case. *Crime and Delinquency, 3*(1), 129–146.

Kline, S. (1993). A profile of female offenders in state and federal prisons. In *Female offenders: Meeting needs of a neglected population* (pp. 1–6). Baltimore, MD: United Book Press.

Kruttschnitt, C. (1980–1981). Social status and sentences of female offenders. *Law and Society, 15*(2), 247–265.

Lewis, D. (1981). Black women offenders and criminal justice. In M. Q. Warren (Ed.), *Comparing female and male offenders* (pp. 89–105). Beverly Hills, CA: Sage.

Mann, C. M. R. (1989). Minority and female: A criminal justice double bind. *Social Justice, 16*(4), 95.

Mann, C. M. R. (1993). *Unequal justice: A question of color*. Bloomington: Indiana University.

Mann, C. M. R. (1995). Women of color and the criminal justice system. In B. R. Price & N. J. Skoloff (Eds.), *The criminal justice system and women* (pp. 118–135). New York: McGraw-Hill.

Mauer, M., & Huling, T. (1995). *Young Black Americans and the criminal justice system: Five years later*. Washington, DC: Sentencing Project.

Miller, J. G. (1996). *Search and destroy: African-American males in the criminal justice system*. New York: Cambridge University Press.

Odubekon, L. (1992). A structural approach to differential gender sentencing. *Criminal Justice Abstracts, 2*, 343–60.

Omole, O. E. (1991). *Clarifying the role of gender in the court dispositions: A LISREL model of pretrial release*. Ann Arbor, MI: UMI Research Press.

Rafter, N. H. (1990). *Partial justice: Women, prisons and social control*. New Brunswick, NJ: Transaction Books.

Simon, R., & Landis, J. (1991). *The crimes women commit and the punishments they receive*. Lexington, MA: Lexington Books.

Simpson, S. (1989). Feminist theory, crime, and justice. *Criminology, 27*(4), 605–631.

Spohn, C., Gruhl, J., & Welch, S. (1987). The impact of the ethnicity and gender of defendants on the decision to reject or dismiss felony charges. *Criminology, 25*(1), 175–191.

Tonry, M. (1995). *Malign neglect*. New York: Oxford University Press.

Visher, C. (1983). Gender, police arrest decisions, and notions of chivalry. *Criminology, 21*(1), 5–28.

Young, V. (1986). Gender expectations and their impact on black female offenders and their victims. *Justice Quarterly, 3*(2), 305–327.

PART IV

THE FEMALE OFFENDER AND INCARCERATION

Before, During, and After Incarceration

Over the past three decades, a correctional system that long ignored women because of their small numbers suddenly confronted a population explosion for which they were totally unprepared. The number of women in prison has nearly doubled the rate of men since 1985 (404 percent versus 209 percent, respectively), and today, more than one million women are under criminal justice surveillance and more than 200,000 are behind bars.[1] Despite the social and economic costs of the increased incarceration of women offenders, women have seldom received equitable treatment in prison or recognition in penological research.

When women enter prison, they do so with all of the problems that led them to the criminal activity itself: poverty, drug and alcohol addiction, histories of sexual and physical abuse, fractured homes, and so on. The following readings highlight the multiple issues surrounding women and prison and examine their lives before, during, and after their incarceration.

The first two readings in this section discuss the lives of female prisoners and life behind bars. Representing research from the early era of feminist criminology, Meda Chesney-Lind and Noelie Rodriguez's seminal work critiques the popular belief that the increase in women's imprisonment is driven by women's desire for equality with male criminals. The authors find that, on the contrary, once women end up on the streets in their escape from abusive households, it is not liberation but rather the lack of education, vocational training, and genuine employment opportunities that force women to commit crimes. Using interviews with female inmates in a Midwest prison, Kimberly R. Greer's chapter animates the culture of women's prisons today and shows that while there exist less violence, racial tension, and gang activity than exist in men's prisons, interpersonal inmate relationships are still filled with high degrees of instability, mistrust, and manipulation. Despite such problematic nature in their relationships, the women in Greer's study also reported substantial familial networks behind bars.

The third reading in this section, by Lisa Pasko, takes a look at how youth corrections controls and constructs girls' sexuality. With a concentration on lesbian, bisexual, and queer (LBQ) girls in custody, Pasko underscores the various ways the system invalidates, pathologizes, and criminalizes girls' same-sex attraction and alternative sexual identity. In particular, she tackles the Prison Rape Elimination Act and its potentially dire consequences for incarcerated girls.

The last reading in this section investigates female offenders' re-entry issues and life on parole. Andrea Leverentz's research with ex-prisoners in Chicago shows how these formerly imprisoned women navigate their old communities and attempt to desist from offending. In order to remain successful on parole, many of the respondents in her study identified with the law-abiding in the community and became a "professional" ex-offender: They gave positive meaning to their past experiences as a way of helping others. Leverentz details the difficulties and the gendered symbolic strategies the women employed in order to stay clean, to resist temptation, and to avoid future criminal activity.

Note

1. The Sentencing Project. (2007). *Women and the criminal justice system*. Washington, DC: Author, p. 2.

Chapter 13

WOMEN UNDER LOCK AND KEY

A View From the Inside

MEDA CHESNEY-LIND AND NOELIE RODRIGUEZ

During the early 1970s, newspapers and periodicals were full of stories on the "new female criminal" (Roberts, 1971; Foley, 1974; Nelson, 1977; Klemesrud, 1978; Los Angeles Times Service, 1975). Presumably inspired by the women's movement, she was beginning to seek equality in the underworld just as her more conventional counterparts were pursuing their rights in more acceptable arenas.

These accounts generally relied on two types of evidence to support the notion of a relationship between the women's rights movement and increasing female criminality: Federal Bureau of Investigation (FBI) statistics showing dramatic increases in the number of women arrested for nontraditional crimes and sensationalistic accounts of the activities of female political activists such as Leila Khaled, Bernardine Dohrn, Susan Saxe, and Emily Harris. Of course, the involvement of women in political or terrorist activity is nothing new, as the activities of Joan of Arc and Charlotte Corday demonstrate.

Arrest data collected by the FBI, however, seemed to provide more objective evidence that dramatic changes in the number of women arrested were occurring. For example, between 1960 and 1975 arrests of adult females went up 60.2 percent, and arrests of juvenile women

increased a startling 253.9 percent. In specific, nontraditional crimes, the increases were even more astounding. For example, between 1960 and 1975, the number of women arrested for murder was up 105.7 percent, forcible rape arrests increased by 633.3 percent, and robbery arrests were up 380.5 percent (U.S. Department of Justice, Federal Bureau of Investigation, 1973:124; U.S. Department of Justice, Federal Bureau of Investigation, 1976:1.91).

Law enforcement officials were among the earliest to link these changes to the movement for female equality. "The women's liberation movement has triggered a crime wave like the world has never seen before," claimed Chief Ed Davis of the Los Angeles Police Department (Weis, 1976:17). On another occasion, he expanded on his thesis by explaining that the "breakdown of motherhood" signaled by the women's movement could lead to "the use of dope, stealing, thieving and killing" (Los Angeles Times Service, 1975). Other officials, such as Sheriff Peter Pritchess of California, made less inflammatory comments that echoed the same general theme: "As women emerge from their traditional roles as housewife and mother, entering the political and business fields previously dominated by males, there is no reason to

Source: Chesney-Lind, M., & Rodriguez, N. (1983). Women under lock and key: A view from the inside. *The Prison Journal, 63,* 47–65.

believe that women will not also approach equality with men in the criminal activity field" (Roberts, 1971).

Law enforcement officials, of course, were not alone in holding this position. Freda Adler, in her book *Sisters in Crime,* also linked increases in the number of women arrested to women's struggle for social and economic equality:

> The movement for full equality has a darker side which has been slighted even by the scientific community. . . . In the same way that women are demanding equal opportunity in fields of legitimate endeavor, a similar number of determined women are forcing their way into the world of major crimes. (Adler, 1975:13)

While Adler's formulation met with wide public acceptance, more careful analyses of changes in women's arrest rate provide little support for this notion. Utilizing national arrest data supplied by the FBI along with more localized police and court statistics, Darrell Steffensmeier (1980:58) examined the pattern of female criminal behavior for the years 1965–1977. By weighting the arrest data for changes in population as well as comparing increases in female arrests to increases in male arrests, Steffensmeier concluded that "females are not catching up with males in the commission of violent, masculine, male-dominated, serious crimes (except larceny) or in white collar crimes" (1980:72). He did note female arrest gains in the Uniform Crime Report categories of larceny; fraud, forgery, and vagrancy but, by examining these gains more carefully, he demonstrated that they were due almost totally to increases in traditionally female criminal areas such as shoplifting, prostitution, and naive check forgery (fraud).

Moreover, Steffensmeier noted that forces other than changes in female behavior are probably responsible for shifts in the numbers of adult women arrested in these traditionally female areas. The increased willingness of stores to prosecute shoplifters, the widespread abuse of vagrancy statutes to arrest prostitutes combined with a declining use of this same arrest category to control public drunkenness, and the growing concern with "welfare fraud" were social factors which he felt might explain changes in female arrests without necessary changes in the numbers of women involved in these activities.

Steffensmeier's findings confirm the cautions that had been voiced earlier by Simon

(1975), Rans (1975), and others about generalizing solely from dramatic percentage increases in the number of women arrested. These reservations are further justified by current arrest data, which suggest that the sensationalistic increases of the early 1970s were not indicative of a new trend. Between 1976 and 1979, for example, the arrests of all women rose only 7.1 percent, only slightly higher than the male increase of 5.8 percent for the same period. Moreover, between 1978 and 1979 arrests of all women actually showed a very slight decline (.7 percent) with arrests of women under the age of 18 dropping more sharply (by 4.4 percent) (U.S. Department of Justice, Bureau of Justice Statistics, 1980:466; U.S. Department of Justice, Bureau of Justice Statistics, 1982:350).

Unfortunately, during the period that female arrest figures were registering little or no change, the number of women incarcerated in state and federal institutions has skyrocketed. Between 1974 and 1982, for example, the number of women in prison jumped 119 percent; for males the increase was a sobering but far less dramatic 70 percent (U.S. Department of Justice, Bureau of Justice Statistics, 1982:350). Since there is virtually no evidence that women have been engaged in more serious kinds of offenses (Steffensmeier and Steffensmeier, 1980), the possibility emerges that what may be occurring is a classic example of "self-fulfilling prophecy" —which suggests that if people believe a situation to be real, it is real in its consequences (Thomas and Thomas, 1928). In this case, law enforcement and criminal justice personnel may be participating in the widespread but largely mythical belief that women are now engaging in more serious criminal misconduct and are sentencing them more harshly for their relatively minor crimes.

The other possibility is, of course, that the new female offender does differ from her earlier counterpart, but in ways more subtle than can be detected from secondary analysis of arrest data. Surprisingly, despite all the rhetoric, there has been very little research conducted on this point (Kassebaum, 1967; Burkhart, 1973). Does the modern woman in prison possess different background characteristics than her earlier counterparts? Is she more violent and versatile in her criminal activities than earlier female offenders? Does she, in her attitudes about crime, represent a new, more liberated, female criminal? Finally, what special problems are associated with being a woman in prison during the 1980s? The present chapter attempts, in an exploratory fashion, to provide some preliminary answers to these questions.

STUDY BACKGROUND

During 1982 in-depth interviews were conducted with 16 of the 22 long-term women convicts at Oahu Community Correctional Center (the largest prison in Hawaii and the only institution in the state with facilities for female offenders).[1] Interviewers were able to break through the cautious reserve of these women in part because of the privacy of the interview setting provided by the prison administration. The women were also reassured by an affidavit of anonymity that was attached to the interview schedule and read to each woman.

It was clear that the success in winning this cooperation of the women inmates was further assisted by the entree given the project when two of the informal leaders among the prisoners endorsed the study. The seven women who refused to be interviewed differed from the sample in two basic ways. They were, by and large, older—averaging 43 years old as opposed to the average age of 28 among the women who chose to cooperate with the study; and, while in general, they seemed to comprise a small, older clique, the group also included the few loners in the women's section, or "module," of the prison.

The interview schedule was dominated by open-ended questions that allowed the respondent the freedom to explore her own thoughts and memories, respond to the interviewer's probes, and to return to earlier questions at her own pace. The actual interviews ranged from a minimum of two hours to a maximum of six hours. In virtually every interview, there appeared to be an initial period of caution and reserve followed by a flood of information once rapport was established and the woman began to relate intimate personal experiences to the interviewer. Because of all of these factors, the researchers feel confident that the women's accounts—even those regarding the sensitive issues of prostitution, incest, rape, and violence—were, in fact, accurate. In virtually all cases, the women prisoners not only cooperated with the interviews, they welcomed the chance

to express themselves and review their personal histories with the interviewers.

The interview schedule, itself, was devised to probe both traditional and new themes relating to the situation of the female offender. She was first asked about her commitment offense, the length of her sentence, and the length of time she had been in prison. She was then asked detailed questions about her prior criminal history (both within the juvenile justice and adult systems).

The interview schedule also solicited exhaustive information on women's background asking for specific data on the woman's characteristics as well as information on the quality of her current social networks (both within and outside of prison). The nature of her relationships with her parents or foster parents was also explored. There were specific questions about both extensiveness of physical punishment in her family and the general level of violence in her family, and another series of questions probed her early sexual experiences and her involvement, if any, in prostitution. Here she was specifically asked about whether she had ever been the victim of incest (or family-related sexual assault) or rape. If she had been involved in prostitution, she was also asked details about her age at entry and length of involvement.

Finally, she was asked about her own assessment of her hopes and opportunities as a woman. Questions solicited both past and present perceptions, asking the woman whom she admired as a child, what her dreams were then about her future, and what her perception, at that age, was of the likelihood that she would achieve those dreams. Following these queries, the woman was asked about her contemporary aspirations and finally she was asked, "What do you think is the main reason most women get into crime?"

The 16 women who consented to be interviewed constituted three-quarters of the sentenced female felons held in the two sections of the Oahu Community Correctional Facility; and a look at their characteristics provides no surprises for those familiar with the literature on female offenders. Indeed, it is remarkable that, despite the unique mixture of cultures and peoples of Hawaii, the women inmates of Hawaii's prison so closely resemble the profile of the female prisoner that has traditionally emerged in earlier studies (Glick and Neto, 1977). Like the typical woman prisoner in previous years, the contemporary woman in prison is young (this sample's average age was about 27). She is also poor,[2] a member of a minority group,[3] a high school dropout,[4] unmarried, and the mother of two or more children for whom she is the sole support.[5] This profile is virtually identical to an earlier one constructed on a national sample by Glick and Neto and to more recent studies in Michigan (Figueira-McDonough, 1981) and Australia (Hancock, 1982).

But behind these familiar facts are the details that provide a genuine understanding of how particular characteristics relate to the women's involvement in criminal activity. Probing into these relationships, the interviews permit the identification of major themes in the backgrounds and current situations of women prisoners serving time in the 1980s.

SPARE THE ROD

Analysis of the women prisoners' responses to questions about the way they were raised provides some of the most dramatic and impressive results of this study. In the case of almost all of the women, it was hard to avoid thinking the cliché question, "How did a nice girl like you end up in a place like this?"

In fact, the data revealed that in many ways these women were much like American women everywhere. As children they had had the same hopes and values as most girls. They had had dreams of happy family lives and of successful careers. However, the biographies of all but three of the 16 inmates spelled out a childhood situation that was far from ideal. Only seven of the 16 women reported that they were raised by both parents. The other nine were raised by only one parent or by foster parents of one form or another (blood relatives or state-appointed guardians). Furthermore, for all nine of these, their home situation was disrupted one or more times by being shifted from their single parent or guardians or relatives.

While the stories of broken homes and foster parents were not surprising, the data about the child-rearing techniques showed an impressive pattern that contradicts the wisdom of the adage "spare the rod and spoil the child." About 80 percent of the women reported having been raised "very strictly" by at least one of their parents. The exception to this was two of the inmates (who, incidentally, were among those

who had been raised by both parents) who complained that their parents had been "too lenient" with them as children. For all of the others, spankings, restrictions,, and punishments of all sorts were the rule.

While there is no way of comparing the sample of women prisoners with other women from similar backgrounds, they report having been the victims of an astonishing amount of severe child abuse. The data on their childhood and adolescent histories are full of incidents of recurrent disciplinary spankings that would escalate to violent beatings. Ten of the 16 inmates told of childhoods filled with "beatings" and "hard lickin's" for even the most mild or innocent misbehaviors.

For these ten women, the beatings they received were not really a matter of discipline. Often alcohol or a fight between the foster parents would trigger a physical attack on the children. For about five of the inmates the beatings were a weekly or even daily ritual. One woman told of "severe beatings" with an ironing cord "every day." Another woman recalled that she would " . . . get a lickin' for about anything. [It was] ridiculous for it didn't matter at all; they just took it out on us kids when they had a dispute with each other . . . we would catch hell." Yet another said that she did not do anything wrong to receive the beatings. "I was just in the way. They would beat me to shut me up."

The irrationality and cold brutality to which some of these women were exposed as children is detailed in their own stories. For instance,. one inmate related how the godfather who raised her would drink and then beat her to the point of once giving her a concussion. Another time she had to have stitches on her eye. She reported that she frequently could not go to school because of the beatings. Another inmate who was beaten with a baseball bat by her mother said " . . . it was real heavy beatings . . . it showed when I'd go to school. The school called for it. I was shamed for it. I squealed." When asked what would provoke the beatings she received from her mother, another inmate answered, "Anything, anything. If you told her she was wrong . . . she'd pull out my hair, bruise me . . . break wooden spoons and brooms on me . . . leave me locked up without food for two or three days."

Another inmate's mother would turn her boyfriends against the little girl and prompt them to give her "lickin's." She was so afraid of the wild parties her mother threw that she'd stay in the closet. In her words her mother " . . . didn't want me around. I stayed in my room. The closet felt safe. I'd sit in the closet later too . . . I was always alone." Another woman told the story of her childhood with a foster parent where

> . . . my half sister was her real granddaughter . . . so she was treated real well . . . I wasn't blood so I was a little house slave. I got all the beatings. [The grandmother] was wealthy but she would make me eat spoiled food. I would get sick as a dog. I was always doing something wrong. Like not ironing a shirt. I went to school with whelps and cuts. She'd use cords, sticks and belts. The neighbors called the cops. I went to court but she threatened to kill me so I lied and told them I'd made it all up.

Finally, when asked about what she was punished for as a kid, one inmate reported recurrent beatings as well as an incident where her foster parents held her over a stove to burn her hands "for an incident where I was accused of stealing Auntie's money." She added, "I didn't do it, it was my brother."

Clearly these reports of violence and physical brutality go beyond the question of discipline. What was obviously missing from the homes of most of the inmates was affection and physical security. The situation seemed to be a great deal worse for the women who had had single or foster parents. It is relevant that all but four of the women now have their own children. The special pain of separation from their children was expressed by every one of the mothers. The irony of the situation lies in the fact that now their (collectively) 24 children, too, are being raised by foster parents while their mothers do time in prison.

OCCUPATION AND CRIME

The women in this sample had worked at a wide array of traditionally female occupations. Indeed, most had tried a good many of these dead-end positions, at least for short periods time. The job history of a 31-year-old part-Hawaiian woman who is serving a 12-year sentence for robbery provides a typical example of the employment patterns found in this group: cannery worker (one and one half months), car wash (one and one half months), interior cleaner (three months), hotel maid (one and one half months), perfume factory (two weeks), bar maid (five months), and go-go dancer (her first job which she obtained at 14 years of age). All but one of these women had been employed at some time, but 88 percent (14 of the 16) were not employed at the time of arrest.

Clearly, as with other recent studies on the occupational backgrounds of female offenders (Figueira-McDonough, 1981; Hancock, 1982), these data do not provide any support for the notion that women's increased participation in the labor force has increased their "opportunity" to commit crimes. If anything, the data suggest that it was the lack of genuine employment opportunities which led these women into criminal careers.

Slightly over half of the women were serving time for theft, and another quarter were committed for robbery; but in many respects their careers in crime parallel their position in the straight job market. They are, at best, minor offenders with lengthy histories in the system; three-quarters had been arrested as juveniles and nearly two-thirds had served time in prison previous to this commitment.

The criminal "careers" of two of these women show this quite clearly. Take, for example, a 27-year-old Puerto Rican woman who is doing a five-year mandatory sentence as a "career criminal" for first-degree theft. A heroin addict, she had engaged in some shoplifting and petty theft (from tourists) when she was caught in a police stakeout of a popular tourist area. She and a friend were attempting to take cameras, money, and jewelry from rented cars and were arrested for first-degree theft. Since this was her second offense, she is serving a mandatory five-year sentence. Another woman, also serving a five-year mandatory sentence as a career criminal, entered the criminal justice system as a runaway at the age of 14. She ran away from home the first time because "no one believed" her when she finally complained of sexual abuse at the hands of her godfather that had been going on for "a couple of years." She had been supporting herself as a prostitute and as an exotic dancer "for ten years off and on" and had also been arrested a few times for prostitution or buffer charges for this offense ("disorderly conduct," "loitering"). She is currently serving time for a burglary of a hotel room.

These women's situations were typical of this group. While most of these women are incarcerated for property offenses, three-quarters had been involved, at least in some way, in prostitution. All had used drugs; half were self-reported addicts, and many others simply answered the question about whether they had used drugs by saying such things as "yes . . . almost all kinds . . . speeds, downs, acid, mescaline, hash, marijuana, and heroin . . . heroin is what got me into prison." It appears that extensive drug use as well as prostitution feature as recurrent themes in the lives of these women prisoners, though these are rarely the offenses for which they are serving time. Clearly, these phenomena, as well as the background experiences that propelled them into these behaviors, need to be examined in detail.

THE OLDEST PROFESSION

According to their interviews, nearly all (88 percent) of the women in prison in Hawaii had been involved in some fashion with prostitution at one time or another in their lives, though none were actually serving time for that specific offense. Of course in Hawaii, as elsewhere, a much larger percentage of the pretrial detainees were being held explicitly for prostitution or for offenses that serve as buffer charges for this activity. Only about a fifth of these women had been found guilty of violent offenses; most were currently serving time for property offenses (theft, robbery, or burglary were the most common), but their associations with prostitution were anything but trivial. Most had been working for years at the profession (eight years was the average), a third had been in the life for more than ten years.

There has been considerable debate about whether all women criminals begin as prostitutes, and while these data cannot ultimately resolve the issue, they do suggest that many of the women prisoners had been involved in the activity. Moreover, the interviews reveal that they got involved at an early age (the average at entry for the group was 17.6). One woman was only 13 when she began working, and only two in the group began working as prostitutes after the age of 20.

Most of the women in this group got into prostitution in their teens, often as an outgrowth of living on the streets as runaways. It was also clear from the women's comments that the reasons for entry were largely financial. For example, one woman's response when asked whether she was employed when she got into prostitution: "Yes, [I] had odd jobs, but [I] made more as a prostitute." Some women were recruited directly out of what might be called bar-related female professions into prostitution. For example, one woman who is currently doing time for burglary, said she had been a "taxi dancer" when she "met a guy that got me into it." Another had been a "topless dancer," and two others had worked as employees in massage parlors. One of these women stated that, for her, there had been "no other employment."

Clearly, these women make more at prostitution than they can at the other straight jobs at which they had also worked. However, half the women were working off and on in these entertainment or bar-related jobs while they were involved in prostitution—indicating that these occupations, themselves, serve as adjuncts rather than alternatives to female criminal activity.

Recently, there has been a fair amount of speculation about the psychological background of young prostitutes with an emphasis on damaged self-esteem that might result from having been victimized by sexual abuse and rape (James, 1976). Certainly, interviews with those involved in prostitution bear out the possibility of this relationship. Half had been raped as children and 63 percent were the victims of sexual abuse. One woman now doing time tor robbery was only six when a childhood friend offered her a "camera" if he could "touch her." At age seven, she said her father "touched her when mom wasn't home [and] as the years went by offered money." At the age of nine, he had sexual intercourse with her in exchange for money. "He would be drunk," she continued. By the age of 11, she felt threatened that he "would beat her up" if she didn't have sex. "He would give [me] from twenty-five cents to $3.00 [but I] began to steal more money from him because [I] felt I was worth more. At the end the money wasn't worth it. [My] half brother was aware of what was going on and wanted 'something' too . . . all he did was touch me."

This pattern of multiple victimization runs through the interviews. One woman currently doing time for manslaughter commented in answer to the question, "When you were a kid did anybody try to fool around with you?" "Yeah, [my] uncle, my oldest brother, oldest cousin, and friends of my uncle. It seemed to be a family affair." Also a recurrent theme among these women was the use of money to attempt to gain the girls' consent to sexual abuse. One girl, after repulsing her grandfather's attack at the age of 14; said she "let him screw my girlfriend for $10.00." Others were seduced, or threatened, into acceding to the requests.

Clearly, these experiences led women to cultivate a certain distance and callousness about their sexuality and to view it as a commodity. For some this damage has been so severe that it has made them want to alter their own bodies. One woman, for example, has chosen to gain weight to lessen her attractiveness: "[I'll] let myself go [get heavy] so men will stay away. . . . [I] was very beautiful and well proportioned when younger."

Another theme among these prostitutes is drug dependency. Though it is clear that not all the women in this group were addicts, all had been in a life that encouraged enormous experimentation with drugs, which then ultimately led some to prostitution to support their habit (half were self-reported addicts). Said one woman, "[I'm] addicted. [I] make money . . . [my] money problems [were] real bad . . . couldn't get enough." Another intimated that she lost her straight dancing job and entered prostitution because she "needed more money" to support her drug habit: "I lost my job because I was busted shooting up in the dressing room. [They] gave me my check first and then told me to leave." Another said "drugs have ruined [my life]: . . . got me into prison . . . to me drugs are the main reason for everything." Clearly, the cost of illegal drugs made prostitution and the money they could earn there irresistible. It is also clear that from prostitution, these women then branched out into other activities such as burglary and theft—again to pay for their drugs.

THE DRUG CONNECTION

When asked directly about what "got them in to crime," over half of these women felt that their problems with the law were caused by their drug dependency. This young woman's comments are typical. In response to the question about the "main reason" women got into crime, she said:

> . . . The way we were brought up and drugs, I think the main reason is drugs, we wanted money, the root is drugs, and we needed money

to get drugs, then that's when crime comes in. People like us don't know of any way of getting money and we don't want to work on any other kind of jobs. Prostitution and stealing is the easy way of making money. I will return to prostitution when I get out of here.

The academic question as to whether drug use should be a medical or a criminal issue touches on the process of the criminalization of almost all the women in the study. All had done drugs (besides alcohol), and all but three reported having had trouble handling the drugs. The connection between their criminal career and drug use is undeniable, but it is not a simple one. For example, one felon reported using speed and cocaine to help "psych" herself up for doing robberies. But she also said that she became addicted to speed and would go through painful withdrawals. Finally, she said, it got her into prison. In fact, most of the women inmates reported that their drug use became unmanageable for them and caused financial, psychological, health, or interpersonal problems of one sort or another. For some, the drugs they liked even became life-threatening. Two of the inmates expressed the idea that they were actually lucky that they had been put into prison since, on the outside, they were out of control on the drugs they were taking. One of them said, "Getting in here probably saved my life."

The obvious interconnection between their drug involvement and prostitution, burglary, and robbery was explicit in many of the interviews. As one woman put it, "it [heroin] started me off . . . I had to have my daily." One of the three inmates from a "good home" explained that the drugs she used " . . . ruined my life." Drugs were the reason for her criminal involvement. She said, " . . . they got me into prison." Another said she'd gotten addicted and had to make money to get a fix. She had to hustle. She got into prostitution to make the money. She couldn't get "enough." (She was doing time for two counts of theft.) In a nutshell, it is apparent from the interviews that their drug addiction pressed these women into economic straits that, in turn, significantly contributed to their criminal involvement. The question of causation, though, is less clear. For example, looking at the data, it is obvious that for most of these women their entry into prostitution predated their heavy drug use. However, drug dependency, perhaps developed as part of life "in the fast lane," quickly made their exit from the profession unlikely and quite probably encouraged them to seek even more money through burglary and theft.

STREETWISE AND SORRY ABOUT IT

There has been considerable speculation that the contemporary woman in prison is, in some respects, a "liberated" woman who is seeking equality in the previously male-dominated field of crime. Yet, when these women prisoners were asked about their feelings about their own situation as women and their career aspirations as they were growing up, there was no evidence that they had considered non-traditional careers in either the straight or the criminal world.

Indeed, what is remarkable about their responses is the naive conventionality of their aspirations. One woman (who is doing time for kidnapping and robbery), for example, said she dreamed of a "house with a picket fence, a man to love, children to love and care for, and living happily ever after." Another woman said of her dreams: "I was a ballerina in a huge house with five kids." The "TV kind of life" had made an impression on many of these women, though one woman did comment that "I don't think I admired anybody, 'cause [there] wasn't no black models or movie stars when I was a kid." Others, however, were deeply affected by the media. When asked whom they admired as girls, they frequently mentioned actresses: Ann-Margret, Sophia Loren, Gidget, Jaclyn Smith, Shirley Temple. "Shirley had everything in her and around her. She had a sense of humor," said one woman.

As for career aspirations, they were similarly and poignantly traditional. Said one woman, "I wanted to be a nurse . . . [I] just like to help people and I wanted to be a nun, too. Don't laugh, but that's really true." Nursing was mentioned by three other women as a career choice, while others had aspired to similarly conventional careers: airline stewardess, actress, secretary. Only two women expressed a desire to be "career" women. All but one (93 percent) wanted to get married ("to meet the right guy, be in love, and not fight"), but only one was married at the time of the interview.

In many of the interviews, the lack of money, which characterized the youth of these women, made them long for financial security and even wealth. Some sought wealth for altruistic reasons: "I wanted to get a good job and get a big house and have all my brothers and sisters [have] a nice life and the things they couldn't have." Most, however, were more interested in the benefits money could bring to them directly. One woman said she dreamed of a "life with all the luxuries . . . not having anything to do [but] having anything I Wanted." Others were equally candid as to the role of money in their dreams: "wanting to be rich," "being around rich people . . . [having] nice clothes" were frequent answers. One woman said that, as a girl, she thought of "having money, that's all, I couldn't wait until I was 18 to do what I want—prostituting to earn more money and do what I want." She began working as a prostitute at the age of 13.

This woman was unusual, however, since most of these women did not, as girls, envision becoming criminals. Indeed, their comments during the interview show that they still cherish and, to some extent, still hope to realize their conventional dreams. For this reason, many of these women feel ambivalent about the fact that they have become tough, streetwise survivors. Said one 27-year-old woman doing time for robbery: "I always wanted to be an actress, even today I still want to be an actress. I guess [the dream] was to be an actress and to be in a kind world, now [there is] too much roughness." Another said that she felt she had almost no chance to achieve her desired future: "I don't think it is possible with the life I had as a kid."

Like most low-income or working-class women, these women possess very traditional and narrow attitudes about appropriate female behavior (Crites, 1976; Rainwater, 1960, 1965). Yet, because of their disrupted family life and early victimization, they have had to develop an impressive array of survival skills. These assertive and even aggressive attributes, while they enabled them to be self-supporting since adolescence, seem, nonetheless, to be held in low esteem. Instead of viewing them as assets, these women view them with ambivalence, perceiving them as possible liabilities in their quest for female careers and conventional sex-segregated marriages.

Exemplifying this is the fact that while some talk vaguely of wanting training for careers, which would give them independence once released from prison, they are also maintaining very traditional and dependent romantic relationships with the type of men who exploited them on the streets. For example, while they were in the coed prison, over half (56 percent) told interviewers they had become "romantically involved" with male inmates. These relationships were largely carried on through correspondence, though there was some communication. Occasionally, according to staff sources, male inmates would pass drugs on to the women. There were also rumors the male inmates were expecting sexual favors in return for the drugs. While such relationships are not unnatural, it should be recognized that these men are not unlike the males (described by one woman as "boyfriend dope fiends") who preyed upon their vulnerability while they were on the streets. Indeed even the women recognized that these men were very skilled at manipulating their very significant needs for acceptance and security. Take, for example, this comment from a longtime prostitute who is now in prison for manslaughter and escape:

I feel, as I mentioned before, drugs was my biggest asset in the downfall of my life and as you know one after the other begin to fall in place, you know getting associated with friends and all of a sudden you're involved . . . sure you're probably thinking why didn't you get out of that situation or problem, but I was too involved, and shit, I thought it was great and people liked me a lot and I could demand and get things through friends and especially my boyfriend at the time who in turn became my husband and we split-up and got a divorce after our two girls which was very sad to me. I wish I'd stayed out of trouble if not I wouldn't have to be in here . . . so I have to do my best now until I get out again.

Perhaps one woman summed up their mixed feelings about their criminal careers best when she said women get in to crime because "there is nothing to do . . . no jobs . . . [they are] with the wrong people. They don't want to work. They, the prostitutes, say it's easy but it isn't . . . it's a front. They don't have anything else they can do." The desire to work at straight, respectable female jobs ("be a secretary with an important boss") and have fairy-tale marriages with the "right" man are constant themes in these interviews. Indeed, one suspects that the search for the "right man" and the desire to establish an

"appropriate" dependency relationship with him is a greater source of female criminality than the desire for independence. These women are a far cry from the "liberated female crooks" envisioned by journalists and academicians.

WOMEN'S LIFE IN A COED PRISON

Hawaii, like many states, has experienced a dramatic increase in the number of women it is confining. In the early 1970s, there were only a handful of women in either jail or prison. For example, in 1973 only six women were incarcerated, but in 1982 the figure was closer to 50, with about half of these women serving time as sentenced felons.

Women incarcerated in Hawaii have also been moved several times in the last decade. In just the last three years, they were moved from an isolated cottage on the grounds of the state youth training school to two modules in the state's largest prison (where these interviews were conducted) and back to another facility at the training school. The express purpose for having moved the women into the coeducational facility was the expectation that the women would be able to participate in the larger number of programs available at the male facility.

This hope was not realized, however, as the women's comments clearly indicate. Indeed their chief concern was about a lack of real programming: one woman put it very succinctly in answer to a question about the conditions in the prison: "F—ed . . . nothing to do. Schooling is for some. I'm going out of here with nothing better than the prostitution I came in here for. [My main] gripe is . . . teach women something that gives them an option." Another echoed this frustration: "I feel that if I was given vocational training while I'm in, I'll go straight when I'm out . . . it's very boring in prison . . . there's nothing to do." Another said: "There is nothing for us . . . no degree programs . . . not enough recreation . . . like today we were supposed to go to recreation but we didn't."

Again and again women scored the lack of meaningful programs and healthful activities. These seem odd give their presence at the coed facility. However, because of both dramatic increases in the male population (the number of men housed in the facility nearly doubled during the time the women were there) and continued excessive official concern about the prevention of sexual activity between male and female inmates, movement of women within the facility was carefully monitored, and interactions between male and female inmates were virtually nonexistent. Since there were far more male than female inmates, this meant that women were gradually denied access to virtually all programs at the facility.

At the time of the interviews, these women inmates had no access to the prison's two vocational programs, no access to the prison's worklines (except janitorial work in the women's visiting area), no ability to enter the prison's furlough program, no access to the large recreation yard, no access to clubs, restricted access to religious services and community excursions, and no voice on the inmate council. When they went to school (their one genuine program opportunity), they were escorted by a matron (male students came to class on their own). Women had no free movement in the facility while many male prisoners moved about with passes. Unwilling to abandon their concern with sexual activity, the prison administration used the women's small numbers (relative to male population) as justification for curtailing female access to the program opportunities available at the facility.

This concern with the prevention of any interaction between the male and female inmates to prevent sexual liaisons did not appear to protect the women inmates from sexual harassment by the male staff. Several of the women who were interviewed indicated that male guards had been exerting pressure on some of the women for sexual favors (something these women understand quite well). As one woman put it: "The male guards were sneaking around at night . . . (but) fooling around works two ways."

The women also complained of excessive and arbitrary enforcement of petty regulations by guards and excessive reliance on lockup as punishment:

> I was locked up for six weeks in a room with nothing to do. [The] only time I could leave was to take a shower. They would bring me my meals. The reason I was locked up was 'cause I was always fighting, fighting for my rights . . . but I am more humble now . . . I have learned you have no rights in here.

She continued saying "the staff forget we're human like them, authority gets to their heads . . . the staff is always right and the inmate always wrong." It should be noted that these descriptions were in stark contrast to general appearance of the facility. One interviewer even commented:

> When I asked how the living conditions were in the prison, I expected a more pleasant answer because when I went I observed that they had a nice place, but the answer I got contradicted my first impression: "They can set you up any time. What they (the guards) say carries a lot of weight. They'll exaggerate to make a charge stick. There's so much squealing—no problems—they set up people versus each other."

Complaints about lack of privacy, poor food, and no fresh air were also common in the interviews. These complaints about limited access to programs and rigid rule enforcement are particularly ironic when the relatively trivial and nonviolent offenses of the female inmates are recalled. They also suggest that the Hawaii approach to coeducation seems to have been different and less positive than some reported in the literature. For example, Ruback (1980:33–60), writing about a coeducational facility in Fort Worth, commented on the amount of energy expended by correctional officers because of the fear of sexual activity, but he gave no indication that women were systematically excluded from programs because of that concern. Moreover, Ruback speaks of the willingness of staff to overlook female infractions at that facility, even going so far as to discuss the "double standard applied in disciplinary proceedings," with women receiving preferential treatment.

Such was clearly not the case at the Hawaii facility. It was common knowledge[6] at the prison that rules were more strictly enforced in the female modules, and women inmates (but not male inmates) were punished if found touching or kissing another inmate. Clearly, women inmates considered themselves the losers in this experience with coeducation, so much so that news reports of their return to an isolated single sex facility (Altonn, 1982) are filled with expressions of women's delight at their separate quarters. The article does close by noting that one woman was "reluctant" to move because she had been involved in the prison's college program;

the new woman's facility, like its counterparts across the country, lacks such programs.

CONCLUSION

The number of women in prison has escalated dramatically in the last decade. Some might assume that the changing nature of female criminality is largely responsible for this phenomenon. These in-depth interviews provide no support for this hypothesis; women in prison today (like their earlier counterparts) are minor offenders, who, while they have extensive histories with the criminal justice system, are imprisoned largely for the same types of nonviolent property offenses as were women offenders in previous years.

A careful look at the backgrounds of these women prisoners also provides little support for the notion that their entry into the criminal world was motivated by a desire to seek equality with male criminals. Instead, the biographies of the women in the study spell out a history of exposure to violence and sexual victimization that began early in life. Their backgrounds reveal an interface between victimization and involvement in the criminal justice system that may constitute a systematic process of criminalization unique to women.

Three-fourths of the women prisoners in this sample were repeatedly arrested as juveniles for recurrent incidents of status offenses like runaway and truancy. The in-depth interviews revealed that these incidents of runaway were often due to a situation of child abuse and sexual victimization at home. The women in the sample told chilling stories of violent and irrational beatings that occurred from their early childhood. It is also quite significant that five-eighths reported early incidents of sexual abuse. Moreover, almost half of the inmates admitted to having been raped in their youth. Many of these incidents of rape involved an adult male in their immediate family—a stepfather or older stepbrother, uncle or one of their mother's boyfriends.

Their impossible situation at home led most of them to run away, but then they were open to arrest. In fact, 13 of the 16 women that were interviewed had spent some time in juvenile detention facilities. Add to this the fact that of those who went into prostitution, nearly all (75 percent) entered before the age of 17; and all of these reported they had no other job (or only "odd jobs") at a time they made that decision. The picture that emerges is one of young girls faced with violence and/or sexual abuse at home who became criminalized by their efforts to save themselves (by running away) from the abuse.

Once on the streets, the position afforded these women in the criminal world indicates that, again, it was not liberation but lack of formal education and genuine employment options that forced them to continue committing crimes. In the sex-segregated world of crime, most began as prostitutes and then graduated to minor property offenses. For many, the transition to crime was made easier by dependence on drugs, which, in turn, then escalated their involvement in illegal activities.

A brief look at the opportunities afforded women in prison today also suggests that, in fact, the overcrowding in the male facilities may have slowed or even halted the meager gains made by women inmates in previous decades. In Hawaii, for example, correctional administrators (whose institutions were just recently integrated) quickly returned the women to an isolated single sex facility when the logistics occasioned by the women's presence in a facility experiencing a dramatic increase in male inmates became troublesome. Even while in the overcrowded coed facility, women were afforded little mobility and virtually no access to program opportunities.

Contemporary woman prisoners, then, are not unlike their earlier counterparts, but they are handicapped by virtue of their numbers. Victims as well as offenders, their backgrounds and current situations, require specialized services that overburdened and underfunded social service and correctional systems will be hard pressed to deliver.

NOTES

1. Unfortunately, access to the imprisoned women who were awaiting trial was not approved. Oahu Community Correctional Center housed, at the time of these interviews, all women inmates in the state who required incarceration in one of two modules or sections of the largely male facility. The coed facility also held roughly 800 male long-term prisoners at that time.

2. Nearly all, 14 of the 16, were not employed at the time of arrest.

3. In Hawaii, being of Hawaiian, Samoan, or mixed ancestry usually means that one is disadvantaged economically and socially. The islands are ethnically stratified with Caucasians and Orientals (most notably Japanese and Chinese) in advantaged positions.

4. Less than a third (five) were high-school graduates, and six had dropped out of school during or after intermediate school (9th grade).

5. Three-quarters of the women in our sample had children.

6. One of the authors (Meda Chesney-Lind) has kept in routine communication with the male and female inmates of the facility as a consequence of having taught sociology courses in the facility. It was common knowledge that the "female side" had enforcement of rules that were largely ignored in the men's sections. Women were also kept out of school for being seen kissing men, but no similar punishment was instituted for the male involved in such incidents.

References

Adler, Freda. *Sisters in Crime*. New York: McGraw-Hill, 1975.

Altonn, Helen. "55 Women Prisoners 'Home' at Olomana," *Honolulu Star-Bulletin*, 10 November 1982, p. 1.

Burkhart, Kathryn. *Women in Prison*. New York: Doubleday, 1973.

Crites, Laura, editor. *The Female Offender*. Lexington, Mass.: Lexington Books, 1976.

Figueira-McDonough, Josephina, et al. *Females in Prison in Michigan, 1968–1978*. Ann Arbor: School of Social Work, 1981.

Foley, Charles. "Increase of Women in Crime and Violence, "*Honolulu Sunday Star-Bulletin and Advertiser*, 20 October 1974, p. 1.

Glick, Ruth, and Neto, V. *National Study of Women's Correctional Programs*. Washington, D.C.: U.S. Government Printing Office, 1977.

Hancock, Linda, editor. *Prisoner and Female: The Double Negative*. Victoria, Australia: Victorian Council of Social Service, 1982.

James, Jennifer. "Motivations for Entrance into Prostitution." In *The Female Offender,* edited by Laura Crites. Lexington, Mass.: Lexington Books, 1976.

Kassebaum, Gene. *Women's Prison*. Chicago: Aldine, 1967.

Klemesrud, Judy. "Women Terrorists, Sisters in Crime." *Honolulu Star-Bulletin,* 16 January 1978.

Los Angeles Times Service. "L.A. Police Chief Blames Libbers," *Honolulu Advertiser,* 7 August 1975.

Nelson, Lois DeFleur. "Women Make Gains in Shady World, Too." *Honolulu Sunday Star-Bulletin and Advertiser,* 23 October 1977, p. G-8.

Rainwater, Lee. *And the Poor Get Children*. Chicago: Aldine, 1960.

Rainwater, Lee. *Family Size: Marital Sexuality, Family Size and Contraception,* Chicago: Aldine, 1965.

Rans, Laurel. "Women's Arrest Statistics." *The Women Offender Report*. Washington, D.C.: Female Offender Resource Center, American Bar Association, 1975.

Roberts, S. "Crime Rate of Women Up Sharply Over Men's." *The New York Times,* 13 June 1971, pp. 1, 72.

Ruback, Barry. "The Sexually Integrated Prison." In *Coed Prison,* edited by John Ortiz. New York: Human Science Press, 1980.

Simon, Rita. *Women and Crime*. Lexington, MA: Lexington Books, 1975.

Steffensmeier, Darrell J. "Sex Differences in Patterns of Adult Crime, 1965–77: A Review and Assessment." *Social Forces* 58(June 1980):58.

Steffensmeier, Darrell J., and Steffensmeier, Renee Hoffman. "Trends in Female Delinquency." *Criminology* 18(1980):1.

Thomas, William I., and Thomas, Dorothy Swaine. *The Child in America*. New York: Knopf, 1928.

U.S. Department of Justice, Federal Bureau of Investigation. *Uniform Crime Reports for the United States, 1972*. Washington, D.C.: U.S. Government Printing Office, 1973.

U.S. Department of Justice, Federal Bureau of Investigation. *Uniform Crime Reports for the United States, 1975*. Washington, D.C.: U.S. Government Printing Office, 1976.

U.S. Department of Justice, Bureau of Justice Statistics. *Sourcebook of Criminal Justice Statistics, 1979*. Washington, D.C.: U.S. Government Printing Office, 1980.

U.S. Department of Justice, Bureau of Justice Statistics. *Sourcebook of Criminal Justice Statistics, 1981*. Washington, D.C.: Government Printing Office, 1982.

Weis, Joseph G. "Liberation and Crime: The Invention of the New Female Criminal." *Crime and Social Justice* 6(1976): 17.

Chapter 14

THE CHANGING NATURE OF INTERPERSONAL RELATIONSHIPS IN A WOMEN'S PRISON

KIMBERLY R. GREER

As of December 1999, approximately 1.4 million individuals were under the jurisdiction of state and federal correctional institutions (Bureau of Justice Statistics, 1999). Of that number, 87,199 were women inmates (www.ojp.usdoj.gov/bjs/correct/htm, July 2000). Currently, women represent about 6% of the total prison population (Bureau of Justice Statistics, 1999). However, the number of female inmates increased 5.5% during a 12-month period preceding June 1999 (www.ojp.usdon.gov/bjs/correct/htm, July 2000). Upward trends in the incarceration rates of women are attributed to a combination of the new mandatory sentencing guidelines and the country's policy regarding intensified sanctions for drug charges (Bloom, Chesney-Lind, & Owen, 1994; Nagel & Johnson, 1994). Women in prison are more likely than their male counterparts to be incarcerated for offenses involving drugs. Thirty-three percent of women in prisons in 1991 were confined for drug offenses, whereas only 21% of male inmates were imprisoned for drug charges (U.S. Department of Justice, 1991).

In 1996, women were convicted in state courts for 13,509 violent felonies, 69,536 property felonies, and 59,027 drug felonies (Bureau of Justice Statistics, 1999). Female and male inmates differ not only in terms of the crimes they commit but also in the backgrounds and personal histories they bring to the institution. Women are three times more likely to have suffered some type of abuse than male inmates; almost 60% of incarcerated women report prior physical and sexual abuse (U.S. Department of Justice, 1997). Female offenders are more likely than male prisoners to have had members of their families imprisoned (Pollock, 1998). In addition, women in prison more often had primary caretaking responsibilities for their children than male inmates. Approximately 7 in 10 women in prison have children under the age of 18 years (Bureau of Justice Statistics, 1999). Therefore, approximately 1.3 million minor children have mothers who are incarcerated in a correctional setting (Bureau of Justice Statistics, 1999). When men are incarcerated, approximately 90% report that their children are in the custody of the mother (U.S. Department of Justice, 1991). On the other hand, when women are confined in prison, only 25% indicate that their children are living with their fathers. Instead, children of incarcerated mothers

Source: Greer, K. (2000). The changing nature of interpersonal relationships in a women's prison. *The Prison Journal, 80*(4), 442–468.

are more likely to be placed in the custody of grandparents. Furthermore, about 6% of the female inmates enter correctional institutions pregnant (U.S. Department of Justice, 1991).

Although prior research has explored the effect of incarceration on prison inmates, most examinations have focused on male offenders. Female offenders now are receiving increased scholarly consideration, but a thorough understanding of the perceptions and experiences of these women is still lacking. Much of the information relevant to female offenders involves possible explanations for their criminality, new criminal trends, sentencing decisions, adjustments to imprisonment, or the differential treatment they receive while confined (e.g., Boritch, 1992; Chesney-Lind, 1991; Fogel, 1993; MacKenzie, Robinson, & Campbell, 1989; Maher & Daly, 1996; Morash, Haarr, & Rucker, 1994; Pollock, 1998; Steffensmeier, 1993).

In addition, earlier studies provide a better understanding of such topics as the history of female penitentiaries and reformatories, possible explanations for increased criminality on the part of women, and the inappropriateness of specific rehabilitative programs for female offenders (e.g., Chesney-Lind, 1991; Morash et al., 1994; Nagel & Johnson, 1994; Rafter, 1990). Although these examinations certainly address important issues related to women in prison and have raised the consciousness of the public with regard to the needs of female offenders, these explorations do not address the interpersonal relationships among female inmates that will be discussed in this study.

Previous research provides a wealth of information related to the description of typical female inmates and treatment issues related to their incarceration. Although there have been several excellent ethnographic examinations of prisons for women, there still seems to be a void in understanding the personal experiences of female inmates and how their perceptions shape their interactions within the prison subculture.

RESEARCH QUESTIONS

The questions this research seeks to answer are as follows:

1. How do women construct the social culture in this particular institution?

2. In what ways might perceptions influence social interactions in the prison?

3. What factors influence relationships in prison?

OUR PREVIOUS UNDERSTANDING OF RELATIONSHIPS IN WOMEN'S PRISONS

Women prisoners are still frequently referred to as forgotten offenders (Chesney-Lind, 1986; Feinman, 1983; Fletcher, Shaver, & Moon, 1993; Goetting & Howsen, 1983; Morash et al., 1994; Pollock-Byrne, 1990; Simon & Landis, 1991). The typical female inmate has never been married, is a woman of color, is 25 to 29 years of age, and is a single parent with one to three children being cared for by her mother or grandparent (Fletcher et al., 1993; Goetting & Howsen, 1983; Merlo & Pollock, 1995).

In addition, these offenders typically have been easily manipulated by their peers, runaways from home, sexually abused as children, high school dropouts, and arrested multiple times for property crimes (Chesney-Lind & Rodriguez, 1983; Fletcher et al., 1993; Goetting & Howsen, 1983; Owen, 1998). Approximately half of the women in prison are African American, even though only one in eight women in the United States is African American (Pollock, 1998).

Despite the recent advocacy for gender-responsive services for adolescent girls and adult women offenders, institutional policy regarding the treatment of female offenders has not followed a well-studied or consistent plan. A review of the literature suggests women offenders receive less appropriate programs and services than male inmates (Chesney-Lind & Rodriguez, 1983; Culbertson & Fortune, 1984; Genders & Player, 1991; Goetting & Howsen, 1983; McCarthy, 1980). Bell (1976) noted that confinement in prison may be a more difficult experience for women than men because they are more likely to find the social isolation insufferable. Similarly, women do not as readily become part of an inmate subculture and do not adhere as rigidly to an inmate code (Bell, 1976).

Sykes (1958) chronicled the "pains of imprisonment" (p. 63) suffered by male inmates and provided a description of the subcultural roles men adopted in prison to cope with such stressors and pressure. Research revealed that men in prison experience numerous deprivations, and to deal with these personal losses, they often develop and assume specific subcultural roles (Sykes, 1958).

Women inmates also experience pains of imprisonment (Faith, 1993; Pollock, 1998). Faith (1993) cites a lengthy list of personal agonies encountered by women in prison (pp. 151–153), a few of which include the stigma of incarceration, the claustrophobia of confinement, anxiety about one's children, physical and emotional problems that accompany withdrawal from alcohol and street drugs, insensitivities and abuses of power both by staff and other inmates, and cognitive dissonance from not knowing how or whether to express their feelings.

Whether women adopt prison subcultural roles is a question somewhat open for debate. Giallombardo (1966) and Ward and Kassebaum (1965) were some of the first researchers to study subcultures in prisons for women. However, until recently, there have been very few studies examining the subcultures in prisons for either men or women (for more current research involving female offenders, see Girshick, 1999; Owen, 1998; Pollock, 1998). Early research (Giallombardo, 1966; Larsen & Nelson, 1984; Leger, 1987; Propper, 1982; Ward & Kassebaum, 1965) identified the existence of "pseudofamilies" that were kinship networks established by women to fulfill lost familial roles such as daughter, wife, father, cousin, and grandmother. Homosexual relationships were also discussed by these prior studies and were found to form a significant aspect of the prison subculture for women. Intimate relationships brought with them social structure demonstrated by marriages and divorces as well as jealousy and power struggles (Pollock, 1998).

Although women do "form affectional ties that have some similarity to familial relationships," questions remain as to how pervasive and extensively defined these kinship networks might be (Pollock, 1998, p. 38). There has been some speculation that these types of prison relationships have diminished in recent years (Pollock, 1998). Those women who are alleged to be involved in the prison subculture are described as "being less inclined to introspection and continue to involve themselves in relationships, drugs, and other distractions to divert their attention away from looking at their own behavior" (Pollock, 1998, p. 39).

In her new book, Barbara Owen (1998) discusses relationships formed by women in prison. Her interviews and observations revealed that female offenders still participate in "play family" and form dyadic sexual relationships (p. 134). Obviously, relationships formed in prison, whether they are friendships among inmates, sexual encounters, or interactions with correctional officers, are quite complex (Owen). Girshick (1999) found mixed reactions; some women still engage in forming kinship networks, but other individuals strongly disapproved of such relationships. Therefore, respected scholars writing as late as 1998 report somewhat contradictory findings (see Owen, 1998; Pollock, 1998).

Although the initial goals of this research focused on obtaining a thorough understanding of how women in prison manage both their identity and emotions while in prison, I was informed by several women who participated in exploratory (pilot) interviews that the one thing my interview schedule omitted was questions related to the intimate relationships between women in prison. These respondents advised me that whether a woman was involved in a sexual relationship with another inmate or not, she would be influenced by the environment that such interactions create in the prison world. Therefore, I added several questions inquiring into the perceptions of respondents related to such relationships. As it turned out, the data generated by these additional questions ultimately resulted in interesting results. The observations of these respondents indicate that the nature of interpersonal relationships between women inmates may be changing.

METHOD

A total of 35 female inmates from a midwestern state correctional institution participated in an in-depth, semistructured interview. To ensure correct, as well as continuous and uninterrupted, data gathering, the research protocol required that all interviews be tape-recorded using a microcassette recorder (Patton, 1990). Taping the interviews was less obtrusive and provided more accurate data gathering than taking notes based on the responses of female offenders or relying on field notes compiled after the interaction (Lofland & Lofland, 1995; Maxwell, 1996; Patton, 1990). Verbatim transcription of the interview data occurred simultaneously with continuous data collection, thus allowing for constant and ongoing comparisons of themes being discussed during the interviews.

Data Analysis

Following transcription of the interviews, the data were then read and analyzed by performing content analysis (see Bogdan & Biklen, 1992;

Lofland & Lofland, 1995; Maxwell, 1996; Miles & Huberman, 1994; Patton, 1990; Strauss, 1987; Strauss & Corbin, 1990). As Patton (1990) noted, "Content analysis is the process of identifying, coding, and categorizing the primary patterns in the data" (p. 381). This analysis reflected a continuous process that began after the first interview had been conducted and was not completed until long after the last interview had been concluded (Maxwell, 1996). The average length of each transcribed interview was approximately 33 pages, resulting in a total of 1,149 pages of data to analyze.

Description of the Respondents

Thirty-five women participated in interviews during the fall of 1997. At the time this study was being conducted, a total of 238 women were incarcerated at this midwestern state correctional facility. In the interest of conserving space, Appendix A provides a comparison between the characteristics of the sample and prison population, and Appendix B portrays descriptive information for respondents related to age, race, type of crime committed, and length of time served.

The Changing Nature of Social Environments in a Women's Prison

During interviews, respondents painted a picture of the interpersonal environment inside the walls of the institution that can best be described as one based on manipulation and mistrust. The women discussed several different types of relationships: (a) friendships among female offenders, (b) sexual relationships among inmates, and (c) lack of kinship networks. All aspects of their interpersonal environment are tainted with perceptions of dishonesty, paranoia, and hostility. Most of the respondents preferred to view themselves as "loners"; however, as the interviews revealed, avoiding any type of interactions with other inmates or correctional officers is nearly impossible in a closed environment.

Friendships Among Female Offenders

One type of relationship discussed by female inmates involved friendships with other inmates. There were several different aspects of the friendships described by the women at this correctional

facility. However, the pervasive attitude held by the respondents regarding prison friendships was that any individual who engaged in this type of interaction did so at her own risk. Most of the women I talked with wanted to demonstrate a rather rigid stance against prison friendships. Twenty-one respondents voluntarily described themselves as "loners" at some point during our conversations. Conversely, there were those individuals who talked about forming intense friendships with other women incarcerated at this and other facilities. Phyllis made the following statement while discussing the differences between friends "on the street" and friendships formed in prison: "It is based purely on feelings in here. Out there, you know you run into each other, you are friends, you talk. In here it just, you get dependent upon each other emotionally."

Many respondents believed they had not formed close relationships with any of the other women who were also incarcerated at this institution. They indicated that this lack of friendship was the result of conscious decisions and behaviors on their part. Repeatedly, women referred to "associates" when asked whether they had formed any friendships in prison. One respondent after another appeared to use the distinction between *friend* and *associate* to distinguish the important difference they perceived between "real" friends and people with whom they simply interacted. For example, Kimberly had this response to a question about friendships:

> I have no friends; I have associates . . . even my MOOR [religion] sisters . . . or my Islam sister . . . even them are not my friends and that is sad to say . . . it is very conscious on my part because I am conscious of the other moves, snake moves. . . . I feel deprived because I know that somewhere you can have a good friend. But at the same time it is okay with me because I know where I am at. I know my surrounding. And I know that I can't really trust anybody here fully.

Explaining why she so strongly distrusts the other women who are incarcerated with her, Kimberly continued,

> You deal with a bunch of people every day with different attitudes and different thoughts. You don't know how they going to be today, you don't know how they going to be tomorrow. Today they're fine, tomorrow they're not. . . . You're really taking a chance on whether you can have a

relationship with someone here and I don't want to take that chance.

Preoccupation with the motives and intentions of other women prisoners caused respondents to forego establishing close relationships with others. Although they might express regret for this forced sense of isolation, they nonetheless thought abstaining was the wisest choice.

Besides the element of mistrust, an additional factor that influenced hesitation at forming friendships had to do with the transitory nature of relationships developed in prison. Respondents indicated that forming friendships takes time, and after an individual leaves the correctional institution, often interpersonal contact is severed. Joan explained why she had chosen not to develop friends in prison:

I don't have any friends in prison. . . . I been here for a while so I have met a lot of women. Some of the same ones come and go, three or four times . . . and they say, "I will write you as soon as I get out." But you never hear from them . . . so they want to be your friend while they are here. You are a friend inside, but probably never see them again and never hear from them again unless they come back through and you are here.

Because these relationships are perceived as being temporary, respondents may attempt to avoid close friendships in an effort to avoid negative feelings associated with those times in which one person or the other is released. Many respondents mentioned the sadness evoked when a friend was either released or transferred to another institution. Also acknowledging the temporary nature of these alliances during her interview, Brenda commented,

I don't think friendships inside could compare with friendships outside . . . if you want to be an acquaintance or whatever, you might as well do it now because once you walk out them gates . . . you have to get your life back on track again. Maybe you might call this person once or twice but eventually it just fades out.

Although the experiences these women share in prison could possibly serve to form tight bonds, the mutual problems that bring them to this facility can also contribute to complicated relationships. As Paula noted in the following remark, women prisoners often share similar backgrounds and perceptions, which logically might forge a strong bond. However, those common experiences can prove simultaneously problematic to healthy, sustained relationships in the real world. While discussing this precarious bond, Paula stated,

I am okay with them [friendships] to a certain extent because I have formed relationships before in prison with women and like I say, most of us that are in prison are some type of users, or addicted to something and when we depart and go back on the street, if I am doing good, they are not doing good. If they are doing good, I'm not doing good . . . it really hurts to see that when the other one is doing good and you aren't.

A few respondents indicated that although they were very selective about the individuals with whom they chose to develop friendships, they nonetheless did allow one or more people in their lives they felt were good, trustworthy companions. While describing her current friends, Molly stated,

The only friends I have now are the friends I have made since I have been down, which is a handful. They are not actually criminals by trade [laughs] . . . they just made some bad choices. Some of them are out now, got their lives pretty well together and we write and we keep in touch. And as far as a really good friendship when I get out, that, time will tell. You don't make a friend overnight and you don't make a friend on this side of the fence either and expect it to be the same out there.

An even smaller number of women discussed relationships in which the friends were portrayed as extremely significant persons in their lives. On the basis of the rather positive interpretation of her friendship, Molly proceeded to reflect on how forming a relationship in prison made her feel:

Everybody has to have someone that they can trust to talk to about certain things in here and well, you know as well as I do that you can't talk to one person about everything. You have one friend that you can talk to about this and you have another friend that you can talk to about that; you just can't talk to one friend about everything because they probably wouldn't understand. You have different friends who fulfill different roles for you definitely, and that makes me feel pretty good in here.

A few women disagreed with popular institutional wisdom regarding a need for remoteness in interpersonal relationships. Barbara was one respondent who seemed to have a fairly strong resistance toward the majority's perception about the negative repercussions that prison friendships can create for an individual. However, she seemed to find this attitude difficult to accept based more on pragmatism rather than some more complicated interpersonal need. While discussing the predominant attitude toward prison friendships, Barbara reported,

> A lot of people say you don't have friends in the penitentiary . . . you don't come here to make friends. Well, I didn't come here to make friends but it is inevitable. You are living with 300 and some women, it is not easy being alone. So you cannot tell me that you will go and spend your whole day not having one friend in this whole institution. I can't see it.

The primary theme that emerged from the conversations about friendships in prison focused on the women's distrust of close interpersonal relationships with other female offenders. Whether their misgivings were based on personal experiences or observations of other interactions is unknown. Comments made by respondents suggested inmates frequently mention the carelessness inherent in allowing other people to know too much about oneself.

Although these women appeared to perceive their peers as being manipulative and self-serving, the majority nonetheless reported having at least one person whom they considered a friend. Those who did not develop friendships had what they described as associates or individuals with whom they interacted with on a superficial basis. Based on the remarks of respondents, it seems doubtful that very many of these friendships survive transfer to other institutions or release from custody altogether. However, comments made by the women often appeared contradictory in that they discussed the apprehension they have about forming friendships, yet they appeared to establish some form of relationship with at least one other female inmate. Such discordant remarks may simply reflect the existence of conflict between attitudes and behaviors. For instance, although they perceived the social environment of the institution as manipulative and dysfunctional, most respondents still did not prevent themselves from developing friendships.

Skeptical attitudes held about prison friendships were also consistent with those sentiments expressed about the sexually intimate relationships between women inmates.

Sexual Relationships Among Inmates

All but three women either described their attitudes toward and participation (or lack thereof) in sexual relationships with other female prisoners. This was a subject that most women felt strongly about, either positively or negatively. However, 28% of respondents reported experiencing relatively neutral feelings toward participation in sexual relationships by other women. These respondents indicated that although they did not wish to become involved in intimate relationships with other women, they did not judge harshly those individuals who did choose to engage in such activity. Interestingly, although most respondents described sexual relationships among women as being extremely prevalent (one woman even guessed the participation level as being as high as 90% of all female inmates), only 10 of 35 women admitted ever having been involved in a sexual relationship in prison. At the time interviews were conducted, 5 respondents reported currently being sexually involved with another inmate. In addition, 2 women identified themselves as lesbians, and 1 woman reported she was bisexual. Of these 3 women, 2 indicated they chose not to participate in sexual relationships in prison because of the manipulative nature of the relationships.

Information provided by these respondents suggests that the nature of sexual relationships in prison may be slowly changing. Burkhart (1973), Giallombardo (1966), Hawkins (1995), and Ward and Kassebaum (1965) concluded that incarcerated women chose to form homosexual relationships with other inmates as one technique for lessening the pains of imprisonment. According to Giallombardo (1966), "The vast majority of inmates adjust to the prison world by establishing a homosexual alliance with a compatible partner as a marriage partner" (p. 136). Although it might have been true that the "vast majority" of inmates at Alderson prison participated in sexual relationships to ease the physical and psychological discomfort of imprisonment by selecting personally compatible partners, that may not presently be the primary motivation. According to responses made by women in this study, homosexual relationships are a fairly significant aspect (both for those who do participate and those who do not approve of such behavior) of the prison culture, but there were a number of respondents who indicated that they have chosen not to participate. Therefore, involvement in these relationships may not be as pervasive as previously discovered and when formed, may be initiated for different reasons. Findings from this study also suggest that these respondents believe sexual relationships are based primarily on manipulation rather than on any perception of compatibility or genuine attraction between partners.

The reactions toward homosexual relationships fell along a continuum, from attitudes that were very accepting to comments indicative of very intolerant perceptions. For instance, Elaine volunteered, "After my divorce . . . I was in a relationship with a female on the street and I have been in one since I was here and it was for 13½ months." Conversely, an example of intolerance was provided by Joan, who stated:

It makes me sick. In the bathrooms, you might be going to take a shower and you . . . open the curtain and you get shocked . . . if you happen to be in the room . . . like a ten-man room and it goes on at night time . . . so you kind of stop up your ears and face the wall . . . and pray that you don't hear it.

Of course, there were a number of women who reported feeling fairly neutral or nonjudgmental about these types of sexual involvement. For example, Paula commented, "I don't have anything against it. I mean if that's their choice then that is their choice. I am not here to judge them."

Throughout the course of this study, these women discussed a number of motivations they considered possible impetuses for participation in sexual relationships. On the basis of their comments, seven categories of motivations emerged from the data: economic motivation, sincere relationship, loneliness, curiosity, sexual identity, peer pressure, and other (sexual release and diversion from the boredom). See Appendix C for a display of respondents' perceptions related to possible explanations for this type of interpersonal relationship.

Economic Manipulation

One element of homosexual relationships that may have changed since the earlier examinations of women's prisons is related to the issue of clearly delineated sex roles. Earlier research (Burkhart, 1973; Giallombardo, 1966, p. 136; Ward & Kassebaum, 1965) strongly suggested that women who became involved in sexual relationships did so by adopting "overtly assumed" sex roles. Such roles have commonly been referred to as *femme* and *stud broad*. Previous scholarly works (Burkhart, 1973; Giallombardo, 1966; Hawkins, 1995; Ward & Kassebaum, 1965) note that inmates even conform their physical appearance to stereotypical assumptions about sex roles. Although I did not specifically ask women whether they played these types of roles, responses did not reflect that these were commonly assumed ways of behaving.

Most respondents did not seem to be trying to portray overly feminine or masculine qualities. During their reflections about the nature of homosexual relationships and the impact these associations have on institutional life, only a couple of women ever referred to other inmates according to clearly defined roles (i.e., "bulldagging"). Giallombardo (1966) thought by adopting either male or female sex roles and establishing sexual relationships, women in prison were reconstructing a "substitute universe" to adapt to the loss of the roles they performed in the real world (p. 103). However, these women did not seem to be involved in trying to recreate alternative social worlds. If anything, these women reported being focused on not forming any close, long-lasting relationships within the institution walls.

My respondents would adamantly disagree with the thought that "mate selection is based upon romantic love" (Giallombardo, 1966, p. 141), as it relates to sexual relationships in prison. Based on the comments obtained by these incarcerated women, the notion that women become involved with each other in prison on the basis of some concept of romance is erroneous in today's correctional institutions for women. Similarly, opinions furnished by respondents would not support the assertion made by Ward and Kassebaum (1965) when they reported, "The process of turning out thus seems to represent socialization of the new inmates into practices which provide support, guidance, and emotional satisfaction during a period when these are lacking" (p. 78).

Although respondents observed that there are numerous motivations for beginning and maintaining a sexual relationship, 25 women (71%) speculated that the primary reason involved what they described as economic manipulation. Repeatedly, female inmates described the element of dishonesty as being pervasive in all prison relationships, but most especially those that involved sexual intimacy. Many women could think of several different reasons why women would pursue or participate in these intimate activities, but foremost in their minds was the issue of unequal access to money and material goods.

Women consistently referred to "canteen whores" or "commissary whores" when describing those inmates who participated in sexual relationships simply to improve their economic standing. All inmates are required to work if they are not in school, but this does not necessarily result in an equal distribution of income. Different job assignments receive varying amounts of financial compensation. The least amount of money an inmate could receive each month was $7.50, and the most was approximately $20.00. This money is credited to an inmate account and can be used by the women to purchase items from the commissary (canteen) or materials can be ordered from approved catalogs. In addition, some inmates have family and friends who send money to their inmate accounts; this money can also be spent by the inmate at the commissary, on catalog orders, or electronic possessions such as televisions and radios that can only be purchased from the state.

As in free society, the inequalities in economic status contributed to power differentials. Women prisoners who have more money are perceived as being more influential in the correctional facility than those individuals who have less monetary support. For example, while discussing possible positive and negative results of sexual relationships between inmates, Joan described how prisoners look for outward signs of financial status before selecting a possible partner. She stated,

> It is canteen for women who don't have money. . . . They always find someone that has got money. . . . Everybody knows when someone has money, and they will sit and watch who has the big bags that comes from the store and who goes to the store every week.

Voicing her agreement that the inequality in terms of what inmates have to spend on the discretionary items within the correctional institution influences relationships, Sarafina remarked, "Some people . . . go to the store and don't have a girlfriend. They try to use people . . . you don't even know this person but you are doing that because you know they got money on the books."

Inmates who receive financial support from significant others may find themselves having more discretion as to whether they become involved in sexual relationships with other women. Sarafina credited her family's economic support with allowing her to not become sexually involved when she commented,

> I am not rich; I am not wealthy, but I'm well looked out [for]. Certain people do certain things around here, that get their little hustle along, have their little cigarettes or buy soap, whatever, because they don't have people looking out for them, and that is hard.

Echoing the consistent concern that these relationships are inherently dishonest and manipulative, Barbara, who had been involved sexually with another inmate, described the majority of women's motivations as being related to this inherent economic inequality when she said,

> A lot of people do it for money. Here it is a money thing. It is not about people's feelings or it is all [a] game really and so, people when you are broke and only get $7.50 a month and somebody may get $250.00 a week or month . . . it begins to be attractive to you.

The fact that money plays a significant role in the perpetuation of at least the more temporary and manipulative sexual relationships did not seem to come as a surprise to any of the women. Although none of these respondents admitted ever being involved in a sexual relationship because of money, they certainly had no compunction about pointing their fingers at their peers. Women who participated in the research indicated that this focus on the exchange of material goods is not a well-kept secret, yet this knowledge evidently does not deter the deceptive behavior. Nor does it prohibit individuals from being taken advantage of during their involvement with others.

Respondents indicated that often women take advantage of each other on more than one occasion. They described instances where one woman will indicate a desire to be with someone else sexually only around the time when canteen orders can be placed. After she has provided the material items, the woman with the money may not see or hear from her friend until the next time she can place an order at the canteen.

Loneliness and Companionship

The economic factor may explain why some women engage in sexual relationships with other inmates, but it surely cannot explain all the possible reasons for such relationships. Eighteen respondents (51%) perceived that loneliness and the need for companionship provided an incentive for some women to participate in sexual activities. For one respondent, it was important that she make it clear that she did not need anyone and preferred not to be involved with anyone; however, she did recognize that some women initiate or succumb to relationships because they need the companionship of others to survive incarceration. Sarafina, who advised me that her prior employment involved stripping and running an escort service, concluded,

> I'm not looking for a relationship. Some people they do look for relationships and they want, they need someone to spend time with. I'm not saying that I have never been with a woman because when I was, it was business and not pleasure. They get into relationships because they have people that have more time and they need to do their time with somebody.

Indicating that individuals may engage in sexual relationships because of a profound need for belonging, Kimberly noted that the desire these women are acting on may have developed prior to their imprisonment. While discussing why women become sexually involved with other female inmates, Kimberly reflected, "Love, they didn't have that when they was coming up [growing up] and they try to find it here. It be false love, but to them it's basically all they've ever had, so they hold on to it."

Somewhat related to the issue of loneliness is the idea, consistent with previous research (Burkhart, 1973; Giallombardo, 1966; Girshick, 1999; Ward & Kassebaum, 1965), that sexual relationships assist women in serving their prison time with the least amount of psychological discomfort. Phyllis stated,

> Women [who] have never done it out on the streets and will never do it again, they usually do it in here and it is a lonely thing and it is also that little dance you do when you fall in love with

somebody . . . that good feeling that you get over somebody pursuing or whatever. They get that charge and they miss that.

Thus, the excitement one may experience when initiating a new love affair can serve to distract one's attention away from the harsh realities of the correctional facility and provide a rationale for engaging in a homosexual relationship. Pressure to conform exists inside a prison as well. Several respondents listed curiosity and the desire to "fit in" as other possible explanations for women's sexual involvement with other inmates. The idea of wanting to fit in suggests a normative aspect to sexual relationships in this prison and many women did suggest that these types of interactions are prevalent.

Sincere Couples Versus Dibbling and Dabbling

For most of these respondents, the nature of prison relationships revolves around deceit, deception, distrust, and manipulation. These qualities were also evident in their thoughts on sexual relationships in the correctional facility. However, there were relationships, including their own, that they could describe more positively.

Women who were perceived as being involved in sincere, long-lasting, committed relationships were accorded a special status by respondents. In the eyes of these women, there was a tremendous difference between those individuals who "play games" with each other for canteen privileges and female inmates who nurture stable, monogamous, and caring relationships with each other. Only 9 of the 35 women (26%) interviewed mentioned genuine affection as being a possible explanation for sexual relationships. While discussing these rare but more respected relationships, Brenda reflected, "There is some that they are in a relationship because they care . . . probably five or six couples on this grounds that have been in a relationship for some years." Several respondents noted specifically that lesbians (those who identified themselves as such before they were imprisoned) sometimes formed the most stable relationships in prison or chose not to participate whatsoever for the duration of their imprisonment. Ashley, who identified herself as bisexual, believed there was a noticeable difference in the behaviors of women who had homosexual experience prior to incarceration and those individuals whose first encounters occur in prison. She commented,

With a lot of them, they come in . . . and they start participating and . . . they don't really know what they are doing anyway so they really get used because they go from individual to individual to individual. But the ones that have been doing it for awhile or had did it before they came to the penitentiary, you can tell it because they might be with one woman for the next six years. You can tell the difference.

While contemplating the nature of relationships among women, Jade reflected on the difference between temporary and long-lasting interactions. After informing me that she was not a lesbian or homophobic, Jade reported,

> There are some women here who have been together almost 10 years. To me, they are real and they are going to do 10 or longer together. They have got 30, they have got life, and if I was in that position, I would probably do the same thing and I would find a companion.

Inmates who are able to maintain caring, sincere interactions are accorded a certain degree of respect. Paula, who indicates she has nothing against individuals who participate in sexual relationships, reported that she can see both positive and negative aspects to their involvement:

> I see both sides . . . because I see the ones that are real about it, that don't play, it is not just a prison game thing. It is a person that is truly a lesbian that truly has a real lover . . . and there is no dibbling and dabbling, you know it is just them two. Now the negative [side], them are the ones that move from one to the other, playing all kind of games in prison.

One of the unfortunate outcomes of intimate relationships mentioned by several women reflected the importation of domestic violence into the correctional facility. Although none of them reported having experienced violence at the hands of intimate others in prison, several women commented on having seen abuse within the prison walls. Some respondents explained that attempts to control others serve as an incentive not to become involved in intimate prison relationships. While describing the downfalls of sexual relationships that often revolve around jealousy and mistrust, Jade asserted,

> They fight . . . and it is jealous like . . . hollering at her, "you don't do this, you don't talk to her, you don't give her nothing, you don't take nothing, you do what I say, I am here for you." I don't think so. You know, I mean personally, I ate enough shit off men [not] to have a woman check [control] me. It is not going to happen.

Throughout the course of these interviews, none of the respondents seemed surprised or offended by the inclusion of questions related to sexual behavior. Obviously, some women were more eager to explore and explain the nature of these relationships than were others. On the basis of their comments, I gathered that intimate personal relationships still are a significant aspect of the interpersonal prison environment. However, rather than being generally neutral or positive strategies to address the harshness of confinement, these relationships are perceived as being interpersonally risky behavior. The unease with which women view these relationships may help explain why there appeared to be a lack of what has previously been described as pseudofamilies in women's prisons.

Lack of Kinship Networks

Observations made by the respondents in this study suggested that changes in the experiences of female inmates have obviously occurred during the past 34 years (since Giallombardo's early research). For instance, although previous research, as well as these respondents, noted that one of the goals of those imprisoned is to do "easy time" rather than focusing on the experiences of friends and family members in the real world, they differ in how that time may be completed with the least amount of psychological grief possible. According to Giallombardo (1966),

> The inmates' psychological transition of self from civil society to the prison world may be considered complete when the individual reacts neutrally to events in the outside world, even when these events concern crucial matters pertaining to close family members. (p. 135)

There may exist a misconception that very few inmates actually maintain contact with their friends and family members once incarcerated. However, respondents indicated through their interview comments that they do perpetuate fairly consistent interaction with family members. Very few women reported consistent visitation with children and family for various reasons. However, through mail and telephone contact, they do remain current on what is taking place with significant others.

Giallombardo (1966) found that among the women at Alderson Federal Women's Prison, same-sex relationships served to form the foundation of the pseudofamily networks. The kinship ties that revolve around the couple help to create barriers around individuals who are not available for the sexual relationships and provide stability and emotional support to these individuals. Giallombardo speculated that without kinship ties, the prison environment could become tremendously chaotic. In addition to determining which individuals are off-limits as romantic interests, family networks can also be advantageous to groups of women by providing a sense of protection, companionship, and mutual aid (Giallombardo, 1966; Hawkins, 1995).

Contrary to much of the early research examining the experiences of women in correctional institutions, these respondents described an individualistic approach to doing time rather than a kinship structure that developed in other facilities. Whereas Burkhart (1973), Giallombardo (1966), Hawkins (1995), Owen (1998), and Ward and Kassebaum (1965) discussed the existence of family kinship networks and same-sex relationships, the findings from this research suggest some subtle changes in the manner in which women in prison go about doing their time.

In her classic study of a women's prison, Giallombardo (1966) explained that women experience similar "pains of imprisonment" (Sykes, 1958, p. 63) as encountered by male prisoners. However, she concluded that women create a "separate universe" (Giallombardo, 1966, p. 103) from which they can maintain an identity or sense of self that is relevant to the outside world. This perception led Giallombardo to recognize that women in prison established relationships with other prisoners that were consistent with, as well as familiar to, relationships they had with significant others outside of prison. In essence, female inmates recreate familial and sexual relationships based on the same cultural expectations of women in the larger society.

Kinship networks might also help provide a larger group of individuals from whom the inmate could receive emotional support and socialization into the role of a prison inmate (Giallombardo, 1966). In explaining the existence of pseudofamily relationships, Giallombardo (1966) stated, "The family group in the female prison is singularly suited to meet the internalized cultural expectations of the female role. It serves the social, psychological, and physiological needs of the female inmates" (p. 185). Giallombardo elaborated that these needs may arise from several different sources, such as the prison environment itself (deprivation model), women's personalities, and a sense of dependence based on the cultural expectations of women. In other words, women experience a need to form relatively close familial relationships, even in a correctional facility, because of previous socialization experiences and gender expectations.

The 35 women interviewed for this research did not relate examples of similar types of prison relationships. In a few occasions, respondents discussed very loosely established familial acknowledgments, but none of these relationships approximated the rather structured and stable kinship networks described by Burkhart (1973) and Giallombardo (1966). Most women either did not refer to these types of relationships based on their experiences and observations or, when asked, responded directly that those kinds of interpersonal interactions really did not occur at this institution. However, a few women discussed knowing women in the prison whom they referred to by some term of endearment such as "Mom," "Grandma," "Sister," or "Cousin." For example, Destiny commented,

> I do that myself [referring to playing family roles]. The trouble is, it's kinda funny because there is this one Black lady, she is like in her 50s and I call her mom. And she, I go "mom" and she comes up to me and gives me a hug and all that stuff. I mean, everybody looked at me, like that ain't your mom is it? I said, "sure." And I got them to believing it and started laughing, and I said, "No, she is just, she is like a mother role in my life here."

This respondent was one of the youngest women interviewed, and she looked even younger than her chronological age. Therefore, the fact that she would want to be mothered was not surprising. During her interactions with correctional officers, she also conducted herself in a rather childlike manner. While she was describing the nature of what she perceives to be a family-like relationship, her remarks indicated that other women found her calling another woman "Mom" confusing. If the establishment of kinship networks were widespread and pervasive within the institution, others would not be surprised at the use of such titles. Respondents suggested that structured or formal family roles were not performed in this prison even though some older women might be perceived as behaving in a motherly fashion.

Hence, even kinship networks suffer from the perception that no one in the institution can be trusted. Again, the overwhelming theme of manipulation and mistrust seemed to permeate all interpersonal interactions inside the walls of this facility. One of the more open and trusting women to participate in this study acknowledged the tug of family bonds. Ashley commented,

> Like I got a roommate and nearly everybody calls her Mom because she is elderly. We got a older White lady and everybody calls her Grandmother. Me and my roommate calls each others sisters all the time. I treat her like my baby sister.

Rather than being highly structured and important responses to the pains of imprisonment, family roles do not appear to play a significant part in the day-to-day lives of respondents. Even for those women who admit referring to others as, or considering someone, a family member, the expressions they make toward each other are more representative of respectful terms of endearment rather than acknowledgment of more formal kinship roles. Respondents do not perceive clearly defined family relationships as part of their interpersonal environment.

DISCUSSION

Themes that emerged during analysis of these data were similar to findings reported previously in literature related to contemporary men's prisons (Irwin, 1980; Irwin & Austin, 1997; Johnson, 1996). Because of changes in the diversity of persons being committed to correctional institutions, as well as the move away from rehabilitation toward a more custodial function for prisons, there no longer exists a singular inmate code or subculture (Irwin, 1980; Irwin & Austin, 1997; Johnson, 1996). Instead, male prisons have become much more volatile and less cohesive institutions than those represented during the 1950s (Irwin, 1980; Irwin & Austin, 1997). Responses provided by these women suggest that, similarly, changes in female prison subcultures may also be occurring. Rather than forming pseudofamilies and relatively caring dyadic relationships, these women demonstrate through their comments a fear of forming close relationships with other female prisoners. "Doing time" was perceived as being a solitary process, especially if one wanted to avoid as many problems as possible. Therefore, respondents really were hesitant about developing friendships with other prisoners. The prison subculture encountered by these women certainly appears different from the one experienced by women incarcerated in the 1960s, 1970s, and 1980s.

In some ways, the reactions of respondents were comparable with the experiences of their male counterparts. Like these women, Irwin (1980) noted that withdrawal also was one technique employed by some male inmates wishing to avoid conflicts in their unstable prison environments. Male prisoners increasingly choose to avoid the more communal areas of the correctional institution and limit their personal interactions to a few trusted friends in an effort to survive their confinement (Irwin, 1980).

Where the interactions among this group of women differ from findings in male prisons was in the area of racial and ethnic tensions, as well as reported gang activity (see also Owen, 1998). Again, literature involving contemporary prisons for men describe the interactions between racially and ethnically diverse groups as being extremely violent and contributing to the demise of a singular, cohesive inmate subculture (Hassine, 1996; Irwin, 1980; Irwin & Austin, 1997; Johnson, 1996). Gang activity is intimately tied to the various racial and ethnic identities represented in men's prisons and also is a significant factor influencing the perception among male inmates that the prison subculture is stratified along lines of power and violence (Irwin, 1980; Irwin & Austin, 1997; Johnson, 1996).

Although a few respondents commented they believed a portion of the correctional officers and other female inmates were prejudiced, overwhelmingly racial differences were not discussed by the women. Only during conversations about whether the two racial groups express their feelings differently did respondents report variations between the two groups of women. Respondents described friendships and sexual relationships involving women of different races. Where pseudofamilies have been found to exist, often "prison families cross racial lines" (Alarid, 1997). Similarly, women portrayed this institution as being relatively free of any gang activity. A few respondents believed there were a small number of women in the prison who might qualify as "gang wannabes," but there was not any recognized gang membership. Only three respondents acknowledged having been members of a gang on the street.

These findings suggest that in some ways the experiences of women in prison coincide with those of their male counterparts. Specifically, the diversified and stratified contemporary prison subcultures present frightening, unstable living environments for both groups of offenders. However, racial conflicts and gang activity have affected women's prisons less than correctional institutions for men.

In summary, comments made by respondents suggest changes in the interpersonal environment of women's prisons. Because this study involves a small sample derived from a single correctional institution, the findings may not be generalizable to other prisons for women. However, based on the results of this examination, future research that further examines the prison relationships of women (and the factors that influence social interaction) might prove fruitful. The overall interpersonal environment was depicted by respondents as being one that is manipulative and distrustful. Intimate sexual relationships are formed primarily on the basis of game playing and economic manipulation. Strong kinship networks previously observed in women's prisons were essentially nonexistent in this facility.

There may be several possible explanations for why the experiences of these respondents differed from those reported by earlier researchers (Burkhart, 1973; Giallombardo, 1966; Ward & Kassebaum, 1965). One factor that may account for the lack of cohesiveness among inmates is the change in the physical environment of women's prisons. Early studies were conducted in the 1960s and 1970s when many women's facilities were built around the cottage system, wherein women were assigned to homelike dwellings. Giallombardo (1966) noted that cottages were remnants of the reform movement during which time the emphasis was placed on rehabilitating fallen

women. Reformers believed these women might be more easily rehabilitated if they were incarcerated in facilities that were reminiscent of home. Perhaps living in a cottage setting facilitated the formation of dyadic homosexual relationships based on more positive motives than economic manipulation.

Likewise, a homelike environment might be more conducive to the formation of family networks than cells or dormitory settings. Individual living rooms, kitchens, and dining rooms would be more conducive to facilitating a family-like environment than more institutional contexts. The prison where this research was conducted used a series of dormitories to house the inmates, with one centralized kitchen and dining room used by all the women. Some of these dormitory rooms held up to 10 women, and the smallest rooms had at least 4 women per room. Perhaps this kind of living arrangement is not conducive for the development of intimate relationships or kinship networks.

Variation in prison sentences might influence the nature of prison relationships. I am not aware of the average length of incarceration of the Alderson Prison women, but perhaps differing periods of time in prison can have an impact on the development of intimate or kinship relationships. Giallombardo (1966) commented that short sentences may contribute to individuals choosing not to participate in homosexual relationships (p. 128). However, these respondents had served an average of 7.08 months at this particular facility and had been in custody for an average of 28.5 months at the time interviews were conducted.

Another plausible explanation for the change is related to the passage of time itself. Early research suggested that the reason for the formation of sexual and kinship relationships was a cultural expectation regarding women. Giallombardo (1966) speculated that by forming these kinds of relationships in prison, female inmates were simply responding to these cultural expectations about gender roles. Perhaps female inmates incarcerated in the 1990s are responding to different cultural expectations for women in general. Perhaps female inmates bring with them alternative perceptions about acceptable roles for women. On the basis of the comments of respondents, one might question whether these individuals additionally are not as strongly tied to their various social roles as might be expected.

These respondents did not seem to be strongly invested in any particular social roles, including those related to gender. Although Owen (1998) is correct in suggesting that scholars must remember the pressures associated with a patriarchal society and the gendered nature of all social roles, these particular women indicated they were much more invested in their personal identities (individuality) rather than social identities (those roles that place them socially). Perhaps this focus made it difficult to create supportive interpersonal relationships and contributed to the prevalent feelings of social withdrawal.

The contradictory nature of relationships experienced in various women's prisons around the country may reflect the complexity of such interpersonal interactions, the social histories that accompany the women, and the changing cultural expectations influencing the subculture of women's prisons. Perhaps changes in the larger society are imported within the walls of the institution and are reflected in the changes described in intimate relationships. Importation of societal attitudes and changes in cultural expectations may provide insights into the altered interpersonal environment of this women's correctional institution (see also Girshick, 1999).

Perhaps the most promising explanations involve the changing nature of prisons in general. As noted previously, the social environment described by the women in this prison is similar in nature to that portrayed in literature pertaining to male correctional institutions. Contemporary prisons are more open systems rather than the stereotypical "total" institution considered representative of all correctional facilities in the past. Inmates are no longer completely closed off from the rest of society. Male and female prisoners can maintain contact with significant others and continue to be influenced by the larger culture through television, radio, movies, correspondence, literature, and visits with family members.

Moreover, the inmate culture has become more complex and complicated due to the importation of various lifestyles and backgrounds by a divergent inmate population. The influences male and female prisoners bring with them to the correctional institution are now considered to be more significant than the indigenous deprivations associated with prisons. Such social influences have contributed to the demise of a singular prison subculture. Both male and female inmates may come to perceive withdrawal and social isolation as the best techniques for adjusting to prison life. Obviously, such a modification in the subculture of women's prisons would not necessarily be viewed as a positive change. Although feminist criminologists have been advocating equality in services for women offenders, creating male-based programs and environments has not been the goal. Supporters of gender-responsive services for adolescent girls and adult women offenders recognize the neccessity of designing institutional programs and environments that address the unique gender and cultural needs of the women confined therein.

Appendix A	Comparison Between Sample and Population Based on Age, Sentence, Length of Time Served, and Race	
Characteristic	*Sample*	*Prison Population*
Age	33.05 years	33.35 years
Sentence	6.68 years	5.86 years
Time served	28.5 months	19.76 months
Time served here	7.08 months	4.98 months
Race	Caucasian = 54%	Caucasian = 45%
	African American = 43%	African American = 55%
	Other = 3%	Other = 0.0%

| Appendix B | Description of Respondents—Age, Race, Type of Crime, Length of Time Served (*N* = 35) | |

Characteristic	Number	Percentage
Age		
25 years or less	7	20
26–39 years	21	60
40 years and older	7	20
Total	35	100
Race		
Caucasian	19	54.29
African American	15	42.86
Other	1	2.86
Total	35	100.01
Type of crime[a]		
Violent	13	32.50
Property	16	40.00
Substance abuse	11	27.50
Total	40	100
Length of time served		
Less than 1 year	19	54.29
1 to 5 years	13	37.14
5 or more years	3	8.57
Total	35	100

a. Four women committed crimes that involved more than one criminal category. Therefore, the total number will exceed 35 and the total percentage will exceed 100 for this characteristic.

| Appendix C | Possible Motives for Involvement in Sexual Relationships | |

Motivation	Number	Percentage
Economic manipulation	25	71.43
Sincere relationship	9	25.71
Loneliness/companionship	18	51.43
Curiosity	3	8.57
Sexual identity	6	17.14
Peer pressure	3	8.57
Other[a]	4	11.43

a. Other included motivations related to sexual release and diversion from boredom. Respondents provided their thoughts on possible motivations for their own relationships as well as the involvement of other women. Many women offered more than one explanation; therefore, totals for number of responses and percentages will exceed 35 and 100, respectively.

References

Alarid, L. F. (1997). Female inmate subcultures. In J. W. Marquart & J. R. Sorensen (Eds.), *Correctional contexts: Contemporary and classical readings* (pp. 134–139). Los Angeles: Roxbury.

Bell, R. R. (1976). *Social deviance*. Homewood, IL: Dorsey.

Bloom, B., Chesney-Lind, M., & Owen, B. (1994). *Women in California prisons: Hidden victims of the war on drugs*. San Francisco: Center on Juvenile and Criminal Justice.

Bogdan, R. C., & Biklen, S. K. (1992). *Qualitative research for education* (2nd ed.). Boston: Allyn & Bacon.

Boritch, H. (1992). Gender and criminal court outcomes: An historic analysis. *Criminology, 30,* 293–321.

Bureau of Justice Statistics. (1999). *Prison statistics.* Retrieved July 27, 2000, from the World Wide Web: http://www.ojp.usdoj.gov/bjs/prisons.htm

Burkhart, K. W. (1973). *Women in prison.* New York: Popular Library.

Chesney-Lind, M. (1986). Women and crime: The female offender. *Signs, 12,* 78–96.

Chesney-Lind, M. (1991). Patriarchy, prisons, and jails: A critical look at trends in women's incarceration. *The Prison Journal, 71,* 51–67.

Chesney-Lind, M., & Rodriguez, N. (1983). Women under lock and key: A view from the inside. *The Prison Journal, 62,* 47–65.

Culbertson, R. G., & Fortune, E. P. (1984). Women in crime and prison. In R. G. Culbertson (Ed.), *Order under law* (2nd ed., pp. 240–254). Prospect Heights, IL: Waveland.

Faith, K. (1993). *Unruly women: The politics of confinement and resistance.* Vancouver: Press Gang.

Feinman, C. (1983). An historical overview of the treatment of incarcerated women: Myths and realities of rehabilitation. *The Prison Journal, 62,* 12–24.

Fletcher, B. R., Shaver, L. D., & Moon, D.G. (1993). *Women prisoners: A forgotten population.* Westport, CT: Praeger.

Fogel, C. I. (1993). Hard time: The stressful nature of incarceration for women. *Issues in Mental Health Nursing, 14,* 367–377.

Genders, E., & Player, E. (1991). Women lifers: Assessing the experience. *The Prison Journal, 70,* 46–57.

Giallombardo, R. (1966). *Society of women: A study of a women's prison.* New York: John Wiley.

Girshick, L. B. (1999). *No safe haven: Stories of women in prison.* Boston: Northeastern University Press.

Goetting, A., & Howsen, R. M. (1983). Women in prison: A profile. *The Prison Journal, 62,* 27–45.

Hassine, V. (1996). *Life without parole: Living in prison today.* Los Angeles: Roxbury.

Hawkins, R. (1995). Inmate adjustments in women's prisons. In K. C. Haas & G. P. Alpert (Eds.), *The dilemmas of corrections: Contemporary readings* (3rd ed., pp. 103–122). Prospect Heights, IL: Waveland.

Irwin, J. (1980). *Prisons in turmoil.* Boston: Little, Brown.

Irwin, J., & Austin, J. (1997). *It's about time: America's imprisonment binge* (2nd ed.). Belmont, CA: Wadsworth.

Johnson, R. (1996). *Hard time: Understanding and reforming the prison* (2nd ed.). Belmont, CA: Wadsworth.

Larsen, J., & Nelson, J. (1984). Women, friendship, and adaptation to prison. *Journal of Criminal Justice, 12,* 601–615.

Leger, R. (1987). Lesbianism among women prisoners: Participants and nonparticipants. *Criminal Justice and Behavior, 14,* 463–479.

Lofland, J., & Lofland, L. H. (1995). *Analyzing social settings: A guide to qualitative observation and analysis* (3rd ed.). Belmont, CA: Wadsworth.

MacKenzie, D. L., Robinson, J. W., & Campbell, C. S. (1989). Long-term incarceration of female offenders: Prison adjustment and coping. *Criminal Justice and Behavior, 16,* 223–238.

Maher, L., & Daly, K. (1996). Women in the street-level drug economy: Continuity or change? *Criminology, 34,* 465–491.

Maxwell, J. A. (1996). *Qualitative research design: An interactive approach.* Thousand Oaks, CA: Sage.

McCarthy, B. R. (1980). Inmate mothers: The problems of separation and reintegration. *Journal of Offender Counseling, Services, and Rehabilitation, 4,* 199–212.

Merlo, A. V., & Pollock, J. M., (1995). *Women, law, and social control.* Needham Heights, MA: Allyn & Bacon.

Miles, M. B., & Huberman, A. M. (1994). *Qualitative data analysis: An expanded sourcebook* (2nd ed.). Thousand Oaks, CA: Sage.

Morash, M., Haarr, R. N., & Rucker, L. (1994). A comparison of programming for women and men in U.S. prisons in the 1980s. *Crime & Delinquency, 40,* 197–221.

Nagel, I. H., & Johnson, B. L. (1994). The role of gender in a structured sentencing system: Equal treatment, policy choices, and the sentencing of female offenders under the United States sentencing guidelines. *Journal of Criminal Law and Criminology, 85,* 181–221.

Owen, B. (1998). *In the mix: Struggle and survival in a women's prison.* Albany: State University of New York Press.

Patton, M. Q. (1990). *Qualitative evaluation and research methods* (2nd ed.). Newbury Park, CA: Sage.

Pollock, J. M. (1998). *Counseling women in prison.* Thousand Oaks, CA: Sage.

Pollock-Byrne, J. (1990). *Women, prison, and crime.* Pacific Grove, CA: Brooks / Cole.

Propper, A. (1982). Make-believe families and homosexuality among imprisoned girls. *Criminology, 20,* 127–139.

Rafter, N. H. (1990). *Partial justice* (2nd ed.). New Brunswick, NJ: Transaction Publishers.

Simon, R. J., & Landis, J. (1991). *The crimes women commit, the punishments they receive.* Lexington, MA: Lexington Books.

Steffensmeier, D. (1993). National trends in female arrests, 1960–1990: Assessment and recommendation for research. *Journal of Quantitative Criminology, 9,* 411–439.

Strauss, A. (1987). *Qualitative analysis for social scientists.* New York: Cambridge University Press.

Strauss, A., & Corbin, J. (1990). *Basics of qualitative research: Grounded theory procedures and techniques.* Newbury Park, CA: Sage.

Sykes, G. M. (1958). *The society of captives: A study of a maximum security prison.* Princeton, NJ: Princeton University Press.

U.S. Department of Justice. (1991). *Women in prison: Survey of state prison inmates.* Washington, DC: Government Printing Office.

U.S. Department of Justice. (1997). *News release.* Washington, DC: Author (http://www.ojp.usdoj.gov).

Ward, D. A., & Kassebaum, G. G. (1965). *Women's prison: Sex and social structure.* Chicago: Aldine.

Chapter 15

"SETTING THE RECORD STRAIGHT"

Girls, Sexuality, and the Juvenile Correctional System

LISA PASKO

In here, having a "relationship" with another girl? And it's sexual? It's a crime. Period.

—Therapist, residential facility

Before the mid-1970s, most formal discussions of juvenile corrections did not include an explicit concentration on girls. Today, however, female juvenile offenders are no longer invisible and have become one of the fastest-growing segments of the juvenile justice system. For example, in 1975 girls represented 15% of juvenile arrests in the United States; 30 years later, they accounted for nearly one-third (Federal Bureau of Investigation, 2008). Juvenile court data suggest a similar trend: girls now comprise nearly one-third of all referred delinquency cases, and their adjudications have increased by 300% over the past three decades (Office of Juvenile Justice and Delinquency Prevention, 2006).

Girls also have become an increasing proportion of juveniles in custody. By the turn of the century, girls' detentions rose by nearly 100%, and their commitments to secure facilities increased by 88% (Sickmund, 2004). In terms of private institutionalization, girl offenders, particularly chronic status offenders (runaway, truancy, and incorrigibility charges), were also more likely to be admitted to residential placements, training schools, or group homes, in comparison to their male counterparts who were more likely to receive day treatment (Chesney-Lind and Sheldon, 2004: 211). As a result, girls now make up 12% to 20% of all youth commitments. Due to the limited number of beds available in long-term state facilities,

Source: Pasko, L. (2010). "Setting the record straight": Girls, sexuality, and the juvenile correctional system. *Social Justice, 37*(1), 7–26.

Author's Note: This chapter uses only LBQ, since the focus is solely on girls; no transgender or intersexed girls were at the facilities and no interviewees made comments about such individuals.

girls often wait nearly five months in detention for a residential placement to open.

These findings have led scholars to examine current custodial conditions for girls, the institutional expectations that can exacerbate their future pathways back into the juvenile justice system, and the rationale behind correctional discretion and the decisions made for them (e.g., Bloom et al., 2002; Chesney-Lind and Sheldon, 2004; Mallicoat, 2007; Schaffner, 2006). Despite the growing academic interest in female juvenile offenders, studies on girls, sex, and juvenile corrections remain neglected and fairly scarce in the field of criminal or social justice. In particular, the literature fails to show how the institution of youth corrections deals with lesbian, bisexual, and questioning (LBQ) youth and how such management techniques consequently affect girl offenders' identities and relationships.[1] This chapter addresses this paucity and uses feminist critical criminology to interrogate correctional professionals' perceptions of LBQ issues. Overall, it shows how staff construct and penalize girls for their within-institution sexual identity and activity.

HISTORY OF GIRLS, SEXUALITY, AND THE YOUTH CORRECTIONAL SYSTEM

In the early years of the juvenile justice system, adolescent offenders were viewed as "little adults," often receiving punishments—in the form of retaliation, retribution, and banishment—commensurate with older lawbreakers. By the late 1800s, increases in immigration, urbanization, and industrial jobs heightened poverty and subsequent societal concerns. Poor became synonymous with delinquent, as poor and neglected children often turned to criminal activity as a means of dealing with familial neglect and abandonment (Platt, 1977; Champion, 2001). Because incarceration with adult offenders did not seem to deter youth from criminal behavior, reform schools—Houses of Refuge—were founded. Their primary intent was to provide discipline and education to incorrigible youth who lacked desirable character—to "save" these children from themselves and their surroundings (Platt, 1977).

The movement to create separate institutions for juvenile offenders was part of the larger Progressive Movement that, among other things, was ardently troubled about "social evils" such as prostitution (Chesney-Lind and Pasko, 2003: 56–57; Rafter, 1990: 54). Spearheaded by privileged women, the child savers' movement and newly established family courts provided an opportunity for these women to patrol the normative boundaries of the social order (Chesney-Lind and Pasko, 2003: 56). Particularly concerned with sexual morality, "fallen" or rescue homes, homes for unwed mothers, and girls' reformatories served the multiple functions of reforming girls, providing prenatal and natal care, and containing girls' sexuality and venereal disease (Knupfer, 2001: 90). Whereas the first juvenile court originally defined "delinquent" as those under 16 who had violated a city ordinance or law, when the definition was applied to girls, the court included "up to the age of eighteen when activities included incorrigibility, associations with immoral persons, vagrancy, frequent attendance at pool halls or saloons, immoral conduct, and use of indecent language" (ibid.: 81).

Throughout transformations and legal changes in juvenile justice, the constitution of the female juvenile offender changed very little, with girls infrequently charged with serious law violations and commonly judged in terms of their moral welfare. For example, Brenzel (1983) writes that in Lancaster, Massachusetts, in the late 1800s, girls were sentenced to reform school "to punish petty larceny; to supply a home; to provide protection from physical abuse; to prevent further lewd acts; and to effect moral salvation" (p. 130). Alexander (1995) similarly traces how delinquent young women in early 20th-century New York—"wayward girls" institutionalized for various morals offenses—contested constraints of female heterosexual norms and were sent to reformatories for indulging in the sorts of freedoms that their wealthy sisters exercised, such as going on unsupervised dates and spending their money as they pleased. Behind reformatory walls, these girls spirited against therapeutic and punitive agendas and programming designed to reform them into proper and respectable women, i.e., good girls.

In her study of juvenile justice in late-19th-century Los Angeles and Oakland, Odem (1995) also found that working-class young women who sought opportunities for social and sexual independence ended up in police holding cells, juvenile courts, and training schools for their morally offensive behaviors. Odem shows that reform efforts led by morally concerned, conservative women to protect girls from marauding men were ineffectual. The girls received judicial penalties for their willfulness and sexual encounters.

Indeed, not only did girls remain sexually vulnerable, but justice professionals and intimates also openly questioned their victimization. Finally, Knupfer (2001: 91) found similar themes in her analysis of the early juvenile court in Chicago; between 1904 and 1927, 60% to 70% of delinquent girls placed on probation or in institutions were first-time offenders; virtually all of them were brought in on charges of incorrigibility. Indeed, judges more frequently institutionalized girls than boys for sexual delinquency or immorality, considering it a "more dangerous" sex offense. Embedded in these deliberations was a dichotomous image of girls—the first, a victim, an errant yet essentially good girl and the second, a "sexualized demon" who was a danger to herself and the larger society (ibid.: 94). Additionally, nearly all girls who had sex with more than one partner were institutionalized, along with nearly 70% of girls who were victims of incest.

An examination of judicial sentiments and sentencing practices of girls throughout the mid-20th century yields few changes. In 1940 in Los Angeles, girls were overwhelmingly referred to family court for status offenses (78%), such as running away from home, truancy, curfew violations, or "general unruliness at home." Nearly half of the status offenders were charged directly with sexual misconduct, although this was usually with a single partner and not prostitution (Odem and Schlossman, 1991). In 1956, according to the President's Commission on Law Enforcement and the Administration of Justice, half the girls petitioned to the juvenile court were appearing for status offenses, as compared with only one-fifth of the boys (Jolly, 1979: 98). In New Jersey in 1970, large numbers of girls were committed to training schools for "their own protection" and as a means of preventing pregnancy (Chesney-Lind and Pasko, 2003). Lastly, Andrews and Cohn (1974) found in New York in 1972 that judges' concerns about girls' sexual morality continued, as did their personal and stereotypical opinions of girls as sexual manipulators and troublemakers. Consequently, girls, in comparison to their male counterparts, were sentenced more harshly for status offenses and, despite the absence of serious law violations, were as likely as boys to be institutionalized.

Beyond the boundaries of the juvenile justice system, research has also documented a broader social movement and struggle among medical, legal, and moral authorities to define and propose solutions to the "problems" posed by the unconventional sexual behavior of young, unmarried women. For example, in her work on girls' sexuality and the control of unplanned reproduction, Nathanson (1991) documents the tremendous claims-making and political conflicts surrounding the "problem" of teen pregnancy. She examines the historical redefinition of nonmarital pregnancy from a moral to a medical problem—one that could be treated through medically overseen contraception rather than religiously imposed moral redemption. She also studies the countermovement that aimed to restore traditional values of sexual morality and to define teen pregnancy as a moral issue to be handled by parents instead of intrusive public health professionals. In conclusion, Nathanson contends that both sides are limited by the underlying assumptions that there is only one accepted sexual path for young women to take and that the source of the problem lies with flawed choices of impish young women rather than in the structural conditions that shape their lives or their male counterparts in such activities.

Contemporary research on girls and sexuality clearly reveals that the pattern of sanctioning and institutionalizing girls for minor offenses, status offenses, and sexual misconduct continues in present-day conservative moral movements and in juvenile justice processing (for example, Schaffner, 2006, and Bond-Maupin et al., 2002). With a focus on their physical appearance and sexuality, the characterization of girls in their official court records and case files regularly obscures girls' agency and deems them to be deceitful, manipulative, hysterical, wildly sexual, and verbally abusive (Bloom et al., 2002; Bond-Maupin et al., 2002; Gaarder et al., 2004; Goodkind, 2005; Inderbitzin, 2007; Kempf-Leonard and Sample, 2000; Mallicoat, 2007; Pasko, 2006; Schaffner, 2006). Under a paternalistic ideology, the current juvenile justice institution—police, courts, and corrections—exercises the repeated need to "protect" their "daughters," usually from sexual experimentation and other dangers on the streets (Chesney-Lind and Sheldon, 2004: 171). At the same time, the court frequently labels girls as sexually promiscuous, untrustworthy, and unruly, without connecting such behaviors to their life histories and social contexts. For example, Gaarder et al.'s study (2004) of 174 girls' case files and 14 interviews with probation officers in Arizona reveals that stereotypical images and negative assessments of girls outweighed the girls' realities. Girls' character flaws were conceived as problematic internal attributes and independent certainties, while links to prior victimization experiences, family disruption, educational deficits, and other current needs were not used as explanations or offered as underlying factors.

Concentrating on the LBQ girl in custody, current research also shows how girls regularly experience heteronormative policies and overall homophobia, from staff and other inmates. Majd et al.'s (2009) and Curtin's studies (2002) demonstrate how lesbian and bisexual identities are often ignored in juvenile court and corrections, with staff assuming youth are always "straight." In addition, girls in lock-up are often encouraged to develop a heterosexual understanding of themselves and their sexuality and to engage in hetero-feminine forms of gender conformity. Such forms of conformity include pressuring them to wear makeup and "feminine" clothing, prohibiting them from shaving their heads, using "reparative therapy" to address sexual identity confusion, and offering them only heterosexual life skills and safe-sex education. When girls in Curtin's study did engage in consensual same-sex relationships and expressed their LBQ orientation, staff treated them with distrust, fear, negative remarks, and occasional punishments, such as being denied roommates, being held in isolation, and being forbidden to shower with other girls (ibid.: 4). Consequently, such policies enforced inmates' homophobic responses: "Every participant reported witnessing openly homophobic peer behavior such as anti-gay name calling and threats of violence. Some reported that girls 'out' lesbian or bisexual girls to staff to get them in trouble or to have them removed from their rooms" (9).

Building on this limited research, this chapter examines the multiple ways in which juvenile corrections respond to girls' within-institution sexuality: psychiatrization, invalidation, and criminalization. It explores two primary questions: How do correctional professionals discuss and manage girls' sexual identity, relationships, and activity? What institutional changes have occurred that affect such management and treatment of LBQ girls? Overall, this chapter shows that a dominant script underscores institutional rules and understanding of LBQ girls. It mandates environments devoid of tolerance for LBQ issues, disallows open and flexible discussion of girls' personal sexual agency, sees difficulty in distinguishing between sexual activity and identity, and stresses heteronormative rules for sexual behavior, essentially setting these girls "straight."

METHODOLOGY

Although the juvenile justice system varies widely throughout the United States, a similar process exists. After juveniles are arrested, their cases are dismissed by the prosecutor, referred to diversion, or formally petitioned; the case then proceeds to court. In rare cases (especially for girls), the case may be waived to adult jurisdiction. Once the state files the delinquency petition, the youth may accept responsibility and admit to the charges (plead guilty). The case then moves toward disposition (sentencing). The youth may also deny the allegations (plead not guilty) and receive an adjudicatory hearing. Once in court, the judge has several options: to adjudicate the case without a disposition (essentially, to dismiss the case), place the juvenile on probation with a set of conditions and requirements (such as house arrest, electronic monitoring, curfew restrictions, psychological evaluations, medical examinations, community service, fines, and/or specialized program attendance), detain (short-term custody), or commit the juvenile (long-term residential sentence). In addition, if the juvenile is part of a child welfare case, the probation officer, judge, attorneys, and other social workers may decide that residential treatment is needed, not as a commitment of the juvenile court but as a social service placement. In some states, funds for child welfare/social service placements and youth corrections commitments come from the same bureaucratic budget and are under one general "human services" division. In other states, commitment and juvenile parole are separate, but the same authority funds probation, social service residential placements, and detention.

Custodial arrangements also run the gamut in most states, from privately run, nonsecure group homelike placements to secure, prison-like, centralized youth correctional facilities. Some states may use a combination of private and public placements, and the decision concerning which to use depends on the severity of the juvenile's offenses, the severity of the juvenile's needs, or both. The decision to commit is not an isolated judicial decision; many juvenile justice professionals contribute to the information known about the juvenile offender and affect the use of discretion. Specifically, probation officers and parole officers undertake risk assessments and social histories on their juveniles and make recommendations to the court. Many times, judges follow their recommendations and arguments when deciding residential placements, as these juvenile justice professionals presumably know the juvenile best.

The data here are a subsection of a larger study that focused on the social and legal constructions of girl offenders and the impact of gendered juvenile justice decision-making. This subsection encapsulates interviews done with juvenile justice professionals who (a) work directly (or formerly did so) with girls on probation whose probation requirements in part include residential treatment, or (b) now (or formerly) work directly in a youth correctional facility (detention and residential placements). Interviews with current and former professionals were completed to capture a contemporary understanding of correctional issues, as well as former (and perhaps, critical) perspectives. The sample includes directors of residential facilities ($n = 5$), correctional therapists ($n = 11$), counselors/line staff ($n = 7$), correctional social workers/case managers ($n = 13$), and probation officers ($n = 19$). All but five interviewees are female and all but 13 are Euro-American. The average occupational length in the juvenile corrections field was eight years (the shortest time was four years, the longest 20 years). This chapter includes 55 in-depth, open-ended interviews performed in the Western United States and in seven facilities (five long term, two short term). Some of the facilities resembled group homes, were privately run, and treated only social service placements (probationers); others contained probation and committed girls; other facilities were public, state-run, and housed only committed girls.

Interviews generally lasted from one to three hours and took place at the residential facility ($n = 17$) or staff member's office ($n = 25$). Thirteen interviewees felt uncomfortable talking about sexuality at their places of work and consequently met me at locations of their choosing. When interviews were completed at residential facilities, staff took me on tours and/or allowed me to sit in on nonconfidential programming. I used these observational opportunities to contextualize and corroborate assertions made during interviews.

Each of the seven facilities varied in terms of daily routine and programming, although some basic rules applied to all of them. When girls entered long-term residential facilities, they were placed on a one-month to 90-day probation, in which staff performed needs assessments and girls were exposed to behavioral expectations and disciplinary rules. In some facilities, staff then organized and separated girls according to their mental health needs, age, or offenses. During the probation period, girls were not allowed to move or speak without permission. As girls showed they could follow rules for appropriate behavior, they slowly gained rewards and privileges, ranging from better (single room) accommodations, choice of daily vocational and educational activities, freedom to move around the campus, off-campus recreational activities, and weekend furloughs. The length of a residential stay for probation and commitment ranged from eight months to four years, depending on their sentence, their age upon entering the facility, their mental health needs, availability of aftercare placement, and the number of girls waiting for an open bed/placement.

Short-term residential facilities (i.e., detention) function much differently from long-term placements. The structure of detention is such that it uniformly accommodates the highest common denominator for boys and girls. Accordingly, girls wear underwear similar to boys (boxers) and never possess their own pairs—laundry from all detained residents is meshed together. Like boys, girls have 90-second daily showers, are offered the same caloric amount of food, and experience lockdown hours, regardless of whether their behavior was positive or negative. In addition, unlike boys, girls of different backgrounds in terms of mental health needs, age, and offense severity are housed in the same series of cells. On the whole, girls who were recently committed by juvenile court stayed in these detention facilities from two to five months, as they waited for an appropriate and open residential placement.

PSYCHIATRIZATION OF LBQ GIRLS' SEXUALITY

Unsurprisingly, interviewees attributed girls' overall delinquent behaviors to addiction or mental health conditions, given that juvenile court essentially placed these girls for "treatment."

In the study's judicial districts, very few girls were committed for serious offenses. Most girls were placed/committed—including the state-run, centralized youth correctional facilities—for failing to comply with the terms of their probation, and this failure was directly linked to psychological/behavioral problems. This meshes with previous feminist research that has shown how women are constructed as mentally ill more often than men are within the criminalized population (e.g., Laberge et al., 2000). When female offenders enter the penal institution, their deviant behaviors are often interpreted in terms of unmitigated psychiatric problems, while the social and economic situations surrounding their actions remain largely unexplored. This accords with the view that "men are bad and normal, women are mad and abnormal."

In this study, regardless of whether the facilities were private or public, secure or open, detention or long-term correctional, the rules and treatment of girls' sexual activity remained virtually uniform. "Psychiatrization" (Conrad, 2007; Monahan, 1973) refers to the process of placing deviant or criminal behavior under the umbrella of psychiatry, resulting in offenders being increasingly likely to receive the label of "mentally ill patient." The process of psychiatrization involves the definition of a behavior as an illness, or the symptom of an illness, syndrome, disorder, or disease, which requires psychiatric attention. As deviance designations shift from crime to illness, the person is no longer defined as bad but comes to be defined as ill. Accordingly, the person is no longer considered to be acting completely under "free will" and is no longer fully responsible for the behavior—which is now the consequence of the "illness." The process of psychiatrization also requires the dominance of psychological and medical technology, including psychoactive medications and behavior modification techniques, as well as collaboration, such as with law enforcement or child welfare agencies (see also Conrad and Schneider, 1980:245).

In their explanations of girls' sexuality and "sexually acting out" behaviors in the facility, all interviewees expressed girls' sexuality as (1) being a problem and (2) resulting from a treatable condition, most notably sexual abuse. Table 15.1 summarizes interviewees' (abbreviated) explanations for girls' LBQ behaviors. Overwhelmingly, interviewees' explanations for why girls "sexually act out" in their facilities were based on general or specific psychological

disorders. Over three-fourths of the interviewees connected LBQ sexuality to sexual abuse, PTSD (post-traumatic stress disorder), and "unhealthy" boundaries.

Table 15.1	Explanations for Within-Institution Girls' Sexual Activity

Explanation	Responses[*]
"General" connection to sexual abuse	$n = 52$
"General" aspect of institutionalization	$n = 51$
As a means of gaining power	$n = 48$
As a means of gaining popularity	$n = 45$
Unhealthy boundaries	$n = 45$
Post-traumatic stress disorder/trauma	$n = 45$
"Unhealthy" relationships/attachment problems	$n = 42$
"Impulse Control Disorder"	$n = 23$
Experimenting/"Cool thing to do now"	$n = 21$
"General" personality disorder comment	$n = 18$
Dependent personality disorder	$n = 12$
Borderline personality disorder	$n = 10$
General "pathology"	$n = 9$
Depression	$n = 8$
LBQ identity ("choice," no link to sex abuse)	$n = 6$
Lonely	$n = 4$
Conduct disorder	$n = 3$
LBQ identity ("born that way")	$n = 2$
Intermittent Explosive Disorder	$n = 1$

[*]Interviewees often merged comments or gave more than one explanation

Several interviewees illuminated the psychiatrization process and advocated "treating" sexual behavior through behavioral modification therapy and medication. For example, both of these interviewees show this connection between abuse and "confused" sexuality, as they advocate for treatment:

When girls are sexually abused, their psychological development is disrupted. All the harmful behaviors we see them do, their actions that brought them here, whether it's drugs, and for a lot of them, we see a lot of drug use, or it's running away a lot, prostitution, whatever it is, it all stems from this abuse. That is why they got into such things and why they continue to confuse sex and love and violence and sex. It's all mixed up for them. It's also why they need somewhere secure, because then it is safe for them to do the intensive therapy they need. . . . We usually do some form of cognitive behavioral approaches, group therapy, vocational therapy; they get lots of services and the girls see a psychiatrist once a month to monitor whatever meds they need.

—Therapist, residential facility

I think it would be nearly impossible to know if any of these girls were born that way [lesbian] because they have such traumatic histories of sexual abuse. Sex and sexuality are confusing. So if they do like girls even after they leave, I think it is impossible to know if they are born that way or . . . made that way, after years of abuse. These are issues that need to be brought up in therapy, I think.

—Line staff, detention facility

Others were adamant that all girls—even when they do not divulge abuse—have histories of sexual victimization if they identity as LBQ:

No, not every girl in here has told us that they were sexually abused. But we know all of them have been. That's just the truth. Whenever a girl exhibits these behaviors (sexual activity with other girls), it is always because of PTSD, impulse control disorders, sometime intermittent explosive disorder . . . there is a history of sexual abuse, whether they tell us or not. But more times than not, it comes out during therapy.

—Director, residential facility

In addition, others attributed (somewhat reluctantly at times) all LBQ activities—inside or outside the penal institution—to being abnormal, the result of some previous trauma. This particular interviewee struggled with her explanation but ultimately offered "pathology" as an explanation for girls' LBQ sexuality:

You know some of these girls are very good at using sex for power. And boy, they can be very charming. Even staff defends them, but I know. I can see it, you know what I mean? I don't trust them. Their charm . . . really manipulative, it is because this is what they have learned about sex. It is because of their abuse, and [looking at stats of girls in the facility], about three-fourths of our girls have sexual abuse histories. So, do I think that a girl is a lesbian because she was sexually abused? No . . . well, that could explain it, but not in the . . . [I offered the word political or identity] . . . yes, it is not like what you hear in the news or anything. The girls are lesbian because they have been abused. I do think that even if it isn't very PC. Not that I think that about all women who are lesbians. I don't think they are all sexually abused, although [referencing a lesbian celebrity] was sexually abused, so I don't know . . . but you know what I mean? For these girls, the reason they like other girls is because they want power over them and because their pathology is such that they do not understand healthy relationships or intimacy. It is part of trauma.

—Social worker, residential facility

This interviewee also illustrates the difficulty correctional professionals have with discussing LBQ issues in general, and of reconciling their personal ideas about LBQ individuals with their education, experiences, and knowledge of the girls under their authority. As this social worker showed, girls under her care suffered from a pathology that affected their choices, including sexual ones, and, accordingly, "what you hear on the news" about lesbian and gay politics and identity does not apply to them. They were not the same as girls and women on the outside, and therefore, general discussions and understanding about alternative sexuality also did not apply.

Similar to other findings on the psychiatrization of women in prison, this interviewee also showed how correctional staffs frequently merge language involving "free will" or "rational choice" with mental health determinants. Qualifying their responses with openness for education on "alternative lifestyles," some interviewees conflated their psychiatric explanations for girls' within-institution sexual activity with a justice imperative of "taking responsibility," "being held accountable," and actively making "better choices." The following interviewees' explanations show this fusion between choice and psychological influences. They also show how, regardless of the tolerance for same-sex relationships on the outside, within-facility intimacy is an element of sickness and, without proper treatment, their impulses could lead to future personal and legal problems:

> I don't care what they are on the outside. I don't judge. In here, though, there is no such thing as a lesbian relationship. There are no relationships. There are intimacy issues. Even if they say, "No, I know I like girls," which we do hear sometimes, we tell them, "not in here you don't." It's not that I have a problem with it, though. It's because these girls do not know boundaries. They have always had their boundaries violated and that abuse . . . leads to confusing sexuality for them. Their PTSD leads to impulse control problems, too. . . . Part of their therapy is to work through that confusion. Maybe not confusion, but to work through these psychological problems and respect boundaries. I tell them, "Yes, it is unfortunate what happened to you before you got here, now you have a chance to make better decisions for your life."
>
> —Therapist, residential facility

> We do teach them appropriate boundaries . . . healthy boundaries and relationships. And we hold them accountable for their actions. The girls in here, well, they use touching and sex for power, sometimes for affection, but usually for popularity, power over others . . . so really, there is no option but to say no touching. Because when they do get outside and they use sex for power and popularity and they push someone's private parts into their hands or press on someone, maybe even someone younger into that, well, they could ruin relationships or worse, get arrested and get on the registry. We really need to work with them on understanding trauma and controlling their impulses.
>
> —Director, residential facility

Whereas striving for popularity and power in relationships may be viewed as a normal adolescent (if not general) interactional process, for committed/institutionalized girls, the strategies for popularity and power were associated with unhealthy, treatable sexual behaviors and mental health conditions. One interviewee (line staff) elaborated on this linkage between gaining popularity and being LBQ: "It's not that girls who are butch are popular. I'm not saying that. It's the opposite actually. It's that when a girl is able to get with a lot of other girls in here, I think she thinks . . . or maybe other girls think she is well-liked, so they try to do that." Indeed, over 80% of the interviewees included "power" and "popularity" as reasons for being LBQ within the facility.

INVALIDATION OF LBQ GIRLS' SEXUALITY

While therapists and other staff pathologize girls' lesbian identity as part of their sexual abuse histories and consequent inability to control impulses and make "healthy" intimacy decisions, they also nullified girls' lesbian activity as simply part of the institutionalization experience. More than nine out of 10 interviewees either based LBQ activities solely on the "natural" institutionalization experience or combined it with their explanation of mental health/sex abuse. As a result, correctional professionals denied girls' sexual identity that was other than heterosexual or assumed it to be an active, temporary choice. Indeed, only eight interviewees attributed girls' same-sex activity to identity. This deniability was functional in many ways because it removed the need for additional aspects in programming and professional development (e.g., incorporation of LBQ treatment groups or professional workshops on LBQ issues) or discussion of potentially uncomfortable subjects (e.g., homophobia). Interviewees who felt some girls would benefit from an institutional LBQ-specific component in therapy, for example, also amended their comments with nullification:

> Okay, sure, yes, some of these girls are gay and I think if some kind of alternative lifestyle education was given to them, they could feel . . . validated. Well, not validated, as much as I think it could help them understand themselves, too. Even for the girls who do not say they are gay, I think it would be helpful. Still, a lot of them will say they love a girl in here and plan on that [relationship] when they get out, and then years later, will come back for a visit and be married with kids.
>
> —Therapist, residential facility

> We are just starting to talk about doing groups for gay and lesbian kids. It's not only good for them, but really helpful for their families. Because a lot of them will go home after here and the groups help

with acceptance, although frankly, I don't see a lot of resistance from families as much anymore. It does seem like it is more acceptable now. But honestly, I really don't think I have met a single girl [in corrections] who is a lesbian. In the sense that you are born that way. It's just part of the experience in here. So it's more like experimenting. Especially now since it's the cool thing to do.

—Director, residential facility

I do wish we had something more formal when it comes to this area. But the system is very conservative for sure. I would think, though, that if a girl really, you know really, knew she were gay and it wasn't an unhealthy way to get power or popularity in here, she would, you know, stick to it. . . . say it. The fact is, though, when they do keep their relationships when they get out and they come back to the facility with their girlfriends, it's almost as if they are just showing the girl off, rubbing it in our faces, "see, see. . . . I am with a girl now and there is nothing you can do about it." So even then, I think it is about power and not about really being gay.

—Therapist, residential facility

The first two quotes demonstrate how staff see an opening for groups about alternative lifestyles and want to address LBQ issues, yet they subsume the within-facility lesbian identity as part of the institutionalization experience—a momentary position that will change upon departure. The therapist shows a reluctance to acknowledge "permanent" LBQ identity within the confines of the residential facility, attributing girls' post-release LBQ relationships to power relations, not orientation or identity.

Acknowledging girls' sexuality only as heterosexual or the result of one form of victimization (sexual) also denies other factors and experiences in girls' trajectories toward delinquency and incarceration. Specifically, staff attributed girls' post-release relationships with men as evidence of "heterosexuality" and not as strategies for emotional and economic survivability (shelter, food, affection, etc.) due to limited skills, educational and vocational deficits, absent families, and the general lack of support and resources. Each of the following interviewees expressed a similar sentiment of "gay while institutionalized":

They are gay on the inside and straight when they get out. I just had a girl who was, "Oh, I am in love with [girl]." And I said, "Yeah right, back to your boyfriend you go when you get out. I am sure of it."

—Probation officer

They will be straight when they leave. I have one girl on my caseload right now who says she thinks she is gay, but I am pretty sure when she leaves here she will end up with her guy. Probably the same pimp who got her in trouble in the first place.

—Probation officer

Yes, I have known girls who say they are lesbian when they are inside and when they get out they have been in relationships with other women. But they have always had some man around, too, so I don't think they are really gay.

—Social worker, detention facility

It's what we call institutional lesbian. It doesn't, I hate to say this, maybe I shouldn't say this, but it doesn't stick when they get out. They go right back to men. It's just something they do on the inside.

—Line staff, detention facility

As these quotes reveal, interviewees equated girls' sexual identity with their activity, and when they had sexual activity with men—regardless of whether the relationship was potentially coercive (such as prostitution)—their sexual identity was therefore heterosexual.

CRIMINALIZATION OF LBQ GIRLS' SEXUALITY

Although interviewees psychiatrized and/or invalidated girls' same-sex behavior, all also recognized that a general hyper-punitive legal response to sexually aberrant behaviors (Zimring, 2004), as well as the overarching policy of recent adult prison reforms, have trumped and replaced previous individualized, case-specific reactions with a general punitive one. Correctional staff expected girls' inability to control hyper-sexualization due to psychiatric pathologies or to the institutionalization experience.

Regardless, they punished and criminally sanctioned girls for such inability. This has primarily been the case since the advent of the Prison Rape Elimination Act (PREA).

In 2003, the United States Congress unanimously passed PREA, a "zero tolerance" policy for prison rape. The act seeks to identify, prevent, and sanction sexual violence in all custodial settings—including juvenile—regardless of whether the facility is federal, state, or local, privately or publicly run. Spearheaded by human rights, faith-based, and prison rape advocacy groups, PREA's genesis can largely be attributed to growing conservative concerns about homosexuality and the spread of AIDS in male prisons, and to concerns over the growing number of white men (who are more frequently victimized) being placed in custody (Smith, 2008). PREA does address sexual misconduct of staff against inmates, although this is a minor focus. After PREA was passed, states and agencies were required to comply with all federal standards and reporting or risk losing 5 percent of criminal justice assistance.

PREA has had the unintended consequence of criminalizing institutionalized girls' sexual activity with each other and, as four interviewees noted, has contributed to the emergence and growth of the female juvenile sex offender population. Indeed, the number of committed girls with registered sex offenses has increased by 120% since 1997 (Sickmund, 2004). PREA is another example of the capillary power of the adult male prison system to spread its policies to lower institutions of social control. It has made the loss of sexual autonomy an apparent corollary to imprisonment (Smith, 2008). For girls, this has meant the disappearance of any continuum of permissible sexual behaviors in institutional settings.

PREA contradicts what we know about how girls and women "do" their time; it also contradicts how friendships among women and girls in general take place through verbal and physical affection. Research on women and prison has shown that sexuality and intimacy are complicated in prison and that consensual sexual relationships, the creation of a pseudo-family, and emotional dyads among inmates are common phenomena (Hensley et al., 2002; Owen, 1998). For some women, their prison relationships are highly transient; when they leave prison, they reenter heterosexual relationships. For other female inmates, their relationships are long-term, through

incarceration and freedom. As such, they may identify as lesbian prior to coming to prison and/or in their post-incarceration social worlds. We can also assume this to be true for girls. For example, in Pasko's (2006) research, one out of six girls in the sample identified as lesbian before incarceration.

Adhering to PREA and what many interviewees ($n = 42$) deemed generally "more conservative" institutional and bureaucratic attitudes, every facility adopted an overarching rule of "no touching allowed," which extended to all physical contact among girls and between girls and staff. This rule was enforced partly to reduce staff exploitation of residents, partly to curtail girls' false accusations of staff abuse, but mostly because staff felt girls could not fully grasp the difference between appropriate and inappropriate physicality. Only with permission were girls allowed some form of physical exchange. The following excerpts illustrate these sentiments:

> Sometimes in groups girls will cry when talking about something bad that happened to them. I think it's natural then to want to give a hug. If they ask permission, they can give the girl who is upset a one-armed hug.
>
> —Therapist, residential facility

> The girls need to learn that on the outside, you cannot be touching each other. People are not sexual in that way on the outside.
>
> —Probation officer

> The system, it really has become so conservative, so afraid. Before, well, we'd expect some sexual activity among the girls. I mean, it is part of their experience here. Ask any of them. And we would just handle it on a case-by-case basis and determine if it really was assault or consensual . . . well, no sex is truly consensual in here, but . . . something we could handle in session, not with the police, but now, any touching, anything sexual, is completely not allowed and we have to report it.
>
> —Director, residential facility

Most staff did not agree with a strict application of PREA in girls' facilities but enforced it anyway. They recognized how arresting and adjudicating girls for sexual activity could lead them to becoming registered sex offenders, further complicating their success upon release:

With PREA . . . it affects girls because of calling police on inappropriate touching, but I am not sure if enforcement really goes anywhere. My sense is that the police still are like, "What? You called us for this?" But still, it is policy, and when an investigation occurs, it could lead some girls' sexually acting out to getting additional charges and when they are released, being on the registry.

—Probation officer

Other interviewees felt that implementing PREA and reducing the possibility of physical and sexual contact turned the work they did into micro-management of behaviors (or threat of behaviors) and took away from larger therapeutic goals:

It seems like now we have so many bureaucratic rules to follow that it really takes up so much of our time and takes away from the good work we used to do.

—Line staff, residential facility

Now we cannot even have girls sit next to each other in our van because of PREA. We have to eliminate any possibility that the girls will sexually act out. So we have a van with four rows, but we either have to have staff sit in between girls or only have one girl in a row. Our van that would normally fit 14 girls and four staff now fits at best five girls with one sitting up front, or if we can spare four other staff besides someone who drives, we can transport nine girls. So much for outings.

—Social worker, residential facility

In addition, the criminalization of girls' sexual activity was at odds with its psychiatrization. Many of the correctional professionals saw their work as treating and addressing girls' sexually aberrant behaviors, abuse histories, and lack of understanding of appropriate boundaries in therapy. However, PREA policies turned their work into the policing of girls' sexual behaviors, which often conflicted with therapeutic goals, as this interviewee explained:

We just had a situation in here where two girls were fondling each other during an activity. Did it behind staff's back. Real sneaky. When we looked into it, the one girl who was a couple years older than the other one seemed to instigate

it. We did call the police to have her arrested. . . . It's not what I would prefer for her. I wish we had more discretion like the old days and could just handle it in session. Getting arrested for something you are supposed to be in therapy for . . . it doesn't work out well sometimes.

—Therapist, residential facility

Lastly, several interviewees, though critical of PREA, rationalized its application by viewing physical affection and sexual identity as privileges that were removed once they became committed/detained. Within the boundaries of normal teenage development, experimentation in and exploration of sex, intimacy, and relationships are deemed normal or only marginally deviant (depending on culture and location). For girls in residential placement and detention, this otherwise acceptable passage through adolescence was truncated. One interviewee, who self-identified as "queer" during the interview, put it candidly:

I do struggle with this sometimes. I want to be supportive of them (referring to LBQ girls in custody). It's hard, though, because I cannot come out to them. I have my own worries. And the bottom line is, you don't get that choice when you are in here. Freedom to express your sexuality is just that, a freedom.

—Therapist, residential and detention facility

As this therapist demonstrated, even when staff can intimately identify with the complexities of sexuality and the difficulties of "coming out," the rules and policies of juvenile corrections keep them from exercising such understanding. When girls enter custody, regardless of their pathway to the facility (court-sentenced commitment or social service placement), they lose sexual agency. Instead, they encounter a system of punitive sanctions for sexual behaviors and identities that fall outside the heteronormative framework.

Conclusion

The juvenile justice system has long been criticized for being a heterosexist, masculinist organization that is only now beginning to recognize the bias, harassment, and abuse experienced by gay and lesbian youth in custody. Despite this small growth in recognition, few legal actors and mental health professionals have expertise in responding to court-involved LBQ youth, and few residential facilities that competently and respectfully incorporate LBQ issues exist nationwide (Majd et al., 2009). This is particularly problematic for girls, given the court's long history of concern over girls' sexuality and the current lack of gender-aware programming (Chesney-Lind and Pasko, 2003). The heteronormative construction of sexuality and the enforcement of heterosexual identity can have profound, often unnoticed, impacts on girls in the youth correctional system.

This chapter has shown the imperatives involved in and the complexities of constructing, controlling, and responding to girls' sexuality in the juvenile correctional setting. It has illustrated the multifaceted tensions created by staff's desire to recognize LBQ issues while creating a treatment-oriented, sexually vapid environment in which alternative sexuality is seen as part of a pathology (stemming from sexual abuse), part of the institutionalization experience, and always criminal. In addition, sexuality is frequently reduced to action and choice, privilege and freedom, which girls in custody are not allowed to "enjoy." Indeed, many staff insisted that girls were heterosexual and that their same-sex attraction was a temporary method of manipulation and power over other girls and staff. Rarely did staff conceptualize or acknowledge girls' LBQ behavior as identity.

However, deniability allowed the staff's work to be uncomplicated by the intricacies of human sexuality and it removed any discussion of homophobia, tolerance of LBQ individuals, or an institutional critique of hetero-affirmative practices and punitive policies, such as PREA. If LBQ identities were not organic or permanent, but fleeting and changing, then recognition of LBQ issues was unnecessary. It allowed staff to place all girls within a "straight" category, with one generic set of rules applicable to all. This study's findings suggest that sexual stereotypes and heteronormative policies leave LBQ girls few options for treatment and services that are more open to and understanding of their experience.

Sexual abuse is an important predictor of girls' delinquency and justice involvement (Acoca, 1998; Alexander, 1995; Chesney-Lind and Shelden, 2004; Gaarder et al., 2004), and any sexual violence perpetrated by girls in residential placement is problematic. As such, this chapter does not deny that girls in the juvenile justice system need girl-responsive and girl-sensitive programming to address victimization issues, and it does not assert that girls are incapable of sexual offense. However, current correctional policies such as PREA, which treat and construct girls' sexual activity as controllable, psychiatric/criminal problems or privileges that only "free" individuals can pursue, serve to alienate LBQ girls and push them further to the margin within the institution and upon release. The nullification and criminalization of their identity also impede and gainsay whatever progress the treatment process hopes to achieve, as it constricts girls' agency in sexuality and sexual decision-making.

Finally, the processes and issues presented here require more serious attention from researchers and practitioners. A key recommendation is to advance research on LBQ girls and their perspectives, as well as to develop LBQ-sensitive programming (see Majd et al.'s 2009 report for more in-depth discussion of policy recommendations concerning gay and lesbian court- and corrections-involved youth). "Best practices" programming for LGBTQ youth is virtually nonexistent, let alone for those incarcerated. This chapter has shown that professionals and other staff, while not outwardly homophobic, could benefit from education about sexuality, heterosexism, and LBQ issues. A final recommendation is that caution is needed in the development of such education and programming, so as to avoid language that initiates the overmedication or prolonged treatment (i.e., incarceration) of such youth.

REFERENCES

Acoca, L. 1998. "Outside/Inside: The Violation of American Girls at Home, in the Streets, and in the System." *Crime and Delinquency* 44: 561–590.

Alexander, R. 1995. *The Girl Problem: Female Sexual Delinquency in New York, 1900–1930*. Ithaca: Cornell University Press.

Andrews, R., and A. Cohn. 1974. "Ungovernability: The Unjustifiable Jurisdiction." *Yale Law Journal* 83: 1383–1409.

Bloom, B., B. Owen, E. P. Deschenes, and J. Rosenbaum. 2002. "Improving Juvenile Justice for Females: A Statewide Assessment for California." *Crime and Delinquency* 48: 526–552.

Bond-Maupin, L., J. Maupin, and A. Leisenring. 2002. "Girls' Delinquency and the Justice Implications of Intake Workers' Perspectives." *Women and Criminal Justice* 13: 51–77.

Brenzel, B. 1983. *Daughters of the State.* Cambridge, MA: MIT Press.

Champion, D. 2001. *The Juvenile Justice System.* Upper Saddle River, NJ: Prentice Hall.

Chesney-Lind, M., and L. Pasko. 2003. *The Female Offender* (2nd Edition).Thousand Oaks, CA: Sage.

Chesney-Lind, M., and R. Sheldon. 2004. *Girls, Delinquency, and Juvenile Justice.* Belmont, CA: Wadsworth.

Conrad, P., 2007. *The Medicalization of Society: On the Transformation of Human Conditions into Treatable Disorders.* Baltimore, MD: The Johns Hopkins University Press.

Conrad, P., and J. Schneider. 1980. *Deviance and Medicalization.* St. Louis: Mosby Press.

Curtin, M. 2002. "Lesbian and Bisexual Girls in the Juvenile Justice System." *Child and Adolescent Social Work Journal* 19: 285–301.

Federal Bureau of Investigation. 2008. *Uniform Crime Reports, 2007.* Washington, DC: Federal Bureau of Investigation.

Gaarder, E., N. Rodriguez, and M. Zatz. 2004. "Criers, Liars, and Manipulators: Probation Officers' Views of Girls." *Justice Quarterly* 21: 547–578.

Goodkind, S. 2005. "Gender-Specific Services in the Juvenile Justice System: A Critical Examination." *Affilia: Journal of Women and Social Work* 20: 52–70.

Hensley, C, R. Tewksbury, and M. Koscheski. 2002. "The Characteristics and Motivations Behind Female Prison Sex." *Women & Criminal Justice* 13: 125–139.

Inderbitzin, M. 2007. "The Impact of Gender on Juvenile Justice Decisions." In R. Muraskin (ed.), *It's a Crime: Women and Justice.* Upper Saddle River, NJ: Prentice Hall: 782–791.

Jolly, M. 1979. "Young, Female and Outside the Law: A Call for Justice for the Girl 'Delinquent.'" In R. Crown and G. McCarthy (eds.), *Teenage Women in the Juvenile Justice System: Changing Values.* Tucson, AZ: New Directions for Young Women: 97–103.

Kempf-Leonard, K., and L. Sample. 2000. "Disparity Based on Sex: Is Gender Specific Treatment Warranted?" *Justice Quarterly* 1: 89–128.

Knupfer, A. 2001. *Reform and Resistance: Gender, Delinquency, and America's First Juvenile Court.* New York: Routledge.

Laberge, D., D. Morin, and V. Armony. 2000. "The Gendered Construction of Expert Discourse: An Analysis of Psychiatric Evaluations in Criminal Court." *Critical Criminology* 9, 1: 22–36.

Majd, K., J. Marksamer, and C. Reyes. 2009. *Hidden Injustice: Lesbian, Gay, Bisexual, and Transgender Youth in Juvenile Courts.* San Francisco, CA: Autumn Press.

Mallicoat, S. 2007. "Gendered Justice: Attributional Differences Between Males and Females in the Juvenile Courts." *Feminist Criminology* 2, 1: 4–30.

Monahan, J. 1973. "The Psychiatrization of Criminal Behavior: A Reply." *Hospital and Community Psychiatry* 24: 105–107.

Nathanson, C. 1991. *Dangerous Passage: The Social Control of Sexuality in Women's Adolescence.* Philadelphia, PA: Temple University Press.

Odem, M., 1995. *Delinquent Daughters: Protecting and Policing Adolescent Female Sexuality in the US, 1885–1920.* Chapel Hill: University of North Carolina Press.

Odem, M., and S. Schlossman. 1991. "Guardians of Virtue: The Juvenile Court and Female Delinquency Cases in Early 20th Century Los Angeles." *Crime and Delinquency* 37: 186–203.

Office of Juvenile Justice and Delinquency Prevention (OJJDP). 2006. *Juvenile Offenders and Victims: 2005 National Report.* Washington, DC: OJJDP.

Owen, B. 1998. *In the Mix: Struggle and Survival in a Women's Prison.* New York: State University Press.

Owen, B., and B. Bloom. 1995. "Profiling Women Prisoners: Findings from National Surveys and a California Sample." *Prison Journal* 75: 165–181.

Pasko, L. 2006. *The Gendered Nature of Juvenile Justice and Delinquency in Hawaii.* Unpublished Dissertation. University of Hawaii at Manoa.

Platt, A. 1977. *The Child Savers.* Chicago: University of Chicago Press.

Rafter, Nicole Hahn. 1990. *Partial Justice: Women, Prisons, and Social Control.* New Brunswick: Transaction Publishers.

Schaffner, L. 2006. *Girls in Trouble With the Law.* Piscataway, NJ: Rutgers University Press.

Sickmund, M. 2004. *Juveniles in Corrections.* Washington, DC: Office of Juvenile Justice and Delinquency Prevention.

Smith, B. 2008. "The Prison Rape Elimination Act: Implementation and Unresolved Issues." *Criminal Law Brief* (Spring): 10–18.

Zimring, F. 2004. *An American Travesty: Legal Responses to Adolescent Sexual Offending.* Chicago, IL: University of Chicago Press.

Chapter 16

PEOPLE, PLACES, AND THINGS

How Female Ex-Prisoners Negotiate Their Neighborhood Context

ANDREA LEVERENTZ

Neighborhoods are a defining feature of self-conception and everyday life. For example, there is an independent effect of neighborhood on depression (Ross 2000), drug use (Boardman et al. 2001), perceptions of self-efficacy (Boardman and Robert 2000), legal cynicism (Sampson and Bartusch 1998), and ex-prisoner recidivism (Kirk 2009; Kubrin and Stewart 2006; Mears et al. 2008). In studies of prisoner reentry, neighborhoods are important in terms of where former prisoners live, how they respond to their neighborhoods, and how others in the neighborhood respond to them. Prisoners are not evenly drawn from, nor released to, neighborhoods; rather, they are concentrated in a relatively small number of predominantly disadvantaged urban neighborhoods (see e.g., Lynch and Sabol 2001). Given the constraints on former prisoners, they often have little choice but to return to such neighborhoods, regardless of their aspirations. Growing attention

Source: Leverentz, A. (2010). People, places, and things: How female ex-prisoners negotiate their neighborhood contexts. *Journal of Contemporary Ethnography, 39*(6), 646–681.

Author's Notes: The author wishes to thank Andrew Papachristos, Shadd Maruna, John Eason, and anonymous reviewers for feedback on previous versions of this chapter.

Points of view in this chapter are those of the author and do not necessarily represent the official position or policies of the U.S. Department of Justice.

The author(s) declared no conflicts of interest with respect to the authorship and/or publication of this chapter.

The author(s) disclosed receipt of the following financial support for the research and/or authorship of this chapter: Grant 2003-IJ-CX-1005, awarded by the National Institute of Justice, Office of Justice Programs, U.S. Department of Justice; research and travel grant of the Center for the Study of Race, Politics, and Culture at the University of Chicago.

to the effect of this neighborhood concentration most often involves an analysis of differential rates of recidivism by neighborhood or the effect of coercive mobility on the community (e.g., Clear 2002; Kirk 2009; Kubrin and Stewart 2006; Mears et al. 2008).

Studies focused on offenders or former offenders' subjective relationship with their environment typically look at the "code of the street" and the need to appear tough (Anderson 1994; J. Miller 2001). Among both male and female offenders, living in high crime, economically disadvantaged, and often racially segregated environments shapes their experiences, and engaging in criminal behavior is one way that offenders respond to these conditions. While many former prisoners value commonly esteemed neighborhood characteristics, such as safety and quiet, rarely do they have the opportunity to live in such neighborhoods. They typically have few options in choosing "better" neighborhoods and so live in neighborhoods characterized by disadvantage, crime, and large ex-prisoner populations. These types of neighborhoods form the basis of our understanding of "the code of the streets" (Anderson 1994; La Vigne, Visher, and Castro 2004; Travis 2005). While many residents of these neighborhoods face similarly limited choices of where to live, desisting ex-prisoners must change their relationship with their neighborhood and their role in it. For those ex-prisoners who aspire to lead a law-abiding life, this can create a conflict, as they negotiate a new self-conception and lifestyle in their old (or similar) neighborhoods. How, then, do ex-prisoners understand and negotiate this tension?

I address two gaps in the literature: (1) former prisoners' perceptions and negotiations of their neighborhood context and (2) women and largely African American prisoners' return to the community. I focus on the narratives that a group of desisting women and predominantly African American ex-prisoners use to describe their neighborhoods, how they frame their experience within their neighborhoods, and how they reconcile their "ex-prisoner" identity with their "bad neighborhood" context. Because their role as women in disadvantaged largely African American neighborhoods shapes these experiences and narratives, I situate their framing within what we know about gender differences and street life. Also, I illustrate the misalignment between the recovery messages the women receive and their social contextual reality. Over time, by negotiating this discrepancy, the women develop a sense of agency and self-efficacy over their ability to "go straight."

SELF-HELP NARRATIVES

Frames give meaning to and organize events (Goffman 1974; Hollander and Gordon 2006). Analyzing the narratives that people use to describe their lives is "one of the best ways to understand a particular subculture or group at a particular point in time" (Maruna 2001, 39). The focus of this chapter is on the narratives that largely African American, urban, female ex-prisoners use to reconcile a "bad" neighborhood context with a coherent and "ex" prisoner identity. This framing allows them to maintain a consistent life narrative, while acknowledging how it diverges from expectation (Gubrium and Holstein 1998, 2000; Howard 2006). The stories they tell make sense of their past relationship with their neighborhood and allow them to continue living, in a very different way, in the same or similar neighborhood.

The rhetoric many ex-prisoners use in constructing these stories comes largely from the self-help programs they are exposed to in prison and in drug treatment programs. As a low cost approach to drug treatment, self-help and 12-step groups are common in prisons, halfway houses, and supportive housing programs. Self-help groups often become popular when other support systems break down (Archibald 2007). With the United States' rapidly expanding prison population, it is not surprising that approximately 75 percent of drug treatment in U.S. prisons consists of self-help groups, like Alcoholics Anonymous and Narcotics Anonymous (Petersilia 2003). Gubrium and Holstein (2000, 110) argue that "each helping profession, with its underlying disciplinary commitment to a particular view of troubles and solutions, is the source of a distinctive kind of troubled identity." Self-help group attendees see drug use as an individual level problem, which can be addressed in part by avoiding those who were connected to one's drug use. For example, one recovery Web site declares

> People, places and things. We stay away from anything we identify that reminds us of using.

Dealers, party/fuck buddies, friends we ran with, or others in our lives who throw off our equilibrium; bars, clubs, baths, certain streets or corners, or other places we associate with copping or using; stems, vials, lighters, cocktail glasses. . . . There's an AA saying: "If you hang out in the barbershop, eventually you'll get a haircut." (http://www.royy.com/toolsofrecovery.html; accessed March 20, 2009)

This rhetoric does not acknowledge the very different social contexts drug users may inhabit. Some former prisoners have little choice but to live in the metaphorical "barbershop" of their neighborhoods, as they have limited incomes and face housing restrictions and stigma in securing housing (Petersilia 2003). This is especially true among former prisoners living in urban neighborhoods with high concentrations of ex-prisoners, which also are characterized typically by high rates of poverty and social disadvantage and are predominantly neighborhoods of color (Lynch and Sabol 2001). Women, in particular, are unlikely to be able to easily avoid "others in their lives who remind [them] of using," as this group often includes family members, children, and romantic partners. These relationships, in addition to being connected to histories of drug use, also are central to their identities and roles as caregivers and to those who may provide them important supports in their reentry and recovery (Leverentz 2010). While avoiding people, places, and things related to drug use may be feasible for a subset of drug users, it is done at significant cost and difficulty for many ex-prisoners.

Alcoholics Anonymous and other self-help programs impose "limitations on the role of the individual, limitations on personal authority, limitations on affiliation and organizational structure, limitations on areas of operation and involvement" (O'Halloran 2005, 537). Similarly, we use rhetoric of dependence—on the "wrong" men, on drugs, and on government aid—to explain women's criminality and poverty (McCorkel 2004). However, some participants use the language of self-help programs to resist or reframe the importance of the lessons of that particular view of their problems (G. Miller and Silverman 1995; Gubrium and Holstein 2000; Maruna and Roy 2007). They continue to draw on the rhetoric but use it to their own ends or to ends that are consistent with their structural constraints. In the case of avoiding old neighborhoods, this includes recognizing the limitations of this admonition and rejecting its value. In doing so, participants may construct an identity that is consistent with their identity as an "ex" drug user/prisoner/offender and their limited choices and competing needs. I discuss several frames through which a group of female ex-prisoners view their neighborhoods. Before turning to these frames, I first discuss briefly the relevance of neighborhood, race, and gender in discussions of prisoner reentry and street life.

NEIGHBORHOODS AND EX-PRISONER REENTRY

Most research on the neighborhood concentration of former prisoners indicates that there are significant potential costs to both ex-prisoners and their communities if they return to their old neighborhoods. Among desisting offenders, neighborhood change is an important self-described turning point (Laub and Sampson 2003; La Vigne, Visher, and Castro 2004). These turning points may "knife off" the offender from their immediate environment and offer them a new script for the future (Caspi and Moffitt 1995, in Laub and Sampson 2003; Maruna and Roy 2007). The change in context provides an opportunity to redefine one's lifestyle, routine activities, and sense of self and to break away from unsatisfactory relationships, all of which are tied to desistance from offending (Giordano, Cernkovich, and Rudolph 2002; Laub and Sampson 2003; Warr 1998). As mentioned earlier, the need to knife oneself off from people, places, and things related to substance use is a common message of 12-step programs.

Changing neighborhoods as a way to change relationships is, in part, contingent on neighborhood-based social networks. For example, Vaillant (1988) found that external interventions that restructure an addict's life in the community were often associated with sustained abstinence. The main factors for success were compulsory supervision, finding a substitute dependence, obtaining new social supports, and membership in an inspirational group and corresponding discovery of new source of hope. None of these changes requires an actual change in residence, but rather a reframing of one's life within a community. Similarly, Maruna and Roy (2007) argue that "environmental knifing off" is one, but not the only, possible source of self-change and is unlikely to be successful without a corresponding cognitive self-transformation (see also Giordano, Cernkovich, and Rudolph 2002). In other words, the community does not need to change, but rather the offender's experience within it.

Even when ex-prisoners want to move, they have limited options and often live in similarly disadvantaged communities. While nearly half of the inmates interviewed for the Urban Institute reentry study in Chicago lived in new neighborhoods after their release, they were still largely concentrated in highly disadvantaged communities (La Vigne, Visher, and Castro 2004). Ex-prisoners are likely to have limited funds to pay for housing, especially immediately after their release, and they often experience discrimination in private housing markets. In addition, formal restrictions often limit their ability to stay with family or in subsidized or public housing. These problems are more pronounced in major urban areas, and many former prisoners experience homelessness (Petersilia 2003; Travis 2005). Programs geared toward helping people out of homelessness or helping ex-offenders or drug addicts can provide some help. However, these programs often are time-limited and have extensive waiting lists and admission requirements (Travis 2005). In addition, many are single-room occupancy buildings (SROs), so those living with children may have additional hurdles to find suitable housing.

GENDER, RACE, CRIME, AND NEIGHBORHOOD

As with most criminological research, much of our attention to neighborhood dynamics and crime focuses on male offenders. Most prison inmates are men, and so the coercive mobility, or forcible removal and return of prisoners, affects more male prisoners (and their female partners and relatives) than female prisoners (Clear 2002). Yet female prisoners come from the same neighborhoods as male prisoners, and similar neighborhood dynamics shape their experiences. In addition, the streets are one place where gendered power relations play out (J. Miller 1995, 2008). Women in the drug economy most often remain in subordinate or peripheral positions and often acquire access to

roles through their relationships with men (Fagan 1994; J. Miller 1995; Maher and Hudson 2007). However, while substantial research demonstrates their continued subordination, many women who are engaged in street life believe in their independence and efficacy within a street culture (J. Miller 1995; Maher and Daly 1996; Maher and Hudson 2007; Steffensmeier 1983; Stewart, Schreck, and Simons 2006).

Crime, drug use, and violence are widespread in the neighborhoods from which female prisoners are drawn and to which they return. Similar to men's experiences, structural conditions in neighborhoods shape women's offending patterns (Anderson 1994; Baskin and Sommers 1998; Hill and Crawford 1990; O'Brien 2007; Reckdenwald and Parker 2008; Simpson 1991; Sterk 1999). African American women are represented disproportionately in prison populations, and women in prison tend to be low income and have limited educational attainment and work histories (Greenfield and Snell 1999). Women's economic marginalization is related both to increased involvement in intimate partner homicides and economically motivated crimes of robbery and drug sales (Reckdenwald and Parker 2008). This impact of structural disadvantage on criminal offending is particularly true for African American women (Hill and Crawford 1990). In addition, African American women in urban contexts are more susceptible to a cultural legitimacy of violence and are more likely to engage in violence than other women (Anderson 1994; Heimer and De Coster 1999; Hill and Crawford 1990; J. Miller 1998). Even so, while women in disadvantaged urban neighborhoods are more involved in crime than other women, fewer women are involved than men. Women offenders can be considered "doubly deviant," violating both gender and legal norms in their pursuit of criminal activity (Heimer and De Coster 1999; Owen 1998; Sterk 1999).

For women reentering the community after incarceration, these race, gender, and power dynamics continue to shape their negotiation of neighborhood life (O'Brien 2007). When female prisoners return to the community, they, like men, return primarily to disadvantaged neighborhoods. The added stigma of being a female offender may make it more difficult to feel accepted and to be able to access resources. As Richie (2001, 383) argues, "the sense of being marginalized within the context of a disenfranchised community has a profound impact on the ability of the women to successfully reintegrate into it." In addition, many women face additional demands. For example, women prisoners are much more likely than male prisoners to be custodial parents at the time of their incarceration and often attempt to reestablish relationships with children and regain custody upon their release (Greenfield and Snell 1999; Hagan and Coleman 2001; Richie 2001). This limits their housing options, as many supportive housing programs have limited resources for families. In addition, mothers who successfully regain custody need to secure child care in order to pursue employment.

In this chapter, I focus on how a group of predominantly African American female former prisoners in Chicago, most with a history of drug use and all with experience in self-help programming, negotiate the constraints of their structural position with their desire to desist and the self-help messages they have received. Specifically, I look at the narratives they use to explain and justify their neighborhood context and discuss how gender, race, and class shape their narratives and their structural positions.

METHODOLOGY

The data I use are part of a larger project designed to understand the social embeddedness of women's reentry experiences. This project included up to four qualitative interviews each with 49 women who have been involved with the criminal justice system and were current or former residents of a halfway house in Chicago. In all, I interviewed 45 women at least twice and 33 women all four times (for a total of 165 interviews).[1] Data collection lasted from August 2003 through December 2004. Most interviews were approximately an hour to an hour and a half and took place most often at the woman's residence. Occasionally, at her request, we met at her place of employment, the halfway house, or a coffee shop or restaurant. I gave the women $20 in cash per interview as compensation for their time. This chapter draws primarily on these interviews but also includes information from fieldnotes I wrote after the interviews. All names used in this chapter are pseudonyms.

I recruited women through their current or past involvement with a halfway house for female ex-offenders in Chicago. I introduced current residents to the project and invited their participation through two group meetings at the halfway house. These meetings were several months apart and captured largely different groups of residents. All women who attended these meetings consented to participate, and several other current residents who missed the meeting approached me later about participating (for a total of 24 current residents). In addition, I mailed letters to the former residents for whom the halfway house had current addresses. I gave these letters to the halfway staff, who added address labels themselves, in order to protect the identity and privacy of those former residents who were not interested in participating. The letter explained the project and included an informed consent form, a return stamped envelope, and contact information. From the 75 valid addresses, I interviewed 25 former residents.

While many of the respondents were on parole or probation at the time of the interviews, their stay at the halfway house was never a requirement—all women go there voluntarily. Because no residents were court-mandated to be at the halfway house, the University Institutional Review Board did not consider these women a protected population. I received written consent from all participants and a federal privacy certificate protected the information in these interviews. I notified respondents of this both verbally and in the written consent form (of which they kept a copy) before the interviews began and again before I asked about past illegal activity. I also told them that the certificate did not cover any possible plans to commit future illegal acts and that they should not tell me of any such plans.

As a childless, middle-class, white woman without a criminal record, there was significant social distance between the women I interviewed and myself. The support of the halfway house administrators in my research gave me some initial credibility with the women. By allowing me to speak with the current residents and to mention their help in a cover letter to former residents, they provided me with an affiliation to a trusted source. I was a frequent presence at the halfway house and several single-room occupancy buildings and I was friendly with staff members. However, I spent most of my time in individual interviews with the women in private settings. I maintained an outsider status with the halfway house, which also increased the women's comfort level. Several women described the interviews as being therapeutic and said they told me things they would not say in group therapy sessions, because they did not want the other women to "know their business." As time went on, and they could see I did not talk about them to other residents or staff members, their trust increased. In some cases, they revealed information in later interviews (e.g., details of offenses or relationships) that they did not tell me initially. My role as an "acceptable incompetent" helped establish rapport and trust (J. Miller 1995; Lofland and Lofand 1994; Twine 2000). In the interviews, I also tried to place myself in an equal proximal position to the woman, for example, by sitting next to them rather than across a desk (when one was present), accepting offers of water or coffee, providing an occasional ride, or offering small details of my life.

In the interviews I sought to understand the subjective experiences of female ex-prisoners and how they negotiated various types of social relationships as they reentered the community. Each interview included a combination of repeated and new questions, which covered a wide range of issues, from basic living situation (where they live, who they live with, their perceptions of their living circumstances), important relationships (romantic, friends, family), their future goals, their experiences with offending and the criminal justice system, and their personal background (education, employment history, significant childhood events). The interviews developed inductively, to learn about issues that were important in the respondents' lives and including these questions in subsequent interview guides. In terms of neighborhood context, I asked the women explicitly about their perceptions of their current neighborhood(s), their ideal neighborhood, and their "home" neighborhood. In addition, neighborhoods came up as they talked about other aspects of their lives. To conduct the analysis for this chapter, I read each interview transcript and set of fieldnotes for mentions of neighborhood and inductively assigned open codes. I then refined these codes based on emerging themes.

The multiple-interview design offers substantial benefits over a purely cross-sectional design. I established more rapport and trust by later interviews, making the women more open to discussing sensitive or painful issues. In addition, I could witness and hear about important changes in the women's lives over the course of the year. This was especially important for those released recently from prison, as they were going through a period of tremendous change. Many of the women who had been out of prison longer had more stable existences during the interviews but could reflect on sometimes lengthy periods during which they established a conventional lifestyle. In many cases, I saw at least two housing situations (the halfway house and a first apartment or two apartments). With all interviews, the multiple interviews also provided some verification of information (i.e., if the same answer was given consistently) and I could see and hear about the progress, or lack of progress, toward professed goals.

Participants

At the time I began interviewing them, the women had been out of prison for between a few weeks to nine years. By the last interview, all women had moved out of the halfway house. The women interviewed were predominantly African American (44 of 49; the remaining were white, two, and Latina, three). Their average age was 41 years old. Almost all of the women (92 percent) were single and most (88 percent) had children. Just over half of the women (53 percent) had minor children, though most were not living with their children. Many of the women came from disadvantaged economic backgrounds and nearly all of them grew up in racially segregated (predominantly African American) neighborhoods. The former residents tended to be older (by about five years on average) than the current residents. They were older than the average Illinois female prisoner (33 years in the Illinois Department of Corrections [IDOC]), more likely to be African American (69 percent in IDOC), and less likely to be white (26 percent in IDOC).[2] The racial composition likely reflects, in part, the urban location of the halfway house; most of the women were originally from Chicago, which has a much larger African American population than the state as a whole.

The women had spent an average of 40 months in prison, with an average of 2.5 sentences each. This is somewhat higher than the female IDOC population, with an average of 1.8 incarcerations. Their average age at first incarceration was 32 years. Almost all of the women had a history of drug use and addiction. Approximately one third of their holding offenses were drug related (e.g., possession) and many more were related to a drug addiction (e.g., theft). Approximately three quarters self-reported drug-related offenses and many made direct connections between their criminal activity and drug addiction. Some of the former residents were reincarcerated after their stay at the halfway house. To account for their varying positions in their life histories and reentry processes, I include details in the analysis about when they were at the halfway house and their pathways leading to their current residence (e.g., halfway house to single-room occupancy to family home).

Halfway House

The women's experience at the halfway house is an important factor that makes their experiences exceptional compared to ex-prisoners more broadly. The halfway house provided access to important resources, including connections to supportive housing programs and assistance with employment placement and education. Most often, women went to the halfway house immediately upon release from prison, though a few came from inpatient drug treatment, and typically stay for six months to a year. Though there is an application and interview process, there are few formal criteria for entry beyond a desire to change their lives. Most women reported hearing about the halfway house from other prisoners (often former residents themselves) or from prison staff. Several had family members who previously had stayed at the halfway house. Most commonly, the women applied to the halfway house because they wanted to change their lives or they had no (adequate) place to go, which was often the case for women who were not from Illinois or whose relatives already had a parolee staying with them, making them ineligible as hosts.

The women had access to numerous self-help and 12-step messages while incarcerated and after that shaped the ways they viewed their experiences and how they articulated them. While at the halfway house, the women were required to participate in outpatient drug treatment. In addition, they participated in self-help groups (e.g., Alcoholics Anonymous, Narcotics Anonymous, and Prostitutes Anonymous). Many of the women also had participated in previous drug treatment programs, either in prison or in other residential or outpatient programs. The women that moved into supportive housing after they left the halfway house (single-room occupancy and scattered-site programs) were required to attend a minimum number of meetings a month. In addition, many of the women worked in the drug treatment field and several took leadership roles in their self-help groups, working as meeting facilitators and leaders. These experiences strongly shaped the way they talked about their experiences, choices, and goals.

NEIGHBORHOOD CHOICES AND CONSTRAINTS

While the women in this study had limited options and limited incomes, they also had a variety of experiences and relationships with their neighborhoods. The rhetoric of self-help groups, advising them to stay away from "people, places, and things" related to their addiction, influenced women's perspectives noticeably. I employ this rhetoric and how they use it to explain their choices and experiences in the second section. Before turning to how the women negotiated their neighborhood context and identity, however, I first describe briefly their ideal neighborhoods, the choices they confronted in choosing where to live, and the neighborhoods where they lived. The neighborhoods, or types of neighborhoods, where the women aspired to live are often in stark contrast to the neighborhoods where they were actually able to live. This provides a context in which to understand how they framed their choices. This section describes both where they wanted to live and where they did live.

Neighborhood Aspirations

When asked where they would like to live, the women typically named characteristics that are common and socially desirable. They valued the same traits in neighborhoods that most people value: striving to find peaceful neighborhoods with minimal crime, drug use, and street activity. When asked to describe their ideal neighborhoods, the women typically mentioned peacefulness, convenience, diversity, and low crime—in short, they strive to live in the same neighborhoods, for the same reasons, most others do (Charles 2000; Harris 1999; Taub, Taylor, and Dunham 1984).

Heidi: The North Side. . . . It's clean. It ain't as much hanging out on corners. It's like, I think it's a good environment. Plus, it's like a majority of economic, you know, people from different races. You know, it's a mixture of people. It ain't all Black or brown. On the West Side you see mostly Black. You know, up North you'll see white people. You'll see African people. You'll see Chinese people. All types of people up there. My cousin lives there.

Shelly: You know I haven't really given that [where to move] any thought. But since you asked me that question I would like to look for a neighborhood where people are working, going to schools, striving to do better. I wouldn't want to see a drug dealer on the corner, or gangbangers. I wouldn't want to see people hanging out on the corners.

Heidi and Shelly are both African American women who grew up in disadvantaged, segregated, and predominantly African American communities on the west side of Chicago. They, and many of the women, would like to live in racially and economically diverse neighborhoods, in which they would feel comfortable and safe and that would provide amenities like quality housing stock and programs for their children. Many named specific neighborhoods in Chicago, while others spoke in more abstract terms. Regardless, they stressed similar ideal neighborhood characteristics.

Neighborhood Choices and Constraints

While many of the women aspired to live in middle-class, low crime neighborhoods, this often was not possible. About half of the women in this study lived in Chicago neighborhoods with the greatest concentrations of ex-prisoners in the state, and nearly all the women in the study lived in neighborhoods characterized by racial segregation and poverty. They all struggled to make ends meet and often relied on subsidized housing (most often a connection they make through the halfway house).

The majority of study participants received referrals, facilitated by the halfway house, to housing programs that provided them more independence yet were still recovery communities and provided rent subsidies. Typically, they moved into the first unit or program into which they were accepted and had limited options in choosing where they would be located. At the end of the data collection period, roughly a third (38 percent)[3] of the women lived in SRO buildings and an additional 10 percent lived in scattered-site studio apartments. Another 10 percent lived in either town homes or scattered-site subsidized multiple-bedroom apartments. Living in supportive and subsidized housing was extremely common among those who were recent halfway house residents. Several of the women stayed in these programs for years; for example, April lived at the halfway house in 1995, Lisa D. in 1998, and Delilah in 1999, and all continued to live in SRO buildings during the interview period. Others transitioned in a year or two. These programs provided women a helpful stepping-stone. These programs allowed for more privacy and independence than the halfway house, but still provided some programming and case management. They also provided a financial cushion; rent was typically calculated at one third of their income and accommodations could be made if the women were out of work. The terms of these programs varied by site; some were permanent housing while others had stricter time limits. The particular program placement depended largely on availability at the time the woman was ready to move. Most of these programs, and the halfway house itself, were in largely African American neighborhoods with high crime and disadvantage, although several were in areas that had recently begun to experience gentrification and redevelopment efforts. In addition, a few of the scattered-site apartments were in more racially and economically heterogeneous neighborhoods.

The remaining women (38 percent) lived either in their own apartment or house or in a family home. This was much more common among the former residents than among those who were still living in the halfway house when I met them. A few of the former residents moved straight into market rate units, while others transitioned from the halfway house to a single-room occupancy or other subsidized units and then to their own apartment. Blanche is a typical example of someone who went through several steps before eventually buying her own house. She was in the penitentiary in the early 1990s, followed by a stay at the halfway house. She then went back to her old neighborhood and was reincarcerated (both times on drug-related charges). Following her second incarceration, she went to another recovery home and then to an apartment. At the time of the interviews, she was living in an "up and coming area" on the west side (for the first time, though working in her old neighborhood) in a multifamily home she bought recently with her husband, who also was in recovery. Several women lived in transitional housing for a year or more before "outgrowing" it or moving back to a family home to help take care of aging parents.

Of the women who moved straight into market rate housing, there were two common reasons for doing so: to live with family and in response to a conflict with the halfway house staff. Many of the women who moved into their own apartment wanted (immediately or in the near future) to live with their children, romantic partners, or other family members. Most of the supportive housing available was single-room occupancy buildings and so few women had the option of living in supportive housing with their children. Others had family members with spare rooms or apartments or they lived with parents (usually mothers) to help care for them. In addition, a few of the women chose to find their own apartments as a response to conflict with the halfway house staff. Bennie, for example, was at the halfway house in the mid-1990s. Because she "didn't see eye to eye" with the then-director, she chose to move out without receiving housing assistance. She had lived in the same market rate apartment with her husband since then. Bennie had limited options in choosing an apartment and neighborhood; she chose an apartment with "reasonable" rent and no required security deposit. The following excerpt from my fieldnotes describes her immediate neighborhood and apartment:

> I looked around and didn't see an address for the building I thought was hers. The building next door had an address, but no apartment names so I couldn't check to see if that was her building. . . . The building was a corner building

with what looked like an old storefront on the corner. Several of the buildings around hers had boarded up windows, but all looked occupied (at least partially). The neighborhood in general was run down, with older, moderately maintained buildings, and no green space (made worse by being the middle of winter). . . . There is a metal gate on her front door (of the apartment) that could be pulled closed and locked with a padlock. It was open, as was the gate on the [apartment door the] floor below. The front door of the building was left open for the mailman, she said. . . . We sat down in a small, cozy front room. Judging from the size of this room, the apartment is quite small but I didn't go beyond it.

While Bennie, and all of the women I interviewed, maintained her apartment well, hers was in a fairly typical neighborhood, particularly for those in private apartments. Boarded-up buildings were common, buildings were sometimes poorly maintained, and (weather depending) there was an active and visible street life.

Housing and Children

A substantial drawback of most of the subsidized housing programs is that they do not allow children (or allow them in a very small subset of the total units they have available). Most of these buildings consist of one-room apartments. For those with minor children, about half of this sample, choosing between a subsidized program and living with their children was often a significant source of stress. While a few women permanently had lost or given up custody of their children, more commonly, their children were living with family members or friends temporarily. Regaining custody of their children was often a priority for the women, though one that was difficult to accomplish.

A small number of women lived in subsidized housing programs that would allow them to live with their children. Two women, Sharon and Iris, were placed in larger apartments in subsidized buildings immediately from the halfway house so that they could live with their children. Andrea and Erica, also both at the halfway house within the past few years, moved into apartments big enough for their children through a program providing rent assistance for up to three years for women enrolled in school. Gertrude moved into a Section 8 apartment with her children after spending several years in a single-room occupancy building. More commonly, the women had to choose between housing programs and living with their children. Sweetness and Marie had typical experiences in making compromises between housing and living with children. Sweetness, a halfway house resident when the interviews began, chose to move into an SRO apartment when her request for a town house did not come through:

Sweetness: I had originally put in for the town home, because I had wanted my baby daughter and my son to come stay with me, but they consider him as grown, because he was 19, and I don't really consider him grown til he is 21. So anyway that was put on the backburner so they offered me the SRO instead of a town home, you know, so that's how it end up that I'm living in here, so I was like I'd stay here for awhile, but I'd still want my daughter to come stay with me and my son. If I'm gonna end up getting an apartment just to get the space, you know, he can stay with me til he's 21, . . . and then, but I didn't want to turn it down or nothing because you know there's other people that need to get in the program [halfway house] you know . . . so I make room for someone else. . . .

AL: So how long do you think you'll stay here?

Sweetness: Well, until I find something bigger. . . .

Sweetness's struggle to find an apartment for her two younger children (who were then staying with her oldest daughter) continued throughout the interview period. She was denied housing through another program because she was not considered homeless (because of her current apartment, which was considered permanent housing). She still was hoping to get into a town home associated with her single-room occupancy building. Similarly, in 1997, Marie moved from the halfway house to a rent-subsidized studio apartment in a gentrifying area on the south side of Chicago. Once the temporary housing assistance ended a year later, she stayed in the apartment, assuming the entire cost of rent. Her teenage daughter moved in with her, while her son remained with her mother. At the time of the interviews, she was looking into the possibility of moving into a one- or two-bedroom apartment but was not sure she would be able to afford to stay in the neighborhood.

To summarize, the women often had very typical desires in where to live but faced significant constraints. While many would like to live in middle-class, heterogeneous neighborhoods with low crime and little street life, most often they moved into high crime, high poverty, and racially segregated (predominantly African American) neighborhoods. They balanced financial limitations, a desire to receive case management and rent subsidies, and family demands. Their family demands, in particular, are a gendered aspect of their existence. Most of the women were mothers, their role as mothers was central to their identity, and many strove to be reunited with children. In addition, they often took on caregiving roles with other family members. These demands created an additional layer of consideration as they sought housing. As a result of these constraints, they often lived in the same or similar neighborhoods as before their incarcerations. Yet many of them thrived in their neighborhoods. In the next section, I discuss how the women framed their neighborhoods and their experiences in them in ways that allowed them to negotiate this apparent discrepancy between their desire to desist from offending and their neighborhood context.

NEGOTIATING NEIGHBORHOOD IDENTITIES

It is not surprising that ex-prisoners face numerous constraints in where they live. These limited options, however, raise questions of how the women viewed their choices and the neighborhoods in which they lived, how they framed their neighborhood context in ways that allowed them to maintain their "ex-offender" status, and how race, class, and gender shaped this. The women's experience with the halfway house and other drug treatment programs strongly shaped the narrative frameworks the women use to talk about their experiences (G. Miller and Silverman 1995; Gubrium and Holstein 1998, 2000). While there was variation in the level of their involvement, commitment, and interest in self-help programs, all of the women could, and did, articulate the program philosophies. They invoked frequently common catch phrases of Alcoholics Anonymous and other 12-step groups, such as "people, places, and things"; "do for me what I could not do for myself"; and "there but for the grace of God." Avoiding "people, places, and things" was a significant theme in how they viewed their apartments and neighborhoods. While they all recited these messages, they translated them into several very different interpretations.

Some women, particularly those newly in recovery, embraced the message and aspired to do as much. In contrast, many women appropriated the phrase but rejected the typical message. Instead, they embraced their old neighborhoods as a neutral or positive force. These women adopted three common frames: drugs were so widespread as to be unavoidable and so neighborhood did not matter, their old neighborhoods were comfortable and desirable because of their familiarity, and that "bad" neighborhoods could be beneficial, as a reminder of their past selves and as an opportunity to give back. These appropriations and reframing of the message allowed them to reconcile their "bad" neighborhood with their "good" self-conception. Through this reconceptualization, they developed a sense of their own agency in the desistance process. In the next sections, I detail these four frames and how the women used them.

Avoiding People, Places, and Things

Several women, especially those in recovery for the first time, embraced the message of avoiding people, places, and things and attempted to start over in a new neighborhood. Commonly, they used this language to describe the desirability both of their current and preferred neighborhoods. These women equated avoiding triggers with avoiding neighborhoods where they had used drugs or offended in the past. Importantly, making a move to get away from "people, places, and things" did not necessitate moving to a crime- or drug-free neighborhood, rather just avoiding areas and people known to them. For some, this included the entire city, or large portions or it, and for others, it was merely staying away from their former block, immediate neighborhood, or people with whom they used drugs.

AL: What made you choose this as a place to live?

Jeanette: I wanted a new start, away from people, places, and things.

AL: What do you like about living in this neighborhood?

Jeanette: I don't know nobody. The only one I know is my landlord. Everybody minds their business. They stick together. It's a community, there's no violence.

AL: What do you like least about living here?

Jeanette: The drugs, you see all the traffic.

Jeanette moved from the halfway house to an apartment in one of the neighborhoods with the highest concentrations of ex-prisoners in the state of Illinois, about a year prior to the interviews. While the neighborhood had been experiencing some redevelopment, it was almost entirely African American and had high rates of unemployment, poverty, and crime. There also was an active street life, as evidenced by this excerpt from my fieldnotes:

As I pulled over to the side of the road, I saw two African American children, roughly age 10. They walked into the yard of the building I was going to. One of them turned around and gave me the finger. . . . About a block up from her apartment, I drove through 6 or 8 black men (young men or teenagers) who were making their way across the street in a mass. One of them banged on my rear driver's side window as I drove through. I kept driving.

Jeanette was aware of the social disorder, crime, and drug activity in the neighborhood. Yet she felt she was in a better area for her, even though it was only two miles away from her previous neighborhood and had many of the same problems, because it was a different neighborhood.

Attempting to avoid known places was especially common among women who were new to the halfway house or in recovery for the first time. Those more experienced with drug treatment or who had been out of prison for longer often learned the limitations of the admonition. This also was true of Jeanette's experience. In the second interview, Jeanette complained of her continued "dope fiend tendencies" and reported using drugs several times in the past few months. Again, from my fieldnotes,

> Last time I talked to Jeanette she seemed pretty willing to talk. This time, she seemed more agitated and was much more terse. I got the sense that she really just wanted the money and wanted to get it as quickly as possible. She wasn't unfriendly and I didn't get the sense that she was editing herself. . . . She just didn't seem very interested in talking at length. The interview went very quickly. At one point, Jeanette seemed emotional, as though she might cry (I think talking about her fear of relapsing).

As I left, Jeanette walked me out and then ran to join a group of men down the street. Between this interview and when I attempted to reach her for the third interview, she received a new drug possession charge, left her apartment, and was living on the street (according to a neighbor, as I could not reach her). While Jeanette knew few people in the neighborhood initially, she seemed to establish ties with those involved in street life. For her the geographic "knifing off" was insufficient, possibly because she formed new criminogenic ties or because she could still easily access her old neighborhood and her old ties (Maruna and Roy 2007).

Several of the women had similar experiences during attempts at recovery. Danielle, for example, believed she needed to avoid people, places, and things and yet also attributed negative experiences to being in an unfamiliar area.

AL: Has your experience here [at the halfway house] been different from what you were expecting?

Danielle: I didn't expect, I don't know I think that for some reason I didn't think that I would accept the program the way I did, but I did, you know. It wasn't as hard as I thought it was going to be. Well, I've lived in that environment [recovery home] before but I was out in the suburbs and I was lonely out there. And I was also afraid to come here because it was in Chicago. And I know Chicago like the back of my hand, you know, at least all the bad areas. And I was scared to come here. And I conquered one of my fears. It wasn't like I thought it was

going to be. You know, I think that if I would have went back out to the suburbs I would have messed up again. You know, because I would be out there and be lonely and it's like, okay, I keep running from it. You know, so I dealt with it, you know.

Danielle was initially wary to come to the halfway house because she believed she needed to avoid familiar places and people. However, when she tried relocating to a new area (the first recovery home), she relapsed, which she attributed to the social and physical isolation she felt in a suburban recovery home. Several other women likewise stressed a desire to avoid the suburbs, which also reflects their experiences as poor urban women of color in an area where "suburbs" often mean "white" and limited public transportation. Given these experiences, Danielle began to reframe the desirable conditions of a neighborhood, beyond the messages she was taught. By "conquering" her fear of being in the city, Danielle also began to emphasize her own agency as she learned to live without using drugs or offending.

Reframing the Role of Neighborhoods in Desistance

As the aforementioned examples illustrate, the women in this study quickly learned that avoiding people and places did not protect them from relapsing or reoffending and may even contribute to it. The women who rejected this message continued to use the language of "people, places, and things" but reframed the messages they were taught so that they were consistent with their living conditions and goals. In doing so, they stressed their control over the desistance process. One argument against the message was the impossibility of avoiding drugs, as they were prevalent and easy to find, though they had the ability to choose whether or not to use drugs. Second, some of the women took comfort in being in familiar surroundings and around familiar people. Third, some women turned the message around, so that being surrounded by known people, places, and things or being in a high crime, high drug use neighborhood was good, both for them and the community. They were reminded of what they did not want and the community had positive role models of women who had changed their lives for the better. With all three of these frames, the women used the rhetoric of self-help to emphasize their ability to thrive in spite of their constraints.

Drugs Are Everywhere

Staying away from "people, places, and things" was rarely easy or possible. These women had limited opportunities when they moved and many returned to neighborhoods (either in single-room occupancy buildings or private apartments or houses) with which they were familiar. In addition to these structural constraints, many learned from firsthand experience (in current and past attempts at recovery) that there often was not a straightforward relationship between place and drug use. If they wanted to use drugs, they had the skills and knowledge to find them, even if they were in an unfamiliar neighborhood or city. Being in a new area may slow them down or add an additional step to the procurement of drugs but would not prevent them from finding them. These women still used the rhetoric of "people, places, and things" but reinterpreted its message as irrelevant or misguided. Abra (a current halfway house resident at the time) described the events leading up to her arrival at the halfway house:

AL: What made you decide to come here [the halfway house]?

Abra: I left Cook County Jail and I went out to my mom's and you know, I love my mom and my family and everything but it's like a place where I used at, you know, so before I knew it I started using again. And I had been clean for a while. You know, I guess my family and stuff like that is a trigger for me. So, I got high for about 13 or 14 days, a bag here, a couple of bags there. . . . Being in Chicago, where I knew, this is the place where I knew where drugs is at everywhere. Every side of town, even in the suburbs. I have been over there. I have tried to do a geographical change, that's why I ended up in [a city in Western Illinois]. You know, to stay away from the blows. O.K., well I stayed away

from the blows because they didn't have none, but they had rocks. You know, so, that's like they say that in the book, that shit doesn't work. Excuse my expression, but it don't work that geographical thing. If you want to find it you're going to get it. I needed a support team in my life. Like a family, and that's what I get from [the halfway house].

Abra grew up in a disadvantaged predominantly African American neighborhood on Chicago's south side and was familiar with the city and where and how to locate drugs. In an earlier attempt at recovery, she had tried to abide by the message of avoiding "people, places, and things" by moving to a new city, where she relapsed. She used that experience to reinterpret the message. At the time of the previous quote, Abra had been staying at the halfway house for approximately two months; both her decision to go there and her interpretation of its value were shaped by her evolving understanding of what it meant to avoid people, places, and things. She now believed that the presence of positive relationships, rather than avoiding negative people or places, was the most important aspect of her recovery. Drugs were omnipresent and she had the skills to find them, even in an unfamiliar setting, so avoiding them was impossible and insufficient.

While many women argued that drugs were inescapable, they also stressed that the presence of drugs need not lead one to use drugs. Several women acknowledged the drug use around them but framed it as a mundane and omnipresent characteristic that was separate from their experience in the neighborhood.

Carrie (a current halfway house resident):   Drug dealers [are] everywhere you go. It's the same old thing over there: people walking the streets selling drugs, selling clothes or whatever. Some people out there selling their bodies out on the street trying to get that drug. It's the same thing but I chose not to go that way.

If I do I just have to choose to be strong. If somebody wants to talk to me I got to say, "I can't talk to you. I got somewhere to go" and just leave them where they at. Just tell them I don't have time. Some people'll say, "You think you all that 'cause you clean now." Then you like, "I don't think I'm all that." You know, it's just that I don't want to be bothered with it. That's not my lifestyle no more; that's what I choose not to do. I don't want to do that, drugs. I want to go shopping, go places, do things, stuff like that. I want to enjoy life.

AL: What do you like about living in this neighborhood here?

Carrie: It's nice. It's what you make of it. It don't matter because everywhere you go they're going to sell drugs. . . .

Carrie used the rhetoric of self-help to explain why the presence of drugs and prostitution did not affect her. She must "leave them where they're at," but she could live her life while surrounded by drug users and sellers, because they were "everywhere you go." Partly this reflects the women's continued presence in neighborhoods that often had visible drug markets and street prostitution, contributing to the impression this was unavoidable. However, it also reflected their drug procurement skills and experiences and the relative ease of moving across neighborhoods in Chicago. Even when surrounded by drugs—she agreed with Abra that they were everywhere—Carrie could choose not to use them. Sheila made a similar argument that even though drugs are everywhere in her neighborhood, "it doesn't matter where you live; it's what you make of your home."

These two perspectives—"if you want it, you'll find it" and "just because it's there, doesn't mean you will use it"—share the idea that the presence of drugs and the use of drugs are two independent phenomena. From this perspective, the women believed that neighborhoods did not matter as much as individual agency and how one defines one's experience in a neighborhood (Gubrium and Holstein 2000; Maruna and Roy 2007). In addition, Abra argued that positive supports were more significant than negative factors and could counteract the influence of people, places, and things related to her drug use and offending (Vaillant 1988). Whether the women were in the same neighborhoods in which they used drugs and offended or in equally disadvantaged and drug-infested neighborhoods, positive social supports, more than negative reminders or triggers, would influence their own behavior. In part, this framing may be a practical response to limited options. By framing their environment and negative influences as less important than their own agency, they retained a sense of control over their life chances (Maruna 2001).

Comfort in the Familiar

While at the halfway house and in other drug treatment, the women learned that avoiding "people, places, and things" was necessary and good. However, this also was unsettling for some. Moving to a new neighborhood allowed them to stay away from drug-using associates and old locations, but the women also sometimes felt anxious and uncomfortable in new and unfamiliar areas, particularly predominantly white and/or suburban neighborhoods. Because of this anxiety, some women chose to move back to their old and familiar neighborhoods. This often was an affective decision; that is, they wanted to go back to neighborhoods that had meaning, history, and familiarity in their lives. These neighborhoods were most often where the women grew up and were typically disadvantaged African American neighborhoods with a high crime rate and common and visible drug use. Moving back to childhood neighborhoods also was sometimes driven by a desire or need to be close to and care for family members. This was useful financially and allowed them to fulfill caregiver responsibilities (Richie 2001). By the last interview, close to 20 percent of the women lived in the same neighborhood in which they grew up.

Mary is one example of someone who moved back to her old neighborhood because of its familiarity. She moved back to an African American neighborhood with one of the highest concentrations of ex-prisoners in Chicago, after leaving the halfway house in 2001. My fieldnotes describe my second experience in the neighborhood:

I arrived at Mary's house about 20 minutes early. I got out and rang her bell but there was no answer. . . . It was cold out, and I was a little uncomfortable standing on the street, so I got back in my car. . . . Mary lives on—, which is not a major thoroughfare. It is largely residential, with a corner store. There was a lot of foot traffic coming through. It was rare that there wasn't someone walking down the street. Most of them were alone, and most were men, though there were some women, and all African

American. . . . Some of the walkers went into the corner store, but many of them it wasn't clear where they were going. A few looked at me curiously but no one said anything to me.

Mary's building is run down, with a short metal fence with a gate that doesn't close smoothly. There is trash in the small unkempt yard, and a vacant lot next door. . . . While I was standing on the porch, a man from a few houses down looked at me curiously. . . . The street looks shabby.

As with Bennie's neighborhood, Mary's neighborhood was rife with boarded-up buildings, rundown houses and apartment buildings, and vacant lots. Mary recognized some of the disadvantages of her neighborhood, citing the crime and the "bad" youth. Yet, while Mary described her neighborhood in what sounds like undesirable terms, she liked living there.

AL: How would you describe this neighborhood?

Mary: Englewood to me, is quiet. I guess since I live at home. It's alright. I've been around here so many years I guess I just adjusted.

AL: What do you like best about living here?

Mary: Mostly because I know people in the area. Because you know crime is real bad in Englewood. So when I leave home I don't have to worry about it being broken into because I know people all around the neighborhood. Somebody's going to see something.

AL: What do you like least about living here?

Mary: Least about it? Let me see. The kids is real bad around here.

AL: How so?

Mary: They're just bad. They like to tear up and destroy things.

Mary was well aware of crime in the area, but her fear of victimization was minimized by her familiarity with the neighborhood. In spite of the problems in the neighborhood, she liked living there and had every intention of staying there, even given the (hypothetical) alternative.

While many of the people that Mary knew in the neighborhood used drugs, she maintained a friendly, but distant, relationship with them. This parallels Carrie's previous response about "leaving people where they at."

Mary: . . . I would say, most people in the neighborhood I know around here I used to get high with them, you know, but I tend to shy away. Well, you know, I can speak to them or something, because you just don't do people like that. You know because they got a problem, you know, because I don't want nobody to do me like that if they was clean and I was still getting high. . . .

This attitude is consistent with the messages they receive in self-help and group drug treatment programs. They learned that they cannot control others' behavior, cannot force anyone to get help, and must avoid people who contribute to their own relapse. Thus, they should avoid close contact with others who are using but also attempt to avoid judgment. In addition, Mary valued the familiarity of her neighbors, even as she distanced herself from their behavior. This was a balancing act, as she strove to distance herself, without coming off as superior. As Carrie said, previously, they do not think they are "all that." The women defined themselves as different because of their actions, but not better than active users and offenders.

A few women did not see their neighborhood or the people around them as part of what led to their offending. For example, Sunshine (a Latina woman) blamed her own stubbornness and the influence of her family, not the influence of her friends or neighborhood context, for her offending.

AL: Okay, and you want to go back to the same neighborhood?

Sunshine: Yeah. My friends were the ones I was fighting with were telling me to quit my shit and stop it. They were the ones that kept telling me, "No, no, no." I mean they were a good influence on me but I was hardheaded. I wouldn't listen. But, yeah, I'd go back over there. Over in my part there's no gangs and nobody selling drugs so it's not a problem.

She did not see a neighborhood influence as an important one in her own offending, so there was no need to avoid any places. Similar to Abra, she desired the positive influences of her friends. While Sunshine may face stigma in her childhood neighborhood, the temptations of "people, places, and things" were most likely to arise in drug use terms. Since Sunshine did not have a history of drug use, she easily dismissed that message. As most women did have a history of drug use, this dismissal was unusual.

Moving to a childhood neighborhood was much more common among those who had been out of prison and the halfway house for longer periods of time. Half of these women lived in the halfway house roughly a decade ago, and only one woman who was a current halfway house resident at the beginning of the interviews moved directly to her old neighborhood. Often, women transitioned from a stay at a single-room occupancy building to their old neighborhoods. This time lapse gives them distance from their old neighborhood and networks early in their recovery, when it may be most necessary (Maruna and Roy 2007). At times, there is practical exigency in the decision to move back to an old neighborhood, as frequently the women moved into a family-owned home or moved to help a sick or elderly parent.

Finding comfort in familiar neighborhoods also reflects the women's race, class, and gender positions. Most of the women grew up in neighborhoods highly segregated by race and class and often had little experience outside of these neighborhoods. As Danielle experienced in her previous drug treatment stay, they often felt socially and physically isolated in largely white suburbs with limited public transportation. The caregiving roles they adopted in their families were gendered pathways for women and strengthened both their affective ties to the neighborhood and family and their perceived need to move back (Covington 2003; Leverentz 2010). Other women, even when they were unable to live in the neighborhoods, maintained strong ties to the neighborhood, considering these neighborhoods "home." The vast majority of the women thought of the area in which they were raised as "home." In contrast, only one woman identified her new, current neighborhood as "home."

Part of the Solution, Not the Problem

Some of the women reframed their neighborhood context as beneficial, both personally and for the community. For these women, they did not need to avoid "people, places, and things" and they believed that being around them is a good thing, for them and the community. For example, in their neighborhoods, the women were constantly reminded of where they did not want to return. Angela, an African American woman originally from western Illinois, described her current neighborhood, an African American neighborhood on Chicago's south side, as "not a destination, but a place on the way." While she said she would move to middle-class and racially diverse neighborhoods or another state if she could afford it, she also said that a benefit of her neighborhood was that "it keeps the addiction up front. I look out the window and see where I don't want to be." Angela talked about the undesirability of her neighborhood and disliking the view of drug dealers out her windows. However, she was reminded constantly of the effects on her life of her own long-term drug use. Her experience in the neighborhood was substantially different from her experiences when she was using drugs; she was working, going to church, and spending little time on the street. Her attitude was similar to Danielle's (aforementioned) experience of facing her fears and learning how to live in high crime neighborhoods with a strong drug presence. In many respects, the women were taught in drug treatment to fear Chicago (or its high crime neighborhoods). Yet, being in a high drug use neighborhood "kept the addiction up front" and demonstrated Carrie's aforementioned point—that drugs being there did not mean they would use them. Learning this lesson was valuable to Angela, Danielle, and others, strengthening the women's sense of self-efficacy and accomplishment.

In addition, the women saw themselves as positive role models for others in the neighborhood. While this contrasts with the common messages of ex-prisoners being a scourge on communities, many of these women saw themselves as living in a realm apart from the drug addicts, prostitutes, and others involved in the street life. Rather, they saw themselves as taking on the role of the "female old head," dispensing advice and providing social control (Anderson 1990). They saw themselves as uniquely situated to play such a role, as their position was distinct from the purely law-abiding individuals precisely because of their experience as part of street life. They could serve as role models and inspiration for other drug users, dealers, and offenders in the community and as a bridge between the criminal and law-abiding members of the community.

Bennie highlighted her changed role, saying "I used to be part of the problem, now I am part of the solution." Women who took on this new identity had elevated themselves to a prosocial status. Bennie stayed at the halfway house in 1996 and had lived in her current neighborhood since. She described her experiences in both her current and former neighborhoods, both of which were predominantly African American and had high rates of drug use, crime, poverty, and other disadvantages.

AL: What was that neighborhood like?

Bennie: Hell. This neighborhood is like hell too, but I'm not a part of the environment, you know, negative wise. . . . It's that I just wasn't into the nice part of it. This is a dope-stroll, a ho-stroll, everything else but I'm not a part of it so it doesn't affect me, you know, unless I be a neighborhood watch and you know and put a too noisy, disturbing the peace or something and put a cease and desist on it or something like that. But other than that.

         I was part of the problem. So it was different because at this point in my life I'm not a part of the problem; you know, I'm part of the solution. So it's different.

         . . .

AL: What do you like least about living in this neighborhood?

Bennie: It needs to come up. There's some nice neighborhoods back east. They got block clubs and everything. It all depends on where you're at in this neighborhood, you know, if you're a home owner or renting. The least thing about it is the prostitutes, the drug trafficking, stuff like that. But, you know, everybody got a part to play in society. You know, they got a place in life. That's their place in life at this time in their lives. So I don't bother them either. I don't knock them. You know, they don't bother me and I don't bother them. You know, because only by the grace of God

there go I. You know, so I just thank God. Then the pastor, he owned this building. Even though he passed on they got the church downstairs so I feel this is holy ground for me too. From where I was at, from where I came from to where I'm at.

While Bennie's current and former neighborhoods were comparable in many ways, her experience in them was vastly different. She recognized the similarities and yet saw the two neighborhoods in very different ways because of her own role in them. While she had relapsed in the past, she had a long period of sobriety and spoke with confidence of her role in the neighborhood. She emphasized her efficacy and her ability to shape the neighborhood, either through a neighborhood watch or merely by not participating in the "dope-stroll, ho-stroll" and other street activities in the neighborhood. Bennie went on to talk about conversations she had with others in her building and neighborhood about her own experiences, stories that may serve as inspiration for others who were in similar positions as to her own, years before. Bennie also emphasized the possibility of change, both in herself and in others. The current drug users, prostitutes, and offenders in the neighborhood were in a certain place "at this time in their lives," a place she had known and moved past. She recognized "where I came from to where I'm at" and the possibility of others to make the same changes and she strived to help them make those changes.

Lisa S. took her new role further by actively engaging with neighborhood youth causing problems in the neighborhood and enforcing social control. Lisa S. went to the halfway house in 1995 because "I wanted more stability first before I went back to the neighborhood." After the halfway house, she moved into a single-room occupancy building, until she "outgrew it" and moved back into her mother's building "on the west side—the only side I've ever lived on," in a predominantly African American area with high poverty and crime. A decade after her stay at the halfway house, she was still living in her family home with her teenage daughter. Her neighborhood had a lot of drug activity, including "disrespectful guys. They stand around on the corner and sell drugs; they do it right in your face." However, Lisa S. said she talked to them. We're not used to this. Almost everyone has been here for 25 or 30 years. They don't live here; this block is our business. I went to them like they were somebody. We've always been able to maintain the neighborhood. Kids here respected their neighbors; we raised each other's kids. I asked them "Is that fair to us?" They said "no." They probably see how people treat me. It's been much better. Where they went, I don't know.

Despite Lisa S.'s own half a dozen stays in jail and nine-month prison stay, she identified herself as someone who was a positive force in the neighborhood, helping raise neighborhood children. In addition, however, she could relate to the local drug dealers by treating them with respect and an absence of fear. Lisa S. had a "passion to get everyone to feel what I felt. I never want to go back," and this was apparent in her interactions and attitudes toward her neighborhood and its residents. These connections and relationships also helped Lisa get a job at a drug treatment facility, when her supervisor, who lived across the street, saw her interacting with the children and invited her to apply for a position.

These women identified themselves primarily with the law-abiding people in the neighborhood, while maintaining some connection and identification with those involved in street life. The women framed this position as uniquely advantageous, because they could relate to the drug dealers and users, prostitutes, and offenders in the neighborhood while contributing to the positive aspects of neighborhood life. In this sense, they took on the role of an informal "professional ex" in their daily lives; they redefined their past experiences as necessary for a meaningful future by helping others with similar problems to their own (Brown 1991; Ebaugh 1988; Maruna 2001). For these women, the neighborhood context was just one area in which they demonstrated the desire to give positive meaning to their offending past. Because of the women's firsthand experience in street life, they could interact with street youth with more authority than residents without that experience. In doing so, they refined their role in the neighborhood as good and beneficial for themselves and the communities, not as a threat to their recovery and desistance. As with the other women who rejected the need or desirability of avoiding people, places, and things, they stressed their own efficacy and agency.

Among the women in this sample, the perspective that their neighborhood context was an asset seemed to develop over time. Both Lisa S. and Bennie had been drug free and desisting from criminal activity for close to a decade and both were in their mid- to late forties. While many of those out of prison for shorter periods emphasized their own agency, they were more clearly in the midst of a process of understanding themselves and their lives as desisting ex-offenders. These women were unlikely to take an active role in neighborhood social control or express as much confidence in their ability to do so. Many first believed they needed to avoid their old neighborhoods, learned through experience that this was difficult and not necessarily beneficial, and then gained confidence in their ability to negotiate neighborhood life, as they did so successfully over time. While not a perfectly linear process and while not all long-time desisters took on an active role in neighborhood life, the order of the frames identified in this chapter reflects growing experience, stability, time, and confidence as desisting former offenders.

While these women talked about the need to negotiate relationships with former co-offenders and drug-using acquaintances, the dominant theme was being careful to not act in ways that would come off as superior, rather than actively having to resist peer pressure to return to the street. Minding their own business, being friendly but somewhat disengaged, and playing an active role in monitoring the behavior of others in the neighborhood are all consistent with female gender norms of street behavior in urban black communities, particularly among adult women (e.g., Anderson 1990). For those women, like Bennie and Lisa S., who took on a more active role in the community, they become like the female old head (Anderson 1990). In desisting from offending, they were not defying expectations, rather they were (finally) conforming to them.

Conclusion

There is increased attention to the problems associated with mass incarceration and prisoner reentry, including the neighborhood concentration of ex-prisoners. This chapter contributes to the discussion by exploring how a group of female ex-prisoners framed their constrained neighborhood choices in ways that are consistent with their desire to desist from offending. Their experiences in drug treatment and self-help programs and their positions as (predominantly) poor women of color shaped how these women viewed their neighborhood. The study participants used the rhetoric of 12-step and self-help groups to reconcile a neighborhood context they have learned is "bad" with their desire to develop a coherent and "ex" prisoner identity (Goffman 1974; Gubrium and Holstein 1998; Hollander and Gordon 2006; Maruna 2001). This reframing allows them to maintain a consistent life narrative, while acknowledging the ways in which it diverges from expectation (Goffman 1974; Hollander and Gordon 2006; Howard 2006; Maruna 2001). The stories they told made sense of their past relationships with their neighborhoods and allowed them to continue living, in a very different way, in the same or similar neighborhood.

These women embraced the rhetoric of self-help programs but reframed the arguments so that they were consistent with their constrained circumstances (G. Miller and Silverman 1995; Gubrium and Holstein 1998, 2000). Over time and through experience, the women used the language of self-help to emphasize their own efficacy and control over their desistance (Giordano, Cernkovich, and Rudolph 2002; Maruna 2001). Race, class, and gender shape these processes. Contemporary criminal justice and welfare institutions often view and respond to incarcerated and poor women (particularly African American women) as weakly dependent (McCorkel 2004). Renegotiating the messages they received gave these women a vocabulary through which to emphasize their agency and independence. Most of the women in this study were from and continued to live in neighborhoods that were predominantly African American, poor, and high crime. This reflects segregation patterns of Chicago, the concentration of returning prisoners in a small number of inner-city neighborhoods, and the intersection of race, class, and gender in these women's lives. Living in high crime, high incarceration neighborhoods and often related and intimately tied to drug users and offenders, the women have little choice but to continue to interact with the people, places, and things related to their offending. At the same time, the new roles they adapted, as women who either avoided street involvement or behaved as "female old heads" enforcing neighborhood expectations, are more consistent with expected roles for women in disadvantaged neighborhoods of color.

While this rhetoric was certainly shaped by their experiences at the halfway house and other drug treatment experiences, these messages are widespread enough to believe that many ex-prisoners attempting to go straight face similar conflicts and may adopt similar frames (Giordano, Cernkovich, and Rudolph 2002; Maruna and Roy 2007). For example, Maruna's (2001) sample of British male and female ex-offenders was chosen because they were "false positives"—given their backgrounds and our understandings of offending and desistance, they should have continued offending. He avoided sampling only those who were involved in drug treatment or self-help programs to minimize the influence of institutionalized rhetoric in their narratives. Still, those who managed to reframe their pasts as meaningful for a positive future desisted and those who "read from a condemnation script" did not. Given the realities most ex-prisoners face, the realities and pressures of returning to their "old" neighborhood and the possible benefits of doing so are important considerations in preparing ex-prisoners to return to their communities. Rather than leaving former prisoners to develop a sense of agency and control on their own, reentry programs may better support and encourage these efforts, while acknowledging the very real constraints in which many former prisoners live.

Notes

1. The most common reason for attrition was losing contact when the women moved from the halfway house or to a new apartment without leaving forwarding information.

2. Information on the Illinois Department of Corrections (IDOC) prisoners was provided by the IDOC Research and Analysis Unit and refers to fiscal year 2002 releasees (as of May 2002).

3. These percentages exclude seven women whom I lost touch with before or when they moved from the halfway house. I do not know where they moved.

References

Anderson, Elijah. 1990. *Streetwise: Race, class, and change in an urban community*. Chicago: University of Chicago Press.

Anderson, Elijah. 1994. "The code of the streets." *The Atlantic Monthly*, May, 80–94.

Archibald, Matthew E. 2007. *The evolution of self-help: How a health movement became an institution.* New York: Palgrave Macmillsan.

Baskin, Deborah R., and Ira B. Sommers. 1998. *Casualties of community disorder: Women's careers in violent crime.* Boulder, CO: Westview Press.

Boardman, Jason D., Brian Karl Finch, Christopher G. Ellison, David R. Williams, and James S. Jackson. 2001. Neighborhood disadvantage, stress, and drug use among adults. *Journal of Health and Social Behavior* 42:151–65.

Boardman, Jason D., and Stephanie A. Robert. 2000. Neighborhood socioeconomic status and perceptions of self-efficacy. *Sociological Perspectives* 43:117–36.

Brown, J. David. 1991. The professional ex-: An alternative for exiting the deviant career. *Sociological Quarterly* 32:219–30.

Charles, Camille Zubrinsky. 2000. Neighborhood racial-composition preferences: Evidence from a multiethnic metropolis. *Social Problems* 47:379–407.

Clear, Todd. 2002. The problem with "addition by subtraction": The prison-crime relationship in low-income communities. In *Invisible punishment: The collateral consequences of mass imprisonment,* ed. M. Mauer and M. Chesney-Lind, 181–93. New York: The New Press.

Covington, Stephanie. 2003. A woman's journey home: Challenges for female ex-offenders. In *Prisoners once removed: The impact of incarceration and reentry on children, families, and communities,* ed. J. Travis and M. Waul, 67–104. Washington, DC: Urban Institute Press.

Ebaugh, Helen Rose Fuchs. 1988. *Becoming an ex: The process of role exit.* Chicago: University of Chicago Press.

Fagan, Jeffrey. 1994. Women and drugs revisited: Female participation in the cocaine economy. *Journal of Drug Issues* 24:179–225.

Giordano, Peggy C., Stephen A. Cernkovich, and Jennifer L. Rudolph. 2002. Gender, crime, and desistance: Towards a theory of cognitive transformation. *American Journal of Sociology* 107:990–1064.

Goffman, Erving. 1974. *Frame analysis: An essay on the organization of experience.* New York: Harper and Row.

Greenfield, Lawrence A., and Tracy L. Snell. 1999. *Women offenders.* Washington, DC: Bureau of Justice Statistics, U.S. Department of Justice.

Gubrium, Jaber F., and James A. Holstein. 1998. Narrative practice and the coherence of personal stories. *Sociological Quarterly* 39:163–87.

Gubrium, Jaber F., and James A. Holstein. 2000. The self in a world of going concerns. *Symbolic Interaction* 23:95–115.

Hagan, John, and Juleigh Petty Coleman. 2001. Returning captives of the American war on drugs: Issues of community and family reentry. *Crime and Delinquency* 47:352–67.

Harris, David R. 1999. "Property values drop when blacks move in, because . . .": Racial and socioeconomic determinants of neighborhood desirability. *American Sociological Review* 64:461–79.

Heimer, Karen, and Stacy De Coster. 1999. The gendering of violent delinquency. *Criminology* 37:277–318.

Hill, Gary D., and Elizabeth M. Crawford. 1990. Women, race, and crime. *Criminology* 28:601–26.

Hollander, Jocelyn A., and Hava R. Gordon. 2006. The processes of social construction in talk. *Symbolic Interaction* 29:183–212.

Howard, Jenna. 2006. Expecting and accepting: The temporal ambiguity of recovery identities. *Social Psychology Quarterly* 69:307–24.

Kirk, David. 2009. A natural experiment of the effect of residential change on recidivism: Lessons from Hurricane Katrina. *American Sociological Review* 74:484–505.

Kubrin, Charis E., and Eric A. Stewart. 2006. Predicting who reoffends: The neglected role of neighborhood context in recidivism studies. *Criminology* 44:165–95.

La Vigne, Nancy G., Christy Visher, and Jennifer Castro. 2004. *Chicago prisoners' experiences returning home.* Washington, DC: Urban Institute.

Laub, John H., and Robert J. Sampson. 2003. *Shared beginnings, divergent lives: Delinquent boys to age 70.* Cambridge, MA: Harvard University Press.

Leverentz, Andrea. 2010. For the love of family: Families of origin in the reentry of female ex-prisoners. Paper presented at the American Sociological Association Annual Meeting, Atlanta, GA.

Lofland, John, and Lyn Lofand. 1994. *Analyzing social settings: A guide to qualitative observation and analysis.* Belmont, CA: Wadsworth Publishing.

Lynch, James, and William Sabol. 2001. *Prisoner reentry in perspective.* Washington, DC: Urban Institute.

Maher, Lisa, and Kathleen Daly. 1996. Women in the street-level drug economy: Continuity or change? *Criminology* 34:465–91.

Maher, Lisa, and Susan L. Hudson. 2007. Women in the drug economy: A metasynthesis of the qualitative literature. *Journal of Drug Issues* 37:805–26.

Maruna, Shadd. 2001. *Making good: How ex-convicts reform and rebuild their lives.* Washington, DC: American Psychological Association.

Maruna, Shadd, and Kevin Roy. 2007. Amputation or reconstruction? Notes on the concept of "knifing off" and desistance from crime. *Journal of Contemporary Criminal Justice* 23:104–24.

McCorkel, Jill. 2004. Criminally dependent? Gender, punishment, and the rhetoric of welfare reform. *Social Politics—International Studies in Gender State and Society* 11:386–410.

Mears, Daniel P., X. I. A. Wang, Carter Hay, and William D. Bales. 2008. Social ecology and recidivism: Implications for prisoner reentry. *Criminology* 46:301–40.

Miller, Gale, and David Silverman. 1995. Troubles talk and counseling discourse: A comparative study. *Sociological Quarterly* 36:725–47.

Miller, Jody. 1995. Gender and power in the streets. *Journal of Contemporary Ethnography* 23:427–52.

Miller, Jody. 1998. Up it up: Gender and the accomplishment of street robbery. *Criminology* 36:37–66.

Miller, Jody. 2001. *One of the guys: Girls, gangs, and gender.* New York: Oxford University Press.

Miller, Jody. 2008. *Getting played: African American girls, urban inequality, and gendered violence.* New York: New York University Press.

O'Brien, Patricia. 2007. Maximizing success for drug-affected women after release from prison—Examining access to and use of social services during reentry. *Women & Criminal Justice* 17:95–113.

O'Halloran, Seán. 2005. Symmetry in interaction in meetings of Alcoholics Anonymous: The management of conflict. *Discourse & Society* 16:535–60.

Owen, Barbara. 1998. *"In the mix" struggle and survival in a women's prison.* Albany: State University of New York Press.

Petersilia, Joan. 2003. *When prisoners come home: Parole and prisoner reentry.* Oxford, UK: Oxford University Press.

Reckdenwald, Amy, and Karen F. Parker. 2008. The influence of gender inequality and marginalization on types of female offending. *Homicide Studies* 12:208–26.

Richie, Beth. 2001. Challenges incarcerated women face as they return to their communities: Findings from life history interviews. *Crime and Delinquency* 47:368–89.

Ross, Catherine E. 2000. Neighborhood disadvantage and adult depression. *Journal of Health and Social Behavior* 41:177–87.

Sampson, Robert J., and Dawn Jeglum Bartusch. 1998. Legal cynicism and (subcultural?) tolerance of deviance: The neighborhood context of racial differences. *Law and Society Review* 32:777–804.

Simpson, Sally. 1991. Caste, class, and violent crime: Explaining difference in female offending. *Criminology* 29:115–35.

Steffensmeier, Darrell J. 1983. Organization properties and sex-segregation in the underworld: Building a sociological theory of sex differences in crime. *Social Forces* 61:1010–032.

Sterk, Claire E. 1999. *Fast lives: Women who use crack cocaine.* Philadelphia: Temple University Press.

Stewart, Eric A., Christopher J. Schreck, and Ronald L. Simons. 2006. "I ain't gonna let no one disrespect me": Does the code of the street reduce or increase violent victimization among African American adolescents? *Journal of Research in Crime and Delinquency* 43:427–58.

Taub, Richard, D. Garth Taylor, and Jan D. Dunham. 1984. *Paths of neighborhood change: Race and crime in urban America.* Chicago: University of Chicago Press.

Travis, Jeremy. 2005. *But they all come back: Facing the challenges of prisoner reentry.* Washington, DC: Urban Institute.

Twine, France Winddance. 2000. Racial ideologies and racial methodologies. In *Racing research, researching race: Methodological dilemmas in critical race studies,* ed. F. W. Twine and J. W. Warren, 1–34. New York: New York University Press.

Vaillant, George E. 1988. What can long-term follow-up teach us about relapse and prevention of relapse in addiction? *British Journal of Addiction* 83:1147–157.

Warr, Mark. 1998. Life-course transitions and desistance from crime. *Criminology* 36:183–216.

INDEX

ABOUT THE EDITORS

Meda Chesney-Lind, PhD, is Director and Professor of Women's Studies at the University of Hawaii at Manoa. Nationally recognized for her work on women and crime and the author of seven books, she has just finished two books on trends in girls' violence titled *Beyond Bad Girls: Gender, Violence and Hype,* written with Katherine Irwin, and *Fighting for Girls,* co-edited with Nikki Jones. *Fighting for Girls* recently won an award from the National Council on Crime and Delinquency for "focusing America's attention on the complex problems of the criminal and juvenile justice systems." She received the Bruce Smith, Sr. Award "for outstanding contributions to Criminal Justice" from the Academy of Criminal Justice Sciences in April 2001. She was named a fellow of the American Society of Criminology in 1996 and has also received the Herbert Block Award for service to the society and the profession from the American Society of Criminology. She has also received the Donald Cressey Award from the National Council on Crime and Delinquency for "outstanding contributions to the field of criminology," the Founders award of the Western Society of Criminology for "significant improvement of the quality of justice," and the University of Hawaii Board of Regent's Medal for "excellence in research."

Finally, Chesney-Lind has recently joined a group studying trends in youth gangs organized by the National Institute of Justice, and she was among the scholars working with the Office of Juvenile Justice and Delinquency Prevention's Girls Study Group. In Hawaii, she has worked with the Family Court, First Circuit advising them on the recently formed Girls Court as well as helping improve the situation of girls in detention with the recent JDAI initiative.

Lisa Pasko, PhD, is Assistant Professor in the department of sociology and criminology at the University of Denver. Receiving her PhD from the University of Hawaii at Manoa, Lisa's primary research and teaching interests include criminology, the female offender, delinquency and the juvenile justice system, sexualities, and punishment. Her dissertation examined juvenile delinquency and justice in Hawaii, with particular attention on the differential impacts institutional policies and decision making have on boys and girls. Recently finishing a Colorado Division of Criminal Justice funded grant titled "In and Out of the System: Understanding and Addressing the Female Juvenile Offender in Colorado," Dr. Pasko's latest research examines correctional attitudes about girls, their sexual behavior, reproductive decision making, and sexual identity issues. As a public sociologist, she is also a board member for the Colorado Coalition for Girls and is performing an ongoing evaluation of InterCept, a girl offender intervention program in Colorado Springs, CO. In addition to being co-author of *The Female Offender,* she has also authored over ten articles and book chapters and several technical reports that focus on girls' experiences, inside and outside the correctional system.